Of Pathics and Evil

A Philosophy against Malice

Compiled, Arranged, and Written

by

Joseph Free*man*

Edited by
Sharon Campbell

"One does not become enlightened by imagining figures of light, but by making the darkness conscious."
-Jung

Of Pathics and Evil
Public Benefit Press

ISBN: 978-1-7350978-6-2 (paper book)

ISBN: 978-17350978-7-9 (electronic book)

To David Nason, in gratitude for our long-standing friendship and for my indebted appreciation for encouraging and supporting me so that this book has been published and on its way of influence.

"To defeat them, first we must understand them"
- Elie Wiesel

Contents

ACKNOWLEDGEMENT

The personal accounts of these passages, which consist of the bulk of this book, are mainly from internet forums; and I am endlessly grateful for each person's story, which, without these forums, this book could not have been compiled. These individuals have contributed immeasurably to the ongoing understanding of the pathic personality.

To keep the authenticity of the personal accounts in this book, I have retained each person's natural way of writing with her-his often nonstandard wording, spelling and usage – for example: "gonna," "for the helluvit," "sooooo seductive," etc; as well as, idiosyncratic words, such as "creepazoids". I retained their use of capital letters for emphasis, since their accounts on these internet forums were written in plain text, which, do not include bolding, italics, underlining, and the like (HTML). Also, since many of these accounts are from England, I retained their standard spellings of such words as, "behaviour" (behavior), "cant" (can't), "favour" (favor) "realise" (realize), etc. I do change punctuation marks, where necessary, so that their sentence arrangements make sense.

PART ONE
Perspectives of Human Evil

Chapter 1
A PRELIMINARY

The title of this book, *Of Pathics and Evil: A Philosophy against Malice*, fairly much tells of its contents. It is about evil – human evil in general, and about pathics – malicious evil in particular; and includes a philosophy aimed to protect ourselves against them. And as used in this book, evil implies destruction, breaking down, undermining, disruption, "trouble ahead," "bad moon rising," to quote a rock song's title.

My purpose in writing – actually *composing* – this book is threefold: First, to serve as an introductory manifesto, of sorts, for those individuals who aspire to do good for others, or for mankind; second, to serve as an introductory guide for those who aspire to be good to themselves by preserving their self-identity and personal integrity; and third, to forge the way to a broadening consciousness toward the gradual ascendancy of justice and wisdom (good) over injustice and ignorance (evil).

By reading the part and chapter sequence in the table of contents, the reader will easily grasp the overall format and development of the book's three basic themes: namely, that evil is an integral part of human nature, more or less

1

according to the individual; that pathics are *more* than *less* evil; and that good can take the ascendancy over evil through a philosophy and wisdom that leads to self-understanding centered in Transcendence. And though this book merely touches on the full spectrum of this wisdom, it nonetheless lays the foundation for the attainment of it; and that in itself is a dawning: to emerge from the night of our minds into the light of day.

All cited passages in this book are preceded by either quotation marks, numbers, or the sources' name. All other passages (besides chapters 2, 17, 18, and 19, which are written by the author), introducing each chapter's contents, are by the author.

NOTE: The following abbreviations are used by the contributors (victims mainly) throughout this book:

N = Narcissist
S = Sociopath
P = Psychopath
NP = Narcissistic Psychopath
NPD = Narcissistic Personality Disorder
PA = Passive Aggressive
NS = Narcissistic Supply (attention, admiration, etc.)
ASPD = Antisocial Personality Disorder
BPD = Borderline Personality Disorder
RAD = Reactive Attachment Disorder

The following preliminary passages introduce the reader to the three main types of pathics – the psychopath, the sociopath, and the naricpath (otherwise known as the narcissist; or more specifically, the malignant narcissist) – and their distinctions. But first let me preface these passages with the following analogy which sums up perfectly the overall pattern of the human predator's (whether psychopath, sociopath, narcissist, psychotic-killer) pursuit of his/her prey.

"My Psychiatrist was wonderfully supportive and knowledgeable. In the course of our discussion he said – 'Ps are Cheetahs in human form.' 'How so?' I asked. He replied...In the wilderness, the Cheetah does not chase an entire herd. Hundreds of gazelles could go past until the Cheetah recognizes the one who is his prey. It is perhaps limping, perhaps slower than the rest, perhaps not paying attention to where the others are going. It doesn't matter what the gazelle is doing, the Cheetah targets it – and it is dead. It doesn't stand a chance. It could be running right beside the fattest, plumpest, juiciest gazelle, but it is not the Cheetah's target. The fattest, plumpest is safe. Only the target dies. 'Ps,' he said 'do that.' They identify their target, put them into the crosshairs and pursue – without being distracted by any peripheral activity or people. Their target is their dead reckoning.' Now, my challenge, as we both agreed, has been to identify what it was within me that recognized the P as desirable. Because he was, at one time, very desirable to me."

The Psychopath

[Those who use and abuse others primarily for the sake of harming them]

1. "My sister scares me even more than my mother because she is simply uneducated with no thirst for knowledge. Her actions are purely thoughtless, malicious and dumb. She was brutal to me as a child although we were only 1 year apart. She would just scream terrible things to me to the point of such belittling, name-calling (slut, because I had nice boyfriends and was thinner than her; tease, because I got the attention from boys she craved; bitch, because her self-esteem was hurt, etc.) I had to watch everything I did, downplay my talents, successes, and good fortunes on a daily basis as to not negatively affect her in any way. My parents supported her nasty behavior and only told me not to listen to her; but words hurt, especially when all I wanted was to see her enjoying her life and [be] happy with who she was. She is a mother of a 9-yr-old and 1-year-old daughter. I see the brutality toward the 9-year-old and it breaks my heart. I see it coming for the 1-year-old, as all she talks about is how impressed she or others are of her average 1-year- old. I love my nieces so much, but I am a mother myself and have had to convince myself that I can't save the world; and it is my main goal to provide the best life for my own children. Every conversation with her is a series of 'subtle' (SCREAMING) putdowns, belittling, and what-is- good-in-her-life scenarios. It is exhausting and I have decided to lessen the communication with her because it is so negative and so competitive. She is always trying to prove something to me. She has nothing to show for anything unless someone else gave it to her. She has no sense of pride, priority or responsibility. It is sick."

2. "It's heart-sickening how ignorant most therapists are when it comes to psychopathy. Excuse me: Antisocial Personality Disorder. Let's be politically correct, here.

"The last therapist I saw with my psychopath husband did not see ASPD at all in him. He dropped out of the 'therapy' after he had thoroughly conned her. This therapist knew he had beaten me, threatened my life, slept with my friends, had affairs with teenagers, peeped, exposed, lied, stolen, abused his positions, turned my community against me; he had admitted to all of this. She also knew he had been accused by some children of molesting them, which he had not denied. He had told her if he did it, he didn't remember. She also knew he probably had molested his own children. She said to me, 'You think he has ASPD. I don't see that.'

"I said, 'Why not?'

"She said, 'Where is the antisocial behavior? What crimes has he committed?'

"I guess she meant he had no criminal record. Therefore, he didn't have ASPD. Most people, including most therapists have a cardboard, insightless, image of a psychopath. They wouldn't know a psychopath if one hit them over the head with a two-by-four.

"They don't think a psychopath is charming, intelligent, attractive, personable, nice. In fact, a successful psychopath is all these things. And that is why a successful one has no criminal record. Nobody ever pressed charges against my husband. The next door neighbors had a talk with him after he window-peeped the wife in the shower, and rang her doorbell and exposed himself to her. When he did it again, they had another talk.

"A successful psychopath can talk himself out of just about anything. ASPD? No way. No psychopath worth his salt would ever get that label.

"Said therapist lectured me, repeatedly, to let Psychopath have his job, to not ruin that for him, to not turn his family against him. She was clearly agonized that I had turned his children against him. In her view, I was taking everything away from him. I did not do any of that. There was a leak into his job community about his office affair. I was not responsible for the leak. I never spoke to his family about the problems at all – ever. (She got the idea I would turn them all against him from Psychopath.); my sin was apparently inviting them to my daughter's baby shower). I did not turn his youngest daughter against him. She put him out of her life after he beat me, for the hundredth time, and held me captive with a knife for many hours; and I called her, afterwards, out of need. Okay, I did that. But I did not mean to turn her against him; I tried to talk her into being chummy with him again. Afterwards, I was sick.

"When we reconciled, briefly, the therapist lectured me, endlessly, that I had better darn well be having sex with him. She was worried that I wouldn't play fair with poor Psychopath. Me, being such a mean, spiteful person.

"And people wonder how we who were so victimized could have stayed so long. Here was a credentialed therapist who was not in love with the man, hadn't had his children, hadn't been his wife for decades, had never suffered any abuse, but knew about it, and blamed it all on me. The psychopath was that good. If he could convince her it was all me, how much more easily could he convince me?

"And she was not the first therapist to blame it all on me. I believe she was the fourth; which is all of them, except for the first and the last.

"The therapy situation is appalling. No one should be permitted to work with a psychopath's victim who is not very specially trained. Better yet, all those who do, should have experience with psychopaths."

The Sociopath

[Those who use and abuse others primarily to their advantage through manipulative control]

1. In my case [my] husband of 12 years, is not exactly malicious. He doesn't set out to hurt me just for kicks, in my opinion. He hurts me as little or as much as it takes to achieve his goal: to make me dependant on him in as many ways, obey him, give him all the [attention, admiration, etc.]. He demands that I abdicate control. So, while his primary goal isn't to hurt me, it becomes a goal if that's what it takes to get [attention, admiration, etc.] out of me."

2. "MEET MY WONDERFUL EX: SHE IS … distant — stories never add up — inconsistencies or unexplained loose ends — cold — doesn't cry — never says sorry — explosive — bad tempered — highly irritable — on edge — feisty — rigid — avoidance — admits she is a control freak — intense eye contact or none at all — lack of remorse or guilt — lack of empathy — insincere or deceitful — deceitful and manipulative — shallow emotions — impulsive — short-tempered or hotheaded — obligations and commitments mean nothing — 'hair trigger' — her aggressive displays are 'cold' — highly reactive to perceived insults — appear completely forthright about the matter — shrug off personal responsibility for actions they cause — indifferent to the rights and suffering of family or loved ones — handy excuses for her behavior or actions — flighty — doesn't show emotion — defensive — flips out — flips things around when confronted — road rage — constant yelling — difficulty compromising — done resentfully — irrational — no sympathy — no compassion — no feelings — no communication —

no commitment — no talking about the future — constant lying — deceitful — always vague — easily annoyed — makes no future plans together — her behaviors become easily predictable — ready with a clever comeback — claims to have specific goals and little or no chance of attaining these goals — everything done on her terms — shuts down when confronted or explodes — avoids confrontation using text or emails or excuses she's busy or napping — offers no explanation for her actions — she mentioned rules about what not to do or say when we first met; for example: 'Don't ever call me a bitch or we will be finished.' — she has a book on the coffee table *Why Men Love Bitches* — things she would say such as 'I love you' don't come across in her actions. — any emotional feeling, while rare, appears fake. — you will often feel shock and disappointment — you are and what you have/own are her possessions — I felt her actions towards me often created a reaction from me that further spoiled the relationship. There often was a feeling of shock or, 'Where the hell did that come from; I just asked you a question!' — high suspicions of cheating; overwhelming evidence is shrugged off as if you are crazy for thinking that way. — she will want you to make decisions so it can't come back on her if things do not go as planned. — smokes while pregnant."

The Narcipath [variant of 'Narcissist]
[Those who use and abuse others primarily to their advantage for the sake of self-aggrandizement]

1. "The Game"
    "The game is a game of hearts. The 'Heartbreaker' is the 'Master' of this game. He leaves gifts and tangible things. He uses his eyes first to catch you; they focus on you, and you feel captured, unable to escape their intense gaze. Then he uses his words. His words are subtle, but they make the point he's trying to get across to you.

His point is that you are in his sights and there is nothing you can do about it. Then he uses this kiss. It's so focused on your heart and your emotions that he takes your breath away and you fall madly in love with him, just because he leaves you no choice. You feel like a captured bird that cannot free itself. He has you under his magical spell and you're left reeling, wondering how it happened so fast.

"(His name) is 'The Master' at this game. After all, I should know. He's done it to me three times now. Even though I tried my best to avoid him, he managed to get to me, again. Nothing worked till he said, 'I want to hold you (my name).' I couldn't resist him when he put it in words like that. And then I let him come over and he stared at me 'till I told him it made me uncomfortable. And then...He kissed me...And Oh! ...That was 'all she wrote.' I started falling right back in love with him. My heart was trapped again, just like a bird in a cage.

"'The Game' worked. After all those years, he's still a Player. A 'Master of the Heartbreakers,' and he's gonna break my heart again....I know it!

2. "My ex girlfriend said I was perfect. She made me feel so special and tried so hard to make her feel loved. After the first year, nothing was ever good enough. On every holiday, she found a way to cheapen the experience and say it was my fault. It was like looking into the abyss. She did the most horrible things to me to make me feel like garbage. When she left me, she just acted like everything I did was nothing to her. It was my fault because she wants a man who will give her 80% of their time to nurture her needs while giving 20% in return, because she said she deserves it, and intends to have it. Her lies were unnecessary and she never seemed to be able to have an in-depth conversation about much of anything. I miss the person she claimed to be. The facade was so great. I don't know what happened to her, but I wish I could find her again. I know it's over; but, god, it hurts to know you spent two years together and it meant nothing."

Chapter 2
THE PATHICS

This chapter explores in some detail the distinctions and variations between the *pathic* individual who is either predominantly narcipathic, sociopathic, psychopathic, or psychoticpathic, depending upon the type and extent of his or her pathic behavior.

---

1. Psychopaths do us harm. Sociopaths also do us harm. Narcissists, too, do us harm. Each harms in his/her own propensities. Psychopaths will do us harm primarily for *the sake of harm*. Sociopaths will do us harm primarily for *the sake of manipulative-dominance*. Narcissists will do us harm primarily for *the sake of self-aggrandizement*. However they may differ in their approach to harming others, they will do so both covertly and overtly.

2. The terms, "psychopath," "sociopath," and "narcissist" are commonly interchanged, and so can be confusing as to the degree and type of harm perpetrated by these individuals. Accordingly, in order to resolve this confusion, my wife has coined a comprehensive term that includes all three terms. The term "pathic" is this comprehensive term that includes the *sociopath*, the *psychopath*, and the *narcissist*. I modify the term, "narcissist" to "narcipath" so that the suffix, "path," is consistent with the other two terms, as well as to avoid the various connotations, unfavorable, and otherwise, of the term "narcissist." One other term included with these three, is what I term *psychoticpath* which refers to the psychic abnormality, derangement, of blood-lust as an habitual frame of mind. Because of its rarity in human behavior, it will not be discussed overall, but will have its own chapter.

3. The term "pathic" is derived from the suffix, *path*, signifying 'disease-producing,' 'suffering'. It is this etymological root of the term 'pathic' which gives these three types of harmful individuals, each in his own way, their commonality: that they cause disease (the breaking down of physical and/or psychological health) and suffering.

4. It is often difficult to determine whether a pathic is a narcipath, sociopath, or psychopath, since most pathic traits (habitual lying, cheating, lack of conscience, lack of remorse, etc.) often overlap, one into the other. Is the pathic essentially sociopathic or essentially narcipathic, or essentially psychopathic? The victim, however, who actually experiences the harm done to him or her would surely recognize whether her victimizer acts from sheer self-aggrandizement (the narcipath), or from sheer dominance (the sociopath), or from sheer malice (the psychopath). Hence the importance of being able to apply the appropriate term to the pathic individual in order to help get to the bottom of the abusive relationship; for consider the complexities involved in the situation in which a pathic who, on the surface, is unjustly controlling (an *apparent* sociopath), but who from a deeper aspect is controlling in order to harm his victim from sheer malice (an *actual* psychopath); or the person who is being willfully malicious (an *apparent* psychopath) might seem to be so for the sake of malice itself, when in fact he is acting maliciously in order to unjustly control (an *actual* sociopath) – and the complexities go on and on.

Yet an obvious scenario would be when a person preens herself on being aggressively superior to others in intelligence, in attractiveness, in expertise, and willfully harms anyone or any situation that threatens that sense of superiority – then there would be no question that that person is a *narcipath*. Relatedly, a person with the same sense of superiority, but whose main *modus operandi* is to use that sense of superiority, not for her own self-aggrandizement, but to control and dominate others and situations and events to their detriment if they don't fit into her schemes – then it would be obvious that that person is a *sociopath*. Again, given a person with the same superiority complex, but whose main concern is neither self-aggrandizement nor controlled dominance, but to harm others for the sheer sake of delighting in, thrilling to, their suffering – then that person would obviously be a *psychopath*. And lastly, given the same superiority complex in an individual, but to such a severe extreme that it is not even a matter of delight or thrill at the suffering he inflicts upon another; but rather it is an orgasmic demonic compulsion he anticipates, and actually experiences, at his victim's physical and mental agony. In such acts, he gratifies his demented superiority complex, his twisted control over another person's life, and his demonic pleasure in the perdition of his act – it would then be obvious that that person is what I term a *psychoticpath*.

5. We all, as humans, have our own share of these three traits: self-aggrandizement, dominance over others, and malice – and dare I say it!: blood lust, at the remotest place of our brain's stem The difference is that these traits (chemically induced) are naturally, innately, *excessive* in pathics, so that their behavior is mostly and consistently destructive rather than constructive. Their "malady," we might call it, is an inner urge that invariably impels them to destroy, breakdown, manipulate, and control the well-being of others. It is considered a malady because we can liken it, analogously, to a strain of virus that, for its own survival and well-being, infiltrates life in order to destroy it. So far as being a *psychological virus-trait*, as I term it, functioning as a destroying agency, it is, of itself, healthy; on the other hand, inasmuch as it destroys the well-being of others, this psychological virus-trait is considered a disease-making agency. And so the root suffix "path" as meaning 'disease' is justifiably affixed to the terms "psychopath" and "sociopath," and, as I term it, "narcipath." But to call a pathic – whether psychopath, sociopath, or narcipath – as "sick" or diseased, misses the point by far; since they themselves are neither sick nor diseased; rather, it is their presence and their behavior that cause malfunction, sickness or disease in others. They themselves are fine just the way they are so long as they are acting effectively from their "center," so to speak. That they often bring destruction upon themselves – self-destruction, more particularly – is not normally of their own doing, but of the social, legal, inter-personal, and self-limiting (misfiring) consequences of their actions. Life has to protect itself from death. It is extremely (excessively?) difficult for us "normal" ones to conceive that a person can be considered normal who can get by "contentedly" through his life without giving or receiving love, and all its variations; who enjoys, revels, in harming others – ["...Villains ... rejoice in their iniquities." Thucydides]. Such a person may not be a well-balanced person – again, as we understand the term "well-balanced" – but can we consider him/her abnormal, "sick"? Is it a natural element of human nature that a person must be loving to some degree, at least, in order to be psychologically normal? Cannot a naturally non-loving person live his life contentedly, satisfactorily, so long as his non-loving ways succeed for him or her? Or consider, are all persons who can love, and are loved, normal and well-balanced? What *is* normal? What is well-balanced? Is there some universal code that answers these questions? Can scientists measure, or predict, normalcy? Is not each human being replete with oppositions: now this, now that? Has nature itself not created in man and woman a quandary of opposing factions so that we seem a mass of contradictions in our thoughts, feelings, and actions, our wants, needs, pleasures and pains?

Yes, we can ask these queries left and right; but when it comes right down to it, these pathics are programmed with (again, analogously speaking) the *virus-trait* that compels them to habitually destroy, break down, undermine, disrupt, the well-being and order of persons and situations. This programming, to repeat myself, does not mean that they are sick, but rather, anti-social; that is, when having to make a decision, they will choose the option that will create conflict rather than harmony to various degrees; and this does not make for easy-going personal and social and political relationships with them; in which case, they are off the norm; thus

12

"abnormal"

6. Another point to consider is the difference between a psychopath and a *psychoticpath*. A psychoticpath may have all the traits of the psychopath, with the addition, however, of an intense bloodlust streak so that it makes it possible for him-her to commit diabolically murder, mayhem, torture, etc. individually or serially compulsively, with hardly a hint of remorse.

The term "psychotic" refers to disease, pathology; and as such, and as I see it, the disease can go in one of two ways: pathically to the extreme, or neurotically to the extreme. When it goes neurotically to the extreme, then the psychosis reveals itself as manic-depression, or hypochondria, or schizophrenia, or delusional disorder, and the like. Such a psychotic person would be considered a *neuropsychotic*. When it goes pathically to the extreme, then the psychosis reveals itself in murder, mayhem, torture, etc., individually or serially, without remorse. Such a psychotic person would be considered a *psychoticpath*.

So, in sum, we have the *pathic nature,* or *character*, who is either predominantly narcipathic, sociopathic, psychopathic, or psychoticpathic, depending upon the type and extent of his or her pathic behavior.

7. *A simplified distinction between the four types of pathics*:

> The **narcipath**: "I'm the best! – no matter what, and to your detriment if you get in my way."

> The **sociopath**: "I'm the boss! – no matter what, and to your detriment if you get in my way."

> The **psychopath**: "I'm the brutalizer! – no matter what, and to your detriment at my whim and impulse."

> The **psychoticpath**: "I'm the archfiend! – no matter what, and   to your agony and/or death."

8. Another point to make is that we have to distinguish between pathics, often hard to tell apart: There is the person who displays pathic behavior by nature, or naturally; and then there is the person who displays pathic behavior, not by nature, but as a result of conditioning or nurture; and so is considered *conditionally* a pathic. So, there is the natural pathic as distinguished from the conditioned pathic.

One almost certain way of determining whether a person is naturally or conditionally a pathic, would be to observe his or her behavior from childhood up, which only a parent can do. There are definite traits that a child displays that almost certainly marks him or her as a pathic. I say "almost certainly," because even then, if a child is abused right from the beginning of life; yet has a hard enough nature – not pathic – to survive, he will display such pathic behavioral patterns. If an abused child has too much of a soft-nature, such abuse would more than likely turn him or her into a neurotic – or neuro*path*, if his conditioned behavior is habitually harmful to others, which is more of a passive response to abuse.

9. All pathics, as a whole, dominate, and prey on the good will and well-being of others, each to his own individual pathic traits. To instill fear into their victims is their secret, and not too secret, glee.

10. The wary person, ever alert to the pathics they may encounter, must keep just as ever in mind the thoughts: *harm* and *dangerous*. It is these that invariably, potentially, result from their behavior, especially when their behavior is frustrated, or threatened, or thwarted.

11. In line with the above discussion of the pathics, it would be appropriate to give the study of the pathic character its own denomination, name; which, accordingly, would be *pathicology*.

12. To repeat, in summary, if we consider the term "evil" generically, as meaning destructive, the breaking down of good, justice, love, peace (peace of mind, as well), then we can define these three variants of pathics in the following general way: The narcipath does evil (deliberate harm) primarily for the sake of self-aggrandizement; the sociopath does evil primarily for the sake of dominance over others; and the psychopath does evil primarily for the sake of evil, or more particularly, of malice – the sheer pleasure derived from inflicting suffering upon others

13. The term "pathic" then will be used in this book as the compre-hensive, generic, meaning for those who willingly, deliberately, do evil – destruction, breaking down, disruption – or malice, upon their fellow man. The type of each person's natural tendencies, will determine in general whether he or she is psychopathic, socio-pathic, or narcipathic (toxic) narcissistic).

Chapter 3
THE EVIL IN HUMAN NATURE

1

Since the doings of pathics are universally destructive to the well-being of others; and since evil is considered a destructive force, it is understood that pathic behavior is considered a form of evil. Malice is the overall term that applies to this form of human evil. So, we can say of a pathic (person) that he or she is evil in general, and malicious in particular.

It is not very likely that a good person could ever *be* a malicious person; but he might very well *act* maliciously under extreme circumstances, such as revenge or self-defense or self-preservation or jealousy ("the green-eyed monster"), or rage, or passion, or drug addiction, or starvation, torture, and on and on. In which case, malice, or evil, is understandably inherent to even the good or moral, person. Which extreme circumstances induce this evil in a basically good or moral person depends on the person and his particular physical and psychological state of mind and body.

Furthermore, considering human nature from an ethical perspective, we could classify people as either basically *moral* (concerned with what is right and good); or, at the other extreme, basically *immoral* (opposed to what is right and good); or, neither moral nor immoral, but basically *amoral* (indifferent to what is right or good). And, as mentioned, if even a good, moral, person could act maliciously in the extreme, then certainly, even more so, would the amoral and immoral person in situations less than the extreme.

To expand on this notion, so as to understand further the evil in human nature, let us say, hypothetically, that, in general, 1/6th of mankind is predominantly moral, another 1/6th of mankind is predominantly immoral, and that 2/3^{rds} of mankind is amoral. Man, as moral, is mainly concerned with justice; man as immoral, is mainly concerned with injustice; man as amoral is mainly concerned with self-interest.

Regarding the immoralists, it is obvious that their evil-doing, in whatever guise, is part and parcel of our humanity. As for the moral-minded, whatever evil-doing they may commit, is relatively minimal compared to the good that they do. It is the amoral-minded who are the wild card in human affairs; since, overall, they will shift indifferently from acting morally or immorally depending on what is in their best interest.

So we have all three classifications of people contributing to the on-going, ever present, ever constant, evils in life. These evils we can classify as either *minor* or *major*: Minor evils are those which cause the least hurt, harm, or disruption to others; major evils are those which cause the most hurt, harm, or disruption to others.

Some descriptions of persons – mostly of the amoralists – that cause the *least* hurt, harm, or disruption to others would be:

---

antagonistic – apathetic – arrogant – avaricious – backbiting – bitchy – bastardly – bullyish – calculating – cagey – combative – cowardly – conceited – covetous – cunning – dishonest – distrustful – dissimulating – domineering – double-tongued – egotistic – faultfinding – fulsome – haughty – hypocritical – ill-mannered – insensitive – insolent – insincere – insulting – intimidating – intolerant – irresponsible – lustful– miserly – opportunistic – petty – pitiless – purse-proud – pretentious – prejudiced – pompous – quarrelsome – given to ridicule – salacious – shameless – sneaky – snide – shrewish – sanctimonious – snobbish – stuck-up – sycophantic – spiteful – thankless – trouble-making – truthless – two-faced – underhanded – unfair – ungrateful – unfriendly

---

Some descriptions of persons – mostly of the immoralists – that cause the *most* hurt, harm, or disruption to others would be:

anti-social – abusive (physically, emotionally, sexually) – barbaric – bigoted – blood-thirsty – blood-lusting – brutish – ruthless – back-stabbing – cold- hearted – churlish – cruel – diabolical – dictatorial – disloyal – envious – faithless – ferocious – fiendish – fraudulent – guileful – heartless – hostile – hell-bent – imperious – lecherous – manipulative – menacing – mendacious – malevolent – merciless – misogynous – murderous – mean-spirited – pitiless – perfidious – ruthless – rapacious – sadistic – self-aggrandizing – serpentine – scheming – vicious – unscrupulous – underhanded – venomous – violent – terroristic – treacherous – tyrannical – vengeful – villainous – vindictive – victimizing – wily

So, roughly speaking, we have 1/6th of mankind willfully committing major evils on mankind, and 2/3rd willfully committing minor, and in some cases, major evils on mankind (and doing *good*, as well, I grant; though mostly in their own self-interest); which clearly spotlights 5/6th of the whole – not to mention the small portion of lesser evils the other 1/6th (the moral-minded) of mankind commit periodically.

2

From this brief overview, it is fairly much a foregone conclusion that evil is an inherent human factor however minimally active it is in any one person, however, buried in the unconscious "id" of human nature.

To support this view, I offer a wide selection of quotations from eminent and perceptive persons from all times and all places. My threefold purpose in including these quotations is (1) as I mentioned, to support the view that evil, relatively speaking, is as much a part of our common human nature as is good; (2) to better prepare the readers' understanding and open-mindedness so as not to judge the pathics in these readings as an anomaly, or "sickness" of human nature; but rather to view them as an opposition to human welfare and well-being; and so, understand more fully the nature of human evil in general, and the pathics as evil in particular; and accordingly, to protect ourselves from them the best we can; and (3) to understand more fully the nature of human evil in general, and the pathics as evil in particular.

———————————

1

Eminent Persons

LITERARY AUTHORS

D.H. Lawrence

1. Intellectual appreciation does not amount to so much; it's what you thrill to. And if murder, suicide, rape is what you thrill to, and nothing else, then it's your destiny — you can't change it *mentally*. You live by what you thrill to, and there's the end of it. Still, for all that, it's a *perverse* courage which makes the man accept the slow suicide of inertia and sterility: the perverseness of a perverse child. — It's amazing how men are like that.

2. This is the very worst wickedness that we refuse to acknowledge the passionate evil that is in us. This makes us secret and rotten.

Churton Collins

We are no more responsible for the evil thoughts that pass through our minds than a scarecrow for the birds which fly over the seed plot he has to guard. The sole responsibility in each case is to prevent them from settling.

George Bernard Shaw

1. When it comes to the point, really bad men are just as rare as really good ones.

2. It is easy – terribly easy – to shake a man's faith in himself. To take advantage of that, to break a man's spirit, is devil's work.

Somerset Maugham

There is no explanation for evil. It must be looked upon as a necessary part of the order of the universe. To ignore it is childish, to bewail it senseless.

John Steinbeck

1. I believe there are monsters born in the world to human parents.... The face and body may be perfect, but if a twisted gene or a malformed egg can produce physical monsters, may not the same process produce a malformed soul?

2. I believe that there is one story in the world, and only one. ... Humans are caught – in their lives, in their thoughts, in their hungers and ambitions, in their avarice and cruelty, and in their kindness and generosity too – in a net of good and evil. ... There is no other story. A man, after he has brushed off the dust and chips of his life, will have left only the hard, clean questions: Was it good or was it evil? Have I done well – or ill?

Stephen King

It's probably wrong to believe there can be any limit to the horror which the human mind can experience. On the contrary, it seems that some exponential effect begins to obtain as deeper and deeper darkness falls – as little as one may like to support the idea that when the nightmare grows black enough, horror spawns horror, one coincidental evil begets other, often more deliberate evils, until finally blackness seems to cover everything. And the most terrifying question of all may be just how much horror the human mind can stand and still maintain a wakeful, staring, unrelenting sanity.

Charles Dickens

1. I have known a vast quantity of nonsense talked about bad men not looking you in the face. Don't trust that conventional idea. Dishonesty will stare honesty out of countenance any day in the

week, if there is anything to be got by it.

2. I know nothing of philosophical philanthropy. But I know what I have seen, and what I have looked in the face in this world here, where I find myself. And I tell you this, my friend, that there are people (men and women both, unfortunately) who have no good in them – none. That there are people whom it is necessary to detest without compromise. That there are people who must be dealt with as enemies of the human race. That there are people who have no human heart, and who must be crushed like savage beasts and cleared out of the way."

Mark Twain

1. Everyone is a moon, and has a dark side which he never shows to anybody.

2. If the desire to kill and the opportunity to kill came always together, who would escape hanging?

3. I have always felt friendly toward Satan. Of course that is ancestral; it must be in the blood, for I could not have originated it.

4. The vast majority of the race, whether savage or civilized, are secretly kind-hearted and shrink from inflicting pain, but in the presence of the aggressive and pitiless minority they don't dare to assert themselves.

Abraham Lincoln

Knavery and flattery are blood relations.

Edgar Allan Poe

I am not more sure that my soul lives, than I am that perverseness is one of the primitive impulses of the human heart – one of the indivisible primary faculties, or sentiments, which give direction to the character of man. Who has not, a hundred times, found himself committing a vile or a stupid action, for no other reason than because he knows he should not? Have we not a perpetual inclination, in the teeth of our best judgment, to violate that which is Law, merely because we understand it to be such?

Anatole France

Nature, in her indifference, makes no distinction between good and evil.

Dostoevsky

Man likes to make roads and to create, that is a fact beyond dispute. But why has he such a passionate love for destruction and chaos also? Tell me that! But on that point I want to say a couple of words myself. May it not be that he loves chaos and destruction (there can be no disputing that he does sometimes love it) because he is instinctively afraid of attaining his object and completing the edifice he is constructing? Who knows, perhaps he only loves that edifice from a distance, and is by no means in love with it at close quarters; perhaps he only loves building it and does not want to live in it, but will leave it, when completed man is a frivolous and incongruous creature, and perhaps, like a chess player, loves the process of the game, not the end of it. And who knows (there is no saying with certainty), perhaps the only goal on earth to which mankind is striving lies in this incessant process of attaining, in other words, in life itself, and not in the thing to be attained, which must always be expressed as a formula, as positive as twice two makes four, and such positiveness is not life, gentlemen, but is the beginning of death. Anyway, man has always been afraid of this mathematical certainty, and I am afraid of it now. Granted that man does nothing but seek that mathematical certainty, he traverses oceans, sacrifices his life in the quest, but to succeed, really to find it, he dreads, I assure you. He feels that when he has found it there will be nothing for him to look for. When workmen have finished their work they do at least receive their pay, they go to the tavern, then they are taken to the police station – and there is occupation for a week. But where can man go? Anyway, one can observe a certain awkwardness about him when he has attained such objects. He loves the process of attaining, but does not quite like to have attained, and that, of course. is very absurd. ...I admit that twice two makes four is an excellent thing, but if we are to give everything its due, twice two makes five is sometimes a very charming thing too. ....

And why are you so firmly, so triumphantly, convinced that only

22

the normal and the positive – in other words, only what is conducive to welfare – is for the advantage of man? Is not reason in error as regards advantage? Does not man, perhaps, love something besides well-being? Perhaps he is just as fond of suffering? Perhaps suffering is just as great a benefit to him as well-being? Man is sometimes extraordinarily, passionately, in love with suffering, and that is a fact. There is no need to appeal to universal history to prove that; only ask yourself, if you are a man and have lived at all. As far as my personal opinion is concerned, to care only for well-being seems to me positively ill-bred. Whether it's good or bad, it is sometimes very pleasant, too, to smash things; I hold no brief for suffering nor for well-being either. I am standing for my caprice, and for its being guaranteed to me when necessary.

I think man will never renounce real suffering, that is, destruction and chaos. Why, suffering is the sole origin of consciousness. Though I did lay it down in the beginning that consciousness is the greatest misfortune for man, yet I know man prizes it and would not give it up for any satisfaction. Consciousness, for instance, is infinitely superior to twice two makes four. Once you have mathematical certainty there is nothing left to do or to understand. There will be nothing left but to bottle up your five senses and plunge into contemplation. While if you tick to consciousness, even though the same result is attained, that is, there is nothing left to do, you can at least flog yourself at times, and that will, at any rate, liven you up. Reactionary as it is, it is better than nothing.

Wilkie Collins
Are there, infinitely varying with each individual, inbred forces of Good and Evil in all of us, deep down below the reach of mortal encouragement and mortal repression-hidden Good and hidden Evil, both alike at the mercy of the liberating opportunity and the sufficient temptation?

Ralph Waldo Emerson
1. The wave of evil washes all our institutions alike.

2. As there is a use in medicine for poisons, so the world cannot move without rogues.

Henry David Thoreau

1. Who, but the Evil One has cried, "Woe! to mankind?"

2. We are conscious of an animal in us, which awakens in proportion as our higher nature slumbers. It is reptile and sensual, and perhaps cannot be wholly expelled; like the worms which, even in life and health, occupy our bodies. Possibly we may withdraw from it, but never change its nature. I fear that it may enjoy a certain health of its own; that we may be well, yet not pure.

Nathaniel Hawthorne

What is there so ponderous in evil, that a thumb's bigness of it should outweigh the mass of things not evil, which were heaped into the other scale!

Joseph Addison

Man is subject to innumerable pains and sorrows by the very condition of humanity, and yet, as if nature had not sown evils enough in life, we are continually adding grief to grief and aggravating the common calamity by our cruel treatment of one another.

Madame de Sable

We so love all new and unusual things that we even derive a secret pleasure from the saddest and most tragic events, both because of their novelty and because of the natural malignity that exists within us.

Samuel Johnson

Wickedness is always easier than virtue, for it takes a short cut to everything.

Jane Austen

There is, I believe, in every disposition a tendency to some particular evil – a natural defect, which not even the best education can overcome.

Rochefoucauld

There is hardly a man clever enough to recognize the full extent of the evil he does.

Publlllus Syrus

He who is bent on doing evil can never want occasion.

Marcellinus Ammianus

Wicked acts are accustomed to be done with impunity for the mere desire of occupation.

Euripides

1. I know indeed what evil I intend to do, but stronger than all my after-thoughts is my fury, fury that brings upon mortals the greatest evils.

2. To all eternity the bad can never be but bad, the good but good; nor in misfortune does man degenerate from his nature, but he is always good. Is this difference from parents or from education?

Menander

It must be that evil communications corrupt good dispositions.

POETS

Charles Baudelaire

Evil is done without effort, naturally, it is the working of fate; good is always the product of an art.

Longfellow

The world loves a spice of wickedness.

Byron

Oh, man! thou feeble tenant of an hour,
Debased by slavery, or corrupt by power,
Who knows thee well must quit thee with disgust,
Degraded mass of animated dust!
Thy love is lust, thy friendship all a cheat,
Thy smiles hypocrisy, thy words deceit!
By nature vile, ennobled but by name,
Each kindred brute might bid thee blush for shame.

Coleridge

And the devil did grin, for his darling sin is pride that apes humility.

Shelley

All spirits are enslaved which serve things evil.

Robert Burns

Man's inhumanity to man
Makes countless thousands mourn!

Kathleen Raine

I couldn't claim that I have never felt the urge to explore evil, but when you descend into hell you have to be very careful.

Michael Drayton

None but the base in baseness do delight.

Pope

Calm, thinking villains, whom no faith could fix,
Of crooked counsels and dark politics.
Destroy his fib, or sophistry – in vain!
The creature's at his dirty work again.

Shakespeare

1. The devil can cite Scripture for his purpose.
    An evil soul producing holy witness
    Is like a villain with a smiling cheek,
    A goodly apple rotten at the heart.
    O what a goodly outside falsehood hath.

3. O villain, villain, smiling, damned villain!
    My tables, – meet it is I set it down,
    That one may smile, and smile, and be a villain:
    At least I'm sure it may be so in Denmark.

4. But then I sigh, and, with a piece of Scripture,
    Tell them that Gods bids us do good for evil:
    And thus I clothe my naked villainy
    With odd old ends stol'n forth of holy writ,
    And seems a saint, when most I play the devil.

5. Wisdom and goodness to the vile seem
        vile;
    Filths savour but themselves.

6. No more be grieved at that which thou hast done:

Roses have thorns, and silver fountains mud;
Clouds and eclipses stain both moon and sun,
And loathsome canker lives in sweetest bud.

7.   Sweetest things turn sourest by their deeds;
Lilies that fester smell far worse than weeds.

8.   The spirit that I have seen
May be the devil: and the devil hath power
To assume a pleasing shape.

9.   And oftentimes to win us to our harm,
the instruments of darkness tell us truths; win us
with honest trifles, to betray's in deepest consequence.

10. A stony adversary, an inhuman wretch,
Uncapable of pity, void and empty
From any dram of mercy.

Dante
She has a nature so malign and evil that she never sates her greedy will, and after food is hungrier than before.

Virgil
There is wickedness in the intention of wickedness, even though it be not perpetrated in the act.

Diphilus
Whoever does not know to blush or be afraid, has the first principles of every kind of baseness. There is no animal more bold than shamelessness.

PHILOSOPHERS / HISTORIANS

Cicero
1. The evil implanted in man by nature spreads so imperceptibly, when the habit of wrong-doing is unchecked, that he himself can set no limit to his shamelessness.

2. Evil is nourished and grows by concealment.

Seneca
No time is too brief for the wicked to accomplish evil.

Herodotus

For insolence is the natural results of great prosperity, while envy and jealousy are innate qualities in the mind of man. When these two devices are combined, they lead to the most enormous crimes: some atrocities are committed from insolence, and some from envy. Princes ought to be superior to all such feelings; but alas! We know that this is not the case. The noble and the worthiest are the object of their jealousy, merely because they feel that their lives are a reproach to them; with the most abandoned they rejoice to spend their time. Calumny they drink in with greedy ears. But what is the most paradoxical of all, if thou showest them merely respectful homage, they take umbrage because thou art not sufficiently humble; whereas if thou bend the knee with the most submissive looks, thou art disordered personalities....

Heraclitus

1. It should be understood that war is the common condition, that strife is justice, and that all things come to pass through the compulsion of strife.

2. Homer was wrong in saying, "Would that strife might perish from amongst gods and men." For if that were to occur then all things would cease to exist.

Polybius

Whoever meditates on these horrible cruelties will not fail to be satisfied that not only are the bodies of men attacked by corrupt and ulcerous humours, which cannot easily be got rid of, but that the minds of men are equally subject to strange disorders. In the case of ulcerated sores, the very medicines which you apply often only tend to irritate and inflame, quickening the progress of the disease; yet, on the other hand, if the disease be neglected and left to its own course, it infects all the neighbouring parts, and proceeds till the whole body becomes unsound. So it is with the mind; when certain dark and malignant passions get possession of it, they render men more savage than the beasts themselves. To men in this state, if you show mercy and kindness, suspecting it to be fraud and artifice, they become more suspicious than before, and regard you with still stronger feelings of aversion. But if you oppose their furious proceedings, there is no crime too horrible for them to perpetrate. They exult and glory in their impieties, and by degrees get rid of every feeling and affection that embellish human nature. There is no doubt that these disorders chiefly arise from a bad education and evil communications, though there are many other causes which may sometimes assist to bring them on, among which none is so likely to be effectual as the insolent conduct and rapacity of public governors.

Plato
False words are not only evil in themselves, but they infect the soul with evil.

Aristotle
1. When devoid of virtue, man is the most unscrupulous and savage of animals, and the worst in regard to sexual indulgence and gluttony.

Thucydides
1. The number of villains is large in this world; and they are more successful in acquiring a name for adroitness than their dupes are for goodness. The latter cannot refrain from blushing; the former rejoice in their iniquities.

2. For so remarkably perverse is the nature of man, that he despises whoever courts him, and admires whoever will not bend before him.

Plutarch
1. There is no beast more savage than man, when he is possessed of power equal to his passions.

2. It is an observation, no less than common, that there is no stronger test of a man's real character than power and authority, exciting as they do, every passion, and discovering every latent vice.

Pascal
1. If all men knew what others say of them, there would not be four friends in the world.

2. It is the fight alone that pleases us, not the victory.

3. Men never do evil so completely and cheerfully as when they do it from religious conviction.

4. We are only falsehood, duplicity, contradiction; we both conceal and disguise ourselves from ourselves.

Erasmus

Nature, more of a stepmother than a mother in several ways, has sown a seed of evil in the hearts of mortals, especially in the more thoughtful men, which makes them dissatisfied with their own lot and envious of another's.

Hegel

This is a deep truth, that evil lies in consciousness: for the brutes are neither evil nor good; the merely natural man quite as little.

Nietzsche

1. [Zarathustra:] But it is with a man as it is with the tree. The more he aspires to the height and light, the more strongly do his roots strive earthward, downward, into the dark, the deep – into evil.

2. [Zarathustra:] You aspire to the free heights, your soul thirsts for the stars. But your wicked instincts, too, thirst for freedom. Your wild dogs want freedom; they bark with joy in their cellar when your spirit plans.

Schopenhauer

Man is at bottom a wild and terrible animal. We know him only as what we call civilization has tamed and trained him; hence we are alarmed by the occasional breaking out of his true nature. But when- ever the locks and chains of law and order are cast off, and anarchy comes in, he shows himself for what he really is.

Bergson

It would take a good deal of time to become a misanthrope if we confined ourselves to the observation of others. It is when we detect our own weaknesses that we come *to* pity *or* despise mankind. The human nature from which we then turn away is the human nature we have discovered in the depths of our own being. The evil is so well screened, the secret so universally kept, that in this case each individual is the dupe of all; however, severely we may profess to judge other men, at bottom we think them better than ourselves. On this happy illusion much of our social life is grounded.

Santyana

1. To fight is a radical instinct; if men have nothing else to fight over they will fight over words, fancies, or women, or they will fight because they dislike each other's looks, or because they have met walking in opposite directions. To knock a thing down, especially if it is cocked at an arrogant angle, is a deep delight to the blood. To fight for a reason and in a calculating spirit is something your true warrior despises.

2. All men are born with a sufficient violent liking for domination, wealth, and pleasure, and with a strong taste for idleness; consequently, all men covet the money, the wives, or the daughters of other men; they wish to be master, to subject them to all their caprices, and to do nothing, or at least to do only very agreeable things.

Kierkegaard

1. Boredom is the root of all evil – the despairing refusal to be with oneself.

2. Since boredom advances and boredom is the root of all evil, no wonder, then, that the world goes backwards, that evil spreads.

Elie Wiesel

Only one enemy is worse than despair: indifference. In every area of human creativity, indifference is the enemy; indifference of evil is worse than evil, because it is also sterile.

Albert Camus

For centuries the death penalty, often accompanied by barbarous refinements, has been trying to hold crime in check; yet crime persists. Why? Because the instincts that are warring in man are not, as the law claims, constant forces in a state of equilibrium.

Eric Hoffer

1. It is by its promise of a sense of power that evil often attracts the weak.

2. It is remarkable by how much a pinch of malice enhances the

penetrating power of an idea or an opinion. Our ears, it seems, are wonderfully attuned to sneers and evil reports about our fellow men.

John Stuart Mill
Absolute fiends are as rare as angels, perhaps rarer: ferocious savages, with occasional touches of humanity, are however very frequent: and in the wide interval which separates these from any worthy representatives of the human species, how many are the forms and gradations of animalism and selfishness, often under an outward varnish of civilization and even cultivation, living at peace with the law, maintaining a creditable appearance to all who are not under their power, yet sufficient often to make the lives of all who are so, a torment and a burthen to them!

Simone Weil
1. In doing good, we are generally cold, and languid, and sluggish; and of all things afraid of being too much in the right. But the works of malice and injustice are quite in another style. They are finished with a bold, masterly hand; touched as they are with the spirit of those vehement passions that call forth all our energies, whenever we oppress and persecute.

2. Evil is neither suffering nor sin; it is both at the same time, it is something common to them both. For they are linked together; sin makes us suffer and suffering makes us evil, and this indissoluble complex of suffering and sin is the evil in which we are submerged against our will, and to our horror.

3. Evil when we are in its power is not felt as evil but as a necessity, or even a duty.

4. A hurtful act is the transference to others of the degradation which we bear in ourselves.

PSYCHOLOGISTS

Jung
1. It is a fact that cannot be denied: the wickedness of others

becomes our own wickedness because it kindles something evil in our own hearts.

2. The man who promises everything is sure to fulfill nothing, and everyone who promises too much is in danger of using evil means in order to carry out his promises, and is already on the road to perdition.

3. It is a frightening thought that man also has a shadow side to him, consisting not just of little weaknesses and foibles, but of a positively demonic dynamism. The individual seldom knows anything of this; to him, as an individual, it is incredible that he should ever in any circumstances go beyond himself. But let these harmless creatures form a mass, and there emerges a raging monster; and each individual is only one tiny cell in the monster's body, so that for better or worse he must accompany it on its bloody rampages and even assist it to the utmost. Having a dark suspicion of these grim possibilities, man turns a blind eye to the shadow-side of human nature. Blindly he strives against the salutary dogma of original sin, which is yet so prodigiously true. Yes, he even hesitates to admit the conflict of which he is so painfully aware.

4. Taking it in its deepest sense, the shadow is the invisible saurian [reptile] tail that man still drags behind him. Carefully amputated, it becomes the healing serpent of the mysteries. Only monkeys parade with it.

Freud

1. I will say nothing of how you may appear in your own eyes, but have you met with so much goodwill in your superiors and rivals, so much chivalry in your enemies and so little envy amongst your acquaintances, that you feel it incumbent on you to protest against the idea of the part played by egoistic baseness in human nature? Do you not know how uncontrolled and unreliable the average human being is in all that concerns sexual life? Or are you ignorant of the fact that all the excesses and aberrations of which we dream at night are crimes actually committed every day by men who are wide awake? What does psycho-analysis do in this connection but

33

confirm the old saying of Plato that the good are those who content themselves with dreaming of what others, the wicked, actually do.

And now look away from individuals to the great war still devastating Europe: think of the colossal brutality, cruelty and mendacity which is now allowed to spread itself over the civilized world. Do you really believe that a handful of unprincipled place-hunters and corrupters of men would have succeeded in letting loose all this latent evil, if the millions of their followers were not also guilty? Will you venture, even in these circumstances, to break a lance for the exclusion of evil from the mental constitution of humanity?

You will accuse me of taking a one-sided view of war, and tell me that it has also called out all that is finest and most noble in mankind, heroism, self-sacrifice, and public spirit. That is true; but do not now commit the injustice, from which psycho-analysis has so often suffered, of reproaching it that it denies one thing because it affirms another. It is no part of our intention to deny the nobility in human nature, nor have we ever done anything to disparage its value. On the contrary, I show you not only the evil wishes which are censored but also the censorship which suppresses them and makes them unrecognizable. We dwell upon the evil in human beings with the greater emphasis only because others deny it, thereby making the mental life of mankind not indeed better, but incomprehensible. If we give up the one-sided ethical valuation then, we are sure to find the truer formula for the relation of evil to good in human nature.

2. In reality, there is no such thing as *eradicating* evil tendencies....The inmost essence of human nature consists of elemental instincts, which are common to all men and aim at the satisfaction of certain primal needs. These instincts in themselves are neither good nor evil. We but classify them and their manifestations in that fashion, according as they meet the needs and demands of the human community. It is admitted that all those instincts which society condemns as evil – let us take as representatives the selfish and the cruel – are of this primitive type.

These primitive instincts undergo a lengthy process of development before they are allowed to become active in the adult being.

They are inhibited, directed towards other aims and departments, become commingled, alter their objects, and are to some *extent* turned back upon their possessor. Reaction-formations against certain instincts take the deceptive *form* of a change in content, as though egoism had changed into altruism, or cruelty into pity. ...

It is not until all these *vicissitudes to which instincts are subject* have been surmounted that what we call the character of a human being is formed, and this, as we know, can only very inadequately be classified as *good* or *bad*. A human being is seldom altogether good or bad; he is usually *good* in one relation and *bad* in another, or *good* in certain *ex*ternal circumstances and in others decidedly *bad*. It is interesting to learn that the existence of strong *bad* impulses in infancy is often the actual condition for an unmistakable inclination towards *good* in the adult person. Those who as children have been the most pronounced egoists may well become the most helpful and self-sacrificing members of the community; most of our sentimentalists, friends of humanity, champions of animals, have been evolved from little sadists and animal tormentors.

William James

1. We are all ready to be savage in *some* cause. The difference between a good man and a bad one is the choice of the cause.

2. For life is evil. Two souls are in my breast; I see the better, and in the very act of seeing it I do the worse.

3. Regarded as a stable finality, every outward good becomes a mere weariness to the flesh. It must be menaced, be occasionally lost. No one knows the worth of innocence till he knows it is gone forever, and that money cannot buy it back. Not the saint, but the sinner that repenteth, is he to whom the full length and breadth, and height and depth, of life's meaning is revealed.

4. The average church-going civilizee realizes, one may say, absolutely nothing of the deeper currents of human nature, or of the aboriginal capacity for murderous excitement which lies sleeping even in his own bosom. ...The water-tight compartment in which the carnivore within us is confined is artificial and not organic. It never

will be organic. The slightest diminution of external pressure, the slightest loophole of licensed exception, will make the whole system leaky, and murder will again grow rampant. It is where the impulse is collective, and the murder is regarded as a punitive or protective duty, that the peril to civilization is greatest. Then, as in the hereditary vendetta, in dueling, in religious massacre, history shows how difficult it is to exterminate a homicidal custom which is once established.

5. The method of averting one's attention from evil, and living simply in the light of good is splendid as long as it will work. It will work with many persons; it will work far more generally than most of us are ready to suppose; and within the sphere of its successful operation there is nothing to be said against it as a religious solution. But it breaks down impotently as soon as melancholy ["depression," in more modern terms] comes; and even though one be quite free from melancholy one's self, there is no doubt that healthy-mindedness is inadequate as a philosophical doctrine, because the evil facts which it refuses positively to account for are a genuine portion of reality; and they may after all be the best key to life's significance, and possibly the only openers of our eyes to the deepest levels of truth.

The normal process of life contains moments as bad as any of which those which insane melancholy is filled with, moments in which radical evil gets its innings and takes its solid turn.

The lunatic's visions of horror are all drawn from the material of daily fact. Our civilization is founded on the shambles, and every individual existence goes out in a lonely spasm of helpless agony. If you protest, my friend, wait till you arrive there yourself! To believe in the carnivorous reptiles of geologic time, is hard for our imagination – they seem too much like museum specimens. Yet there is no tooth in anyone of those museum-skulls that did not daily through long years of the foretime hold fast to the body struggling in despair of some fated living victim. Forms of horror just as dreadful to their victims, if on a smaller spatial scale, fill the world about us today. Here on our very hearths and in our gardens the infernal cat plays with the panting mouse, or holds the hot bird fluttering in her jaws. Crocodiles and rattlesnakes and pythons are at this moment vessels of life as real as we are; their loathsome existence fills every minute of every day that drags its length along; and whenever they or other wild beasts clutch their living prey, the deadly horror which an agitated melancholiac feels is the literally right reaction on the situation. It may be that no religious reconciliation with the absolute totality of things is possible. Some evils, indeed, are ministerial to higher forms of good; but it may be that there are forms of evil so extreme as to enter into no good system whatsoever, and that, in respect of such evil, dumb submission or neglect to notice is the only practical resource. ...[S]ince the evil facts are as genuine parts of nature as the good ones, the philosophic presumption should be that they have some rational significance, and that systematic healthy-mindedness, failing as it does to accord to sorrow, pain, and death any positive and active attention whatever, is formally less complete than systems that try at least to include these elements in their scope.

6. A few summers ago I spent a happy week at the famous Assembly Grounds on the borders of Chautauqua Lake. The moment one treads that sacred enclosure, one feels one's self in an atmosphere of success. Sobriety and industry, intelligence and goodness, orderliness and ideality, prosperity and cheerfulness, pervade the air. It is a serious and studious picnic on a gigantic scale. Here you have a town of many thousands of inhabitants, beautifully laid out in the forest and drained, and equipped with means for satisfying all the necessary lower and most of the superfluous higher wants of man. You have a first-class college in full blast. You have magnificent music – a chorus of seven hundred voices, with possibly the most perfect open-air auditorium in the world. You have every sort of athletic exercise from sailing, rowing, swimming, bicycling, to the ball-field and the more artificial doings which the gymnasium affords. You have kindergartens and model secondary schools. You have general religious services and special club-houses for the several sects. You have perpetually running soda water fountains, and daily popular lectures by distinguished men. You have the best of company, and yet no effort. You have no

symotic diseases, no poverty, no drunkenness, no crime, no police. You have culture, you have kindness, you have cheapness, you have equality, you have the best fruits of what mankind has fought and bled and striven for under the name of civilization for centuries. You have, in short, a foretaste of what human society might be, were it all in the light, with no suffering and no dark corners. I went in curiosity for a day. I stayed for a week, held spellbound by the charm and ease of everything, by [witnessing a] middle-class paradise, without a sin, without a victim, without a blot, without a tear.

And yet what was my own astonishment, on emerging into the dark and wicked world again, to catch myself quite unexpectedly and involuntarily saying: "Ouf! what a relief!" Now for something primordial and savage, even though it were as bad as an Armenian massacre, to set the balance straight again. This order is too tame, this culture too second-rate, this goodness too uninspiring. This human drama without a villain or a pang; this community so refined that ice-cream soda-water is the utmost offering it can make to the brute animal in man; this city simmering in the tepid lakeside sun; this atrocious harmlessness of all things, – I cannot abide with them. Let me take my chances again in the big outside worldly wilderness with all its sins and sufferings. There are the heights and the depths, the precipices and the steep ideals, the gleams of the awful and the infinite; and there is more hope and help a thousand times than in this dead level and quintessence of every mediocrity.

Such was the sudden right-about-face performed for me by my lawless fancy! There had been spread before me the realization – on a small, sample scale of course – of all the ideals for which our civilization has been striving: security, intelligence, humanity, and order; and here was the instinctive hostile reaction, not of the natural man, but of a so-called cultivated man upon such a Utopia. There seemed thus to be a self-contradiction and paradox somewhere, which I, as a professor drawing a full salary, was in duty bound to unravel and explain, if I could.

So, I meditated. And, first of all, I asked myself what the thing was that was so lacking in this Sabbatical city, and the lack of which kept one forever falling short of the higher sort of contentment. And I soon recognized that it was the element that gives to the wicked outer world all its moral style, expressiveness and picturesqueness, – the element of precipitousness, so to call it, of strength and strenuousness, intensity and danger. What excites and interests the looker-on at life, what the romances and the statues celebrate and the grim civic monuments remind us of, is the everlasting battle, of the powers of light with those of darkness; with heroism, reduced to its bare chance, yet ever and anon snatching victory from the jaws of death. But in this unspeakable Chautauqua there was no potentiality of death in sight anywhere, and no point of the compass visible from which danger might appear. The ideal was so completely victorious already that no sign of any previous battle remained, the place just resting on its oars. But what our human emotions seem to require is the sight of the struggle going on. The moment the fruits are being merely eaten, things become ignoble. Sweat and effort, human nature strained to its uttermost and on the rack, yet getting through alive, and then turning its back on its success to pursue another more rare and arduous still – this is the sort of thing the presence of which inspires us, and the reality of which it seems to be the function of all the higher forms of literature and fine art to bring home to us and suggest. At Chautauqua there were no racks, even in the place's historical museum; and no sweat, except possibly the gentle moisture on the brow of some lecturer, or on the sides of some player in the ball-field.

Such absence of human nature in *extremis* anywhere seemed, then, a sufficient explanation for Chautauqua's flatness and lack of zest.

7. [The following letter to his wife describes in brief his reaction to his "Chautauqua week," as stated in the above passage.]

The Chautauqua week, or rather six and a half days, has been a real success. I have learned a lot, but I'm glad to get into something less blameless but more admiration-worthy. The flash of a pistol, a dagger, or a devilish eye, anything to break the unlovely level of 10,000 good people – a crime, murder, rape, elopement, anything would do.

8. Everyone must at some time have wondered at that strange paradox of our moral nature, that, though the pursuit of outward good is the breath of its nostrils, the attainment of outward good would seem to be in suffocation and death. Why does the painting of any paradise or utopia, in heaven or on earth, awaken such yawnings for nirvana and escape? The white-robed harp-playing heaven of our sabbath-schools and the ladylike tea-table elysium represented in Mr. Spencer's *Data of Ethics*, as the final consummation of progress, are exactly on par in this respect – lubberlands, pure and simple, one and all. We look upon them from this delicious mess of insanities and realities, strivings and deadnesses, hopes and fears, agonies and exultations, which forms our present state, and *tedium vitae* is the only sentiment they awaken in our breasts. To our crepuscular natures, born for the conflict, the Rembrandtesque moral chiaroscuro, the shifting struggle of the sun-beam in the gloom, such pictures of light upon light are vacuous and expressionless, and neither to be enjoyed nor understood. If this be the whole fruit of the victory, we say; if the generations of mankind suffered and laid down their lives; if prophets confessed and martyrs sang in the fire, and all the sacred tears were shed for no other end than that a race of creatures of such unexampled insipidity should succeed, and protract in *saecul saeculorum* their contented and inoffensive lives, – why, at such a rate, better lose than win the battle, or at all events better ring down the curtain before the last act of the play, so that a business that began so importantly may be saved from so singularly flat a winding-up.

9. In many respects man is the most ruthlessly ferocious of beasts. As with all gregarious animals, "two souls," as Faust says, "dwell within his breast," the one of sociability and helpfulness, the other of jealousy and antagonism to his mates. Though in a general way he cannot live without them, yet, as regards certain individuals, it often falls out that he cannot live with them either. Constrained to

be a member of a tribe, he still has a right to decide, as far as in him lies, of which other members the tribe shall consist. Killing off a few obnoxious ones may often better the chances of those that remain. And killing off a neighboring tribe from whom no good thing comes, but only competition, may materially better the lot of the whole tribe. Hence the gory cradle, the *bellum omnium contra omnes,* in which our race was reared; hence the fickleness of human ties, the ease with which the foe of yesterday becomes the ally of today, the friend of today the enemy of tomorrow; hence the fact that we, the lineal representatives of the successful enactors of one scene of slaughter after another, must, whatever more pacific virtues we may also possess, still carry about with us, ready at any moment to burst into flame, the smouldering and sinister traits of character by means of which they lived through so many massacres, harming others, but themselves unharmed.

SAGES /SEERS

From THE OLD TESTAMENT

from Lamentations 3:38
1. I form the light, and create darkness: I make peace, and create evil: I the LORD do all these things. (*Isaiah 45:7, KJV*) Shall a trumpet be blown in the city, and the people not be afraid? shall there be evil in a city, and the LORD hath not done it? (*Amos 3:6, KJV*) Out of the mouth of the most High proceedeth not evil and good?

2. Is it not from the mouth of the Most High that both calamities and good things come? (*Lamentations 3:38, NIV*) Is it not from the mouth of the Most High That both good and ill go forth? (*Lamentations 3:38, NASB*)

Isaiah 5:20-21
1. Woe to those who call evil good, and good evil; who substitute darkness for light and light for darkness; who substitute bitter for sweet, and sweet for bitter! Woe to those who are wise in their

own eyes, and clever in their own sight!

2

Psalm 64

Hear me, a God, as I voice my
    complaint;
    protect my life from the threat of
    the enemy.
 Hide me from the conspiracy of the
    wicked,
    from that noisy crowd of evildoers.
They sharpen their tongues like
    swords
    and aim their words like deadly
    arrows.
They shoot from ambush at the
    innocent man;
    they shoot at him suddenly, without
    fear.
They encourage each other in evil
    plans,
    they talk about hiding their snares;
    they say, "Who will see them?"
They plot injustice and say,
    "We have devised a perfect plan!"
Surely the mind and heart of man
    are cunning.

Psalm 73

But as for me, my feet had almost
    slipped;
 I had almost lost my foothold.
For I envied the arrogant
  when I saw the prosperity of the
    wicked.
    They have no struggles;
  their bodies are healthy and strong.
They are free from the burdens

42

common to man;
   they are not plagued by human ills.
Therefore pride is their 'necklace;
they clothe themselves with
      violence.
From their callous hearts comes
      iniquity;
the evil conceits of their minds
      know no limits.
They scoff, and speak with malice;
   in their arrogance they threaten
   oppression.
Their mouths lay claim to heaven,
   and their tongues take possession of
   the earth.
Therefore their people turn to them
   and drink up waters in abundance.
They say, "How can God know?"
   "Does the Most High have
   Knowledge?"

from **Proverbs**
1
My son, if sinners entice you,
   do not give in to them.
If they say, "Come along with us;
   Let's lie in wait for someone's blood,
   let's waylay some harmless soul;
let's swallow them alive, like the
      grave,
      and whole, like those who go down
      to the pit;
we will get all sorts of valuable things and fill
our houses with plunder;
throw in your lot with us,
      and we will share a common

purse."
My son, do not go along with them,
do not set foot on their paths;
for their feet rush into sin,
they are swift to shed blood.

2

Wisdom will save you from the ways
of wicked men,
from men whose words are
perverse,
who leave the straight paths
to walk in dark ways,
who delight in doing wrong
and rejoice in the perverseness of
evil,
whose paths are crooked
and who are devious in their ways.
It will save you ,also from the
adulteress,
from the wayward wife with her
seductive words,
who has left the partner of her youth
and ignored the covenant she made
before God.
For her house leads down to death
and her paths to the spirits of the
dead.
None who go to her return
or attain the paths of life.

From **The Wisdom of Solomon**

1

For they reasoned unsoundly,
saying to themselves,
"Short and sorrowful is our life,

44

and there is no remedy when a man
comes to his end,
and no one has been known to return
from Hades.
Because we were born by mere
chance,
and hereafter we shall be as though
we had never been;
because the breath in our nostrils
is smoke,
and reason is a spark kindled by the
beating of our hearts.
When it is extinguished, the body
will turn to ashes,
and the spirit will dissolve like empty
air.
Our name will be forgotten in time,
and no one will remember our works;
our life will pass away like the traces
of a cloud,
and be scattered like mist
that is chased by the rays of the sun and overcome by its heat.
For our allotted time is the passing of
a shadow,
and there is no return from our death."

2

"Come, therefore, let us enjoy the
good things that exist,
and make use of the creation to the
full as in youth.
Let us take our fill of costly wine and
perfumes,
and let no flower of spring pass by us.
Let us crown ourselves with rose
buds before they wither.
Let none of us fail to share in our

revelry,
everywhere let us leave signs of
enjoyment,
because this is our portion, and this
our lot.
Let us oppress the righteous poor
man
let us not spare the widow
nor regard the gray hairs of the aged.
But let our might be our law of right,
for what is weak proves itself to be
useless.
Let us lie in wait for the righteous
man,
because he is inconvenient to us and
opposes our actions;
he reproaches us for sins against the
law,
and accuses us of sins against our
training.
He professes to have knowledge of
God,
and calls himself a child of the Lord.
He became to us a reproof of our
thoughts;
the very sight of him is a burden to
us,
because his manner of life is unlike
that of others,
and his ways are strange.
We are considered by him as some
thing base,
and he avoids our ways as unclean;
he calls the last end of the righteous
happy,
and boasts that God is his father.

Let us see if his words are true,
   and let us test what will happen at
   the end of his life;
for if the righteous man is God's son,
   he will help him,
   and will deliver him from the hand
   of his adversaries.
Let us test him with insult and
   torture,
   that we may find out how gentle
   he is,
and make trial of his forbearance.
Let us condemn him to a shameful
   Death,
For, according to what he says, he will
   be protected."

3

For the fascination with wickedness
   Obscures what is good,
And roving desire perverts the innocent mind.

4

Afterward it was not enough for
them to err about the knowledge
   of God,
but they live in great strife due to, ignorance,
and they call such great evils peace.
For whether they kill children in
   their initiations, or celebrate secret mysteries,
or hold frenzied revels with strange
   customs,
they no longer keep either their lives
   or their marriages pure,
   but they either treacherously kill one
another, or, grieve one another by
   adultery,

and all is a raging riot of blood and murder, theft and deceit,
  corruption, faithlessness, tumult,
  perjury,
confusion over what is good, forgetfulness of favors,
    pollution of souls, sex perversion,
    disorder in marriage, adultery, and
    debauchery.
    For the worship of idols not to be
    named
    is the beginning, and cause and end
    of every evil.
For their worshipers either rave in
    exultation, or prophesy lies,
    or live unrighteously, or readily commit perjury;
  for because they trust in lifeless
    idols
    they swear wicked oaths and expect
    to suffer no harm.
    But just penalties will overtake them
    on two counts:
    because they thought wickedly of
    God in. devoting themselves to
    idols,
    and because in deceit they swore
    unrighteously through contempt
    for holiness.
    For it is not the power of the things
    by which men swear!
    but the just penalty for those who sin,
    that always pursues the transgression of the unrighteous.

From **THE NEW TESTAMENT**

1. Beware of false teachers who come disguised as harmless sheep, but are wolves and will tear you apart. You can detect them by the way they act, just as you can identify a tree by its fruit. You need never confuse grapevines with thorn bushes or figs with thistles.

Different kinds of fruit trees can quickly be identified by examining their fruit. A variety that produces delicious fruit never produces an inedible kind. And a tree producing an inedible kind can't produce what is good. So the trees having the inedible fruit are chopped down and thrown on the fire. Yes, the way to identify a tree or a person is by the kind of fruit produced. (Matthew 7:15-23)

2. The good man brings good things out of the good stored up in his heart, and the evil man brings evil things out of the evil stored up in his heart. For out of the overflow of his heart his mouth speaks. (Luke 6:45)

Jesus

1. "But if anyone causes one of these little ones who believe in me to sin, it would be better for him to have a large millstone hung around his neck and to be drowned in the depths of the sea. Woe to the world because of the things that cause people to sin! Such things must come, but woe to the man through whom they come!" (Matthew 18:6-7)

2. "The good person brings good things out of a good treasure, and the evil person brings evil things out of an evil treasure." (Matthew 12:35)

3. "It is what comes out of a person that defiles. For it is from within, from the human heart, that evil intentions come: fornication, theft, murder, adultery, avarice, wickedness, deceit, licentiousness, envy, slander, pride, folly. All these evil things come from within, and they defile a person." (Mark 7:20-23)

4. "For all who do evil hate the light and do not come to the light, so that their deeds may not be exposed. But those who do what is true come to the light, so that it may be clearly seen that their deeds have been done in God." (John 3:20-21)

St. Paul

And if you are sure that you are a guide to the blind, a light to those who are in darkness, a corrector of the foolish, a teacher of children, having in the law the embodiment of knowledge and truth, you, then, that teach others, will you not teach yourself? While you preach against stealing, do you steal? You that forbid adultery, do you commit adultery? You that abhor idols, do you rob temples? You that boast in the law, do you dishonor God by breaking the law?

Buddha

1. An insincere and evil friend is more to be feared than a wild beast; a wild beast may wound your body, but an evil friend will wound your mind.

2. It is a man's own mind, not his enemy or foe, that lures him to evil ways.

Krishna / from **The Bhagavad Gita**

1. It is greedy desire and wrath, born of passion, the great evil, the sum of destruction: this is the enemy of the soul.

2. Evil men know not what should be done or what should not be done. Purity is not in their hearts, nor good conduct, nor truth. They say: 'This world has no truth, no moral foundation, no God. . .' Firm in this belief, these men of dead souls, of truly little intelligence, undertake their work of evil: they are the enemies of this fair world, working for its destruction. ...They are bound by hundreds of vain hopes. Anger and lust is their refuge; and they strive by unjust means to amass wealth for their own cravings.

From **The Upanishads**

As one acts and conducts himself, so does he become. The doer of good becomes good. The doer of evil becomes evil. One becomes virtuous by virtuous action, bad by bad action.

From **The Tao**

The Tao doesn't take sides; it gives birth to both good and evil. The Master doesn't take sides; she welcomes both saints and sinners.

Chinese Proverb

The evil-doer accuses first.

Gandhi

In a strictly scientific sense God is at the bottom of both good and evil.

Ramakrishna

Men are like pillow-cases. The colour of one may be red, that of another blue, and that of the third black; but all contain the same cotton within. So it is with man; one is beautiful, another is ugly, a third holy, and a fourth wicked; but the Divine Being dwells in them all.

PERCEPTIVE PERSONS

Stephen A. Diamond

Selection from *Anger, Madness, and the Daimonic: The Psychological Genesis of Violence, Evil, and Creativity*

Hostility, hatred, and violence are the greatest evils we have to contend with today. Evil is now – ever has been, and ever will be – an existential reality, an inescapable fact with which we mortals must reckon. In virtually every culture there has existed some word for evil, a universal, linguistic acknowledgment of the archetypal presence of "something that brings sorrow, distress, or calamity...; the fact of suffering, misfortune, and wrongdoing." Yet another of Webster's traditional definitions links the English word *evil* with all that is "angry... wrathful...[and] malignant." The term *evil* has always been closely associated with anger, rage, and, of course, violence. But today we seem uncomfortable with this antiquated concept. Our discomfort resides largely in the religious and theological implications of evil, based on values, ethics, and morals that many today find judgmental, dogmatic, and passé. In a secular society like ours, we Americans have tended to avoid biblical characterizations such as "sin," "wickedness," "iniquity," and "evil." Nevertheless, as Jungian analyst Liliane Frey-Rohn rightly remarks: "Evil is a phenomenon that exists and has always existed only in the human world. Animals know nothing of it. But there is no form of religion, of ethics, or of community life in which it is not important. What is more, we need to discriminate between evil and good in our daily life with others, and as psychologists in our professional work. And yet it is difficult to give a precise definition of what we mean psychologically by these terms."

Evil is an actuality, whether or not we choose to deny it. In their

51

1971 anthology, *Sanctions for Evil,* social psychologists Nevitt Sanford and Craig Comstock cogently justify resurrecting the religiously tainted term 'evil': "In using the word *evil,* we mean not that an act or pattern of life is necessarily a sin or a crime according to some law, but rather that it leads to damage or pain suffered by people, to social destructiveness of a degree so serious as to call for use of an ancient, heavily freighted term." When employed in this sense, *evil is* synonymous with "senseless violence." But, on a still subtler level, evil can be considered *that tendency which – whether in oneself or others – would inhibit personal growth and expansion, destroy or limit innate potentialities, curtail freedom, fragment or disintegrate the personality, and diminish the quality of interpersonal relationships.*

The fact that evil, as defined above, exists more or less throughout our world seems incontrovertible. We see evil every day in its infernally multifarious forms. First, there are the cosmic, supernatural, trans-personal, or natural evils like floods, famine, fire, drought, disease, earthquakes, tornadoes, hurricanes, and harmful, unforeseeable accidents that wreak untimely death havoc, and unmentionable suffering on humanity. This is the metaphysical or "existential evil" with which the biblical Book of Job concerns itself, and which religions worldwide try mightily to explain. Existential evil is an inescapable part of our human destiny, and one with which we must reckon as best we can, without closing ourselves off to its tragic, intrinsic reality. But there is, of course, another kind of evil at large: human evil, "man's inhumanity to man" in the most panoramic sense. By "human evil," I mean those attitudes and behaviors that promote excessive interpersonal aggression, cruelty, hostility, disregard for the integrity of others, self-destructiveness, psychopathology and human misery in general. Human evil can be perpetrated by a single individual (personal evil) or by a group, a country, or an entire culture (collective evil). The Nazi atrocities directly or indirectly engaged in by the German people dramatically exemplify the latter.

...

We Americans need desperately to better understand, constructively relate to, and meaningfully communicate about the perennial problem of evil. In the absence of adequate symbols and myths to express and contain our modem experience of evil, we must either modify our existing myths or create completely new, symbolic conceptualizations of evil. Failing to do so forces us into a reactionary and regressive return to outdated myths like the "devil." Symbols and myths have always provided a means of making sense of evil, and putting it in its proper perspective. Symbols and myths make a meaningful niche for evil in our worldview; without them, we cannot contextually grasp the gross reality of evil; nor can we comprehend its psychological significance. Hence, the indispensable role of wicked stepparents, witches, ghosts, and other malevolent creatures in traditional children's fairy tales, and in all myths and legends of lands far and near, each one symbolizing some salient aspect of evil.

Patrick Mcgoohan
But what is the greatest evil? If you are going to epitomize evil, what is it? The greatest evil that one has to fight constantly, every minute of the day until one dies, is the worst part of oneself.

James Oliver Curwood
In every man's heart there is a devil, but we do not know the man as bad until the devil is roused.

Rod Serling
1. I happen to think that the singular evil of our time is prejudice. It is from this evil that all other evils grow and multiply. In almost every- thing I've written there is a thread of this: a man's seemingly palpable need to dislike someone other than himself.

Jake Thoene
1. Apathy and evil. The two work hand in hand. They are the same, really. ...Evil wills it. Apathy allows it. Evil hates the innocent and the defenseless most of all. Apathy doesn't care as long as it's not personally inconvenienced.

Anonymous

Apathy is the glove in which evil slips its hand.

Suzanne Massie

Evil is near. Sometimes late at night the air grows strongly clammy and cold around me. I feel it brushing me. All that the Devil asks is acquiescence ... not struggle, not conflict. Acquiescence.

Ellen Glasgow

When this immediate evil power has been defeated, we shall not yet have won the long battle with the elemental barbarities. Another Hitler, it may be an invisible adversary, will attempt, again, and yet again, to destroy our frail civilization. Is it true, I wonder, that the only way to escape a war is to be in it? When one is a part of an actuality does the imagination find a release?

Dean Koontz

1. I've got evil in me as much as anyone, some desires that scare me. Even if I don't give in to them, just *having* them scares the living bejesus out of me sometimes. I'm no saint, the way you kid about. But I've always walked the line, walked that goddamned line. It's a mean mother of a line, straight and narrow, sharp as a razor, cuts right into you when you walk it long enough. You're always bleeding on that line, and sometimes you wonder why you don't just step off and walk in the cool grass.

2. Many human beings need no supernatural mentoring to commit acts of savagery; some people are devils in their own right, their tell-tale horns having grown inward to facilitate their disguise.

Louis Becks

Of what use are good words to an evil heart?

ON EVIL IN PARTICULAR

Malice

Malice definition: active ill will; desire to harm another or
to do mischief; spite

Eric Hoffer

1. There is probably an element of malice in our readiness to overestimate people – we are, as it were, laying up for ourselves the pleasure of later cutting them down to size.

2. It is remarkable by how much a pinch of malice enhances the penetrating power of an idea or an opinion. Our ears, it seems, are wonderfully attuned to sneers and evil reports about our fellow men.

Mark Twain

1. There is more real pleasure to be gotten out of a malicious act, where your heart is in it, than out of thirty acts of a nobler sort.

2. Malice and malignity faded out of me – or maybe I drove them out of me, knowing that a malignant book would hurt nobody but the fool who wrote it.

3. Of all the creatures [man]...is the only one – the solitary one – that possesses malice. ... He is the only creature that inflicts pain for sport, knowing it to be pain...all creatures kill...man is the only one...that kills in malice, the only one that kills for revenge.

4. You take the lies out of him, and he'll shrink to the size of your hat; you take the malice out of him, and he'll disappear.

Victor Hugo

The malicious have a dark memory.

Anatole France

He who undertakes to guide men must never lose sight of the fact that they are malicious monkeys.... The folly of the revolution was in aiming to establish virtue on the earth. When you want to make men good and wise, free, moderate, generous, you are led inevitably to the desire of killing them all.

Melville

All that most maddens and torments; all that stirs up the lees of things; all truth with malice in it; all that cracks the sinews and cakes the brain; all the subtle demonisms of life and thought; all evil, to crazy Ahab, were visibly personified, and made practically assailable in Moby Dick.

He piled upon the whale's white hump the sum of all the general rage and hate felt by his whole race from Adam down; and then, as if his chest had been a mortar, he burst his hot heart's shell upon it.

Aldous Huxley
Luckily, in the long run, malice is always self-destructive.

Thomas Jefferson
Malice will always find bad motives for good actions.

Riitta Uosukainen
I'm just honest and open, although that may not always be wise. Openness is often responded to with cruelty. One thing that I have learned in this is that truly malicious people exist. -

H. G. Bohn
Malice seldom wants a mark to shoot at.

William Gilmore Simms
But for that blindness which is inseparable from malice, what terrible powers of evil would it possess! Fortunately for the world, its venom, like that of the rattlesnake, when most poisonous, clouds the eye of the reptile, and defeats its aim.

George Stillman Hillard
The venom that chills and curdles the warm current of life in man is secreted only in creeping and cold-blooded creatures; and the inveterate malignity that never forgets or forgives is found only in base and ignoble natures, whose aims are selfish, whose means are indirect, cowardly, and treacherous.

Thomas Wtson
Malice is the devil's picture. Lust makes men brutish, and malice makes them devilish. Malice is mental murder; you may kill a man and never touch him; "Whosoever hateth his mother is a murderer."

Edmund Burke
In doing good, we are generally cold, and languid, and sluggish; and of all things afraid of being too much in the right. But the works of malice and injustice are quite in another style. They are finished with a bold, masterly hand; touched as they are with the spirit of

those vehement passions that call forth all our energies, whenever we oppress and persecute.

Sir Philip Sidney
Malice, in its false witness, promotes its tale with so cunning a confusion; so mingles truths with falsehoods, surmises with certainties, causes of no moment with matters capital, that the accused can absolutely neither grant nor deny, plead innocence nor confess guilt.

William Hazlitt
Ignorance of the world leaves one at the mercy of its malice.

Burns
Vengeful malice, unrepenting.

Blaise Pascal
When malice has reason on its side, it becomes proud, and parades reason in all its splendour.

Walter Raleigh
False and malicious reports which vex the spirit, and consequently impair health, is a degree of murder.

Max Heindel
Evil and malicious lies can kill anything that is good, if they are strong enough and repeated often enough. But, conversely, seeking for the good in evil will, in time, transmute the evil into good.

Macaulay
There is no malice like the malice of the renegade.

Johan Lavatar
He, who cannot forgive a trespass of malice to his enemy, has never yet tasted the most sublime enjoyment of love.

Francis Iles
It was not until several weeks after he had decided to murder his wife that Dr Birkleigh took any active steps in the matter. Murder is a serious business (Malice Aforethought)

William Camden
Malice never spoke well.

Patrick Kavanaugh
Malice is only another name for mediocrity.

Shakespeare
1. Venomous malice.

2. The very fangs of malice..

3. In the great hand of God I stand, and thence
   Against the undivulged pretense I fight
   Of treasonous malice.

Racine
A noble heart cannot suspect in others the pettiness and malice that it has never felt.

Moliere
There is no rampart that will hold out against malice.

Montaigne
Even in the midst of compassion we feel within I know not what tart sweet titillation of malicious pleasure in seeing others suffer; children have the same feeling.

Rabelais
Wisdom entereth not into a malicious mind.

Plutarch
When malice is joined to envy, there is given forth poisonous and feculent matter, as ink from the cuttle-fish.

Socrates
Malice drinketh up the greater part of its own poison.

Cicero
1. Malice is cunning.
2. Malice is pleasure derived from another's evil [misfortune] which brings no advantage to oneself.

Livy
Malice is blind.

Ovid
Malice feeds on the living.

Puiedrus
Biting malice.

Terence
There is such malice in men as to rejoice in misfortunes and from another's woes to draw delight.

Publilius Syrus
1. Malice tells that which it sees, but not the causes.
2. The malice of one man quickly becomes the ill word of all.
3. The malicious mind has hidden teeth.

Gracián
Man's life is a warfare against the malice of men.

VARIATIONS OF EVIL

The following sections: "The Aesthetics of Evil," "The Degradation of Evil," "The Culture of Evil, "The Egoism of Evil," "The Politics of Evil," present evil in its various aspects besides its obvious, ordinary, destructiveness in human affairs.

THE AESTHETICS OF EVIL

Jean Genet

1. Repudiating the virtues of your world, criminals hopelessly agree to organize a forbidden universe. They agree to live in it. The air there is nauseating: they can breathe it.

2. Crimes of which a people is ashamed constitute its real history. The same is true of man.

3. We know that their adventures are childish. They themselves are fools. They are ready to kill or be killed over a card-game in which an opponent – or they themselves – was cheating. Yet, thanks to such fellows, tragedies are possible.

4. When the judge calls the criminal's name out he stands up, and they are immediately linked by a strange biology that makes them both opposite and complementary. The one cannot exist without the other. Which is the sun and which is the shadow? It's well known some criminals have been great men.

5. Anyone who hasn't experienced the ecstasy of betrayal knows nothing about ecstasy at all.

6. To achieve harmony in bad taste is the height of elegance.

7. What we need is hatred. From it our ideas are born.

8. I made up my mind to live with my head bowed and to pursue my destiny toward darkness, in an opposite direction to yours, and to exploit the underside of your beauty.

9. Murder is not the most effective means of reaching the subterranean world of abjection. Quite the contrary. The blood he has shed, the constant danger to which his body is exposed of eventually losing its head (the murderer withdraws but his withdrawal is upward), and the attraction he exerts for he is assumed to possess, in view of the way he defies the laws of life, the most easily imagined attributes of exceptional strength – prevent people from despising the criminal.

Other crimes are more degrading: theft, begging, treason, breach of trust, etc.; these are the ones I chose to commit, though I was always haunted by the idea of a murder which would cut me off irremediably from your world.

10. My solitude in prison was total. Now that I speak it is less so. Then I was alone. At night I would let myself be bourne along by a current of abandon. The world was a torrent, a rapid of forces come together to carry me to the sea, to death. I had the bitter joy of knowing I was alone.

11. My talent will be the love I feel for that which constitutes the world of prisons and penal colonies. Not that I want to transform them or bring them around to your kind of life, or that I look upon them with indulgence or pity: I recognize in thieves, traitors and murderers, in the ruthless and the cunning, a deep beauty – a sunken beauty – which I deny you.

12. I have…been that little wretch who knew only hunger, physical humiliation, poverty, fear and degradation. From such galling attitudes as these I have drawn reasons for glory.

13. "That's probably what I am," I would say to myself, "but at least I'm aware of it, and such awareness destroys shame and affords me a feeling that few know: pride." You who regard me with contempt are made up of nothing else but a succession of similar woes, but you will never be aware of this and thus will, never possess pride, in other words, the knowledge of a force that enables you to stand up to misery – not your own misery, but that of which mankind is composed.

14. When Java cringed with fright, he was stunning. Thanks to him, fear was noble. It was restored to the dignity of natural movement, with no other meaning than that of organic fright, panic of the viscera confronted with the image of death or pain. Java trembled. I saw a yellow diarrhea flow down his monumental thighs. Terror stalked and ravaged the features of his splendid face that had been so tenderly and greedily kissed. It was mad of that cataclysm to dare disturb such noble proportions, such inspiring, such harmonious relationships, and those proportions and relationships were the source of the crisis, they were responsible for it. So lovely were they that they were even its expression, since what I call Java was both master of his body and responsible for his fear. His fear was beautiful to see. Everything became a sign of it: his hair, muscles, eyes, teeth, penis, and the child's manly grace.

15. "These heroes [of treason]," I said to myself, "must have reached such a state of perfection that I no longer wish to see them live, so that their lives may be climaxed by a brazen destiny. If they have achieved perfection, behold them at the brink of death, no longer afraid of the judgment of men. Nothing can spoil their amazing success. May they therefore grant me what is denied the wretched."

16. "It's [Nazi Germany] a race of thieves," I thought to myself. "If I steal here, I perform no singular deed that might fulfill me. I obey the customary order; I do not destroy it. I am not committing evil. I am not upsetting anything. The outrageous is impossible. I'm stealing in the void."

17. [H]is power acted from a distance and I was held back, not by fear but by the attraction of the violence of this mature man, matured in evil, a genuine bandit, capable, and he alone, of drawing me, almost carrying me, into the frightening world from which I felt he had emerged.

18. Bernard knew about my life and never reproached me. Once, however, he tried to justify his being a cop; he talked to me about morality. Merely from the aesthetic viewpoint with regard to an act, I could not listen to him. The good will of moralists cracks up against what they call my dishonesty. Though they may prove to me that an act is detestable because of the harm it does, only I can decide, and that by the song it evokes within me, as to its beauty and elegance; only I can reject or accept it. No one will bring me back to the path of righteousness. ...Since rectitude was your domain, I would have none of it, though I often recognized its nostalgic appeal. I had to fight against its charms.

19. I wish for a moment to focus attention on the reality of supreme happiness in despair: when one is suddenly alone, confronting one's sudden ruin, when one witnesses the irremediable destruction of one's work and self. I would give all the wealth of this world – indeed it must be given – to experience the desperate – and secret – state which no one knows I know. Hitler, alone, in the cellar of his palace, during the last minutes of the defeat of Germany, surely experienced that moment of pure light – fragile and solid lucidity – the awareness of his fall.

20. I am in danger not only when I steal, but every moment of my life, because I have stolen. My life is clouded by a vague anxiety which both weighs upon and lightens it. To preserve the limpidity and keenness of my gaze, my consciousness must be sensitive to every act so that I can quickly correct it and change its meaning. This anxiety keeps me on the alert. It gives me the surprised attitude of a deer caught in the clearing. But the anxiety, which is a kind of dizziness, also sweeps me along, makes my head buzz and lets me trip and fall in an element of darkness where I lie low if I hear the ground beneath the leaves resounding with a hoof.

21. In order to desert Lucian I shall organize an avalanche of' catastrophes around the desertion so that he will seem to be swept away by them. He will be a straw in the midst of a tornado. Even if he learns that I have willed his misfortune and hates me, his hatred will not affect me. Remorse, or the expression of reproach in his lovely eyes, will have no power to move me, since I shall be in the center of a hopeless sadness. I shall lose things which are dearer to me than Lucian, and. which are less dear than my scruples. Thus, I would readily kill Lucian to engulf my shame in great pomp. Alas, a religious fear turns me from murder and draws me to it. Murder might very well transform me into a priest, and the victim into God. In order to destroy the efficacy of murder, perhaps I need only reduce it to the extreme by the practical necessity of a criminal act. I can kill a man for a few million francs. The glamour of gold can combat that of murder.

22. Will anyone be surprised when I claim that crime can help me ensure my moral vigor?

23. Splendid depravity, sweet and kindly, which makes it possible to love those who are ugly, dirty and disfigured!

24. [Armand] seemed to me intelligent. That is, he had dared, not unconsciously, to depart from moral rules, with the deceptive ease of men who are unaware of them. In fact, he had done so at the cost of a mighty effort, with the certainty of losing a priceless treasure, though with the further certainty of creating another, more precious than the one he had lost.

25. I said earlier that the only criterion of an act is its elegance. I am not contradicting myself in asserting my choice of betrayal. Betrayal may be a handsome, elegant gesture, compounded of nervous force and grace. I definitely reject the notion of nobility which favors a harmonious form and ignores a more hidden, almost invisible beauty, a beauty which would have to be revealed elsewhere than in objectionnable acts and things. No one will misunderstand me if I write: "Betrayal is beautiful," or will be so cowardly as to think – to pretend to think – that I am talking about cases in which it is necessary and noble, when it makes for the realization of Good. I was talking of low betrayal. The kind that cannot be justified by any heroic excuse. The sneaky, cringing kind, elicited, by the least noble of sentiments: envy, hatred (though a certain ethic dares class, hatred among the noble sentiments), greed. It is enough that the betrayer be aware of his betrayal, that he will it, that he be able to break the bonds of love uniting him with mankind. Indispensable for achieving beauty: love. And cruelty shattering! that love.

26. I love neither cowardice, nor stupidity; I do not love Java *for* one or *for* the other of these qualities; but their meeting within him fascinates me.

It may surprise the reader that the union of such flabby qualities should produce the sharp edges of rock crystal; it may surprise him that I compare not acts, but the moral expression of acts to attributes of the measurable world. I have said that I was fascinated. The word contains the idea of a sheaf – or rather of a luminous sheaf of beams, like the sparkling of crystal. These sparkles are the result of a certain arrangement of surfaces. It is to these sparkles that I am comparing the new quality – virtue – achieved by slackness, cowardice, etc.

This virtue has no name, unless it be that of the one from whom it emanates. Having found an inflammable substance, these fires which issue from him set me ablaze. That what love is. Having applied myself to the quest of what I compare within me to this substance, I achieve, by reflection, the absence of such qualities. Encountering them in Java dazzles me. He sparkles. I burn, for he burns me. As I hold up my pen for a brief meditation, the words which crowd into my mind suggest light and heat, by means of which we usually speak of love: dazzlement, rays, fire, beams, fascination, burning. However, Java's qualities – those which make up his fires – are icy. Each of them separately suggests an absence of temperament, of temperature.

27. If I had to live – perhaps I shall, though the idea is untenable – in your world [of morality and goodness], which, nevertheless, does welcome me, it would be the death of me. At the present time, when, having won by sheer force, I have signed an apparent truce with you, I find myself in exile.

28. My love for Lucian, and my happiness in this love are beginning to induce me to recognize a morality more in conformity, with your world. Not that I am more generous (I have always been that), but the rigid goal toward which I am moving, fierce as the iron shaft at the top of a glacier, so desirable, so dear to my pride and my despair, seems to me a great threat to my love. Lucian is not aware that I am headed for infernal regions. I still like to go where he takes me. How much more intoxicating, to the point of dizziness, falling and vomiting, would be the love I bear him if Lucian were a thief and a traitor. But would he love me then? Do I not owe his tenderness and his delicate merging within me to his submission to the moral order? Yet I would like to bind myself to some iron monster, smiling though icy, who kills, steals, and delivers father and mother to the judges. I also desire this so as to be myself the monstrous exception which a monster, delegate of God, allows himself to be, and which satisfies my pride as well as my taste for moral solitude. ...

The more I love Lucian, the more I lose my taste for theft and thieves. I am glad that I love him, but a great sadness fragile as a shadow and

heavy as the negro, spreads over my entire life, just barely rests upon it, grazes it and crushes it, enters my open mouth: it is regard for my legend. ...

... Nor can I bear to see his physical person in pain either. At times, in certain moments of tenderness, his gaze is slightly veiled; his lashes come together; a kind of mist clouds his eyes. His mouth then takes on a poignant smile. The horror of this face, for it does fill me with horror, means a plunge into my love for the child. I drown in it as in water. I see myself drowning. Death thrusts me into it. When he is asleep, I must not gaze down on it too often; I would lose my strength. And the strength I draw from it is meant only to ruin me and save him. The love I bear him is composed of a thousand signs of a deep tenderness which comes from him, from the depths of his heart, signs which seemingly emitted by chance, are caught only by me.

29. Oh let me be only utter beauty! I shall go quickly or slowly, but I shall dare what must be dared. I shall destroy appearances, the casings will burn away and. one evening I shall appear there, in the palm of your hand, quiet and pure, like a glass statuette. You will see me. Round about me there will be nothing left.

30. Though saintliness is my goal, I cannot tell what it is. My point of departure is the word itself which indicates the state closest to moral perfection. Of which I know nothing, save that without it my life would be in vain. Unable to give a definition of saintliness – no more than, I can of beauty – I want at every moment to create it, that is, to act so that everything I do may lead me to it, though it is unknown to me, so that at every moment I may be guided by a will to saintliness until I am so luminous that people will say, "He is a saint," or, more likely, "He was a saint." I am being led to it by a constant groping. No method exists.

THE DEGRADATION OF EVIL

De Sade

1. Wolves which batten upon lambs, lambs consumed by wolves, the strong who immolate the weak, the weak victims of the strong: there you have Nature, there you have her intentions, there you have her scheme: a perpetual action and reaction, a host of vices, a host of virtues, in one word, a perfect equilibrium resulting from the equality of good and evil on earth.

2. Get it into your head once and for all, my simple and very fainthearted fellow, that what fools call humanness is nothing but a weakness born of fear and egoism; that this chimerical virtue, enslaving only weak men, is unknown to those whose character is formed by stoicism, courage, and philosophy.

3. All, all is theft, all is unceasing and rigorous competition in nature; the desire to make off with the substance of others is the foremost – the most legitimate – passion nature has bred into us and, without doubt, the most agreeable one. Destruction, hence, like creation, is one of Nature's man-mandates.

4. The more defects a man may have, the older he is, the less lovable, the more resounding his success.

5. The mechanism that directs government cannot be virtuous, because it is impossible to thwart every crime, to protect oneself from every criminal without being criminal too; that which directs corrupt mankind must be corrupt itself; and it will never be by means of virtue, virtue being inert and passive, that you will maintain control over vice, which is ever active: the governor must be more energetic than the governed.

6. For mortal men there is but one hell, and that is the folly and wickedness and spite of his fellows; but once his life is over, there's an end to it: his annihilation is final and entire, of him nothing survives.

7. Hope is the most sensitive part of a poor wretch's soul; whoever raises it only to torment him is behaving like the executioners in Hell who, they say, incessantly renew old wounds and concentrate their attention on that area of it that is already lacerated.

8. How delightful are the pleasures of the imagination! In those delectable moments, the whole world is ours; not a single creature resists us, we devastate the world, we repopulate it with new objects which, in turn, we immolate. The means to every crime is ours, and we employ them all, we multiply the horror a hundred-fold.

9. Man's natural character is to imitate; that of the sensitive man is to resemble as closely as possible the person whom he loves. It is only by imitating the vices of others that I have earned my misfortunes.

10. No lover, if he be of good faith, and sincere, will deny he would prefer to see his mistress dead than unfaithful.

11. Lust is to the other passions what the nervous fluid is to life; it supports them all, lends strength to them all: ambition, cruelty, avarice, revenge, are all founded on lust.

12. Lust's passion will be served; it demands, it militates, it tyrannizes.

13. Nature, who for the perfect maintenance of the laws of her general equilibrium, has sometimes need of vices and sometimes of virtues, inspires now this impulse, now that one, in accordance with what she requires.

14. Humane sentiments are baseless, mad, and improper; they are incredibly feeble; never do they withstand the gainsaying passions, never do they resist bare necessity.

15. Prejudice is the sole author of infamies: how many acts are so qualified by an opinion forged out of naught but prejudice!

16. In libertinage, nothing is frightful, because everything libertinage suggests is also a natural inspiration; the most extraordinary, the most bizarre acts, those which most arrantly seem to conflict with every law, every human institution...even those that are not frightful, and there is not one amongst them all that cannot be demonstrated within the boundaries of nature.

17. I've already told you: the only way to a woman's heart is along the path of torment. I know none other as sure.

18. Here am I: at one stroke incestuous, adulteress, sodomite, and all that in a girl who only lost her maidenhead today! What progress, my friends ... with what rapidity I advance along the thorny road of vice!

19. Ah, Eugene, have done with virtues! Among the sacrifices that can be made to those counterfeit divinities, is there one worth an instant of the pleasures one tastes in outraging them?

20. Behold, my love, behold all that I simultaneously do: scandal, seduction, bad example, incest, adultery, sodomy! Oh, Satan! one and unique God of my soul, inspire thou in me something yet more, present further perversions to my smoking heart, and then shalt thou see how I shall plunge myself into them all!

21. Woman's destiny is to be wanton, like the bitch, the she-wolf; she must belong to all who claim her.

THE CULTURE OF EVIL

Octavio Paz

1. One of the most notable traits of the Mexican's character is his willingness to contemplate horror: he is even familiar and complacent in his dealings with it. The bloody Christs in our village churches, the macabre humor in some of our newspaper headlines, our wakes, the custom of eating skull-shaped cakes and candies on the Day of the Dead, are habits inherited from the Indians and the Spaniards and are now an inseparable part of our being. Our cult of death is also a cult of life, in the same way that love is a hunger for life and a longing for death. Our fondness for self-destruction derives not only from our masochistic tendencies but also from a certain variety of religious emotion.

....

We are nihilists – except that our nihilism is not intellectual but instinctive, and therefore irrefutable. ... We believe that sin and death constitute the ultimate basis of human nature.

2. The North American system only wants to consider the positive aspects of reality. Men and women are subjected from childhood to an inexorable process of adaptation; certain principles, contained in brief formulas, are endlessly repeated by the press, the radio, the churches and the schools, and by those kindly, sinister beings, the North American mothers and wives.

A person imprisoned by these schemes is like a plant in a flowerpot too small for it: he cannot grow or mature. This sort of conspiracy cannot help but provoke violent individual rebellions. Spontaneity avenges itself in a thousand subtle or terrible ways. The mask that replaces the dramatic mobility of the human face is benevolent and courteous but empty of emotion, and its set smile is almost lugubrious: it shows the extent to which intimacy can be devastated by the arid victory of principles over instincts. The sadism underlying almost all types of relationships in contemporary North American life is perhaps nothing more than a way of escaping the petrifaction imposed by the doctrine of aseptic moral purity. The same is true of the new religions and sects, and the liberating drunkenness that opens the doors of "life." It is astonishing what a destructive and almost physiological meaning this word has acquired: to live means to commit excesses, break the rules, go to the limit (of what?), experiment with sensations. The act of love is an "experience" (and therefore unilateral and frustrating). But it is not to my purpose to describe these reactions. It is enough to say that all of them, like their Mexican opposites, seem to me to reveal our mutual inability to reconcile ourselves to the flux of life.

3. A study of the great myths concerning the origin of man and the meaning of our presence on earth reveals that every culture – in the sense of a complex of values created and shared in common – stems from the conviction that man the intruder has broken or violated the order of the universe. He has inflicted a wound on the compact flesh of the world, and chaos, which is the ancient and, so to speak, *natural* condition of life, can emerge again from this aperture. The return of "ancient Original Disorder" is a menace that has obsessed every consciousness in every period of history.

4. The Mexican views life as combat. This attitude does not make him any different from anyone else in the modern world. For other people, however, the manly ideal consists in an open and aggressive fondness for combat, whereas we emphasize defensiveness, the readiness to repel any attack.

5. The harshness and hostility of our environment, and the hidden, indefinable threat that is always afloat in the air, oblige us to close ourselves in, like those plants that survive by storing up liquid within their spiny exteriors. But this attitude, legitimate enough in its origins, has become a mechanism that functions automatically. Our response to sympathy and tenderness is reserve, since we cannot tell whether those feelings are genuine or simulated. In addition, our masculine integrity is as much endangered by kindness as it is by hostility. Any opening in our defenses is a lessening of our manliness.

6. The North American hides or denies certain parts of his body and, more often, of his psyche: they are immoral, ergo they do not exist. By denying them he inhibits his spontaneity.

7. In certain fiestas the very notion of order disappears. Chaos comes back and license rules. Anything is permitted: the customary hierarchies vanish, along with all social, sex, caste, and trade distinctions. Men disguise themselves as women, gentlemen as slaves, the poor as the rich. The army, the clergy, and the law are ridiculed. Obligatory sacrilege, ritual profanation is committed. Love becomes promiscuity. Sometimes the fiesta becomes a Black Mass. Regulations, habits and customs are violated. Respectable people put away the dignified expressions and conservative clothes that isolate them, dress up in gaudy colors, hide behind a mask, and escape from themselves.

Therefore the fiesta is not only an excess, a ritual squandering of the goods painfully accumulated during the rest of the year; it is also a revolt, a sudden immersion in the formless, in pure being. By means of the fiesta society frees itself from the norms it has established. It ridicules its gods, its principles, and its laws: it denies its own self.

The fiesta is a revolution in the most literal sense of the word. In the confusion that it generates, society is dissolved, is drowned, insofar as it is an organism ruled according to certain laws and principles. But it drowns in itself, in its own original chaos or liberty. Everything is united: good and evil, day and night, the sacred and the profane. Everything merges, loses shape and individuality and returns to the primordial mass. The fiesta is a cosmic experiment, an experiment in disorder, reuniting contradictory elements and principles in order to bring about a renascence of life. Ritual death promotes a rebirth; vomiting increases the appetite; the orgy, sterile in itself, renews the fertility of the mother or of the earth. The fiesta is a return to the remote and undifferentiated state, prenatal or presocial. It is a return that is also a beginning, in accordance with the dialectic that is inherent in social processes.

The group emerges purified and strengthened from this plunge into chaos. It has immersed itself in its own origins, in the womb from which it came. To express it in another way, the fiesta denies society as an organic system of differentiated form and principles, but affirms it as a source of creative energy.

. . .

Thanks to the fiesta the Mexican opens out, participates, communes with his fellows and with the values that give meaning to his religious or political existence. And it is significant that a country as sorrowful as ours should have so many and such joyous fiestas. Their frequency, their brilliance and excitement, the enthusiasm with which we take part, all suggest that without them we would explode. They free us, if only momentarily, from the thwarted impulses, the inflammable desires that we carry within us. But the Mexican fiesta is not merely a return to an original state of formless and normless liberty: the Mexican is not seeking to return, but to escape from himself, to exceed himself.

Our fiestas are explosions. Life and death, joy and sorrow, music and mere noise are united, not to re-create or recognize themselves, but to swallow each other up. There is nothing so joyous as a Mexican fiesta, but there is also nothing so sorrowful. Fiesta night is also a night of mourning.

If we hide within ourselves in our daily lives, we discharge ourselves in the whirlwind of the fiesta. It is more than an opening out: we rend ourselves open. Everything – music, love, friendship – ends in tumult and violence.

...The somber Mexican, closed up in himself, suddenly explodes, tears open his breast and reveals himself, though not without a certain complacency, and not without a stopping place in the shameful or terrible mazes of his intimacy. We are not frank, but our sincerity can reach extremes that horrify a European. The explosive, dramatic, some- times even suicidal manner in which we strip ourselves, surrender ourselves, is evidence that something inhibits and suffocates us. Some- thing impedes us from being. And since we cannot or dare not confront our own selves, we resort to the fiesta. It fires us into the void; it is a drunken rapture that burns itself out, a pistol shot in the air, a sky-rocket.

8. In our daily language there is a group of words that are prohibited, & secret, without clear meanings. We confide the expression of our most brutal or subtle emotions and reactions to their magical ambiguities. They are evil words, and we utter them in a loud voice only when we are not in control of ourselves. In a confused way they reflect our intimacy: the explosions of our vitality light them up and the depressions of our spirit darken them. ...They are the bad words, the only living language in a world of anemic vocables. They are poetry within the reach of everyone.

Each country has its own. In ours, with their brief, aggressive, electric syllables, resembling the flash given off by a knife when it strikes a hard opaque body, we condense all our appetites, all our hatreds and enthusiasms, all the longings that rage unexpressed in the depths of our being. The word is our sign and seal. By means of it we recognize each other among strangers, and we use it every time the real conditions of our being rise to our lips. To know it, to use it, to throw it in the air like a toy or to make it quiver like a sharp weapon, is a way of affirming that we are Mexican.

9. In all civilizations, God the Father becomes an ambivalent figure once he has dethroned the feminine deities. On the one hand, the Father embodies the generative power, the origin of life, whether he be Jehovah, God the Creator, or Zeus, king of creation, ruler of the cosmos. On the other hand, he is the first principle, the One, from whom all is born and to whom all must return. But he is also the lord of the lightning bolt and the whip; he is the tyrant, the ogre who devours life. This aspect – angry Jehovah, God of wrath, or Saturn, or Zeus the violator of women – is the one appears almost exclusively in Mexican representations of manly power. The *macho* represents the masculine pole of life. The phrase "I am your father" has no paternal flavor and is not said in order to protect or to guide another, but rather to impose one's superiority, that is, to humiliate. Its real meaning is no different from that of the verb *chingar* and its derivatives. The *macho* is the *gran chingon.* One word sums up the aggressiveness, insensitivity, invulnerability and other attributes of the *macho*: power. It is force without the discipline of any notion of order: arbitrary power, the will without reins and without a set course.

Unpredictability adds another element to the character of the *macho*. He is a humorist. His jokes are huge and individual, and they always end in absurdity. The anecdote about the man who "cured" the headache of a drinking companion by emptying his pistol into his head is well known. True or not, the incident reveals the inexorable rigor with which the logic of the absurd is introduced into life. The *macho* commits *chingaderas,* that is, unforeseen acts that produce confusion, horror and destruction. He opens the world; in doing so, he rips and tears it, and this violence provokes a great, sinister laugh. And in its own way, it is just: it re-establishes the equilibrium and puts things in their places, by reducing them to dust, to misery, to nothingness. The humor of the *macho* is an act of revenge.

THE POLITICS OF EVIL

Machiavelli

1. Whoever desires to found a state and give it laws, must start with assuming that all men are bad and ever ready to display their vicious nature, whenever they may find occasion for it.

2. A prince should therefore have no other aim or thought, nor take up any other thing for his study but war and it organization and discipline, for that is the only art that is necessary to one who commands.

3. Since love and fear can hardly exist together, if we must choose between them, it is far safer to be feared than loved.

4. It is necessary to take such measures that, when they believe no longer, it may be possible to make them believe by force.

5. For injuries ought to be done all at one time, so that, being tasted less, they offend less; benefits ought to be given little by little, so that the flavour of them may last longer.

6. Therefore a wise prince ought to adopt such a course that his citizens will always in every sort and kind of circumstance have need of the state and of him, and then he will always find them faithful.

7. A man who wishes to act entirely up to his professions of virtue soon meets with what destroys him among so much that is evil.

8. Hence it is necessary for a prince wishing to hold his own to know how to do wrong, and to make use of it or not according to necessity.

9. We have not seen great things done in our time except by those who have been considered mean; the rest have failed.

10. You must know there are two ways of contesting, the one by the law, the other by force; the first method is proper to men, the second to beasts; but because the first is frequently not sufficient, it is necessary to have recourse to the second. Therefore, it is necessary for a prince to understand how to avail himself of the beast and the man.

11. If men were entirely good this precept would not hold, but because they are bad, and will not keep faith with you, you too are not bound to observe it with them. Nor will there ever be wanting to a prince legitimate reasons to excuse this nonobservance.

12. One prince of the present time, whom it is not well to name, never preaches anything else but peace and good faith, and to both he is most hostile, and either, if he had kept it, would have deprived him of reputation and kingdom many a time.

13. And here it should be noted that hatred is acquired as much by good works as by bad ones, therefore, as I said before, a prince wishing to keep his state is very often forced to do evil; for when that body is corrupt whom you think you have need of to maintain yourself – it may be either the people or the soldiers or the nobles – you have to submit to its humours and to gratify them, and then good works will do you harm.

14. And a prince ought, above all things, always to endeavour in every action to gain for himself the reputation of being a great and remarkable man.

15. Because fortune is a woman, and if you wish to keep her under, it is necessary to beat and ill-use her; and it is seen that she allows herself to be mastered by the adventurous rather than by those who go to work more coldly. She is, therefore, always, woman-like, a lover of young men, because they are less cautious, more violent, and with more audacity (bold, daring) command her.

16. A prince must imitate the fox and the lion, for the lion cannot protect himself from traps, and the fox cannot defend himself from wolves. One must therefore be a fox to recognize traps, and a lion to frighten wolves. Those that wish to be only lions do not understand this. Therefore, a prudent ruler ought not to keep faith when by so doing it would be against his interest, and when the reasons which made him bind himself no longer exist. If men were all good, this precept would not be a good one; but as they are bad, and would not observe their faith with you, so you are not bound to keep faith with them.

17. I'm not interested in preserving the status quo; I want to overthrow it.

18. Men sooner forget the death of their father than the loss of their patrimony.

19. If an injury has to be done to a man it should be so severe that his vengeance need not be feared

20. The end justifies the means.

21. A son could bear with great complacency, the death of his father, while the loss of his inheritance might drive him to despair.

22. A prince never lacks legitimate reasons to break his promise.

23. Men worry less about doing an injury to one who makes himself loved than to one who makes himself feared. The bond of love is one which men, wretched creatures they are, break when it is to their advantage to do so; but fear is strengthened by a dread of punishment which is always effective.

THE EGOISM OF EVIL

La Rochefoucauld

1. We behave politely to be treated politely, and to be considered polite.

2. Pity is often a way of feeling our own misfortunes in those of other people; it is a clever foretaste of the unhappiness we may someday encounter. We help others to make sure they will help us under similar circumstances, and the services we render them are, properly speaking, benefits we store up for ourselves in advance.

3. We make promises to the extent that we hope, and keep them to the extent that we fear.

4. Self-interest turns to account all kinds of virtues and vices.

5. Gratitude is like business credit: it keeps trade brisk, and we pay up, not because it is the honorable thing to do but because it makes it easier to borrow again.

6. Not all those who pay off debts of gratitude can, for doing so, flatter themselves that they are grateful.

7. Our excessive eagerness in paying off an obligation is a of ingratitude.

8. Even though, in showing ingratitude, the fault may be more our benefactor's than our own, we are ingrates nonetheless.

9. Pride which arouses so much envy on our part, often helps to hold it in check as well.

10. If vanity does not quite topple the virtues, it leaves every last one of them swaying.

11. There is often more pride than kindness in our pitying the misfortunes of our enemies; we give them proofs of our compassionateness to bring home to them our superiority.

12. We are so prejudiced in our own favor that what we often assume to be virtues are only vices with a similar look that we mistake for virtues through vanity.

13. Selfishness which we blame for all our crimes, often deserves to be praised for our good deeds.

14. The most dangerous thing about pride is its way of blinding us; the more pride swells, the more we lose sight of the remedies for solacing our misfortunes or for curbing our faults

15. It appears that Nature, which has so wisely disposed the parts of our body to keep us happy, has also endowed us with pride to spare us the pain of knowing our imperfections.

16. It is hard to tell whether a clear, candid and honest act springs from probity or shrewd judgment.

17. We should often be ashamed of our noblest actions if the world but
knew all the motives that helped shape them.

18. It is as easy to deceive ourselves without knowing it as it is hard to deceive others without their finding it out.

19. We get so much in the habit of wearing a disguise before others that we finally appear disguised before ourselves.

20. When our enemies deceive us, when our friends betray us, we are not to be consoled; yet we are quite willing to deceive and betray ourselves.

21. Men would not get on for long in society if they did not fool one another.

22. If we had no faults, we should not take much pleasure in calling attention to other people's.

23. In the business of living our faults are often more attractive than our virtues.

24. We confess to small faults to create the impression that we have no great ones.

25. The same pride that makes us condemn those faults we think we lack leads us to scorn the good qualities we fail to possess.

26. When our vices desert us, we flatter ourselves that we are deserting our vices.

27. The ills of the soul are like wounds in the body: however hard we try to cure them, they always show scars and are at any moment in danger of reopening.

28. What often prevents our being enslaved by a single vice is that we have a number of others.

29. We easily forget our faults when no one but ourselves knows them.

30. There are men the world approves of whose only merit is that their vices enhance sociability.

31. Virtues are swallowed up by self-interest as rivers are lost in the sea.

32. There are people so superficial and frivolous that they no more have real faults than real virtues.

33. We wish to make virtues of the faults we do not wish to correct.

34. However we may question the sincerity of the people we meet, we always suppose them more truthful with us than with others.

35. We should not be offended that other people conceal the truth from us, seeing how often we conceal it from ourselves.

36. Dislike of lying is often an unconscious desire to enhance the value of our testimony and to give a sacred importance to our words.

37. There are dressed up lies which imitate the truth so well that it would be poor judgment not to let them deceive us.

38. The desire to talk about ourselves and to exhibit our faults in the best possible light accounts for a great part of our sincerity.

39. Sincerity comes directly from the heart. One finds it in very few people; what one usually finds is but a deft pretence designed to gain the confidence of others.

40. Love of justice, in most men, is only a fear of encountering injustice.

41. Justice is but a lively fear of losing what belongs to us: hence our consideration and respect for our neighbour's rights and our great care not to cause him damage. Because of such fear, men stay within the bounds set for them by birth and fortune, where otherwise they would continually prey upon others.

42. We condemn injustice not from a horror of the thing itself but for the damage it can do to us.

43. The love of glory, the fear of disgrace, the incentive to succeed, the desire to live in comfort, and the instinct to humiliate others are often the cause of that courage so renowned among men.

44. There are few cowards who know how really cowardly they are.

45. A fool has not character enough to be good.

46. Good nature which boasts of its sensitive feelings is often crushed by the merest selfish whim.

47. It is very hard to distinguish between benignity extended toward all mankind and consummate cleverness.

Chapter 4
PATHICS AS EVIL

From the following personal accounts it is clear that pathics, as a whole, are emissaries of evil; who are wired neurologically, chemically, and psychologically to oppose, off-set, upset, agitate in the extreme, the moral and social order that prevails in any given situation; yet it is perhaps not so clear that without such pathics, our humanity would fall into a debilitating stagnation of listless automatism; this idea has been around at least since Nietzsche and William James.

And you might protest: "But these pathics cause so much unjustifiable suffering to countless innocent victims. Wouldn't life be so much better without them; and why would such a life be a "debilitating stagnation of our humanity?" And I reply, Theoretically, ideally, life *would be* much better without them; but then, there would remain only the good and loving with no opposition whatsoever: a utopian world. All would be well and good, so it would seem. Yet on second thoughts,, all would not – *could* not – be well and good simply from the living realities of pain and pleasure, wants and needs, self-consciousness; or of sexual selection that spawn rivalry, jealousy, lust, etc.; or of physical and mental variations that spawn competition, aggression, moods, etc.; or of fatigue, of disease and aging that spawn fear of our mortality; and the situations goes on and on.

All these living realities with which we are faced, are inescapably part and parcel of our human condition. Hence there can be no one-sided perspective of human nature. Strife inevitably comes with love; that is to say, creation with destruction. There is no annihilating the one without annihilating the other. Life, human life in particular consists of necessary dualities, or opposites: good and bad, light and dark, male and female, pain and pleasure, good and bad; and all the rest.

And here we return to our topic of the pathics of evil destroying the good, the "claw and fang" side of life. And does not this "claw and fang" side of life apply to the good as well? For the good must protect itself from the bad; and so, often enough must apply the "claw and fang" side of life, though with good on its side. In either case, life remains "claw and fang." There is no way out, however we twist and turn.

So the ever-repeating mantras of "peace on earth," and "universal brotherhood," are no less than illusions – often becoming delusions – so long as life is as it is: patterns of dualities. Hence we are stuck with the pathics as they are stuck with the nonpathics; they need us as we need them so far as life as we know it is structured and patterned; and apparently, evolving. The following passage referring to a pathic's viewpoint relates to this point: "We have had some interesting chats. He [the pathic] tells me that predators are necessary so that prey can develop survival skills – and that assists the human race in becoming smarter. Sometimes I can't really follow his logic."

Hence, the fight, the struggle, one against the other goes on without stop; yet what could very well change for the better is for the good (justice and wisdom) to one day take the ascendancy over the bad (injustice and ignorance). Then we will have a "brave new world" to look forward to; for then we will have fought the *good* fight.

---

1. "And the reptilian stare of those eyes. You cannot escape the uniqueness of that stare, no matter what the color. Once you've seen it, you'll never forget it...how they drill into you, draw you in and capture you."

2. "Also what I have observed is the truly evil end of the spectrum both in human and animal is always displayed in those deep, dark hole for eyes. Can that be the easiest clue to tune into?"

3. "This evil seeks and finds anything and everything that is sacred, special, or cherished and seeks not only to destroy it; but to do so in the most agonizing, never-ending, worst way imaginable."

4. "Even now I find it difficult to fathom how you can give so much of yourself to a person and have them so totally wipe it all away as if it never happened with no remorse and go on their merry way leaving a path of destruction behind them."

5. "The first time I pissed him off, I looked into those piercing blue eyes and felt like I was looking at the evil himself. Those eyes were so full of evil and so dark."

6. "Is it evil to belittle, denigrate, scapegoat, and make fun of someone until they are demoralized, subjugated, and traumatized? Is the verbal and emotional abuser who keeps his victim in suspense and fear with pounding heart and nightmares an evil person? Is the person with the need to control others an evil person?"

7. "Evil leaves its mark on us at the cellular level. There is a physiology to evil. Cells are imprinted at the moment terror engulfs us. Brain cells are destroyed by stress and facing evil is never-ending stress. The body never leaves flight or fight mode. Children silently suffer the slings and arrows of the narcissistic parent who is unable to care. What happens to the child is of no concern to the narcissist; for he must prevail no matter the cost. The child as collateral damage is unimportant. Winning is everything."

8. "Can you survive the evil and the abuse? Yes, though it won't be easy. Stay with the narcissist and you may be damaged. Some choose this, others remain. Some can leave. They are the lucky ones. Changed, but stronger. Wounded, but wiser. Educated in the techniques of disengaging and mindfulness. These are the survivors who can turn the pain into pathways for strength, determination, and finally accept themselves as functioning human beings without the burden of evil on their psyche. A journey, deep and dangerous has been made by those of us who have been companions with 'the people of the lie'."

9. "I believe very much in the concept of evil. Although not all young psychopaths torture animals, I have to believe this is an evil act. Torturing their other siblings is indeed evil and causes terror in the family structure. I think when a person has a young psychopath, and feel like they can't take their eyes off of them for fear of what they will do, I suspect the parent/caregiver is afraid of an evil act being done. It would be my best guess that evil and psychopathy go hand in hand."

10. "There have been a few recent court cases of young kids killing parents and grandparents. Do I think these kids were psychopaths? More than likely. Do I think they are evil? Definitely. They both laid in wait for their victims before murdering them, cold and calculating."

11. "One incident I can remember from my past, is when I left my ex.. One of his friends, who happened to be a juvenile prison warden, actually rang me, and warned that he knew exactly what pain he was inflicting on the children, and would continue to hurt them until he got what he wanted; and that was me. He would play emotional mind games and gut-wrenching scenarios where he would try to kill himself in front of them. He was playing; he knew the pain he was causing too."

12. "It's hard to believe, but I'm beginning to think they're purely evil. They are taught right from wrong and they normally are predators to people they know they can overtake. They'll beat on a woman or child, but won't try to do it to a six-foot bodybuilder. It's almost like their soul is a totally different species from our souls. They're just little monsters with human bodies. They probably don't want to change because they normally get what they want by being their ruthless selves. I know that some of you are also parents of a P or N, and I don't want you to be hurt by my comments. We've just been through so many years and so much hatred from our daughter that I'm really beginning to see the light."

13. "My friend also said that my ex-p is doing the devil's work. That even his planning of the address that would be found when I began my search for him was evil. He said that is beyond cruel, it is pure evil. He said some people's minds get so consumed with evil that there is no turning back, not ever; and that it appears that my ex-p is one of those. When you think like the devil, you have to act like the devil too. You are so right."

14. "I have had a body reaction the couple of times I have seen an unmasked evil being."

15. "I think evil runs through most of nature probably to some degree. Ever had a pit bull stare at you? I can still see a vivid image of the one who was next to me in his car at a stop sign several years ago, the memory is fresh."

16. "I've been reading a lot, and I can't help but see the link between the psychopathic and the demonic. Not to have a religious debate here, but there has just got to be some kind of horrible, evil thing living in a p's [mind]; especially, the more sadistic ones!"

17. "And I've noticed that since I've learned about my boundaries, that I get really nauseous around ps. Then I've also read about people who get nauseous when they feel an evil presence, like a presence they cannot see?!"

18. "I won't debate whether demons or devils are real or not. But one way to look at it is this: all our archetypes, our myths, all come from human experience, from the most sanctified to the most evil."

19. "If you look at Lucifer, for example, as an archetype, it is very much like a very well socialized P: beautiful, in control, master of lies and manipulation, completely selfish and amoral, completely without compassion or empathy, always holding out the promise of wealth and riches and beauty and power untold – but never following through, cut off from God for his arrogance and pride (grandiosity), etc.."

20. "Ps are on one end of the human experience continuum, saints on the other. Most of us are somewhere in the middle and that makes us 'normal'. The farther down that continuum you go, the more demonic and evil the person will seem, just as the higher on the continuum the more godly and saint-like the person will seem."

21. "This was one of the most surprising and disheartening experiences throughout my life with psychopath. It seemed that no matter what heinous thing he did, all of our friends and associates wanted to be neutral, and not judge him; in fact, be supportive of him. Most of the time, I was treated as less than him because I was being negative by focusing on evil, at all. There is a warped condition, a sort of lie, that pervades our culture, that being neutral and nonjudgmental is the highest virtue."

22. "When people align themselves with this 'virtue' (that being neutral and nonjudgmental is the highest virtue), they feel superior to those who speak of evil. They feel superior to us, and we have experienced that condescension, sometimes subtle, sometimes not, always heart- breaking, invalidating, hurtful. I know that part of what kept me enmeshed with the psychopath for so many years was me taking in this invalidation, and feeling like the bad person, instead of him. It supports the psychopathic dynamic, which is that the evil acts are not the problem; the problem is, the victim's negative reaction to them. Our culture very much supports this psychopathic illusion. It is an evil lie which holds most in sway, at this time."

23. "It's true it (that being neutral and nonjudgmental is the highest virtue) doesn't have to involve psychopathy. This principle operates, in general, where good and evil are concerned, in lesser situations of evil, too. But it operates most glaringly in the psychopathic dynamic. Almost everyone in my environment, who I tried to turn to in the worst, most horrible time, the end, pointed to Psychopath's wonderful personality, his extraordinary empathy, how good he made others feel; and said that, for them, these things were just as important (actually more) and that they considered his faults as only a small part of who he was. And they weren't going to judge. After all, we all have faults. Yes, we all do, I thought. But doesn't beating a wife nearly to death, and molesting children disturb something deep inside you? Nope, it didn't.

Wouldn't want to judge."

24. "This is a terrible thing, entrenched. Evil has our culture under a hypnotic spell so that most cannot recognize evil, unless it is embodied by 'other': other cultures, other countries, other belief systems. It is not us. It is 'them'."

25. "Keep reading the posts in here. They are invaluable. My only question now is: Are there 'degrees' of psychopathy? I'm fairly certain there are... but, know that the bottom line is ... It simply doesn't matter. The evil is too much to bear, no matter the degree..."

26. "As I look back at my life (I'm now 45) I see that the few serious long term relationships I've had have all been with very bad people. And my love has had to be bigger and purer to accept them. That was true with my father as well. And I wonder, do I try to balance out the evil they do in the world by being better, more loving, more empathic, more accepting than someone not raised this way?"

"And then when I see that this is enabling behavior, and accept that I allowed myself to become just another mask for them to hide behind, and that it is EVIL that I have loved and supported and tried to nurture; it is almost as though I have contaminated something meant to be pure. Can that be? Or is this just the final betrayal of the psychopath that they make this also, the highest ideal, the one thing that truly connects one to another, into something vile and false?"

27. "The first time he raped me, the mask fell off completely. I'm at a loss for words here... I'm sorry... I don't know how to describe the absolute horror. The distortion of his features at the time...the demonic shape... the black holes of his eyes. It happens in a moment... I know I had to close my eyes against it. You have to understand that this is a man who is strikingly attractive – he could literally take my breath away when he entered a room. The few times he would actually rest, I would stay awake and sketch him, or just watch him, or stroke his beautiful, beautiful face. That night when I saw the 'real' him, I couldn't have been more horrified if his face had been covered in maggots. ...

"About the time this happened, I began to question my sanity. I had been so exhausted, and so overwhelmed, and in such utter despair for such a long time...I questioned what I saw, convinced myself that it was something my poor tired brain had imagined. The boogey man doesn't exist. Demons reside in hell. Yes, he's messed up, or sick, or maybe even just bad...but not...evil. I forgive him the rape. He tells me it was just an extension of the passion he has always felt for me... his need for me."

28. "...I never could make sense of it, because there never is sense to having pure evil just show up out of the depths of a person like that. I set that knowledge away, split it to someplace labeled, 'I don't know' and just went on, more wary, but still with him. No one who hasn't seen that pit that shines in their eyes can know what that utter betrayal is like. I've tried so many times to describe it and you can't do it in such a way that others who haven't witnessed can understand. But this is the embodiment of the archetype of the Light bringer/Devil, Sun god/Hades, Angel/demon ... a thing indeed ... horrible!"

29. "This is the first time in my life I'm not terrified of the dark or feel of a sense of foreboding in my own home. It always seemed like everywhere I lived was full of a dark force I could never put my finger on. Now, I understand the power, the negative energy, a P/N has on everything around them. Living with them is like living in a non-stop horror movie. I really mean this. It makes me sick to even admit this or to discuss it openly."

30. "Seeing my wife and what she had become, it was like looking at the face of Satan and being able to recognize the mask as such. If any- one out there is ever confronted by a person like this, run, do not walk; run just as fast as you can."

31. "It's hard to believe there are people among us that our so diabolical, so calculated, so callous and would do almost anything if they could get away with it."

32. "He is a person of deep evil. Why did I let him do that to me?"

33. "I believe I've been to Hell and met the Devil!!"

PART TWO

Profiles of The Pathic

Individual

Chapter 5
THE PATHICS IN THEIR OWN WORDS

The title of this chapter fairly much explains its contents; which, in addition, clearly portrays the distinctions between the narcipath, the sociopath, and the psychopath, each through his — males exclusively — own self-expression, as I have grouped them. Since the passages consist mostly of one or two sentences, there is obviously not enough information to *categorically* declaim that the particular person is in fact this or that type of pathic. However, the reader will at least glean an impression of these distinctions, categorized as either psychopathic, sociopathic, or narcipathic.

The importance of making these distinctions should advance a fuller understanding of the pathics as either psychopath, sociopath, or narcipath (I exclude the psychoticpaths, since this type of pathic stretches beyond the psychic normalcy of human evil.).

In making these distinctions, as mapped out in chapter 2, and presented also in chapters 8 and 10, I hope I have closed the gap a little more in our pool of knowledge and understanding regarding the study of pathicology, as I term it.

The Narcipath

1. "I'm right back at the center of attention – where I belong!"

2. "It's all about me now. I don't care about you or what the kids want or what they need."

3. "I don't care if you have been sitting in traffic all this time because of a wreck on the Interstate! I have been sitting here waiting for you for 2 hrs! You have no regard for ME!"

4. "If you are not on the train to reach MY goals then I want you off."

5. "You'll never find anybody as good as me. You could never replace me. Men like me only come once in a lifetime."

6. "When people say I'm in love with myself I just shrug my shoulders and say – who wouldn't be!"

7. "I cannot even pass a mirror without wearing sunglasses, otherwise I would get too dazzled by my own appearance."

8. "I am not special or entitled. I merely ask to be treated the same as any other great man."

9. "I am perfect."

10. "I am entitled to the best."

11. "Your life is SO much better with me in it!"

12. "Well, what's in that for me?"

13. "You are always supposed to be trying to get my mood up."

14. "Why do you have to have your own opinions!"

15. "The more you do for me the less I appreciate it."

16. "Childbirth without drugs, natural childbirth, yeah, yeah, 11 hours – ok it may have been hard for you, but it was extremely hard for me too to watch."

17. "I do love you, but I'm looking for a woman who makes enough money to support my life style."

18. "I'm an addiction. You'll never get me out of your head. I'm here to stay, Baby."

19. "I can't be with a smart woman anymore. I need to find a woman who is stupid and easy going."

20. I said to my ex 'Isn't our little girl gorgeous; don't you just love her?' He replied, "What's there to love; she just lies there doing nothing. Boring."

21. "I mean, come on, do you honestly think I would do something that wasn't in my own best interest?"

22. "He tells me long stories about his life, on a regular basis. Sometimes they are half hour monologues or more. One time I listen to one of his stories and it reminds me of something that happened to me that I decide to tell him about. I say less than one sentence before he says, 'Did you feed the dogs?' 'Yes,' I say, and remain silent. 'Go on, go on,' he says impatiently, without looking at me, rotating his hand in the air. I say another sentence, and he interrupts, 'Will you hand me that newspaper?' I hand it to him. He begins to read it. 'Did you not have the slightest interest in what I was saying?' I ask him, after a while. 'I might,' he says, 'if you didn't go on and on, endlessly. Conversation should be a dialogue.'"

23. "When youngest child was 15, he and Dad had a falling out. Youngest child told him how angry he was at him for things he had done. Dad's response? 'If you aren't going to agree with me and tell me I am right, then I don't want you to come to see me anymore!' Hasn't seen or spoken to youngest son for 3 years now."

24. "Why do I need to get life insurance for you? I'm the one that needs it, not you."

25. "I'll get rid of you like a piece on a chess board if I decide you aren't valuable to me anymore."

26. I was heavily pregnant with our son. I was in the shower and N came in and said "Just thought I would let you know that I am starting to look at other women. Just so you know where my mind is at. I find pregnant bodies a turn off."

27. "Paying child support is like buying oats for a dead horse."

28. "Just tell me if you're going bankrupt; I'll have to trade you in then."

29. [When his father died]: "Hey if my mom dies, we'll probably get the house."

30. "I expect to be THE beneficiary of your will; your kids can have something."

31. "I can do anything I want and if you don't like it you can kiss my A**."

32. Even on our first date he said: "I cleaned my car; you'd better be worth it."

33. At Valentine's dinner he says, "You know I'm not obligated to do this for you."

34. "How you feel doesn't matter."

The Sociopath

1. "I don't get mad, I get even. I am the Master Manipulator."

2. "I'm a taker not a giver."

3. "I tell you things on a need-to-know basis. If I think you need to know, I'll tell you"

4. "Get them while they're sick!"

5. "You have to anticipate what I want."

6. "Make a list of what you want back, and I'll decide what you can have."

7. "If people are stupid enough to let me run all over them...I'm gonna take advantage."

8. "I hate holidays and birthdays, including my birthday. It is because I hate it when other people are happy if I am not the cause of it. I have to be the prime mover and shaker of EVERYONE's moods. And no one will tell me HOW I should feel. I am my own master. I feel that their happiness is false, fake, forced. I feel that they are hypocrites; dissimulating joy where there is none. I feel envious, humiliated, by my envy, and enraged by my humiliation. I feel that they are the recipients of a gift I will never have: the ability to enjoy life and to feel joy."

9. "I love pulling one over on someone."

10. "You can't have my cell phone number because it's private; but I'll need yours so that I can check up where you are at any time."

11. "The world is my ashtray."

12. "I will continue to criticize you if you don't cook better meals, The only way to get you to listen to me is to yell and swear; so what else can I do?"

13. "You're like a tool in my tool belt, I take you out when I need you and leave you in the tool box when I don't."

14. About his mother: "She's there for me, to be used and abused."

15. "If you can't screw over your friends then who can you screw over?"

16. "My management style? Fear!"

17. "I can smell fear at a hundred yards."

18. "I want dinner NOW."

19. "It's none of your business what I do."

20. "I can't stay here 'cause you are not under control."

21. "I'll give you up when I'm ready, but first I want to play with you."

22. "What's mine is mine and what's yours is mine."

23. "When I arrive home, you are supposed to be waiting at the door for me with something cold to drink and a cloth to wipe my brow."

24. "My ability to be manipulative was-is not strategic. It's like an INSTINCT. No dossiers, no surveillance. Just as a lion can instinctually pick the one or two weak wildebeest from the herd and chase THEM down, so can narcissists pick the lonely, the gullible, the intellectually lazy 'dummies' and suck 'em dry. I've done it all my life, but I don't know HOW. Really. It just seemed to happen. My mom can do it too."

25. [a con artist] "When I'm on the job the first thing I do is size you up. I look for an angle, an edge, figure out what you need and give it to you. Then it's pay-back time, with interest. I tighten the screws."

26. I said 'I felt like you were a charmer, you know, a con-artist!' His reply was "A CON-artist! Are you SERIOUS?! I'm the nicest guy you'll ever know! You couldn't be more WRONG!" Of course, I just said 'Oh, I know, you are nice!' Then I ended the conversation quickly and never answered his calls since.

27. "She's the best work I've done yet!"

28. "One of the things that triggers my rage more than anything else is the inability to control another person, the inability to dominate them and force my reality on them. I feel impotent, humiliated, forced back on my empty self. Part of what I'm feeling here is envy: that person who can't be controlled clearly has a self and I don't, and I just hate them for it. But it's also a power struggle – I want to get narcissistic supply by being in control and on top and having the other person submissive and compliant."

29. "By the time I was a teenager, I was engaging in exploits that would cause me to be labeled a lying attention whore if I chronicled them here. Suffice it to say that I definitely excelled at manipulating people, and that as I developed certain persuasive skills – becoming a nationally ranked public speaker, for example – I was able to play 'games' of increasing breadth and scale. I didn't torture animals or engage in simple acts of brute sadism anymore. I found it much more satisfying to own and dominate 'people'."

Psychopaths

1. "I will kill you if it takes me 20 years. When you least expect it."

2. "I'd like to beat the sh**t out of you!"

3. "I just have this sudden urge to punch you right in the face."

4. "The BEST time to kick a man is WHEN he's down!"

5. I asked why he was being so verbally abusive. His response was "Because I can!" Didn't that say it all?

6. "Do whatever you want to do to whomever you want to do it. Just don't leave any bruises."

7. "I can only hurt you as much as you allow me to."

8. He told me, "It is like when you put an animal in a cage, I like to poke at you, because I like to watch you get mad,"

9. "That's what you do with hot girls; break them down until they don't think they're pretty anymore – just like I did with you."

10. "You aren't allowed to get mad."

11. I said, 'I have had people treat me bad before, but I have never had someone be as cruel and sadistic as you.' He said, "I told you that I couldn't be compared to everyone else, didn't I."

12. When I asked him to pick me up at the subway at night because there were gang members at the exit: "You interrupted my movie downloading for this?"

13. "I'm going to build you up and build you up, just to knock you down." Of course later, he adamantly denied saying it.

14. When I heard him say "Are you awake?" I said 'Yes!' and he said "No, you weren't"; and he said, "I did a test to see if you were asleep (and he started drawing on my chest) and said "I was saying, 'This is where I'm going to cut your heart out, this is where I'm going to cut your spleen out, and this is where I'm going to cut your kidney out." I jumped up and called him a f.....ing weirdo and he started laughing saying "I was only joking."

15. "I remember peeling the skin off a live baby rabbit that I'd unearthed in the woods behind our house. I remember being briefly fascinated watching this little piece of bloody meat try to scream. 'Why doesn't it realize that it's going to die?' I remember getting bored and leaving it there, and washing my hands before dinner. I was still in elementary school then – maybe seven or eight years old."

16. When asked if he had any regrets about stabbing a robbery victim who subsequently spent time in the hospital as a result of his wounds, one of our subjects replied, "Get real! He spends a few months in the hospital and I rot here. If I wanted to kill him I would have slit his throat. That's the kind of guy I am; I gave him a break."

17. "I've always thought I was different from others. As if I was one in a million, and I must admit I like the thought. I want your opinion, doctor, is there something different about my mind then the rest of society or is it all in my head? Let me start by giving you a bit of background history of my own tendencies. As a child I was constantly getting into trouble with authority figures. Many adults at the time of my childhood would tell you I was a fine boy, but with a temper. I wouldn't hold my tongue when being disciplined by my teachers or parents. I recall many a time actually when my father would try to 'Spank' me (whip with a leather belt); and I would just look at him without a cry or a tear until he was finished. I believe it was then I noticed something was different about me. I, unlike my brothers and sisters, would turn inward when these things were happening, I was totally indifferent. I have considered myself an anti-social personality for quite some time now. However, I don't know if my behavior is that of one you would call a sociopath [more specifically, a psychopath]. I prefer to spend my time alone in my room instead of going out with friends. I call them friends because this is the word the English language deems as the proper term for people you hang around with on occasion. The time I spend with these people, the things I do for them, are solely for my own gain. Like, for instance, a childhood friend of mine has fallen into some trouble with his mother, so I have invited him to stay with me a bit. I did this not because I care about his situation but because I know he has marijuana and a really big bong. Simple as that. When I talk to people, I might be looking at you. I might even follow the conversation and seem as if I'm interested. I'm not; I just have no interest in other people... I don't care about them...I have been known to be unkind to animals, sometimes choking a kitten just to see its eyes bulge a bit. On one occasion, a cat was stupid enough to enter my house unwelcomed, I treated the cat as if [it were] a burglar, and attacked it. The cat escaped into the cold of the night soaking wet, I had tried to drown it. A more recent incident would be when me and my mother where driving, a cat crossed the road and I practically floored it to hit the cat. This of course brought up a wonderful conversation with my mother about how I shouldn't be doing that. She gave a disgusted look when I readily justified my actions...she told me something about how I wasn't normal. I found humor in that. I've been taught right from wrong; but that won't stop me from stealing from right under your nose. I'm not a fool or stupid though; I won't take what can be traced back to me; and many of the lies I tell are to cover up my thievery. I have a habit of stealing from people who anger me. I have little relationship with my father or mother and this doesn't bother me. I find them more useful than anything else. I would equate our relationship with that of a parasite and a host. I get everything from them; they get nothing in return. And I don't know if this has anything to do with anything, but you're the doctor; I'll leave it to you. In my mind where anything is possible, I think about things like murdering people in the woods... just to see what it's like to be a murderer...you know: see what the big fuss is about. I have also thought about a military career for the prospect of killing someone legally."

18. "I'm 23 and a true sociopath [more specifically, a psychopath]. On top of that I am a mimic, I mimic what I see from others to try and fit in and look normal, because if people know who I really am, which only one person in my life truly knows, they treat you different."

"I have no feelings whatsoever. I am married and feel nothing for my wife. At age 5 I started torturing and killing animals. It started out as small ones and then got to be bigger ones. I have thoughts about killing but never have acted upon them. I don't worry about dying, I love pain, and to actually feel something I resort to cutting. I have no remorse, regret, sympathy, or empathy. I fake every emotion that I show ... love, care, sympathy is harder because those I try to show it to can see right through me and know I'm a fake. I lie constantly. I am constantly bored. I'm conceited and usually only think of myself. I consider myself to be quite an intellectual."

"I am sadistic and love causing other to feel pain, not necessarily physical but emotional pain, just to see their reaction to it. When I was 8, I had made the decision to be a professional soldier, 'mercenary'. I figured it would be the perfect career seeing as that I'm cut off from emotions. A physical problem kept me from it."

"I am compulsive when it comes to being clean and everything has to be in its own place. I don't know what makes us this way; most days I love it, there are no worries, but other days, I sometimes wonder what it would be like to feel something."

18. While I have not been diagnosed nor seen anyone for this disorder I do believe I am a psychopath. I am not a maniac or some crazed killer but someone that is attempting to lead a normal life. I have only just begun to realize that I fit the profile of a psychopath and it has been very disturbing but comforting realization for me.

Psychoticpaths

MEN

Thomas Dillon
"Paxton was killed because of an irresistible compulsion that has taken over my life, I knew when I left my house that day that someone would die.... This compulsion started with just thoughts about murder and progressed from thoughts to action. I've thought about getting professional help but how can I ever approach a mental-health professional? I just can't blurt out in an interview

that I've killed people (Paxton was not the only one). Technically I meet the definition of a serial killer (three or more victims with a cooling-off period in between) but I'm an average-looking person with a family, job, and home just like yourself."

Albert DeSalvo

1. "I did this not as a sex act...but out of hate for her. I don't mean out of hate for her in particular, really I mean out of hate for a woman."

2. "It wasn't as dark and scary as it sounds. I had a lot of fun...killing somebody's a funny experience."

Albert Fish

1. "I always had the desire to inflict pain on others and to have others inflict pain on me. I always seemed to enjoy everything that hurt. The desire to inflict pain; that is all that is uppermost."

2. I am not insane, I'm just queer."

3. "I saw so many boys whipped, it took root in my head."

Andrei Chikatilo

"What I did was not for sexual pleasure. Rather it brought me some peace of mind."

Dennis Rader

"When this monster entered my brain, I will never know, but it is here to stay. How does one cure himself? I can't stop it, the monster goes on, and hurts me as well as society. Maybe you can stop him. I can't."

David Berkowitz

1. "A 'possessed' dog in the neighborhood won't let me stop killing until he gets his fill of blood."

2. "I always had a fetish for murder and death."

3. "I am a monster. I am the Son of Sam. I love to hunt."

4. "I didn't want to hurt them; I only wanted to kill them."

5. "I was literally singing to myself on my way home, after the killing.

The tension, the desire to kill a woman had built up in such explosive proportions that when I finally pulled the trigger, all the pressures, all the tensions, all the hatred, had just vanished, dissipated, but only for a short time."

6. "I wasn't going to rob her, or touch her. I was just going to kill her."

David Gore
"All of the sudden I realized that I had just done something that separated me from the human race and it was something that could never be undone, I realized that from that point on I could never be like normal people. I must have stood there in that state for 20 minutes. I have never felt an emptiness of self like I did right then and I never will forget that feeling. It was like I crossed over into a realm I could never come back from."

Dennis Nilsen
"I wish I could stop but I could not. I had no other thrill or happiness."

Ed Kemper
1. "I just wanted to see how it felt to shoot Grandma."

2. "I remember there was actually a sexual thrill . . . you hear that little pop and pull their heads off and hold their heads up by the hair. Whipping their heads off, their body sitting there. That'd get me off."

3. "It was an urge. . . a strong urge, and the longer I let it go the stronger it got, to where I was taking risks to go out and kill people – risks that normally, according to my little rules of operation, I wouldn't take because they could lead to arrest."

4. "One side of me says, I'd like to talk to her, date her. The other side of me says, I wonder what her head would look like on a stick?"

Rudolf Pliel
"What I did is not such a great harm, with all these surplus women nowadays. Anyway, I had a good time."

Gary Ridgeway
"I'm a murderer, not a rapist."

H.H. Holmes

"I was born with the devil in me. I could not help the fact that I was a murderer, no more than the poet can help the inspiration to sing. I was born with the evil one standing as my sponsor beside the bed where I was ushered into the world, and he has been with me since."

Carl Panzram

1. "All of my family are as the average human beings are. They are honest and hard working people. All except myself. I have been a human-animal ever since I was born. When I was very young at 5 or 6 years of age I was a thief and a liar and a mean despicable one at that. The older I got the meaner I got."

2. "I don't believe in man, God nor Devil. I hate the whole damned human race, including myself... I preyed upon the weak, the harmless and the unsuspecting. This lesson I was taught by others: Might makes right."

Henri Blot

"Every man to his own tastes. Mine is for corpses."

Henry Lee Lucas

1. "I hated all my life. I hated everybody. When I first grew up and can remember, I was dressed as a girl by mother. And I stayed that way for two or three years. And after that was treated like what I call the dog of the family. I was beaten. I was made to do things that no human being would want to do."

2. "I was death on women. I didn't feel they need to exist. I hated them, and I wanted to destroy everyone I could find. I was doing a good job of it."

3. "Killing became the same thing as having sex."

4. "Sex is one of my downfalls. I get sex any way I can get it. If I have to force somebody to do it, I do. ... I rape them; I've done that. I've killed animals to have sex with them, and I've had sex while they're alive."

Herbert Mullin

1. "Satan gets into people and makes them do things they don't

want to."

2. "I saw the light over the confessional and the voice said: That's the person to kill."

Ian Brady

1. "Contrary to popular perception, the so-called Moors Murders were merely an existential exercise of just over a year, which was concluded in December 1964."

2. "Obviously and logically, I wish to end it. I have, in effect, been kept in suspended animation since 1965."

John Reginald Halliday Christie

1. "'The sixth commandment – 'Thou Shalt Not Kill' – fascinated me . . . I always knew that someday I should defy it."

2. "For me a corpse has a beauty and dignity which a living body could never hold ... there is a peace about death that soothes me."

3. "My first murder was thrilling because I had embarked on the career I had chosen for myself, the career of murder."

4. "When I murdered my wife I removed the one obstacle which for ten years had apparently held me in check. After she had gone the way was clear for me to fulfill my destiny."

Peter Sutcliffe

1. "Killing prostitutes had become an obsession with me. I could not stop myself. It was like a drug."

2. "The women I killed were filth-bastard prostitutes who were littering the streets. I was just cleaning up the place a bit."

Ted Bundy

1. "I haven't blocked out the past. I wouldn't trade the person I am, or what I've done – or the people I've known – for anything. So I do think about it. And at times it's a rather mellow trip to lay back and remember."

2. "I just liked to kill, I wanted to kill."

3. "I want to master life and death."

4. "I'm the most cold-blooded son of a bitch you'll ever meet."

5. "I want to master life and deat. . . . Possessing them physically as

one would possess a potted plant, a painting, or a Porsche. Owning, as it were, this individual."

6. "Sometimes I feel like a vampire."

7. "The fantasy that accompanies and generates the anticipation that precedes the crime is always more stimulating than the immediate aftermath of the crime itself."

8. "We all go a little mad sometimes."

9. "You feel the last bit of breath leaving their body. You're looking into their eyes. A person in that situation is God!"

Tommy Lynn Sells

1. "I went in and, and, and I don't know if it was her room, don't know if it was his room, I don't, I just knew I wanted to go in there and hurt someone."

2. "My life don't make a lot of sense. ... It don't make sense that I go around the country killing people. Period. It don't make sense doing that."

3. "Take your worst nightmares, and put my face to them."

Vincenz Verzeni

"I had an unspeakable delight in strangling women, experiencing during the act erections and real sexual pleasure. The feeling of pleasure while strangling them was much greater than that which I experienced while masturbating. It never occurred to me to touch or look at the genitals. It satisfied me to seize the women by the neck and suck their blood."

Adolf Eichmann [of the third Reich]

"It is very sad that I can no longer fill my daily quotas in the gas chambers. I have neither enough staff nor enough supplies. Every night I go to bed with a nagging conscience, because I have been unable to do my duty."

Alexander Pichushkin

"For me a life without murder is like a life without food for you. I felt like the father of all these people, since it was I who opened the door for them to another world."

William Heiress

"For heaven's sake catch me before I kill more I cannot control myself."

Richard Ramirez

1. "Killing is killing whether done for duty, profit or fun."

2. "We've all got the power in our hands to kill, but most people are afraid to use it. The ones who aren't afraid, control life itself."

3. "You maggots make me sick, I will be avenged. Lucifer dwells within us all."

4. I'm pretty set in my ways. I doubt anything short of a miracle would change me."

5. "I believe in Satan. I believe evil is a force that is beyond us, and that we just have to invite him in, and he will."

6. "It is in no way beyond understanding [his crimes as 'cruelty, callousness and viciousness beyond any human understanding.']. Mankind has been like that throughout history. In today's society, people use those qualities – I call them qualities – for all things. It is for self-gratification. It is for sex. It is for excitement. This kind of fervor servers its own purpose. It doesn't obey rules. It runs amok. You see it on the news every day, but society cannot hang it's moral and ethical values on me to survive. I do what I must in all ways, and I'm proud of it. The necessity to be myself passes all moral barriers."

7. "Everybody has got good and evil in them. I'd like to be 100% evil, but I can't. I'm too easy-going sometimes. Then again, while anger and hate are two things some people can cope with, I cannot. My anger and hate grow to a level that I cannot live comfortably with it. It causes me headaches and stuff. When I get angry, it's an extreme form. It is the extreme. There is no in between. But there is with good and evil, and I am there."

Donald Harvey

"I controlled other people's lives, whether they lived or died. I had that power to control. After I didn't get caught for the first fifteen, I thought it was my right. I appointed myself judge, prosecutor and jury. So I played God."

A serial killer, explaining his motives
"The most important radical aim is to make her suffer, since there is no greater power over another person than that of inflicting pain on her."

Charles Manson
[Manson had bragged to him about killing people:] "We knocked off five of them just the other night."

WOMEN

Jane Toppan
1. "That is my ambition, to have killed more people – more helpless people – than any man or woman who has ever lived."

2. "I carried it too far, that's for sure."

3. "I made my fantasy life more powerful than my real one."

4. "I think in some way I wanted it to end, even if it meant my own destruction."

5. "My consuming lust was to experience their bodies. I viewed them as objects, as strangers. It is hard for me to believe a human being could have done what I've done"

Aileen Wuornos
1. "They say it's the number of people I killed, I say it's the principle."

2. "To me, this world is nothing but evil, and my own evil just happened to come out because of the circumstances of what I was doing."

Barbara Louise Huxley
1. "After spending so long watching deranged men climb straight to the top of the FBI's Most Wanted list, it was hard to get up the energy to go into work every day and suffocate another frail diabetic. ... "I started to think, 'What's the point? What am I doing here?'"..." I just want to be treated like any other homicidal sociopath."... 'Even when the news finally gets around to reporting on us, it's only to talk about how 'rare' it is to see women do the

awful things we do,' Huxley said. 'It's never because we're just good murderers.'"

2. "There's nothing more upsetting than strangling someone with surgical tubing, only to have them look at you in shock and disbelief. It's like, 'Why are you so surprised? Is it because I'm a woman?!'"

Carol Bundy
"I can't take it anymore; I'm supposed to save lives not take them."

Agnes Pandy
[Explaining how she had eviscerated one of her own stepdaughters] "It was my task to take out the organs while Pandy was cutting up the remains. I just used a kitchen knife. You have to exercise strength. It's not that easy."

Regarding The Manson Family Murders

Susan Atkins
1. "We wanted to do a crime that would shock the world, that the world would have to stand up and take notice.""

2. "Sharon was the last to die," Susan said with a laugh as she described how Sharon was begging her, "Please don't kill me. Please don't kill me. I don't want to die. I want to live. I want to have my baby. I want to have my baby."

3. [Susan said she just looked at Sharon straight in the eye and said,] "Look, bitch, I don't care about you. I don't care if you're going to have a baby. You had better be ready. You're going to die and I don't feel anything about it. ... In a few minutes I killed her."

4. [Susan said she saw that there was Sharon's blood on her hand and she tasted it.] "Wow, what a trip! To taste death, and yet give life."

5. Susan explained. She had wanted to cut out Sharon's baby but there wasn't enough time. She had also wanted to take out all the victims' eyes and squash them against the walls and cut off and mutilate all of their fingers, but they didn't have the chance.

6. [On being asked if she felt sorry for her murders] "Sorry for doing what was right to me? I have no guilt in me. ...What I did was what I did with those people, and that's what I did. [Questioner: Just one of those things, seven dead bodies?] "No big thing."

6. "He was full of blood," she said and claimed that she had stabbed him three or four times. "He was bleeding and he ran to the front part, and would you believe that he was there hollering 'Help, help, somebody please help me,' and nobody came? Then we finished him off."

Chapter 6
THE VICTIMS: DESCRIPTIONS OF PATHICS

The following quotation fragments are further indications of the lack of clarity as to whether who is being referred to is either a narcissist, sociopath, or psychopath. Because of this, these persons use the three terms indiscriminately because each category has shared traits, such as lack of conscience and remorse, lying, irresponsibility, etc.. Much more information would be needed to derive a full picture of the type of pathic (narcipath, sociopath, psychopath) an individual is according to our grouping. Accordingly, for now, the idea to keep in mind is that each victim's description of an individual pathic refers to the basic shared traits of *all* pathics.

---

1. "You say your guy might actually be an NPD. Sometimes I don't think there's a dime's worth of difference between the P and the N. So if he is violent, unpredictable and a chronic liar he's more likely to be a P; more needy of admiration, more likely to be an N. In most other respects they are quite similar."

2. "Of course, as normal human beings, we search inside ourselves for answers. That is precisely what the N never does. If he did, he would go for therapy forthwith. It is natural to wonder how we could be fooled so easily and so ruthlessly. Ever watch sleight of hand? Well, it is the same. You are fooled by the speed and skill of the 'magician' or the card shark. But, and this is the 'but', it is only an illusion."

3. "Looking back on all the Ns I've ever known and merged with, I see there were signs within minutes of meeting the N that they were grossly selfish, immoral, sex-addicted or something was definitely 'off' that I couldn't explain. I didn't honour my intuition, gut feelings, and instinct. The truth is that I had almost no experience setting healthy boundaries."

4. "They simply cannot sustain 'niceness' for any period of time – to anyone – unless they want something from them, or unless that person can offer them something."

5. "Life is a superficial game for him and you are a pawn on his board. Is that what you want to be, a pawn in the hands of a madman?"

6. "My ex-N knew how to hook me by drawing me into her sad stories ... Some Ns like to be MYSTERIOUS because it keeps them in control while you're dancing to FIGURE them out."

7. "The N will not change; you must absolutely keep this before your mind."

8. "The N is like bog-fire (jack-o'-lantern). You race after him, and race into the marsh, where you are swallowed up and suffocated. The N will suffocate all that is good in you, will twist your psyche until you don't know who you are yourself. Eventually your own face will not seem your own in the mirror. Yes, it gets that bad, believe me."

9. "The N is bad even for your looks – reason enough in itself to leave him quickly. He will make you feel ugly, unwanted, inadequate, not up to his standards, no matter how intelligent, good-looking, or smart you are. He makes you feel like this so that you are in line with his dreadful feelings about himself."

10. "I can only offer a comparison: a person who has been in a wheelchair since infancy cannot have any notion of what it feels like to walk, run, jump, do gymnastics, ride a bike etc.. The person with NPD (narcissistic personality disorder) is in the same position, an emotional cripple, whose experience of life bears no resemblance to the ordinary person's."

11. "When I asked him why he had stopped terrifying me, he said:

'It didn't work.' What this says about him is that his behaviour was not out of control, as one might think because it was so bizarre, but a strategy. He stopped using that strategy when it didn't achieve his ends. That's important to remember when dealing with a true N."

12. "Ns are notoriously bad gift-givers. My ex-N only used to give gifts to me he had received as free samples from representatives."

13. "Any apparent (and spurious) remission of NPD is just that – fake. The individual is marshalling his/her forces for the next round, which will be one hundred times worse than what went before. Believe me."

14. "He has never been empathetic towards anyone, and has no idea how much pain he causes people when he makes choices that affect them."

15. "He has this vindictive, mean streak in him. He knows exactly which buttons to push and can tell you to go to hell and you'll look forward to the trip."

16. "Don't tell them ANYTHING you aren't prepared to get shoved up your butt later...or down your throat, or in your heart in the form of a dagger. And of course there are those things you tell them that you have to be prepared to have TWISTED into things they can shove..."

17. "My Ns love to try verbal manipulation. They're very good at it and most people fall for it time and again. It takes Ns 20-40 minutes of running the gamut of all their whining, complaining, argumentative and other persuasive tactics."

18. "Ex-N was always insensitive about what he said to me and he always chose his words carefully as to obtain a look of shock and hurt in my face."

19. "I know the pain of hearing horrible, insulting remarks only to be told that it was merely a 'joke' and how I have 'no sense of humour...' I tell him that his jokes aren't funny to me, but I realize now that that's exactly what he wants to hear. I spend my days in constant anxiety because I know the next blow up is just around the corner."

20. "With an N, you cannot accumulate a store of MEMORIES of what you have meant to them. Your meaning is only in the here and now. This is why a husband can immediately abandon a wife who becomes crippled or has a life-threatening illness or who otherwise is no longer 'Miss step & fetch it', and who might even (HORRORS of HORRORS) need something from the N."

21. "It is not surprising then, to discover that the N has many alters [egos], many secret lives, and they count on others to reinforce the idea that they 'would never do such a thing' and that they 'are not like that'."

22. "If a past girlfriend or wife dumped him, in the new location he may say that his wife recently died of cancer! This is to generate a little community sympathy for himself and opens doors for him to be accepted into the community. Then he gets busy, finding one or more targets to abuse. Stripped naked, the N is an ugly picture, without all of his/her illusions, and the fantasies dissolve."

23. "My daughter is starting to show the toll of just being witness to my mother's treatment of me. She will strike when you least expect... she will lure you in with sweetness and tricks, and when you are feeling hopeful... she will bring you down with one cruel perfectly-timed remark... and you will crash in heartbreak again and again. They do not improve...they get worse."

24. "They tell lies, even when there is no need to tell a lie. But telling the lie makes the game more interesting, for them, but leaves others in a state of confusion; since they do this all the time and seldom tell the truth which makes them pathological liars. With many years of practice, they become very convincing liars."

25. "The lies, the flirting, the lies, the comparing, the lies, the ambivalence, the lies, the belittling, the lies, the teasing, the lies, the built up promises, the lies, the setting up for disappointment. Did I mention the lies?"

26. "I now realise that he is such a pathological liar that just by asking him a question I invite him to lie."

27. "Please give up trying to figure out why he says what he says…does what he does. It's truly a pointless pursuit and it offers little comfort in the end."

28. "Many hours I have spent (wasted) trying to appease, settle down, quiet, succor, help, understand, calm the N….and defend myself to outrageous, untrue, hurtful, lying words and actions. This is the crazy-making process where you think it's your fault and try ANYTHING and EVERYTHING to make it stop."

29. "Final closure for me is the fact that HE IS WHAT HE IS."

30. "Do they every change? NO! They just get better at hiding it!"

31. "When WE look in the mirror we know who is looking back at us. What does the N see when he looks for the millionth time in his mirror. Best not to dwell too much on what he sees."

32. "Every once in a while, somebody actually gets through to them and makes them see what they have done. Then the next day it's as if the revelation never happened."

33. "Yes, they are frustrating, but they are giving you an advanced course in self control. You cannot argue or even have a conversation with them. There is no satisfaction in telling them off, they just do the kindergarten 'No, *you*-are' thing. There is no closure, you just have to walk away and focus on yourself. The whole purpose of their existence is to get attention FROM you, and they will do it any way they can. As long as you are paying attention to them, they win. Any time you spend on N is that much of your life wasted."

34. "N would always change the subject and say, 'I promise we will get right back to that, hold that thought.' And of course when I would bring it up later he would say that I was nagging him."

35. "Ns will always rage to avoid a question – it is like a 'how dare you question me,' and of course you are questioning N and N thinks he will be caught, so what better way to deal with it but rage."

36. "You can love, will always be able to love. He can't, and never will. He is an emotional cripple who cannot even love himself. You will move forward in life, but he will remain, always, in the shadowlands of his disorder."

37. "Verbally sparring with an N is like teaching a pig to sing. It is an exercise in futility and infuriates the pig."

38. "My P is a master with words, an absolute genius."

39. "This guy's capacity to jog through vocabulary was aerobic! He would gallop through people's heads taking twists and turns and confusing their direction until they experienced the 'deer-in-headlights' disorder. That is the point! – to stop you from thinking."

40. "At first the little verbally abusive things went right past me. I thought he was joking."

41. "Trying to figure out how a crazy person thinks is like trying to figure out what a fly is thinking. Ns are so far removed from normal thought that you couldn't possibly do it unless you are crazy too. He will probably try to make you so."

42. "In my view, as long as Ns can find prey and victims to feed off of they will not, nor cannot, change."

43. "They adopt the 'silent treatment' waiting game. The rough translation is they will try to wear you down, and wait to see what, when, and how you do something for them."

44. "The problem with the narcissist's lack of attachment is not just a fear of commitment; it means they are capable of walking away at ANY POINT when there are better options elsewhere. A narcissist is a huge risk for anyone to have as a partner. They will leave when we need them the most."

45. "The bottom line it seems to me, is if you lost your leg, a P would find that a personal inconvenience somehow and be complaining about it."

46. "Normal rules of conduct between normal human beings do not apply with a person like this."

47. "If my ex-P and I were ship-wrecked at sea with one life ring to swim for, he would have pushed my head under water whilst telling me how sorry he was and how much he had always loved me."

48. "They throw out a huge net. Like a big fishing net, hoping to pull in a few gullible ones. What I saw were 75 women on his network and he was writing them all, better chances with more numbers I guess. Quantity over quality, by golly. Yeah, these guys are WORK-ING IT!"

49. "They memorize body language and can spot a person who might feel a little vulnerable a mile away."

50. "He appears to the outside world to be loving, considerate, helpful, charming, knowledgeable and hardworking. They think he's boy wonder. He tells everyone of his deep religious commitment, attends church, and has little old ladies bringing him religious writings. His business is a source of NS [narcissist supply] for him (big time) and puts him in contact with many people where he is able to garner much NS. It works beautifully. And, I have never met a more evil, cunning, ruthless predator in my life."

51. "Sometimes I really believe he thinks he loves these women until their money runs out, and he suddenly has glitches in the relationship and that is when he tells these women 'Oh, sorry, but this isn't going to work out.' Where he finds these women with money I don't know, but this is the 3rd. He must have a radar."

52. "Anything I valued he put down or disregarded – anything, from human life or where I bought gas to a simple restaurant choice."

53. "They are personal poison; they send it to everyone in their path."

54. "I think a female-to-female friendship with an N is so damaging because as women we tend to bond by confiding and revealing personal information. This gives them an incredible arsenal to use against us."

55. "I think the Ns in our life constantly test us to see if they are still in control."

56. "To most people he is the harmless, lovable, proud father and caring partner. At home he was lazy, selfish, money-grabbing, abusive, obsessive and critical."

57. "The N never mourns."

58. "The more vulnerable you are the more abusive he will be."

59. "It is sad because when he's the sweet guy, I'm weak. But something I read recently describes that as 'Come closer ... so I can slap you'."

60. "The problem with these idiots is that they really don't know what the hell they want out of life, but the one thing they do know is THEY LOVE TO TORTURE and to PROLONG THE TORTURE. Somehow sadistic behaviour ensures their control and validates their existence. If he lets you have your life back, who will he torture?"

61. "Never ever forget that they TOTALLY drain you...emotionally, physically and sometimes financially. You do not even know who you are any longer as they methodically take over your basic being. Stay as far away as possible and love yourself again!!! The very smart ones use you up SLOWLY and deliberately. You may not even know what is going on until they suddenly crush you by abruptly leaving for no reason."

62. "NPs particularly favor emotional types who are in touch with their feelings as targets. Two reasons – they are such a rich source of NS and they are easiest to spot. And, at the end of a relationship they can stir up more NS [narcissistic supply] with their cruelty. So, what do we do? We need to shut down that emotional part of ourselves to heal and detach from them. Now isn't that just the darndest thing?"

63. "I have been slowly coming to accept the fact that there is absolutely NOTHING that I can do to help him. It's just so painful to realize that I have to 'give up' on someone I once loved."

64. "He's managed to ruin my reputation, my education, my freedom at the workplace and around town."

65. "These guys will damage your credit, put you in thousands of dollars in debt, collection agencies will be at your door, you won't have a penny to your name when they are done."

66. "Never back a N in a corner; avoid causing a narcissistic injury unless you are willing to engage in their retaliatory rage...A narcissist operates on a level of fear most of us cannot even understand."

67. "In all honesty and bluntness, they tend to get away with it due to the complacency and backpedaling of their victims."

68. "These people are emotionally, mentally, morally and spiritually dead! Can the dead remember what is going on around them? Can the dead feel what they are doing wrong? Can the dead feel at all? They are the walking dead! Don't ever expect an apology or a change unless they find Life! I agree with this and it helped me to understand how someone can commit such horrible things. It also made it much easier to forgive when I was told this: 'Carrying the dead with you is what you are doing by not forgiving! To forgive is not to forget, it's only to release a person from a debt, a debt that can NEVER be repaid! By carrying this you allow them to control you for LIFE and through LIFE!'"

69. "What's scary isn't the sociopaths themselves, but the people who vehemently support them should you or anyone else try to challenge this individual."

70. "They plug into us and breaking away is like a territorial fight. They want our energy, our very lives and we have to stand our ground and fight for what is ours. It is a battle of boundaries and they will find every way possible to get in. If one approach doesn't work they will try another."

71. "They want to suck out our goodness and dump their badness in its place."

72. "I think psychopaths have some sort of 'thing' that makes them able to read what a person wants in order to reel them in. I would guess the nicer a person is the better chance of falling into their traps."

73. "Ns install a mental filter in our heads a little bit at a time. Before we know it, everything we do, say, or think, goes through this filter. 'Will he get upset if I do/say/think this? Will he approve/disapprove? Will he feel hurt by this?' Until we can uninstall this filter, our actions are controlled by them to some degree."

74. "They're always scheming, conniving, plotting. How do we stand a chance against what they make a career of."

75. "One word comes to me when I think of them: 'imposter'."

76. "I am obsessed beyond normal...almost envious of their 'super powers'. How do I wean myself away from this evil fixation?"

77. "THAT is a very interesting idea to me [pathics' allure]. It's how writers create 'atmosphere'. They speak about something as if the reader ALREADY knew what they were talking about. Once this is done, one is drawn into this 'atmosphere' and is led by the words into the world of Jurassic Park, Frankenstein...whatever the imaginary world is. N does this in his writing in ways that I didn't realize before and I think this is what Ns do; not only psychopaths, but lots of Ns too. In a way, we ALL do it with our speaking patterns. We draw others into our 'world' with our tone of 'voice'. When an N does this certain concepts are taken for granted right from the beginning. Like when Clarice goes up to the prison cell where Hannibal is sitting. He speaks with a voice that is elegantly articulate. But he is in a cage so one feels intrigued to listen to this upper-class accent behind bars; one is drawn into wondering what makes this caged, elegantly intelligent man tick. I think women enjoy their complexity and levels and when a man is either without apparent complexity and seems to transcend complexity by brute strength, I think women are turned on by that power. But when a man is complex and mischievously self-aware of his complexity, I think that is also very alluring to women. It feels as if that complex man knows one better than an 'ordinary' man. But all the complexly intriguing men I've met in my life have either been psychopaths or Ns. Maybe only women can understand each others' complexity and we need to leave men to be as they are in their OWN layers that are different from a woman's? I don't know. Hannibal's observing Clarice's cheap handbag and the subtle details of her bearing is sooo seductive. The illusion is that Hannibal KNOWS her in all her details, that he SEES her like no 'ordinary' man on the street. His hawk-like subtle observation, done seemingly off the cuff make this caged man seem to have transcended the bars of his cage, to almost be there unjustly. Then he speaks about cooking the human liver with the fava beans with that num num sucking in his lower lip sound, so horrifying and fascinating! One can't take one's eyes off that glistening mouth, nor forget his malice. It's woven into one's being with such an exotic mixture of romance, the wounded lion in a cage. The horror, oh the horror, and the seductiveness of his glorious mind, those laser-like sinful syn- apses ... sooooo seductive. All the rest of the movie either leads up to that seduction or away from it. Hannibal and Clarice locked into that moment of classic N and N-Co-enmeshment. ...I felt the same rush, the allure. It felt sexual. That charged. My hormones went wild with wanting to be had by this powerful mind. The singer and the song one and the same but trying to separate them, so I could work on my healing, understanding who the Hannibals were, what they had done to me in my own life. But somewhere the rush of fascination disturbed me. It felt sick. It sickened me. But I didn't have words for it. I see now that I was drawn in by the allure of his having set up an 'atmosphere' that I bought into. I felt physically sick. He seemed that repugnant and twisted."

78. "He was the most charming, romantic, witty, charismatic and handsome man I had ever met. I had never before been so attracted to someone. He made my knees go weak; I was completely in his thrall. He called me all the time, texted me continuously, declared his love for me perpetually. We walked in rhythm, we fit together like jigsaw pieces. The sex was a spiritual experience. I suddenly knew what Holly- wood was all about; I felt that my new romance was like something from the silver screen, a veritable fairytale. Then the hell happened. It has taken me ages to recover."

79. "The other day I was 'lured' back into conversation with 'the voice'... he took me by surprise, calling me at work from a pay-phone (I didn't recognize the number) and his 'alluring, polite, warm, sexy voice' had me responding to him before I even knew what I was doing! I know that sounds weak and inexcusable, but it's the God's honest truth! At first, I truly didn't know it was him... it was just a very familiar, friendly, trusting, yet seductive voice and before I realized it was him, I was 'hooked'... Well, once again, as always when I 'engage' in conversation with him... he 'beats around

the bush' and twists things until I am so baffled and confused I am speechless and worn out. So... back to the 'drawing board' once again... NO CONTACT. What's the point? I don't want him in my life AT ALL (he scares me) and he brings nothing to me but disharmony, distrust, confusion, aggravation, and frustration that there is NO way to get through to him that he and I have NOTHING in common! Thank God! But, I just wanted to also say, I understand about feeling sorry for 'them' because they do seem so lost, lonely, strange and sad. But, I truly believe that is just one more way they have to 'hook' our compassion and trust... Don't be fooled."

80. "Despite the million horrific things this man did...that one stupid glance or kind word...or whatever... can wipe the bad memories out in an instant ... is absolutely amazing to me. How does that happen? How is that possible?"

"We ARE NOT stupid people. Before my P ... I was considered one of the strongest women in my circle: Single ... defiant ... strong ... out-spoken ... independent ... intelligent ... attractive... successful ... etc ... like so many of us..."

"I definitely didn't want or need a man in my life ... I saw them as a complication ... rather than something good ... I didn't want the 'trouble' of trying to navigate a relationship ... so up until the P...I just 'dated men' on and off ... just saw them as something to pass the time with ... just for fun ... and that's it ..."

"Until the P of course ... and while I embarked upon the relationship with him with those same intentions...he single handedly manipulated and brainwashed me into thinking I wanted a relationship...that I wanted it with him ... that he was EVERYTHING I WAS MISSING IN MY LIFE ... that he could fill the void (you know ... the void that up until now I wasn't even aware existed) ... and you guys know how the rest of the story goes ..."

"But again ... my main point here is just ... HOW ON EARTH ARE THEY STILL ABLE TO GET TO US. I mean...ok.... in the beginning, we were unarmed ...we didn't have the knowledge ... we were unknowing ... unprepared ... trusting ... loving ... giving people ... who ... just like anyone else ... have our insecurities (that's normal) ... and these vultures come and prey on us ... and use every tactic in

119

their arsenal to twist us into shell's of human beings to do their will...to the point where we no longer have our own identity.

"BUT how on earth ...now ... after time has passed ... the reality revealed ... the knowledge gained ... the distance achieved...the support system developed ... and so on and so forth ... how are they still able to have this effect on us ... and I understand the NO CONTACT thing and why that is important (although not a real option for me); but I just feel like I have to believe that aside from the no contact rule ... that there has to be a way for us to get to a place where we ARE completely and totally UNAFFECTED by them ... NO MATTER WHAT THEY DO. Maybe that's 5 or 10 or 20 years down the line ... but I need to know it's possible and that it can happen."

Chapter 7
THE AUTHORITIES:
AN OVERVIEW OF PATHICS

The three selections in this chapter professionally substantiate the insights, descriptions, and experiences of the nonprofessional contributors (mostly victims of pathics) to this book. Section 1 includes Dr. Robert Hare's noted 20-item checklist that is used extensively in psychopathic literature and therapy. Section 2, includes pertinent passages on psychopathic descriptions from Dr. Hervey Cleckley's seminal masterwork, *The Mask of Sanity*. Section 3 includes recent findings of psychopathy by Dr. Kent Kiehl, one of the world's leading younger investigators in psychopathy.

1

Hare's PCL-R 20-item checklist
Hare's PCL-R 20-item checklist is based on Cleckley's 16-item checklist.

1. GLIB and SUPERFICIAL CHARM – the tendency to be smooth, engaging, charming, slick, and verbally facile. Psychopathic charm is not in the least shy, self-conscious, or afraid to say anything. A psychopath never gets tongue-tied. They have freed themselves from the social conventions about taking turns in talking, for example.

2. GRANDIOSE SELF-WORTH – a grossly inflated view of one's abilities and self-worth, self-assured, opinionated, cocky, a braggart.

Psychopaths are arrogant people who believe they are superior human beings.

3. NEED FOR STIMULATION or PRONENESS TO BOREDOM – an excessive need for novel, thrilling, and exciting stimulation; taking chances and doing things that are risky. Psychopaths often have a low self- discipline in carrying tasks through to completion because they get bored easily. They fail to work at the same job for any length of time, for example, or to finish tasks that they consider dull or routine.

4. PATHOLOGICAL LYING – can be moderate or high; in moderate form, they will be shrewd, crafty, cunning, sly, and clever; in extreme form, they will be deceptive, deceitful, underhanded, unscrupulous, manipulative, and dishonest.

5. CONNING AND MANIPULATIVENESS – the use of deceit and deception to cheat, con, or defraud others for personal gain; distinguished from Item #4 in the degree to which exploitation and callous ruthlessness is present, as reflected in a lack of concern for the feelings and suffering of one's victims.

6. LACK OF REMORSE OR GUILT – a lack of feelings or concern for the losses, pain, and suffering of victims; a tendency to be unconcerned, dispassionate, coldhearted, and unempathic. This item is usually demonstrated by a disdain for one's victims.

7. SHALLOW AFFECT – emotional poverty or a limited range or depth of feelings; interpersonal coldness in spite of signs of open gregariousness.

8. CALLOUSNESS and LACK OF EMPATHY – a lack of feelings toward people in general; cold, contemptuous, inconsiderate, and tactless.

9. PARASITIC LIFESTYLE – an intentional, manipulative, selfish, and exploitative financial dependence on others as reflected in a lack of motivation, low self-discipline, and inability to begin or complete responsibilities.

10. POOR BEHAVIORAL CONTROLS – expressions of irritability, annoyance, impatience, threats, aggression, and verbal abuse; inadequate control of anger and temper; acting hastily.

11. PROMISCUOUS SEXUAL BEHAVIOR – a variety of brief, superficial relations, numerous affairs, and an indiscriminate selection of sexual partners; the maintenance of several relationships at the same time; a history of attempts to sexually coerce others into sexual activity or taking great pride at discussing sexual exploits or conquests.

12. EARLY BEHAVIOR PROBLEMS – a variety of behaviors prior to age 13, including lying, theft, cheating, vandalism, bullying, sexual activity, fire-setting, glue-sniffing, alcohol use, and running away from home.

13. LACK OF REALISTIC, LONG-TERM GOALS – an inability or persistent failure to develop and execute long-term plans and goals; a nomadic existence, aimless, lacking direction in life.

14. IMPULSIVITY – the occurrence of behaviors that are unpre-meditated and lack reflection or planning; inability to resist temptation, frustrations, and urges; a lack of deliberation without considering the consequences; foolhardy, rash, unpredictable, erratic, and reckless.

15. IRRESPONSIBILITY – repeated failure to fulfill or honor obliga-tions and commitments; such as not paying bills, defaulting on loans, performing sloppy work, being absent or late to work, failing to honor contractual agreements.

16. FAILURE TO ACCEPT RESPONSIBILITY FOR OUR OWN ACTIONS – a failure to accept responsibility for one's actions reflected in low conscientiousness, an absence of dutifulness, antagonistic mani-pulation, denial of responsibility, and an effort to manipulate others through this denial.

17. MANY SHORT-TERM MARITAL RELATIONSHIPS – a lack of commitment to a long-term relationship reflected in inconsistent, undependable, and unreliable commitments in life, including

marital.

18. JUVENILE DELINQUENCY – behavior problems between the ages of 13-18; mostly behaviors that are crimes or clearly involve aspects of antagonism, exploitation, aggression, manipulation, or a callous, ruthless tough-mindedness.

19. REVOCATION OF CONDITION RELEASE – a revocation of probation or other conditional release due to technical violations, such as carelessness, low deliberation, or failing to appear.

20. CRIMINAL VERSATILITY – a diversity of types of criminal offenses, regardless if the person has been arrested or convicted for them; taking great pride at getting away with crimes.

2

From *Mask of Sanity*, by Hervey Cleckley

More often than not, the typical psychopath will seem particularly agreeable and make a distinctly positive impression when he is first encountered. Alert and friendly in his attitude, he is easy to talk with and seems to have a good many genuine interests. There is nothing at all odd or queer about him, and in every respect he tends to embody the concept of a well-adjusted, happy person. Nor does he, on the other hand, seem to be artificially exerting himself like one who is covering up or who wants to sell you a bill of goods. He would seldom be confused with the professional backslapper or someone who is trying to ingratiate himself for a concealed purpose. Signs of affectation or excessive affability are not characteristic. He looks like the real thing.

Very often indications of good sense and sound reasoning will emerge and one is likely to feel soon after meeting him that this normal and pleasant person is also one with high abilities. Psychometric tests also very frequently show him of superior intelligence. More than the average person, he is likely to seem free from social or emotional impediments, from the minor distortions, peculiarities, and awkwardnesses so common even among the successful. Such superficial characteristics are not universal in this group but they are very common.

Here the typical psychopath contrasts sharply with the schizoid personality or the patient with masked or latent schizophrenia. No matter how free from delusions and other overt signs of psychosis the schizoid person may be, he is likely to show specific peculiarities in his outer aspect. Usually there are signs of tension, withdrawal, and subtle oddities of manner and reaction. These may appear to be indications of unrevealed brilliance, perhaps even eccentricities of genius, but they are likely to complicate and cool easy social relations and to promote restraint. Although the psychopath's inner emotional deviations and deficiencies may be comparable with the inner status of the masked schizophrenic, he outwardly shows nothing brittle or strange. Everything about him is likely to suggest desirable and superior human qualities, a robust mental health.

The so-called psychopath is ordinarily free from signs or symptoms traditionally regarded as evidence of a psychosis. He does not hear voices. Genuine delusions cannot be demonstrated. There is no valid depression, consistent pathologic elevation of mood, or irresistible pressure of activity. Outer perceptual reality is accurately recognized; social values and generally accredited personal standards are accepted verbally. Excellent logical reasoning is maintained and, in theory, the patient can foresee the consequences of injudicious or antisocial acts, outline acceptable or admirable plans of life, and ably criticize in words his former mistakes. The results of direct psychiatric examination disclose nothing pathologic – nothing that would indicate incompetency or that would arouse suspicion that such a man could not lead a successful and happy life.

Not only is the psychopath rational and his thinking free of delusions, but he also appears to react with normal emotions. His ambitions are discussed with what appears to be healthy enthusiasm. His convictions impress even the skeptical observer as firm and binding. He seems to respond with adequate feelings to another's interest in him and, as he discusses his wife, his children, or his parents, he is likely to be judged a man of warm human responses, capable of full devotion and loyalty.

There are usually no symptoms to suggest a psychoneurosis in the clinical sense. In fact, the psychopath is nearly always free from minor reactions popularly regarded as "neurotic" or as constituting "nervousness." The chief criteria whereby such diagnoses as hysteria, obsessive-compulsive disorder, anxiety state, or "neurasthenia" might be made do not apply to him. It is highly typical for him not only to escape the abnormal anxiety and tension fundamentally characteristic of this whole diagnostic group but also to show a relative immunity from such anxiety and worry as might be judged normal or appropriate in disturbing situations. Regularly we find in him extraordinary poise rather than jitteriness or worry, a smooth sense of physical well-being instead of uneasy preoccupation with bodily functions. Even under concrete circumstances that would for the ordinary person cause embarrassment, confusion, acute insecurity, or visible agitation, his relative serenity is likely to be noteworthy.

It is true he may become vexed and restless when held in jails or psychiatric hospitals. This impatience seems related to his inability to realize the need or justification for his being restrained. What tension or uneasiness of this sort he may show seems provoked entirely by external circumstances, never by feelings of guilt, remorse, or intrapersonal insecurity. Within himself he appears almost as incapable of anxiety as of profound remorse.

Though the psychopath is likely to give an early impression of being a thoroughly reliable person, it will soon be found that on many occasions he shows no sense of responsibility whatsoever. No matter how binding the obligation, how urgent the circumstances, or how important the matter, this holds true. Furthermore, the question of whether or not he is to be confronted with his failure or his disloyalty and called to account for it appears to have little effect on his attitude.

If such failures occurred uniformly and immediately, others would soon learn not to rely upon psychopaths or to be surprised at their conduct. It is, however, characteristic for them during some periods to show up regularly at work, to meet their financial obligations, to ignore an opportunity to steal. They may apply their excellent abilities in business or in study for a week, for months, or even for a year or more and thereby gain potential security, win a scholarship, be acclaimed top salesman or elected president of a social club or perhaps of a school honor society. Not all checks given by psychopaths bounce; not all promises are uniformly ignored. They do not necessarily land in jail every day (or every month) or seek to cheat someone else during every transaction. If so, it would be much simpler to deal with them. This transient (but often convincingly) demonstrated ability to succeed in business and in all objective affairs makes failures more disturbing to those about them.

Furthermore, it cannot be predicted how long effective and socially acceptable conduct will prevail or precisely when (or in what manner) dishonest, outlandish, or disastrously irresponsible acts or failures to act will occur. These seem to have little or no relation to objective stress, to cyclic periods, or to major alterations of mood or outlook. What is at stake for the patient, for his family, or for anybody else is not a regularly determining factor. At the crest of success in his work he may forge a small check, indulge in petty thievery, or simply not come to the office. After a period of gracious and apparently happy relations with his family he may pick a quarrel with his wife, cuff her up a bit, drive her from the house, and then throw a glass of iced tea in the face of his 3-year-old son. For the initiation of such outbursts he does not, it seems, need any great anger. Moderate vexation usually suffices.

The psychopath's unreliability and his disregard for obligations and for consequences are manifested in both trivial and serious matters, are masked by demonstrations of conforming behavior, and cannot be accounted for by ordinary motives or incentives. Although it can be confidently predicted that his failures and disloyalties will continue, it is impossible to time them and to take satisfactory precautions against their effect. Here, it might be said, is not even a consistency in inconsistency but an inconsistency in inconsistency.

The psychopath shows a remarkable disregard for truth and is to be trusted no more in his accounts of the past than in his promises for the future or his statement of present intentions. He gives the impression that he is incapable of ever attaining realistic comprehension of an attitude in other people which causes them to value truth and cherish truthfulness in themselves.

Typically he is at ease and unpretentious in making a serious promise or in (falsely) exculpating himself from accusations, whether grave or trivial. His simplest statement in such matters carries special powers of conviction. Overemphasis, obvious glibness, and other traditional signs of the clever liar do not usually show in his words or in his manner. Whether there is reasonable chance for him to get away with the fraud or whether certain and easily foreseen detection is at hand, he is apparently unperturbed and does the same impressive job. Candor and trustworthiness seem implicit in him at such times. During the most solemn perjuries he has no difficulty at all in looking anyone tranquilly in the eyes. Although he will lie about any matter, under any circumstances, and often for no good reason, he may, on the contrary, sometimes own up to his errors (usually when detection is certain) and appear to be facing the consequences with singular honesty, fortitude, and manliness.

It is indeed difficult to express how thoroughly straightforward some typical psychopaths can appear. They are disarming not only to those unfamiliar with such patients but often to people who know well from experience their convincing outer aspect of honesty. After being caught in shameful and gross falsehoods, after repeatedly violating his most earnest pledges, he finds it easy, when another occasion arises, to speak of his word of honor, his honor as a gentleman, and he shows surprise and vexation when commitments on such a basis do not immediately settle the issue. The conception of living up to his word seems, in fact, to be regarded as little more than a phrase sometimes useful to avoid unpleasantness or to gain other ends.

The psychopath apparently cannot accept substantial blame for the various misfortunes which befall him and which he brings down upon others, usually he denies emphatically all responsibility and directly accuses others as responsible, but often he will go through an idle ritual of saying that much of his trouble is his own fault. When the latter course is adopted, subsequent events indicate that it is empty of sincerity – a hollow and casual form as little felt as the literal implications of "your humble and obedient servant" are actually felt by a person who closes a letter with such a phrase. Although his behavior shows reactions of this sort to be perfunctory, this is seldom apparent in his manner. This is exceedingly deceptive and is very likely to promote confidence and deep trust. More detailed questioning about just what he blames himself for and why may show that a serious attitude is not only absent but altogether inconceivable to him. If this fails, his own actions will soon clarify the issue.

Whether judged in the light of his conduct, of his attitude, or of material elicited in psychiatric examination, he shows almost no sense of shame. His career is always full of exploits, any one of which would wither even the more callous representatives of the ordinary man. Yet he does not, despite his able protestations, show the slightest evidence of major humiliation or regret. This is true of matters pertaining to his personal and selfish pride and to esthetic standards that he avows as well as to moral or humanitarian matters. If Santayana is correct in saying that "perhaps the true dignity of man is his ability to despise himself," the psychopath is without a means to acquire true dignity.

Not only is the psychopath undependable, but also in more active ways he cheats, deserts, annoys, brawls, fails, and lies without any apparent compunction. He will commit theft, forgery, adultery, fraud, and other deeds for astonishingly small stakes and under much greater risks of being discovered than will the ordinary scoundrel. He will, in fact, commit such deeds in the absence of any apparent goal at all.

Despite the extraordinarily poor judgment demonstrated in behavior, in the actual living of his life, the psychopath characteristically demonstrates unimpaired (sometimes excellent) judgment in appraising theoretical situations. In complex matters of judgment involving ethical, emotional, and other evaluational factors, in contrast with matters requiring only (or chiefly) intellectual reasoning ability, he also shows no evidence of a defect. So long as the test is verbal or otherwise abstract, so long as he is not a direct participant, he shows that he knows his way about. He can offer wise decisions not only for others in life situations but also for himself so long as he is asked what he would do (or should do, or is going to do). When the test of action comes to him we soon find ample evidence of his deficiency.

The psychopath is always distinguished by egocentricity. This is usually of a degree not seen in ordinary people and often is little short of astonishing. How obviously this quality will be expressed in vanity or self-esteem will vary with the shrewdness of the subject and with his other complexities. Deeper probing will always reveal a self-centeredness that is apparently unmodifiable and all but complete. This can perhaps be best expressed by stating that it is an incapacity for object love and that this incapacity (in my experience with well-marked psychopaths) appears to be absolute.

In a sense, it is absurd to maintain that the psychopath's incapacity for object love is absolute, that is, to say he is capable of affection for another. ... He is plainly capable of casual fondness, of likes and dislikes, and of reactions that, one might say, cause others to matter to him. These affective reactions are, however, always strictly limited in degree. In durability they also vary greatly from what is normal in mankind. The term absolute is, I believe, appropriate if we apply it to any affective attitude strong and meaningful enough to be called love, that is, anything that prevails in sufficient degree and over sufficient periods to exert a major influence on behavior.

True enough, psychopaths are sometimes skillful in pretending a love for women or simulating parental devotion to their children.

What part of this is not pure (and perhaps in an important sense unconscious) simulation has always impressed this observer as that other type of pseudo-love sometimes seen in very self-centered people who are not psychopaths, which consists in concern for the other person only (or primarily) insofar as he enhances or seems to enhance the self. Even this latter imitation of adult affectivity has been seldom seen in the full-blown psychopath, although it is seen frequently in those called here partial psychopaths.

The psychopath seldom shows anything that, if the chief facts were known, would pass even in the eyes of lay observers as object love. His absolute indifference to the financial, social, emotional, physical, and other hardships which he brings upon those for whom he professes love confirms the appraisal during psychiatric studies of his true attitude. We must, let it never be forgotten, judge a man by his actions rather than by his words. This old saying is especially significant when it is the man's motivations and real feelings that we are to judge. This lack in the psychopath makes it all but impossible for an adequate emotional rapport to arise in his treatment and may be an important factor in the therapeutic failure that, in my experience, has been universal.

In addition to his incapacity for object love, the psychopath always shows general poverty of affect. Although it is true that he sometimes becomes excited and shouts as if in rage or seems to exult in enthusiasm and again weeps in what appear to be bitter tears or speaks eloquent and mournful words about his misfortunes or his follies, the conviction dawns on those who observe him carefully that here we deal with a readiness of expression rather than a strength of feeling.

Vexation, spite, quick and labile flashes of quasi-affection, peevish resentment, shallow moods of self-pity, puerile attitudes of vanity, and absurd and showy poses of indignation are all within his emotional scale and are freely sounded as the circumstances of life play upon him. But mature, wholehearted anger, true or consistent indignation, honest, solid grief, sustaining pride, deep joy, and genuine despair are reactions not likely to be found within this scale.

Even in the situations of squalor and misery into which he repeatedly works himself, when confined in jails and what he regards as lunatic asylums, after throwing away fortunes or catching and transferring gonorrhea to his bride — even under these circumstances he does not show anything that could be called woe or despair or serious sorrow. He becomes vexed and rebellious and frets in lively and constant impatience when confined, but he does not grieve as others grieve.

Psychopaths are often witty and sometimes give a superficial impression of that far different and very serious thing, humor. Humor, however, in what may be its full, true sense, they never have. I have thought that I caught glimpses of it in psychopaths and, despite a typical history, was inclined to question the diagnosis. Further observation of these patients gave convincing evidence that the apparent humor, like the apparent insight, was really an artifact.

The emotional poverty, the complete lack of strong or tragic feeling universally found in all the psychopaths personally observed, has caused me considerable bewilderment in connection with frequent references in the literature to the powerful instinctual drives and passions said to be manifested in such people. Although weak and even infantile drives displaying themselves theatrically in the absence of ordinary inhibitions may impress the layman as mighty forces, it is hardly to be concluded that wise and deeply experienced psychiatrists would be similarly deceived.

Usually, instead of facing facts that would ordinarily lead to insight, he projects, blaming his troubles on others with the flimsiest of pretext but with elaborate and subtle rationalization. Occasionally, however, he will perfunctorily admit himself to blame for everything and analyze his case from what seems to be almost a psychiatric viewpoint, but we can see that his conclusions have little actual significance for him. Some of these patients mentioned spoke fluently of the psychopathic personality, quoted the literature, and suggested this diagnosis for themselves. Soon this apparent insight was seen to be not merely imperfect but a consistent and thorough artifact. Perhaps it was less a voluntary deception than a simulation in which the simulator himself fails to realize his lack of emotional grasp or that he is simulating or what he is simulating. The patient seems to have little or no ability to feel the significance of his situation, to experience the real emotions of regret or shame or determination to improve, or to realize that this is lacking. His clever statements have been hardly more than verbal reflexes; even his facial expressions are without the underlying content they imply. This is not insight but an excellent mimicry of insight. No sincere intention can spring from his conclusions because no affective conviction is there to move him.

Such a deficiency of insight is harder to comprehend than the schizophrenic's deficiency, for it exists in the full presence of what are often assumed to be the qualities by which insight is gained. Yet the psychopath shows not only a deficiency but apparently a total absence of self-appraisal as a real and moving experience. Here is the spectacle of a person who uses all the words that would be used by someone who understands, and who could define all the words but who still is blind to the meaning. Such a clinical picture is more baffling to me than any of the symptoms of schizophrenia, on which attempts have been made to throw some light by psychopathologic theories. Here we have a patient who fulfills all the ordinary theoretical criteria of a "sound mind," and yet with this apparently sound mind is more incomprehensible than the psychotic patient.

The psychopath cannot be depended upon to show the ordinary responsiveness to special consideration or kindness or trust. No matter how well he is treated, no matter how long-suffering his family, his friends, the police, hospital attendants, and others may be, he shows no consistent reaction of appreciation except superficial and transparent protestations. Such gestures are exhibited most frequently when he feels they will facilitate some personal aim. The ordinary axiom of human existence that one good turn deserves another, a principle sometimes honored by cannibals and uncommonly callous assassins, has only superficial validity for him although he can cite it with eloquent casuistry when trying to obtain parole, discharge from the hospital, or some other end.

As in attempting to delineate other aspects of the psychopath, we find ourselves again confronting paradox. Although he can be counted on not to be appreciably swayed in major issues by these basic rules, we often find him attentive in small courtesies and favors, perhaps even habitually generous or quasi-generous when the cost is not decisive. Occasionally his actions may suggest profound generosity in that large sums are involved or something presumably of real value is sacrificed. Usually, however, these appearances are deceiving.

In relatively small matters psychopaths sometimes behave so as to appear very considerate, responsive, and obliging. Acquaintances who meet them on grounds where minor issues prevail may find it difficult to believe that they are not highly endowed with gratitude and eager to serve others. Such reactions and intentions, although sometimes ready or even spectacularly facile, do not ever accumulate sufficient force to play a determining part in really important issues. The psychopath who causes his parents hardship and humiliation by repeatedly forging checks and causes his wife anguish by sordid (and perhaps halfhearted) relations with the housemaid, may gain a considerable reputation in the community by occasionally volunteering to cut the grass for the frail old lady across the street, by bringing a bottle of sherry over now and then to bedridden Mr. Blank, or by leaving his work to take a neighbor's injured cat to the veterinarian.

Outward social graces come easy to most psychopaths, and many continue, throughout careers disastrous to themselves and for others, to conduct themselves in superficial relations, in handling the trivia of existence, so as to gain admiration and gratitude. In these surface aspects of functioning, the typical psychopath (unlike the classic hypocrite) often seems to act with undesigning spontaneity and to be prompted by motives of excellent quality though of marvelously attenuated substance.

Although some psychopaths do not drink at all and others drink rarely, considerable overindulgence in alcohol is very often prominent in the life story. Delirium tremens and other temporary psychoses directly due to alcohol were not commonly found in the hundreds of patients observed by me.

... A peculiar sort of vulgarity, domineering rudeness, petty bickering or buffoonish quasi-maulings of wife, mistress, or children, and quick shifts between maudlin and vainglorious moods, although sometimes found in ordinary alcoholics with other serious patterns of disorder, are pathognomonic of the psychopath and in him alone reach full and precocious flower. Even in the first stages of a spree, perhaps after taking only two or three highballs, he may show signs of petty truculence or sullenness but seldom of real gaiety or conviviality. Evidence of any pleasurable reaction is characteristically minimal, as are indications that he is seeking relief from anxiety, despair, worry, responsibility, or tension.

... Although his most theatrical exploits in public are usually carried on when drinking, the psychopath, even after he has been free from all alcohol for months, as for instance, when he is in a psychiatric hospital, retains all the essential personality features which have been mentioned. These show little or no tendency to diminish when he cannot drink. These words translated from Aeschylus, "Bronze is the mirror of the form; wine of the heart," express something pertinent about alcohol and man, whether the man be ill or well.

... Most of this asocial, unacceptable, and self-defeating behavior associated with the psychopath's drinking seems to occur without the benefit of extreme inebriation. If actual confusion from alcohol prevailed or states of genuine amnesia were induced before the grotesque shenanigans began, intoxication could more plausibly be suspected of playing a larger causal role. The psychopath often reacts in this typical way while in perfect orientation, with unclouded awareness and in anything but the deeply drugged state thought by some to be a prerequisite.

Despite the deep behavioral pattern of throwing away or destroying the opportunities of life that underlies the psychopath's superficial self-content, ease, charm, and often brilliance, we do not find him prone to take a final determining step of this sort in literal suicide. Suicidal tendencies have been stressed by some observers as prevalent. This opinion, in all likelihood, must have come from the observation of patients fundamentally different from our group, but who, as we have mentioned, were traditionally classified under the same term. It was only after a good many years of experience with actual psychopaths that I encountered my first authentic instance of suicide in a patient who could be called typical.

Instead of a predilection for ending their own lives, psychopaths, on the contrary, show much more evidence of a specific and characteristic immunity from such an act. This immunity, it must be granted, is, like most other immunities, relative.

Although suicide, then, cannot be named an impossibility among this group, its unlikelihood still merits strong emphasis. Since most psychopaths do not remain hospitalized or under other protective supervision, the rarity of this act becomes more significant. Also worth noting is the fact that most real psychopaths, not once or a few times but habitually, work themselves into situations that might strongly prompt the normal man to end his own life. Since suicidal threats, like promises and well-formulated plans to adopt a new course, are so frequently offered by these patients, there is good reason to keep in mind the fact that they are nearly always empty. Many bogus attempts are made, sometimes with remarkable cleverness, premeditation, and histrionics.

Unmistakable psychopaths who do not show evidence of strong or consistent deviated impulses but who nevertheless occasionally carry out abnormal sexual acts have been seen much more often than those in whom the two fundamental patterns seem to overlap. This is not surprising in view of the psychopath's notable tendencies to hit upon unsatisfactory conduct in all fields and his apparent inability to take seriously what would to others be repugnant and regrettable.

As might be expected, in view of their incapacity for object love, the sexual aims of psychopaths do not seem to include any important personality relations or any recognizable desire or ability to explore or possess or significantly ravish the partner in a shared experience. Their positive activities are consistently and parsimoniously limited to literal physical contact and relatively free of the enormous emotional concomitants and the complex potentialities that make adult love relations an experience so thrilling and indescribable. Consequently, they seem to regard sexual activity very casually, sometimes apparently finding it less shocking and enthralling than a sensitive normal man would find even the glance of his beloved.

... None of the psychopaths personally observed have impressed me as having particularly strong sex cravings even in this uncomplicated and poverty-stricken sense. Indeed, they have nearly all seemed definitely less moved to obtain genital pleasure than the ordinary run of people. The impression one gets is that their amativeness is little more than a simple itch and that even the itch is seldom, if ever, particularly intense.

The male psychopath, despite his usual ability to complete the physical act successfully with a woman, never seems to find anything meaningful or personal in his relations or to enjoy significant pleasure beyond the localized and temporary sensations. The female, whether or not she has physiologic orgasm, behaves in such a way as to indicate similar evaluations of the experience. Even these sensations seem to wither precociously and leave the subject a somewhat desiccated response to local stimuli. Sensations so isolated are, no doubt, peculiarly vulnerable to routine and to its justly celebrated antidotes for excitement.

... What is felt for prostitute, sweetheart, casual pickup, mistress, or wife is not anything that can bring out loyalty or influence activities into a remedial or constructive plan, Not do sexual desires always seem to compete successfully against such trivial impulses as wanting to hang about street corners or idle in juke joints where the psychopath may, by tampering with slot machines or cheating at dice or cards, pick up a little change and demonstrate his cleverness to the other fellows. So little is apparently found in heterosexual experience that deviate impulses (even when weak) are sometimes accepted and acted upon largely because of reasons like the reason why all cats look gray at night.

... For the person who has ever known even one mature and normal erotic fulfillment, it is impossible to imagine turning by choice to a biologically inappropriate partner or placing partial or deviated aims above what has been so obviously well designed for the purpose. What the human organism shows anatomically is scarcely more clear than the emotional evidence, at physiologic as well as at broader interpersonal levels of reactivity. Even from more remote and less tangible sociologic aspects, nature has left no room here for doubt. It is difficult, without postulating an extremely dulled or otherwise inhibited sensual response in heterosexual experience, to account for the psychopath who can drift into deviate pranks as approximations or acceptable novelties in the same field. It has been said that "the thalamus outdid itself in devising pleasures to go with the conjugating act itself." Without great support from ethics or convention, it seems these would suffice for normal choice in the intact personality.

... The familiar record of sexual promiscuity found in both male and female psychopaths seems much more closely related to their almost total lack of self-imposed restraint than to any particularly strong passions or drives. Psychopaths sometimes seem by preference to seek sexual relations in sordid surroundings with persons of low intellectual or social status. Often, however, the convenience by which what is little more than a whim can be gratified may play a greater part in this than specific preference. Another and more serious kind of sordidness also seems to constitute real inducement.

... Entanglements which go out of their way to mock ordinary human sensibility or what might be called basic decency are prevalent in their sexual careers. To casually "make" or "lay" the best friend's wife and to involve a husband's uncle or one of his business associates in a particularly messy triangular or quadrilateral situation are typical acts. Such opportunities, when available, seem not to repel but specifically to attract the psychopath. Neither distinct appeal of the sex object nor any formulated serious malignity toward those cuckolded or otherwise outraged seems to be a major factor in such choices. There is more to suggest a mildly prankish impulse such as might lead the ordinary man to violate small pedantic technicalities or dead and preposterous bits of formality as a demonstration of their triviality.

... Sexual exploits often seem chosen almost purposively to put the subject himself, as well as others, in positions of sharp indignity and distastefulness. The male psychopath who goes through legal matrimony with the whore he has picked up for the evening furnishes a clear example. And so does the well-born woman who submits to several men in rapid succession, none of whom takes the least trouble to conceal his contempt for her. I have seen psychopaths who seriously attempted to seduce sisters, mothers-in-law, and even their actual mothers. One boasted to his wife in glowing detail of his erotic feats with her mother and with his own. His excellent talents at lying lead me to doubt the truth of his claims. I have little doubt, however, that he would have hesitated to carry out all that he boasted of if the ladies had allowed him to proceed.

... Beneath his outwardly gracious manner toward women and his general suavity and social charms, the male psychopath (or part psychopath) nearly always shows an underlying predilection for obscenity, an astonishingly ambivalent attitude in which the amorous and excretory functions seem to be confused. He sometimes gives the impression that an impulse to smear his partner symbolically, and even to wallow in sordidness himself, is more fundamental than a directly erotic aim, itself hardly more to him than a sort of concomitant and slightly glorified back scratching.

The psychopath shows a striking inability to follow any sort of life plan consistently, whether it be one regarded as good or evil. He does not maintain an effort toward any far goal at all. This is entirely applicable to the full psychopath. On the contrary, he seems to go out of his way to make a failure of life.

... By some incomprehensible and untempting piece of folly or buffoonery, he eventually cuts short any activity in which he is succeeding, no matter whether it is crime or honest endeavor.

...At the behest of trivial impulses he repeatedly addresses himself directly to folly. In the more seriously affected examples, it is impossible for wealthy, influential, and devoted relatives to place the psychopath in any position, however ingeniously it may be chosen, where he will not succeed eventually in failing with spectacular and bizarre splendor.

... Considering a longitudinal section of his life, his behavior gives such an impression of gratuitous folly and nonsensical activity in such massive accumulation that it is hard to avoid the conclusion that here is the product of true madness — of madness in a sense quite as real as that conveyed to the imaginative layman by the terrible word lunatic.

...With the further consideration that all this skein of apparent madness has been woven by a person of (technically) unimpaired and superior intellectual powers and universally regarded as sane, the surmise intrudes that we are confronted by a serious and unusual type of genuine abnormality.

...Not merely a surmise but a strong conviction may arise that this apparent sanity is, in some important respects, a sanity in name only. When we consider his actual performance, evidence of mental competency is sorely lacking. We find instead a spectacle that suggests madness in excelsis, despite the absence of all those symptoms that enable us, in some degree, to account for irrational conduct in the psychotic

3

Selections from *The search for the roots of psychopathy.* by John Seabrook, The New Yorker, November 10, 2008

At thirty-eight, [Dr. Kent] Kiehl, is one of the world's leading younger investigators in psychopathy, the condition of moral emptiness that affects between fifteen to twenty-five per cent of the

North American prison population, and is believed by some psychologists to exist in one per cent of the general adult male population. (Female psychopaths are thought to be much rarer.) Psychopaths don't exhibit the manias, hysterias, and neuroses that are present in other types of mental illness. Their main defect, what psychologists call "severe emotional detachment"—a total lack of empathy and remorse—is concealed, and harder to describe than the symptoms of schizophrenia or bipolar disorder. This absence of easily readable signs has led to debate among mental-health practitioners about what qualifies as psychopathy and how to diagnose it. Psychopathy isn't identified as a disorder in the *Diagnostic and Statistical Manual of Mental Disorders*, the American Psychiatric Association's canon; instead, a more general term, "antisocial personality disorder," known as A.P.D., covers the condition.

There is also little consensus among researchers about what causes psychopathy. Considerable evidence, including several large-scale studies of twins, points toward a genetic component. Yet psychopaths are more likely to come from neglectful families than from loving, nurturing ones. Psychopathy could be dimensional, like high blood pressure, or it might be categorical, like leukemia. Researchers argue over whether tests used to measure it should focus on behavior or attempt to incorporate personality traits—like deceitfulness, glibness, and lack of remorse—as well. The only point on which everyone agrees is that psychopathy is extremely difficult to treat. And for some researchers the word "psychopath" has been tainted by its long and seamy relationship with criminality and popular culture, which began with true-crime pulps and continues today in TV shows like CBS's "Criminal Minds" and in the work of authors like Thomas Harris and Patricia Cornwell. The word is so loaded with baleful connotations that it tends to empurple any surrounding prose.

Kiehl is frustrated by the lack of respect shown to psychopathy by the mental-health establishment. "Think about it," he told me. "Crime is a trillion-dollar-a-year problem. The average psychopath will be convicted of four violent crimes by the age of forty. And yet hardly anyone is funding research into the science. Schizophrenia, which causes much less crime, has a hundred times more research money devoted to it." I asked why, and Kiehl said, "Because schizophrenics are seen as victims, and psychopaths are seen as predators. The former we feel empathy for, the latter we lock up."

In January of 2007, Kiehl arranged to have a portable functional magnetic-resonance-imaging scanner brought into Western—the first fMRI ever installed in a prison. So far, he has recruited hundreds of volunteers from among the inmates. The data from these scans, Kiehl hopes, will confirm his theory, published in *Psychiatry Research*, in 2006, that psychopathy is caused by a defect in what he calls "the paralimbic system," a network of brain regions, stretching from the orbital frontal cortex to the posterior cingulate cortex, that are involved in processing emotion, inhibition, and attentional control. His dream is to confound the received wisdom by helping to discover a treatment for psychopathy. "If you could target the brain region involved, then maybe you could find a drug that treats that region," he told me. "If you could treat just five per cent of them, that would be a Nobel Prize right there."

...

In order to distinguish psychopaths from non-psychopaths among the Western volunteers, Kiehl and his students use the revised version of the Psychopathy Checklist, or PCL-R, a twenty-item diagnostic instrument created by Robert Hare [see section 1, this chapter], a Can- adian psychologist, based on his long experience in working with psychopaths in prisons. Kiehl was taught to use the checklist by Hare himself, under whom he earned his doctorate, at the University of British Columbia.

...

Psychopaths are as old as Cain, and they are believed to exist in all cultures, although they are more prevalent in individualistic societies in the West. The Yupik Eskimos use the term *kunlangeta* to describe a man who repeatedly lies, cheats, steals, and takes sexual advantage of women, according to a 1976 study by Jane M. Murphy, an anthropologist then at Harvard University. She asked an

Eskimo what the group would typically do with a *kunlangeta*, and he replied, "Somebody would have pushed him off the ice when nobody else was looking."

The condition was first described clinically in 1801, by the French surgeon Philippe Pinel. He called it "mania without delirium." In the early nineteenth century, the American surgeon Benjamin Rush wrote about a type of "moral derangement" in which the sufferer was neither delusional nor psychotic but nevertheless engaged in profoundly antisocial behavior, including horrifying acts of violence. Rush noted that the condition appeared early in life. The term "moral insanity" became popular in the mid-nineteenth century, and was widely used in the U.S. and in England to describe incorrigible criminals. The word "psychopath" (literally, "suffering soul") was coined in Germany in the eighteen-eighties. By the nineteen-twenties, "constitutional psychopathic inferiority" had become the catchall phrase psychiatrists used for a general mixture of violent and antisocial characteristics found in irredeemable criminals, who appeared to lack a conscience.

In the late nineteen-thirties, an American psychiatrist named Hervey Cleckley began collecting data on a certain kind of patient he encountered in the course of his work in a psychiatric hospital in Augusta, Georgia. These people were from varied social and family backgrounds. Some were poor, but others were sons of Augusta's most prosperous and respected families. Cleckley set about sharpening the vague construct of constitutional psychopathic inferiority, and distinguishing it from other forms of mental illness. He eventually isolated sixteen traits exhibited by patients he called "primary" psychopaths; these included being charming and intelligent, unreliable, dishonest, irresponsible, self-centered, emotionally shallow, and lacking in empathy and insight.

"Beauty and ugliness, except in a very superficial sense, goodness, evil, love, horror, and humor have no actual meaning, no power to move him," Cleckley wrote of the psychopath in his 1941 book, "The Mask of Sanity," which became the foundation of the modern science. The psychopath talks "entertainingly," Cleckley explained, and is "brilliant and charming," but nonetheless "carries disaster lightly in each hand." Cleckley emphasized his subjects' deceptive, predatory nature, writing that the psychopath is capable of "concealing behind a perfect mimicry of normal emotion, fine intelligence, and social responsibility a grossly disabled and irresponsible personality." This mimicry allows psychopaths to function, and even thrive, in normal society. Indeed, as Cleckley also argued, the individualistic, winner-take-all aspect of American culture nurtures psychopathy.

The psychiatric profession wanted little to do with psychopathy, for several reasons. For one thing, it was thought to be incurable. Not only did the talking cure fail with psychopaths but several studies suggested that talk therapy made the condition worse, by enabling psychopaths to practice the art of manipulation. There were no valid instruments to measure the personality traits that were commonly associated with the condition; researchers could study only the psychopaths' behavior, in most cases through their criminal records. Finally, the emphasis in the word "psychopath" on an internal sickness was at odds with liberal mid-century social thought, which tended to look for external causes of social deviancy; "sociopath," coined in 1930 by the psychologist G. E. Partridge, became the preferred term. In 1958, the American psychiiatric Association used the term "sociopathic personality" to describe the disorder in its *Diagnostic and Statistical Manual of Mental Disorders*. In the 1968 edition, the condition was renamed "general antisocial personality disorder."

Cleckley's book fell out of favor, and Cleckley described himself late in life as "a voice crying in the wilderness." When he died, in 1984, he was remembered mostly for his popular study of multiple-personality disorder, written with Corbett Thigpen, "The Three Faces of Eve."

In 1960, Robert Hare took a job as the resident psychologist in a maximum-security prison about twenty miles outside Vancouver. ...After receiving his doctorate, in 1963, and returning to Vancouver, he set about what would be his life's work: the study of psychopathy, and the creation of the Psychopathy Checklist, the twenty-item diagnostic instrument that Kiehl is using at Western.

Thanks to the checklist, scientists working in different places can be confident that the subjects they are studying are taxonomically similar. The PCL also has a wide variety of forensic applications. It is employed throughout Canada in parole-board hearings and is gaining popularity in the U.S. In the thirty-seven states that allow the death penalty, a high psychopathy score is often used by prosecutors as an "aggravating factor" in the penalty phase of capital cases. Psychopathy scores have also been used in child-custody cases; a high score may result in one parent's loss of custody. Hare's influence on the field of psychopathy is profound. Today, Hare's former students hold important administrative positions throughout the Canadian prison system, and are prominently represented in the next two generations of psychopathy researchers around the world.

...

Hare's Psychopathy Checklist now exists in three variations. (There's one for juveniles, the PCL-YV, and one designed for the general population—the "screening" version.) He collects a royalty fee every time the official PCL scoring sheet is used. The complete psychopathy kit, which includes a book-length manual on how to administer the checklist, costs two hundred and sixty-three dollars. It has been translated into more than twenty languages. The Albany seminar was one of roughly half a dozen that Hare conducts each year. He was giving a talk on psychopathy and culpability in Las Vegas the following week; then he was off to Rome, to instruct the carabinieri in the use of the checklist, and in profiling psychopaths. In Albany, his audience was composed mostly of psychologists and other mental-health professionals.

Hare sees himself as continuing the work that Cleckley started \ warning society of a devastating and costly mental disorder that it mostly continues to ignore. Hare's forensic experience has taught him that psychopathy is of vital concern to mental-health workers in prisons as well as to people in law enforcement and on parole boards; people who come into daily contact with dangerous and destructive individuals need an instrument that will allow them to identify psychopaths and make risk assessments based on their

145

predictive behavior.

...

"Am I happy about the way the checklist can be used?" Hare asked rhetorically. "No, not always. Am I happy it is used to help condemn people to death? No, I am not." Nor does he approve of its use in child-custody cases. However, he believes that, when properly used as a predictor of risk in forensic settings, the social benefits of the checklist far outweigh its drawbacks. Hare rejects the notion that a distinction ought to be made between a violent psychopath, like Ted Bundy, and a nonviolent one who commits financial crimes. Both, he said, are willing to do whatever it takes. He went on, "Can you say Ted Bundy caused more disaster than the guys at Enron? How many destroyed lives and suicides followed as a result of so many people losing their savings?"

...

In a landmark 1991 E.R.P. study conducted at a prison in Vancouver, Robert Hare and two graduate students showed that psychopaths process words like "hate" and "love" differently from the way normal people do. In another study, at the Bronx V.A. Medical Center, Hare, Joanne Intrator, and others found that psychopaths processed emotional words in a different part of the brain. Instead of showing activity in the limbic region, in the midbrain, which is the emotional-processing center, psychopaths showed activity only in the front of the brain, in the language center. Hare explained to me, "It was as if they could only understand emotions linguistically. They knew the words but not the music, as it were."

Since then, cognitive neuroscience has come to be dominated by brain scans, although they are not as widely used in psychopathy research. So far, fMRI studies of psychopaths have only reinforced different models of psychopathy that were in place before fMRI became popular, theories that Kiehl studied while pursuing a doctorate in Hare's lab at the University of British Columbia. Some scientists think that psychopaths suffer from an extreme and far-reaching attention deficit, which causes them temporarily to forget the moral and social consequences of certain antisocial actions.

Joseph Newman, who chairs the psychology department at the University of Wisconsin at Madison, is the leading advocate of this theory. His model is based on traditional research methods, such as lab work using rats with brain lesions, and studies of humans using a well-known card-playing task, in which players gradually start to lose money; the players in the control group stopped as their earnings diminished, but the psychopaths could focus only on the outcome of the next card choice. Another hypothesis is that psychopaths lack fear of personal injury and, more important, moral fear – fear of punishment. David Lykken pioneered this theory in the nineteen-fifties, and it has been taken up by James Blair, Christopher Patrick, and others. The updated version of this model posits that psychopathy is a result of a dysfunction of the amygdala, the almond-shaped bundle of gray matter situated in the midbrain, which is another area instrumental in emotional processing.

...

Hare wants to disassociate psychopathy from the *DSM's* catchall diagnosis of antisocial personality disorder. "It's like having pneumonia versus having a cold," he said. "They share some common symptoms, but one is much more virulent." Before the fourth edition of the *DSM* came out, in 1994, Hare published several articles pointing to field research that showed a difference between psychopathy and A.P.D. John Gunderson, the psychiatrist who chaired the personality-disorders work group for the revision, told Hare that, intellectually, he had "won the battle," Hare recalls; even so, in *DSM-IV* "psychopathy" appears only as a synonym for A.P.D. (Gunderson says this was a function of institutional inertia.) Hare has continued to follow preparations for the next edition, due out in 2012, and recently sent an e-mail to a senior member of the task force inquiring about what revisions, if any, were planned for A.P.D. The reply, Hare said, was noncommittal.

Hare has published two books that translate some of the concepts of psychopathy for a general audience and attempt to teach people how to identify the "successful psychopaths" in their midst. In the introduction to "Without Conscience," he writes, "It is very likely that at some point in your life you will come into painful contact with a psychopath. For your own physical, psychological, and financial well-being it is crucial that you know how to identify the psychopath." Among the professions likely to attract psychopaths, he writes, are law enforcement, the military, politics, and medicine, although he notes that these have norms and are self-policing. The most agreeable vocation for psychopaths, according to Hare, is business. In his second book, "Snakes in Suits: When Psychopaths Go to Work," written with Paul Babiack, Hare flirts with pop psychology when he points out that many traits that may be desirable in a corporate context, such as ruthlessness, lack of social conscience, and single-minded devotion to success, would be considered psychopathic outside of it.

...

"It is very likely that at some point in your life you will come into painful contact with a psychopath. For your own physical, psycho-psychological, and financial well-being it is crucial that you know how to identify the psychopath." Among the professions likely to attract psychopaths, he writes, are law enforcement, the military, politics, and medicine, although he notes that these have norms and are self-policing. The most agreeable vocation for psychopaths, according to Hare, is business. In his second book, "Snakes in Suits: When psycho- Psychopaths Go to Work," written with Paul Babiack, Hare flirts with pop psychology when he points out that many traits that may be desirable in a corporate context, such as ruthlessness, lack of social conscience, and single-minded devotion to success, would be considered psychopathic outside of it.

...

Hare rejects the notion that a distinction ought to be made between a violent psychopath, like Ted Bundy, and a nonviolent one who commits financial crimes. Both, he said, are willing to do whatever it takes. He went on, "Can you say Ted Bundy caused more disaster than the guys at Enron? How many destroyed lives and suicides followed as a result of so many people losing their savings?"

...

Although psychologists don't call minors "psychopaths" – they are "youths with psychopathic traits" – there is considerable evidence that the condition manifests itself at ages earlier than eighteen; in a much cited 2005 paper, "Evidence for Substantial Genetic Risk for Psychopathy in Seven-Year-Olds," published in the *Journal of Child Psychology and Psychiatry*, Essi Viding suggests that the condition can be detected in early childhood. Fledgling psychopaths are particularly interesting to researchers, because their brains are thought to be more malleable than those of adults. In a landmark 2006 study of a specialized talk-therapy treatment program, conducted at a juvenile detention center in Wisconsin, involving a hundred and forty-one young offenders who scored high on the youth version of the checklist, Michael Caldwell, a psychologist at the treatment center and a lecturer at the University of Wisconsin at Madison, reported that the youths that were treated were much more likely to stay out of trouble, once they were paroled, than the ones in the control group. "In other words," Kiehl told me, "psychopathy is treatable after all, if you can catch it young enough." Of course, as he pointed out in an e-mail, even with very violent young offenders we have to accept that "the only way to know if the treatment worked or not is to return the youths to the community once they have finished their sentence. . . . Perhaps you put them in a specialized community/monitoring program once they are released again."

...

While Kiehl and his colleagues are looking for a biological marker for psychopathy, molecular biologists have been analyzing DNA, in an attempt to identify a genetic marker. In a recently published study in the *British Journal of Psychiatry*, Guillermo Ponce and Janet Hoenicka report that two genes that have already been associated with severe alcoholism may also be linked to psychopathy. Efforts are also ongoing in other areas of neurobiological inquiry, including behavioral, neurochemical, pharmacological, and psychophysiological research.

If a biological basis for psychopathy could be established and pharmacological treatments developed, the idea that many people have at least a little of the psychopath in them could well become accepted. As Kiehl points out, "It used to be the case that it was very hard to meet clinical criteria for depression in the fifties and sixties. However, the definition of depression has been broadened so much with *DSM-IV* that nearly every person will meet the criteria at some point in their lives. One reason for this is that drug companies have lobbied to change the criteria – because they have a treatment, a drug, that can help people even with moderate levels of depression. It's a completely different issue whether this is appropriate." He added that "even moderate levels of psychopathy may someday be considered a disorder – especially if we can treat it."

Like many in the field of psychopathy research, Kiehl is aware of the enormous social implications of accepting psychopathy as a form of mental illness. What, for example, would you do with the young psychopaths who don't respond to treatment? The stigma would be profound. It's not hard to imagine a day when everyone's personal psychopathy risk will be assigned early in life—a kind of criminal-potential index. Kiehl was recently appointed as a scientific member of the MacArthur Foundation's Law and Neuroscience Project, which will study some of the legal implications of neuro-imaging.

...

Over the next ten years, Kiehl hopes to amass a database of ten thousand psychopaths – men, women, and juveniles, from a broad array of ethnic groups – complete with brain scans, DNA, and case histories. This database would serve psychopathy researchers in something of the same way that Dr. Johnson's dictionary served linguists – as a founding reference. Whether the data will guarantee the acceptance of psychopathy as a mental disorder is another matter. Hare said, "You're still going to have to collect a massive amount of biographical data from the subjects and link it all to the brain scans in order for them to make sense." And even then we probably won't know what makes people act without conscience.

CHAPTER 8
NATURE AND/OR NURTURE

To be sure, the most compelling issue surrounding pathics is whether their behavior results only, or mainly, or equally, or proportionately, from birth or environment or both. This is the perennial nature/nurture controversy, which I believe is coming to a close in our times. The following selections from nonprofessionals give their views, mainly from personal experience.

The following professional article precedes the nonprofessional perspectives on this controversial topic of nature-or-nurture-or-both. I include it here to set the stage, so to speak, so that the reader will better appreciate the layman's views following the article.

From: *The Journal of Child Psychology and Psychiatrist:* by Dr Essi Viding, from the Medical Research Council's Social, Genetic and Developmental Psychiatry Centre at the Institute of Psychiatry, King's College, London

PSYCHOPATHS are born anti-social, not corrupted by bad parenting, scientists reveal today.

A study of twins showed that anti-social behaviour was strongly inherited in children with psychopathic tendencies. In children without psychopathic traits, being anti-social was chiefly the result of environmental factors.

The findings support previous research indicating that children with psychopathic tendencies often remain an anti-social problem. Psycho- paths are generally recognized by a lack of empathy and weak con- science. If a psychopath does something that hurts another person, he or she is less likely to feel remorse than other people.

These tendencies are a recognized warning sign of anti-social behaviour in young children.

To help identify the genetic components of anti-social behaviour, a team of British psychiatrists studied 3,687 pairs of seven-year-old twins.

Twins are often used by researchers investigating inherited traits. Identical twins share the same genes, and, therefore, the same inherited influences, whereas non-identical twins do not. By comparing the two groups, it is possible to see if a trait is or is not carried in the genes.

In the new study, teacher ratings for anti-social behaviour and psychopathic tendencies were obtained for the children. Those in the top 10 per cent of the sample for anti-social behaviour were separated into two groups, with and without psychopathic ten- dencies. Analysis showed that anti-social behaviour was only strongly inherited in the psychopathic children.

An Introduction: Two Male Viewpoints

1. "Are these children just born bad? Environment alone cannot ex- plain deranged behavior – too many abused and neglected children grow up to be law-abiding citizens. If there is a genetic explanation, it's a slippery, discreet mutation. We don't see entire families of serial killers. There is no such thing as a 'kill gene', but research is revealing some genetic tendencies to violent behavior. In other words, bad seeds blossom in bad environments.

"The position I favor is that psychopathy emerges from a complex

– and poorly understood – interplay between biological factors and social forces. It is based on evidence that genetic factors contribute to the biological bases of brain function and to basic personality structure, which in turn influence the way the individual responds to, and interacts with, life experiences and the social environment. In effect, the elements needed for the development of psychopathy – including a profound inability to experience empathy and the complete range of emotions, including fear – are provided in part by nature and possibly by some unknown biological influences on the developing fetus and neonate. As a result, the capacity for developing internal controls and conscience and for making emotional 'connections' with others is greatly reduced.

"This doesn't mean that psychopaths are destined to develop along a fixed track, born to play a socially deviant role in life. But it does mean that their biological endowment – the raw material that environmental, social, and learning experiences fashion into a unique individual – provides a poor basis for socialization and conscience formation. To use a simple analogy, the potter is instrumental in molding pottery from clay (nurture), but the characteristics of the pottery also depend on the sort of clay available (nature).

"Although psychopathy is not primarily the result of poor parenting or adverse childhood experiences, I think they play an important role in shaping what nature has provided."

2. Psychology is just an awful mess of a science, in my view. Obviously, research into brain chemistry and composition is useful, but that might be called neurology or some other science. Things like the DSM-V and probably Hare's 40-point scale for psychopathy have pretty big problems, in that they don't seem to have much predictive value. Hare goes on to say he thinks being a psychopath is genetic, but to me it seems like it wouldn't be very difficult to drive what people call "humanity" out of a person via their environment. Solders in war kill people easily, and if these (most likely) normal people can be conditioned to do it, why couldn't a "normal" person lose their "humanity" as well? Especially if they're abused and conditioned in that way as children?

What evidence does Hare have that the different brain structure isn't caused by some environmental thing, rather than genetics?

An Introduction: A Woman's Viewpoint

"Most parents will tell you that their children exhibit general behaviors very early in their development. Some may be stubborn, others happy, and still others may be grumpy. We see these general emotional responses in infants and can often see a trend by the time the child is only a few months old. Many of these parents will also assert that these responses, or temperaments, seem to continue throughout the child's development.

"The stubborn infant who cries when put down for a nap may become the stubborn adolescent who rebels against authority or resists society's norms. The happy and content infant may be the adult who finds friends easily and has a knack for seeing the good in others. When these temperaments are present shortly after birth and continue throughout a person's life, it is difficult to not see a biological connection."

TOPIC TITLE: What Are Your Views that Psychopathy Can Be Inherited?

1. "One article I read pointed out that a certain gene combined with a bad environment can bring out this behaviour. If so, how come other siblings with the same genetic makeup or biology and environment do not have the p's [psychopath's] traits? The other question is this then, why is it that some of these Ps come from really good homes?"

2. "As far as I've been able to tell, it's not inherited. It just strikes at random. I've been in a discussion and it seemed that people with Ns or Ps in their family have ancestors who may have had schizophrenia, although, it's not scientific and it's not at   all the

same thing. I don't know why, but it just seemed to be present in a lot of the extended families of Ps. They've done MRIs on Ps and the prefrontal cortex of their brain has little color or activity. In many cases, it seems like they were born that way. That's an interesting point that both the Dad and Grandpa to this girl have had P-ism.

3. "The suggestion that there are 'different routes to psychopathy' really resonates with me. That's why I've never particularly cared for the "nature vs. nurture" title – it seems to imply the two are mutually exclusive and I believe there's too much evidence showing that environ- mental factors do play a significant part to discount or dismiss them."

4. "I've always believed that childhood abuse/rejection is a strong driver towards psychopathy (for some); and the fact that most serial killers seem to have abusive parents (usually the mother) seemed to support that point of view. I've also observed it anecdotally, actually, it's glaring.

"However, I had a bit of a light bulb moment yesterday though when I realized that this very fact (the abusive parent creating a psycho- path theory) may also support the nature argument. Surely, it can be said that the coldness and lack of empathy traits that an abusive parent must have are ones that are passed down to the offspring genetically. I bet it's not some huge discovery in the field of research (it seems too obvious), just one I didn't really think about before probably because I was focused on the abuse.

"Then when you consider that many serial killers are found to have frontal lobe damage, the absence of which would normally cause them to mediate their behaviour, it's as if there's a perfect storm of conditions from which a psychopath is spawned.

"There are so many serial killers that seem to have brutally abusive or rejecting parents (Bundy, Gacy, Henry Lee Lucas, Danny Rollings) that I'm almost more curious to read about one that came from a stable family background."

5. "As you know, I am a nature advocate, the way I see it and this is only my 2 cents: abused psychopaths are the ones that end up in the prison population and those raised in a more "normal" environment probably end up in high positions and are clever enough to not be in the prison system."

6. "Something I've been keeping an eye out for ... there doesn't seem to be any clear cut evidence for a genetic basis for psychopathy ... at least not any that I've seen. My thinking is that it's usually a mix of nature and nurture...a genetic propensity, which is 'developed' by environmental influences, mostly something going horribly wrong with the mother-child bond at a very early age...That's just guesswork though... there might be several routes to psychopathy, some of which may have no genetic component, some which might be purely genetic."

7. "Unlike some other syndromes, such as Downs Syndrome, where the genetic cause is clear-cut, nothing seems very clear about the causes of psychopathy."

8. "I really think there is a huge amount of developmental growth that happens that last month before birth and shortly after birth that is profoundly affected by stress and affection. I think a child that doesn't get even the bare necessities for connection in the early weeks turns its back on the word and never ever develops the capacity to connect. This child is a psychopath. I don't think psychopathology develops as the child ages, but is rather a lack of brain development because the stimulation for that development was just not there."

9. "It seems like living in such grotesquely abusive and oppressive conditions must evoke some fairly primal survival instincts and perhaps this response sort of crystallizes in some people's personalities and becomes a key part of their make-up. Also, perhaps they have some genetic component that predisposes them to that outcome if exposed to those conditions. For me anyway, that makes the most sense. Besides, we know that people often react and are affected very differently by the same set of circumstances even in other situations. It is both fascinating and unsettling at the same time."

10. "Humans, in my belief, are at least born good. Unless some sort of psychological disorder is present. I really think that humans inherently want good for themselves and others, just based upon how much progress the world has made, despite all the bad things that have happened."

11. "I don't think there's any gene that makes people 'mean' or 'nice,' aside from psychological disorders. Who knows, though? We still don't know that much about our genes."

12. "Nature vs. Nurture is an age-old argument, but in this case I believe nurture wins out. The way we act when we're grown up is based a lot on things we learned, saw and had happen to us when we were children. You'd be surprised at how much a seemingly insignificant event in a person's childhood could affect them when they get older. For example, I nearly choked on a pill when I was about 6 years old. To this day I have a deep-rooted fear of swallowing pills. I could swallow a Skittle whole, but not a pill the same size."

13. "A person's personality is the result of heritage (genes) and environment (learned). So you could say both contribute to creating an 'evil' personality. Not that such an archetype exists. The human mind is more complex than that."

14. "The way I see it is that genetics can set someone up with a predisposition towards certain types of behaviour, but environmental factors and upbringing are ultimately responsible for whether or not these behaviour come out."

15. "One thing that always trips me up about nurture is the studies of identical twins. I read an article about studies they did with identical twins separated at birth. There was a lot of amazing similarities between them, even though they had never met before. I think our genes control a lot more than we realize right now."

16. "I think that I am an example that surroundings don't always influence the type of person you become. I have been shown nothing but lots of extreme hatred due to my race and growing up in the Southern US. Most of your personality is predetermined by your genes, and your surroundings have the potential to bring them out more."

17. "I'm prone to believe in a mixture of genes and environment. Then again, there has to be more than that. Some people who originate from the 'worst' genes out there, and who live in horrible environments, still turn out fine, and good."

18. "Perhaps it's more of dealing with how experiences shape a person's personality. Everybody has an amount of savagery/evil within them, there is no doubt about that. However, it's likely that the breaking point between inhibiting those evil tendencies and exhibiting them publicly derives itself from how we deal with experiences, our environment, and our genes. Most of the 'most incredibly evil people' out there have had a catalyst, some event, or a number of events, that drive them to commit evil deeds."

19. "I remember my biology teacher discussing a study done to determine this. Unfortunately, I cannot find any evidence of the study being done, but he was a credible man. He told of a study tracking down identical twins separated at birth, and observing what they had in common years down the road. Supposedly these twins who had never been in contact would often have the same jobs, wear their hair in a similar fashion, marry spouses that looked alike, and other similarities that seem too bizarre for coincidence."

20. "I agree that it's really a mixture of both nature and nurture that make people who they are. This argument always makes me think of Chinese foot-binding. Feet are born to be a certain size, but trained to be another. I've actually seen people beat both nature and nurture, born into drug-addicted families and raised in ghettos, but growing up to be business owners and professors. [author's note: but then how do we know that these business owners and professors are in fact not pathics of one type or another].

"I think it can also depend on how much you want to 'fall victim' (I can't think of a better phrase) to nurture. Mentally, if one is strong enough to do so, he or she can stop him/herself from doing anything, as well as start doing something. It just depends on how willing the person is to take the extra step to break out of the mold environment has put him/her in."

21. "Neither. They are always interacting. One is not subjectively more important than the other, and I think it is scientifically impossible to quantitatively put an amount of significance of one or the other."

22. "You all (I hope) are aware of DNA, correct? In DNA exists many deciding factors in your life. Namely, genetic diseases and such are all encoded in your DNA. Your DNA also encodes how your body should be put together (i.e., legs attached to your hips, nose on your face). This includes the brain. Now, DNA holds the codes for the different enzymes that make your body 'work', and different protein chains that will affect your cells. I won't go over the process, because I assume you have a vague idea on how it works.

"Now, this is the big question: Does DNA encode your personality? Does it encode how you will act as a person? In short, does it encode YOU? Here are the facts:

"No human brain is alike. Each one has slightly varied neuron connections and axon lengths. Basically, the order your brain is in is decided by your DNA (presumably). This means that your 'personality' is already decided before birth. This includes how smart you are, how well you are in athletic events, and various other things. Children have been tested, and those with high IQs all share the same slightly altered DNA in the same region. This is 'Nature'.

"However, you also have to take into account the environment. This is 'Nurture'. The way you are raised decides who you are, not who your parents were. This means that two human with less that 100 IQ could have a baby, raise it, and the child has an IQ of 160. Genetics play no part in the development of the child's attitude and physical abilities (assuming no genetic disease is inherited).

"Then what is it more of? I agree, it's definitely not one or the other. But one has to be dominant over the other. Think of it this way: Intelligent humans can learn better than the average human. Why? Because their brain is 'wired up' better, thusly they can learn easier. Their brain is shaped by their DNA. So, quite indirectly, their parents' DNA has decided their intelligence. However, people of average intelligence can still go to a better school and be smarter than someone hard wired to be intelligent.

"To rephrase the question, which do you think dominates?

"Yay for Randomness!"

23. "You need to take a look around you. We have modern genetics pinned down. Human nature is just now being shown to be nothing more than complicated chemistry. Oh, and the egg came first if you don't believe in the Old Testament.

"For example, let's take motherly love. All mothers 'love' their young, correct? Now, you would be led to believe that love is just an emotion, forever shrouded and never to be found out. Well, experiments have proven this false. There is a gene (fos-B), that when removed from mother rats, will stop them from caring for the young. They will simply ignore them. Now, we know that the gene produces an enzyme which works on the brain. In what way? We don't know. But we know what causes mothers to be so caring. It's in your DNA."

24. "I say nature is a huge overriding factor...it chooses how your body is set up in the beginning. However, the environment you grow up in is always a factor...but its small compared to nature. However depressing it may be, I think nature shapes a person's 'self'."

25. "I don't think we have enough information to really answer this question, nor do I think we ever will. A person's upbringing is just too subjective to be quantified, and genetics are just too complex for us to pin down with absolute certainty. The entire question has about the same hope of being solved to everyone's satisfaction as whether the chicken or the egg came first."

26. "The whole nature/nurture thing is a false dichotomy. Our genetics and brain structure are formed to a large degree on the people and environment in which we are raised. So we can't speak to what we are 'born' with, but at the same time, I believe we are born with specific capacities for becoming analytical, compassionate, gregarious, introverted, etc. But all this can be modified significantly by the people, occurrences and environment of our childhood."

27. "I believe it to be probably about 85% nature, 15% nurture."

28. "I guess it's because seeing such a strong genetic tie between parents and their kids when it comes to physical qualities (skin color, facial features, height, etc.), I figure it's bound to be pretty much the same when it comes to personality, intelligence, etc.."

29. "I think the intelligence thing is probably the largest thing causing me to believe more in nature (versus nurture). I mean, for the most part, kids tend to be about as intelligent as their parents. I see intelligence as part of human behavior, so it would make sense that personality would follow suit & be largely dependent on genetics."

30. "I'd say 60% Nature, 40% Nurture."

31. "At this point in scientific research and study, it seems that nothing is conclusive. It's been virtually impossible to test/study the SAME person in a 'nurturing' versus a 'natural' state. And unless it's precisely the SAME person, how can we ever know for sure? Identical twins have been studied, but that's only a very, very few people ... not conclusive at all.

"As to my opinion, I'd have to lean heavily to nurturing versus nature simply because I think a person's morality and ethical behavior is the more influential. I.e., a person might have natural tendencies, but their nurturing might prevent them from acting upon those tendencies."

32. "It's not a one or the other proposition, but probably more like some of each. Certainly not a 50/50 breakdown, either. Each child is unique. Furthermore, some kids are influenced more by outside influences than others. Hence, the 'bad' kid from the 'good' family. It's just too complex to try to place into a few categories, IMHO."

33. "I think children start off with 'leanings' in behavior that are set by genetics. But it's the environment in which children are raised and the influence of their parents and peers that mold them into what they are."

34. "As a biologist this always fascinates me. The problem with the whole nature vs. nurture thing is that you can't separate them out. How much of nurture is controlled by nature anyway? Maybe the genetic transfer includes the information transfer. Where do you separate them? How do you even test the theory? Whenever you do analysis the more variables you introduce the more garbage you get into the answer. This is why humans are SO hard to study. Too many variables."

35. "I like the conclusion 'nurture *is* nature'! I've always thought that the nature *vs.* nurture argument was too simplistic – the two are so intertwined that separating them out is next to impossible. For example, is the 'motherly love' induced by genetics or is it something that's learned or a combination of both?"

36. "One article I read pointed out that a certain gene combined with a bad environment can bring out this behaviour.

"I doubt that a single gene is responsible. The patterns of occurrence would have been easy to spot in family trees if that was the case.

"If so, how come other siblings with the same genetic makeup or biology and environment do not have the p's traits. Because normal siblings do 'not' have the same genetic makeup. I am not the same as my brother (Thank goodness! we both cry!) Your genetic makeup is a random mixture – 50% from your mother and 50% from your father. Your sibs get a 'different' random mixture. Only identical twins are genetically identical – this is where a single egg spits in two 'after' it has been created by the fusing together of one sperm and one ovum. the two eggs which result carry the same gene set.

"If psychopathy is totally genetically determined (like Down Syndrome) 'both' identical twins would 'always' end up either psychopathic or not.

"The other question is this then, why is it that some of these Ps come from really good homes?

"This relates to my belief that there are a number of routes to psychopathy. With some individuals the genetic mix - they inherit 'might' produce a very strong predisposition toward the development of psychopathy. Or maybe it's a developmental abnormality – an accident which happens in the womb which prevents normal brain development, not genetic. Either way, with

162

some individuals it seems that nothing the parents can do makes any difference."

37. "My view (and it is just an opinion, not something that I can back up with many facts) is yes, there is a genetic component, but that is not a simple single gene / two allele case like blue eyes / brown eyes. I think it's likely to be a whole suite of genes which interact with the environment in a complex way which will be very difficult to disentangle.

"I also think of 'psychopathy' or 'psychopathic' as the same way as I think of 'cough' or 'headache' it's a collection of symptoms, which point to a proximate cause, emotional dysfunction, for which we have no etiology.

"There are a number of reasons why a person might get a cough or a headache. I think the same may apply to psychopathy. I think there are probably a number of 'routes' to psychopathy. Some mainly or even possibly wholly genetic, some a mixture of genetics and environment, and some maybe almost entirely environmental.

"For example, some individuals who might otherwise develop normally, if subjected to extreme trauma at a young age, might not thereafter develop emotionally in the normal way. Environmentally induced psychopathy."

"This is all just guesswork. What is really needed is a large scale research project using the Hare PCL-R test on several thousand identical twins to start sorting this out. The results from the even smaller subset of identical twins separated at birth would be particularly interesting."

38. "I think psychopaths excel at using some terrific tricks to trap a victim and keep the situation going. It is like psychopaths are humans of prey, that is how I view dogs like pit bulls, animals of prey. The rest of us are fortunately missing the 'prey chip' in our brain."

39. "Anyone who has more than two children will tell you that there are dominant character traits that are present at birth. My own son, for example, came from [the] womb 'quiet and comfortable' as he still is today, years later."

40. "I definitely agree, some people become numb as a result of nurture. With me though it seems to be a nature thing. My childhood environment was very supportive and healthy. The combination of factors that create our dispositions are fascinating to try to get to the root of.

"I think I've accumulated some strong reinforcing influences in my life that no doubt have galvanized my nature. To some degree, I think this might simply be an effect rather than a cause. I think I have at times looked for people who shared aspects of my disposition.

"Actually running into a dangerous situation without fear is a trait that I share. Your motives may be more properly motivated than mine. I will often do very altruistic things. But only because deep down inside I'm a firm believer that things always work out to my advantage when I do.

"I don't have any children. I always want to be able to uproot my life at any moment. I suppose I'm too self absorbed to have children.

"I can feel very passionately about people, I just don't think twice when they aren't around. I'm very 'in the moment' that way.

"My libido is very strong and I enjoy sex immensely. I tend to think of sex a lot like a great meal – it can be delicious.

"I definitely enjoy questions that push the line. And I generally don't take offense at all. I prefer for things to be stimulating and interesting. Often things that push the line are just that."

41. "All of my family are as the average human beings are. They are honest and hard-working people. All except myself. I have been a human-animal ever since I was born. When I was very young at 5 or 6 years of age I was a thief and a liar and a mean despicable one at that. The older I got the meaner I got."

42. "I was born with the devil in me. I could not help the fact that I was a murderer, no more than the poet can help the inspiration to sing. I was born with the evil one standing as my sponsor beside the bed where I was ushered into the world, and he has been with me since."

43. "I always had the desire to inflict pain on others and to have others inflict pain on me. I always seemed to enjoy everything that hurt. The desire to inflict pain, that is all that is uppermost."

PART THREE:

Pathics in Relationships
PART FIVE: Against the Evil in Pathics

Chapter 9
GENDER DISTINCTIONS

The material in this chapter places into perspective pathic behavior as a human attribute including men, women, and children. Its overall point is that pathic traits result in pathic behavior, however differently expressed in men, women, and children. Except for the children's section, these selections have been separated into the three subdivisions of pathics; namely, narcipaths, sociopaths, and psychopaths; which give fairly clear distinctions of the behavioral patterns of each type of pathic. I leave out the psychotic-paths, in these selections as this type of pathic is more anomalous than pertinent to the central significance of this chapter and book.

———————

I: MEN

The Narcipath

1. "We met on the internet. When I read his profile I remember thinking 'Boy, is this guy a cocky bastard.' He was saying how handsome he was and that he would be a good catch basically. Well, he contacted me first – I almost didn't respond after reading his profile but I did. We talked for about a week on the phone and then met. One of his first comments to me when he met me was 'You've got potential.' Should have gotten up then and ran."

2. "They mix people up by screwing up the issues up so we get confused. Then they reprioritize everything for us by getting angry so we have to look at them first, we think and we worry about them first. It becomes all about them. Everything else, especially ourselves, and things once important to us, becomes second fiddle. No wonder we feel something isn't right and we don't realize how we got ourselves into such a predicament."

3. "He is angry that I show the children so much care and love and him so little. He accuses me of NEVER LOVING HIM. Until a year ago I was very devoted to him, I did everything I could to make his life easier. I was very loving and caring to him but it got to a point when I was tired of all this giving when I got nothing but nastiness back. I now want him to go and get help for himself. He is another thing for me to worry about, not only does he do nothing to help me and my quest for help for M, he makes matters worse by telling the kids I need help, that I am tired out. He thinks nothing about shouting in the middle of the night, waking kids up. He is always saying to me 'What about me'? I cannot comprehend a parent who puts themselves before their children, who is jealous when he sees his wife, their mother, cuddling them".

4. "We go to the grocery store. We buy something. We stand at the checkout stand together, watching the lady bag the groceries. I pay, as always. We are only 'dating', so I pay for everything, because he thinks it is wrong for women to expect him to 'take them out'. He eats for free, at my house, three days per week. We carry the food out to my car, together. We get home, ready for the Expert N Chef to prepare a meal, with me in the role of scullery maid. Something we bought is missing."

"'How could you forget that, it was so important?', he asks me impatiently, and goes on. 'I don't forget things when I go to the store, I watch to see that they put everything in the bag!'

"'But you were there, too, and had equal responsibility,' I protest. He says, 'How can you say that, when you were the one paying for them?'

"He tells me long stories about his life, on a regular basis. Sometimes they are half hour monologues or more. One time I listen to one of his stories and it reminds me of something that happened to me that I decide to tell him about. I say less than one sentence before he says, 'Did you feed the dogs?' 'Yes,' I say, and remain silent. 'Go on, go on,' he says impatiently, without looking at me, rotating his hand in the air. I say another sentence, and he interrupts, 'Will you hand me that newspaper?' I hand it to him. He begins to read it. 'Did you not have the slightest interest in what I was saying?' I ask him, after a while. 'I might,' he says, 'if you didn't go on and on, endlessly. Conversation should be a dialogue.'

"I buy everything we eat when he is at my house, three days a week. We need some milk, which we both take in our coffee, and he says, 'I want a walk, I'll go out for it.' 'Do you want some money,' I say, heading for my purse. He laughs derisively, looking right at me, hands in his pockets as I try to hand him some money. 'Why are you laughing,' I ask. 'It is so ridiculous,' he says. 'Here I am going out to buy you some milk, and you ask me if I want money: Would I like some money? 'What do you think, I want to pay for your milk as well as going to get it?'"

5. "When youngest child was 15, he and Dad had a falling out. Youngest child told him how angry he was at him for things he had done. Dad's response? 'If you aren't going to agree with me and tell me I am right, then I don't want you to come to see me anymore!'

Hasn't seen or spoken to youngest son for 3 years now."

6. "Yes, I told him exactly what I think of him, his lies, his deceit, his lack of emotions, he is just an image not a real person … and I realize that not only did this not bother him, it actually made him feel great! He knows that he has a dramatic impact on my feelings and since he won't let me love him anymore, now he makes me hate him. This must really make him feel like he's one damn special and unforgettable person!"

The Sociopath

1. "In my case [my] husband of 12 years, is not exactly malicious. He doesn't set out to hurt me just for kicks, in my opinion. He hurts me as little or as much as it takes to achieve his goal: to make me dependant on him in as many ways, obey him, give him all the [attention, admiration, etc.] he demands, abdicate control. So, while his primary goal isn't to hurt me, it becomes a goal if that's what it takes to get [attention, admiration, etc.] out of me."

2. "My father was violent, controlling, and childish at home, and a total charmer in public. He was a philanderer, a misogynist, a hater of children and anyone not directly under his control."

3. " … Now he's resorted to note-leaving, telling me how he sacrificed for our family, slaved away, and he is not selfish (just a control freak in what he considers his domain), I am 'etc'. How I took and took from him. How I pursued my crafts while he slaved (never mind that I paid some bills though he makes easily 20 times what I do) and he never minded.....what was I supposed to do instead … CLEAN BETTER, MAKE BETTER DINNERS!!!!"

4. "I too became lost in HIS world, started walking on eggshells and worrying if I said or was behaving the right way for him. He was so methodical in his control over me and like you, he would throw a bone at me (usually some old flowers on their way out), and I like a jerk would get so excited that he thought a little about me with the award of almost dead flowers. So sad."

169

5. "I married my ex when I was 20 years old and couldn't see what a control freak he was – a forest and tree thing because of my all-about-herself mother. I lived a relatively miserable life with him for 18 years, knowing it and yet NOT knowing it at the same time. We had two children, built a house together and from the outside looked like a perfectly happy family. What no one outside that house knew was that everyone inside was being devalued and undermined every moment of every day. There was no real physical abuse to point at, the abuse came in UNDER THE RADAR instead – in the form of mind games and verbal abuse. My children and I were treated either as slaves or extensions of himself to be bragged up – disorienting to say the least."

6. "He used to say that nothing was mine. He actually told me that I really had no personal belongings. That he believed everything I owned was really his. I couldn't believe what I was hearing. And I internalized this also as part of his brainwashing, crazy-making technique. So if he took something that I believed was mine and I got upset...that I was in the wrong for being hurt or angry or insulted, etc. All in all, the way I NOW see it is that he … is all about destruction. It gives him reason to live. And if I have nothing and I'm his too, then he believes he has the right to destroy me."

7. "When I sprained my ankle so badly they said it would have been better if I had broken it...he said, as I hobbled in on crutches.... 'Well, you're not so hurt that you can't cook me dinner.' I thought he was joking … he wasn't. He had been upset at not getting dinner because my mother had just started with her nearly five years of illness, and I was currently in NYC almost every day, packing up her apartment … no help from him. He didn't like her so refused to help with the four moves during those years, nor did he ever ONE TIME visit her with me. I tried to explain that helping her move (especially while I was alone on crutches and in a cast!) was helping ME not her! Zero empathy. We are divorcing; still in same house, and I think all his girlfriends have not come through [to help him]. They were just on the road playthings, and I believe he intended to keep his home life untouched. Keep me dumb and happy. But I followed my gut and found out. Now he is 59, not in the best health (but too obnoxious to die and put me out of my misery) and mopes around all the time."

8. A LETTER TO HER [SOCIOPATH]

"Today is the day I stop being a fool and take control of me and this situation once and for all. Today is the day you no longer have any control or effect on my life. Today is the day you cease to exist for me.

"At first I was very angry at myself for allowing all of this to happen and letting it go on for so long. But I realize now that I shouldn't be angry at myself. The reality is, this was able to happen because I was a good person who believed in you and what you said, trusted you, loved you, and wanted to give you a chance. You used that and so many other things about me against me to control and manipulate me, and it worked. So, you were able to do your damage. But it's not my fault. It's not because I did anything wrong. I didn't. It's just because I acted as though I was dealing with a normal person and behaved accordingly. I never dreamed that I was dealing with such a dangerous and evil being who could be so toxic. I wasn't even aware that people like that existed. But now I know that they do and you are one of them.

"You are an extremely damaged person. I know that. I know you experienced horrendous things as a child but that is not an excuse for what you've done nor does it give you the right to cause this damage to others.

"I believe now that you hate yourself and because of the things done to you growing up, you also hate women. Because of this, I believe that you either consciously or subconsciously try to overpower, control, and destroy any woman in your life and that in some sick deluded way you think that makes you better and stronger than them. You are so wrong. No matter how many women you victimize you are still NOTHING and will never be anything.

"I now know that you never loved me or cared about me no matter how many times you tell me or try to convince me that you do. You are not capable of loving or caring about anyone, not even yourself. I was just another person to be conquered and destroyed, another pawn in this sick lifelong game of yours. You used me, manipulated me, hurt me, and then left without care or concern and you were on to the next victim, yet for some sick reason still wanting to string me along and keep me under your control.

"I will never again make the mistake of thinking you are a normal human being. I will never again make the mistake of believing that you are capable of feeling. I will never again give you the slightest bit of thought, consideration, emotion or energy. You are nothing and that is how you will be treated.

"I am everything – everything you wanted to be and couldn't and so you had to suck the life out of me to make yourself feel better. But no matter how evil you are and no matter how much you try, you cannot take away the essence of who I am. I'm good, I'm loving, I'm caring, I'm beautiful, I'm strong, I'm intelligent, I'm successful, I'm kind, I'm loved, I'm supported, I'm wanted, and the list goes on. These are all things you cannot even begin to understand much less ever have the joy of experiencing. You cannot be me and no matter what you do you cannot take any of those things away from me.

"I allowed you to have power over me for a while, but not one more day. Today is a new day and it's a beautiful day! You have no power here anymore.

"Not only could you not destroy me, but you actually succeeded in making me stronger! You have no idea how amazing I really am but you will know."

9. "I was with this guy for 3 torturous years. When my daughter's dad was killed in a motor vehicle accident she came to live with me again. I told him I really needed him to step up to the plate and support me and my daughter through this very challenging time. I told him exactly what I needed, what I expected and that if he could not follow through, that I would have to leave. To this date, it was like I was having an out-of-body experience. He reported me to social services for child endangerment because I yelled at her, talked to my estate lawyer into quitting my case and left me and my daughter with no money and no home and then took personal

belongings from my dead husband's home. This guy is a monster. It is done – FINISHED. No phone calls, no missing him. If anyone out there thinks they can love [such a person] into recovery they need recovery themselves. [They] are animals – cruel to the core. RUN!!!!!!

10. "My brother is abusing his rights as my Mother's conservator. He has told me that he doesn't love her and that he wants what money is his – straight up. However, in the public eye, he brings up that I stole $30,000 from my mother. (My Mom gifted me $30,000 from my father's estate when he passed away to help me buy a house). Mom has plenty of money to take care of her in a comfortable manner and I'm willing to take over her care right now – but, also when the savings account that he has runs out...Thereby, returning the gift...but absolutely not while he is in charge. My brother has turned over all personal dealings with my Mom to his wife. She has never liked my Mom either. They never visit. Mom is an hour away and an hour back. I'm the only one who brings her home with me to stay. I have to drive there and back = twice. Now, they've moved her three times in three years. Every place they've moved her to winds up ready to cry 'abuse' – they've talked to me. Not physical (yet) but mental and emotional. My brother has not filed any of the required paperwork. They have alienated every person on the 'notification' list next-of-kin. I have alerted the Investigator at the County Courts that was appointed to my Mom. Third party guardianship was mentioned. After reading this article, I'm scared. Does my stepping up and calling attention to this travesty put my Mother in even more danger? HELP me now before we become a statistic!!!

11. A COURT CASE

Ritter's One-Man Show Is Over. Prison Awaits

Paula Simons, The Edmonton Journal, Tuesday, October 31 2006

It's Halloween, a day when people dress up and pretend to be something they're not. Fittingly, it's also the day an Edmonton court will pass sentence on Michael Ritter, the debonair thief and fraud artist at the centre of one of the largest white-collar crime schemes in Alberta history.

Alberta's former chief parliamentary counsel pleaded guilty last week in a deal to avoid extradition to the United States. The Crown and the defense made a joint sentencing recommendation of 10 years – much less than he might have received from a U.S. court.

For years, Ritter masqueraded as a lawyer, a scholar, an international expert in parliamentary tradition and banking law. The Edmonton financial consultant created a larger-than-life persona, as crusader for civil liberties and government accountability, as a noble philanthropist and patron of the arts.

E-mail to a Friend:

He was charismatic. He was courtly. Tall, handsome, always elegantly dressed, he charmed people – politicians, directors, academics and journalists – with his wit and savoir-faire. Meeting him, it was hard not be impressed with his breadth of knowledge, his force of personality. But it seems Ritter did not graduate with a law degree from the London School of Economics, as he had claimed. Scotland Yard and the RCMP could find no records to support claims that he served a legal internship with the British House of Lords, attended the University of Geneva, or worked for the Swiss Bankers Association. The man who was once head legal adviser to the Alberta legislature wasn't even a lawyer.

Yes, he was generous to his friends and to the arts groups he supported. But it's easy to be munificent, when you're giving away stolen money.

And the man who could be so charming had a mercurial temperament – the polished facade masked a master manipulator who lived to beguile and outwit others. Late last week, Ritter pleaded guilty to stealing $10.5 million US from an American client, Dan Gordon, a former senior executive at Merrill Lynch.

Gordon was also a thief, who had embezzled $43 million US from Merrill Lynch. Court records show Gordon hired Ritter and his consulting firm, Newport Pacific, to set up an intricate web of off-shore bank accounts and trusts to hold Gordon's money – though the agreed statement of facts presented in court indicates Ritter had no actual knowledge the monies were proceeds of a fraud on Merrill Lynch.

Ritter used much of what he stole from Gordon to finance his lavish lifestyle. He leased a $128,000 Edmonton Oilers luxury box. He made big donations to Pro Coro Canada, the Banff Calgary International Writers Festival, the Metamorphosis Concert Society.

He bought two private planes. And he spent $40,000 to purchase Belizian citizenship.

He also took $4 million US of stolen funds to invest in a global Ponzi scheme. The fraud, set up by two California con-artists, convinced victims to buy promissory notes, supposedly invested in the accounts receivable of latex glove factories in Malaysia and China. It was all a hoax – any "investors" who did get any money were simply paid with funds scammed from new investors.

The Psychopath

1. "My son is a psychopath. The doctors and psychologists and counselors he's seen since the age of 4 were never able to confirm the diagnosis until he turned 18 – and my research confirms it takes that long. He had been in and out of mental facilities and medicated for many years and when he turned 18 he quit his meds – which didn't work too well by that time. He would whisper to my daughter in her bed at night that he was going to kill her before morning. I took tough love classes and was finally able to put him out of our house – all the locks were changed – we'd been robbed blind and in fact he also broke in and robbed one of my dearest friends who lives on my street. That was over 10 years ago and to this day – I have little or no contact with any of my neighbors. As time went on he continued to commit crimes but was always able to con his way out. He did do time in jail but always got out early. I always felt that my son wouldn't reach his 30th birthday before something really serious happened – he's soon to be 26.

"I want to urge all of you who suspect their son is 'out of control' to research the life of a Psychopath. As ugly as it is, it's really helped me to deal with all of this.

"Do you recognize your son or daughter with these symptoms:
- No regret or remorse for what they've done to anyone
- The blame is always on someone else
- Unable to hold a job – my son had over 60 jobs in one year
- Pathological liar – we kept hoping to believe him but it's never true
- Masterful con artist – my son not only conned his family and friends but also detectives who were able to reduce his sentences because they believed he could testify as a witness against someone in jail with him – although he never did
- unable to accept "no" as an answer
- violent
- abusive – we urged my son's girlfriend for years to leave him and he always convinced her he'd change so she came back
- they will chew you up and spit you out, time after time
- their eyes are usually dead or angry looking

"The list goes on and on and I can recommend websites for those of you that want to research this. So many of our children are never diagnosed as a Psychopath or Anti-Social so we keep wondering if things will get better.

"The sad truth is that there is little or no cure for these poor tortured souls. While they can be placed on meds in a controlled environment they rarely if ever change – I've read that they may settle down a little after the age of 40."

2. "My [P] never hit me in the 18 months we were on/off. He did however hit his dog whenever she didn't 'listen.' Made me cringe. ... He would justify by saying it was for her own good because she was a 'gun' dog... WHATEVER!!! I truly think he broke that poor dog's spirit. The 'light' in her eyes seemed to just go out sometimes. My therapist says it would have been just a matter of time before he hit me."

3. "My brother's violence certainly escalated over the years – at least to the extent that he was able to get away with it. He was often in fights, and beat my younger sister once (chipping a tooth) because she didn't do something he asked. He always had a strong sense of self-interest though (an understatement), so he always knew exactly how far he could go without jeopardizing himself."

4. "I was certainly always afraid of my brother – there was an aura of danger about him, and I never knew for sure what he might be capable of doing if provoked. He died several years ago, and I will admit that lying under the terrible grief for such a wasted life was deep relief that I wouldn't have to look over my shoulder anymore."

5. "I stood there thinking: 'He can't mean it.' I had the shudders, my skin was crawling. This [P]-from-hell exuded pure evil. Over the next 5 years he kicked his father out of the house, cut off his pension and slandered him. He cheated his first wife and his kids of money he should have paid, manipulated his business(s), lied to his separate little groups, split away from former friends and family, got 'religion,' verbally abused his kids, turned other people into his little evil-doer proxies, hired and fired people on a regular basis. He'd cheat himself to satisfy his own greed if he could. About every three months I'd hear about some treachery he was inflicting on someone, somewhere."

6. "I went along with him once and he said: 'Hey I like the way you talk!' He actually praised me when I agreed with him that a person who causes an accident should be left on the highway to die and just drive on by. What a polished piece of work! I swear I met the devil."

7. "When I first met him he was wonderful, then he came into my apartment and took over my life. It started out by just a slap in the face and apologizing that it wouldn't happen again. Then he started controlling every move I made. He started to choke me until I passed out, smothered me with a pillow and dragging me around by my hair. If I ever said anything to him about how he was treating me he would punch me, slap, and put his hand over my mouth and nose until I passed out. Then the day came when he wanted me to get his name tattooed on my arm, if I didn't he said he would beat the hell out of me, so I did, well after I did that things got much worse because the abuse got worse. He started hitting me with the metal handle of his cane, chasing me with a knife, threatening to kill me, hitting me with a homemade beater that had metal on it. Things were so bad that I had to ask permission to talk, take a bath, go to the bathroom, he had to pick out my clothes, and if I wanted to sleep it was rare that I got to because he wouldn't allow me to sleep. For months I went without food because his drugs were more important than I was. Because of the abuse I lost my daughter in a case I was fighting to get her back through cps. I lost my car because it was seized by the cops for drugs; I lost my apartment, clothes, furniture, and a lot of my life. For a month and a half he held me hostage in four different hotels and beat me. I ended up with black eyes, I have a broken tooth, and a damaged ear because he kicked me with steel toed boots. Then finally the fights got so bad that someone over heard us in the hotel and the manager came when he heard a knock on the door he left, I knew this was the only chance I had, and if I didn't leave he would come back and kill me, so I left and called my mom to come and get me. I had a friend take me to a truck stop and my mom had the police and ambulance waiting for me. I filed charges and then went to the ER that night since then I am trying to gain the 35 lbs. I lost (which I am supposed to weigh 145; but when my mom found me I was 110-115) my mom says I have the symptoms of a prisoner of war. I run and hide when I'm scared or see someone arguing. Or if I see a knife I hide. I never thought that I would ever get into that kind of situation and because of the things he did and said to me I'm a completely different person then I used to be. I was told because of me going to the cops that he had a contract out for me to kill me so I had to go into hiding and moved out of state where all my friends and family are at."

8. "I have had restraining orders, civil and criminal ongoing for over two years. He told me he would kill me but that would be too good for me, first he wants to watch me lose everything and become homeless, then he will kill me. I don't believe he will ever stop until he does kill me."

9. "My children had watched him beat me on more than one occasion (when they were not locked out of the area where the beating was taking place) and if they cried, this man would tell them to 'shut up, or they would get the same thing.' None of this was taken into consideration when the judge made his decision. He would not even look at the pictures his own system had taken."

10. "My son is in jail on 4 counts of attempted murder – he is guilty; and it was me, his mother, that turned him in. He has not been sentenced yet. He tried to kill his former girlfriend, shot her new boyfriend in the face and arm, and also tried to kill his 2 cousins. He has since found out that I turned him in – I had no other choice – he had fled the state and in fact made it as far as Tennessee. With the help of his father and my daughter we were able to talk him back home – we knew he still had a 45 caliber plus 30 shells. Fortunately, no one else was injured and as the police told us – it was a peaceful end.

"My son's sole goal now is to get out of jail and kill me, and also my daughter, because we were instrumental in his arrest."

11. "It's about a year plus few months since my ex hit me. The last time he hit me, I was admitted to the hospital for unconsciousness, loss of memory because he hit me repeatedly in the head. Literally. He just took hold of my head, and banged it on the floor. When I was about to pass out, I saw images of him stomping on my tummy, also repeatedly, and full of hatred. This fight was fueled by his jealousy, just because I was asking my course-mate for my book over the phone, and to him this was adultery.

"That was one of those hundreds of fights which I really can't forget. He always tells me I caused him all the misery, that he has to beat me to make him feel better, and then when he feels bitter about hitting me, he blamed me for not being good enough. Not being a virgin, that is.

"I kept asking myself when he locked me up in his house (not letting me run away), that: Why has this all happened to me? Is this Karma? Was it really my fault that I am not a virgin, that it's okay for a guy who has slept with numerous prostitutes before to judge my loss of virginity? I attempted suicide, cut myself repeatedly, during those moments of hunger when he wouldn't let me eat. When he even isolated me from everything, including my family by taking away the phone, and my handset.

"For all the times that he has bruised me, he kept saying it was my fault. For all the times he raped me and yelling into my face that he loved f***ing whores than me. For all the times I bled not only from the skin, but from the anus (from the stompings), my dignity got sliced off. Slice by slice. Until it was barely there.

"The hospitalization was the only way I could get out of the house. That was it. I could breathe without him telling me to. I could cry without him slapping me numb. I could think without the pain in the heart, knowing that I've loved a beast."

"Many, including friends, and the doctor who examined me, advised me to lodge a police report. My mother was against it, because she believed it was my fault to have been causing the anger in him. What could I say?"

"Until today, I still live with the scars, emotionally, and physical-ly."

"I know I can go on, I am strong."

12. "He is cold blooded towards all animals but tries to hide this unless his sadistic streak is showing. Then he can get pleasure out of shocking a child with his crude comments and behaviors towards pets and other living things."

13. COURT CASE: Narrogin: A New Zealand-raised man has been

convicted in Australia for sadistic abuse of his three-year-old son, including deliberately burning the boy's finger with a lighter and pulling his nail out with pliers. Jason David Ogier, 37, was yesterday jailed for two years and seven months for repeatedly assaulting the boy.

Magistrate Elizabeth Hamilton said the man, a father of nine, had little empathy for his children and the offences were part of an "ongoing and entrenched form of behavior".

Ogier, from the Perth suburb of Welshpool, was sentenced in the Narrogin Magistrates Court, southeast of Perth, where he and his family previously lived.

Ogier's wife, Belinda Ogier, 43, of Guilford, was given a six-month suspended sentence for neglecting her son, by failing to protect him from his father, warn the authorities or seek medical help for his injuries.

"The seriousness of the offences is in the gross breach of trust," Mrs Hamilton said during sentencing.

Ogier pleaded guilty in February to three counts of assault occasioning bodily harm, four of common assault and one of breach of protective bail conditions between October 2004 and December 2006.

He had also admitted to stealing and possessing stolen property.

Ogier committed the worst offences in October 2004 while his wife was in hospital giving birth and he was entrusted with the care of their children.

To discipline his son for not eating his dinner, Ogier rubbed chilli powder on his back, causing the skin to blister.

He burned his son's hand with a cigarette lighter and when the finger became infected pulled the nail out with pliers, causing it to bleed.

Ogier also kicked his son with steel-capped boots and slapped his head from side to side, asking his other children if they wanted to join his game of "tennis".

When the three-year old had supposedly not finished his house chores, Ogier repeatedly beat him with a clenched fist, knocking him to the ground.

At no time did Ogier or his wife seek medical help for the boy.

Police prosecutor Sergeant David Murphy said Ogier had shown no remorse.

"(They are) barbaric acts of cruelty perpetrated on his own child, a defenceless, three-year-old boy," Mr. Murphy said.

Earlier, Mrs. Hamilton had stood the matter down because the couple denied some charges against them in pre-sentence reports, although they later agreed with the police facts.

At the time of the offences, the Ogiers were on community orders for a 2005 assault on their 11-year-old son.

In addition to his 31 months' jail, Ogier was ordered to pay a $A1800 ($NZ2070) fine.

II: WOMEN

A Woman's View of Female Pathics

1. "In reading some of the literature about psychopathy I've seen statistics that state how the percentage of male psychopaths is greater than that of females. I wonder how the studies were done to come up with that information. For example, 'Did they study women prison populations like they did men?' 'What are the differences or similarities in style and *modus operandi* between male and female psychopaths?'

"Just taking the main marker of a psychopath: lack of con-science and empathy. How does this manifest as regards the sexes? What about the differences in the way boys and girls are raised as children and what is considered 'appropriate behavior.'"

"I think that there may be more female psychopaths than have possibly been calculated due to the fact that their violence may be so covert that it passes undetected. They may be the more 'silent partner' in a family or business structure. Just food for thought.

...

"Some more thoughts on the gender thing and psychopaths. I had a friend who became my friend during a time in my life when I was very ill and sad. I welcomed this friendship and was so GRATEFUL that this woman understood and sought me out during this time. I felt indebted to her and over time when I noticed things about her that were red flags (like she would really yell at her children for the slightest irritation that she felt, or that she was never really nice to me again like she was in the beginning of our friendship). In fact, it was all turned around. She was needy forever more and called upon me whenever she needed something from me. The friendship that I had initially felt was gone. And over time it got worse. She got increasingly needy and unavailable, sneaky, and then the cruelty and rage started to rear their ugly head. Sigh.

"As I've been writing this I am even more aware of what this woman was about. She unmasked as all the psychopaths that I've known have. Finally, when I could no longer make excuses to myself for her bad behavior and confronted the demon, she turned it all around and played the victim herself. I have a very strong instinct that this woman is a psychopath. Looking back I can think of more events. Things that she did that hurt my feelings, or things that she did to her children. How manipulative she was and without conscience in her actions, but so sly and with such slick speech; but I had learned that if I ever spoke about my feelings or questioned her that it would get turned around into what a horrible person I was. Always. Of course, psychopaths never accept responsibility for anything that they say or do to cause pain.

"I think I was more unaware, confused, and blindsided because she was a woman."

2. "I personally believe there are fewer female psychopaths than male ones. I think this has to do with innate gender differences.

Psychopathy (in my view) is a total disconnection from the inner self, from feelings, conscience, soul, spirit. Women are notoriously 'more in touch with their feelings' than men. Some of this is probably conditioning, but I think it goes deeper than that, into what a woman is, spiritually, and what a man is spiritually. And I think biology reflects these differences. Women are softer, men are harder. Women's sex points inward. Men's sex points outward. Women's biology creates urges to nest and nurture. Men's testosterone-dominated biology creates urges to be aggressive, fight over territory, and mate many females. I just think men are more prone to psychopathy than women."

A Man's View of Female Pathics

1. "Abuse and violence are behaviors chosen by a woman to cause physical, sexual, or emotional damage and worry or fear. Women who behave this way are often promiscuous, selfish, and narcissistic. Such a woman uses her moods, rage, and impulses to control the people around her and she is not satisfied until they have noticed her. These women choose deceit, fury, and assault to get their own way and then revels in the addicting exhilarating emotional unrest they create. Others, more insidiously, present a personable public image to conceal their true character and behavior.

"These women lie, connive, and extort. To insult and humiliate their partner, some argue and use offensive language in the presence of others including their children. Many steal or destroy their partner's possessions. These women are driven by jealousy and view others as rivals. They treat their partners as possessions and strive to isolate them from friends and family.

"Many abusive women falsely accuse their partners of infidelity while they have affairs. These women often abuse children or animals. Nearly all exhibit erratic mood changes, feign illnesses or injuries, and most are practiced actresses. They are not sick; they play the triple roles of a terrorist, a tyrant, and a victim.

"At some point, she will falsely accuse her husband or partner of a crime. False allegations of child abuse continue to be a common feature in divorce proceedings and the courts ignore the problem. Now, the domestic violence accusation has become the woman's weapon of choice. Apart from the monetary and property gains, domestic violence is so easy to fabricate and these women crave the pleasure that comes from destroying their husband or partner."

"Persons who have experienced an abusive relationship often experience fear or shame or bewilderment. They have tried everything and nothing works. These people have found themselves not knowing what will happen next, riding on an emotional roller coaster that they cannot escape. Most are sad, depressed, humiliated, and just plain exhausted. Many have lost everything they had in the world and are worried about their future. However, these women have no limits. Their outrageous behavior escalates to unbelievable levels and so, no one believes the victim."

"Once your wife or companion has chosen abuse or violence, end the relationship promptly and irrevocably. U.S. and British studies support this view. Domestic battery, theft, and destruction of property are private and civil wrongs. The victim can sue for damages. Get a restraining order now and change the locks, sue in civil court now and, when the assailant is your spouse, file for divorce now."

"When faced with the breakup of a relationship, especially a mar-riage, some women become vindictive, and abusive women become very dangerous. When others (friends, relatives, police, attorneys, and judges) believe her, they join in, and the frustrated husband or partner finds himself a victim of undeserved hatred, defamation, and abuse.

"The other dangers are that some women kill their partner, or the partner's new companion, or the children, or the relatives, or stage unsuccessful suicides. Sometimes, women fake or inflict injuries on themselves, or use an accomplice, a relative or new lover, to frame her husband or partner. The most common behaviors are pressing false criminal charges, stealing or destroying property, snatching children, and engaging in bad faith litigation.

"In divorce, husbands must treat their abusive wives with steeled resolve and the courts must understand this. These women cannot see and reason beyond themselves, so negotiation is impossible. Mediation is pointless. Unfortunately, the legal process regarding divorce requires negotiation and mediation providing yet another way for these women to abuse their husbands. Husbands must not accept telephone calls, conversation, visitations, reconciliation, or appeasements from these abusive wives for this only bolsters their belief that they remain in control of their husbands. The court must realize that these women have no limits and derive pleasure from destroying their husbands. Only unswerving firmness of purpose shows these women that their power has ended."

2. "How would you guys like to don a dress and then ride a donkey backwards down the main street of your town? Everyone could line the street snickering and making fun of you."

"I doubt if you would even consider it. Yet, in medieval France, a man who had been physically abused by his wife was forced to do this so everyone could see how weak he was."

"We probably all accept the fact that both men and women can be the victim of emotional abuse. The 'hen-pecked' man has been the brunt of jokes forever."

"Physical abuse is another story. In our society we think of women as the victims and men as the aggressors in physical abuse."

"But that is not true. Equally as many, if not more, men are assaulted by their girlfriends or wives as vice versa."

"A 1997 survey conducted among dating couples showed almost 30% of women admitting that they had used some form of physical aggression against their male partners within the dating cycle. This runs counter to official documentation of female abuse against men."

"Why?"

1. Less men report abuse. They are ashamed to report being abused by women.

2. Health care and law enforcement professionals are more likely to accept alternative explanations of bruises and other signs of injury from a man.

3. Our justice system sometimes takes the word of the woman above the word of the man. It is just more believable that the aggressor was the man, not the woman.

4. Men will tolerate more pain than women. They are more likely to 'grin and bear it' And again, many are ashamed to seek medical help.

5. Unless a woman uses a weapon (and many do), a woman usually does not have the strength of a man.

6. Our society still sees women as nonviolent peacemakers, the victims of men, perhaps, but not as aggressors against men. The fact that women are more likely to be severely injured in domestic violence adds to the problem of recognizing male abuse.

7. Health care professionals often do not even think of abuse as a potential explanation. When they see an injury, they accept even a fairly lame explanation. For example, on seeing a bruised man, they are quick to accept a work-related accident or 'a week-end game of football with the guys'.

8. Men find it harder to discuss pain than women and even harder to admit to being a victim. In addition, men often have more hazardous occupations than women and certainly show more physical aggression to each other than women show to other women. All of this makes it easy for the health care professional to accept an injury explanation other than domestic violence.

9. Even a mugging might be more acceptable than a female beating. Unless the report is of a woman wielding an iron skillet, of course.

10. When a man does report domestic violence, he often encounters law enforcement professionals who are quick to believe his female aggressor rather than him.

11. Abused men are as likely as their female counterparts to have low self-esteem. In addition, a male victim also has to deal with

the examination of his masculinity.

12. Men and women often come to believe that it is their fault that they are abused; they are somehow responsible for what happened.

13. Men are also in denial! This should not happen to a masculine man, therefore it is not happening.

14. And men, as well as women, hope things will get better. The woman he 'loves' will quit when they are better adjusted, or her job is not so frustrating, or the children get more responsible. Pretty much the same excuses women make for remaining with men who batter them."

The Narcipath

1. "For as long as I remember, [my sister] has always had a need to be center of attention. Because there are only us girls in the family, there has always been some underlying competition. Sometimes she can be the sweetest person alive, but she can suddenly turn and become very aggressive. She insults my appearance, my friends, my career choice and just about everything else about me. It is mostly verbal abuse, but it has been physical and because she is stronger than me now (even though she is a couple of years younger) she always threatens to beat me up."

"She can twist the most innocent things to make me look really bad. She can lie so well and is so convincing."

"This is beyond petty sibling rivalry as sometimes I feel scared of her. I have to live with her day in, day out and can't wait for her to move out for college."

"Since reading up on P's, I feel kinda sorry for her, she just comes across as shallow and manipulative. My advice for anyone living in a situation similar to mine is:

"I just keep myself busy with my life and just try and ignore her (but anyone living with a P knows how difficult it is to ignore them, especially when they want something)."

2. "The NP females are very coy and use past abandonment issues and need for a knight in shining armour to sweep them off their feet and rescue them from their 'downtrodden' world. We, as caring men, tend to rise up to the challenge and promise them the world and more. I can't tell you how many people I told that marriage vows meant forever, that I would be the one. Well, I was wrong. These 'damsels in distress' are as phony as a three dollar bill. Once we are taken for granted they rail against us and the whole devaluation process begins."

3. "My marriage to 'N' began to unravel over a number of years, but things took a turn for the worse following the birth of our daughter. Over time it seemed as though N was jealous of my relationship with my daughter. She demanded more and more attention, and withdrew from family activities involving all three of us. She said she should be 'worshipped'. She referred to herself as the 'head of the household.' She became obsessed with maintaining a youthful appearance, and would make statements like 'I have a body that teenagers would die for,' or 'men fall all over me.' While she would say that she loved me, the words sounded detached and cold. She became unsupportive of my hobbies and interests, while I was constantly pressured to do things for her. Things continued to get out of balance. I started to fall into a depression and withdrew from the things that once gave me meaning, though I continued to maintain a loving and close relationship to my daughter. I was trying to hold the family together, while in denial about the dysfunction.

"In 1998 N seemed to take on another personality. She jokingly called herself 'Wynetta', drove a pickup truck, bought cowboy boots, and began listening to country music. She wrote short fictional stories based on actual people in her life, and the stories became more and more vicious and mean-spirited. Wynetta was the main character in the stories; a sexually-dominating and abusive woman.

"N asked me for a divorce in the summer of 2000. She refused counseling, became hostile, and began to alienate me from our close friends by portraying herself as a victim and me as an unloving and lifeless man. She was a master of coercion. She refused to go to a marriage counselor, saying she no longer loved me. I moved into an apartment (she said that things might work out, that she needed some 'space' as I became weakened by depression, and she seemed to become stronger and more hostile and controlling. She changed the locks on the house, hired an attorney. In time, I learned there had been at least two affairs during our marriage."

4. "She was never around and when she was she would physically hurt me until I could barely walk. When I got older it was less physical and more mental and emotional. She doesn't care about anyone except herself and she puts on this front for people."

5. "Having N parents myself, I have come to the same conclusion and given up. I humor them now, just to keep peace. I listen to them talk endlessly about their recent vacation or other triumph. I don't know if this is the case with your parents, but my mother will actually interrupt a person mid sentence and start another subject entirely. It's as if she didn't hear a word I or someone else was saying. I am still a little shocked every time she does this because it takes such colossal nerve! Anyway, I just let them be the star of the show, so to speak, then I make my exit as soon as I can. I am finished trying to get through to them. Nothing will, so why bother?"

The Sociopath

1. "First red flag: I met NP for coffee after matching up on an internet dating site. She was drop-dead gorgeous, dressed to nines, and appeared normal to a naive small-town guy like me. But looking back I can see that during that first hour together she talked of her past failed marriages and how she had been taken by her husbands. Of course, the opposite is true, she milked them for all she could."

2. "From the very beginning she had control in the relationship. Maybe it wasn't forceful at first because I remember thinking it was cute but she definitely had control. She dictated when we talked and for how long. It was up to her when she wanted to come over

my place. I think in the 6 months that we dated I probably ended a phone conversation 2 or 3 times. I felt bad telling her I had to go.

"Most of what we talked about was her life or her work. At first I didn't mind this because I figured she had a new job and it was normal to be excited and to talk about it. But as days went by I started feeling dejected that she would rarely ask how my day was going or what my plans were. I don't know that I tried enough to tell her about what was going on in my life but I do know she didn't seem interested. She knew that I was there to be with when she wanted me. We rarely ever made plans as she would go home after work and then text me that she was on her way over.

"I started to notice that when she came over she wouldn't seem very interested in how I was doing or how my day was. She would jump into what happened to her and tell me stories about her past and things like that.

"Early I was interested to hear it but for some reason it wore on me. I would start to express my feelings not in conversation but in reaction. When I was really annoyed I would lean back, stare at the TV and not pay attention to her. I guess I was hoping that she would realize this and pay some attention to me. The opposite happened. She would get mad at me, tell me that I don't pay attention to her and multiple times stormed out of my house. It just felt one-sided to me and I've never been able to figure out if this was true or if it was my insecurities getting in the way of things.

"Everything always had to be about her. I remember her specifically telling me that I need to pay more attention to her. Very often told me that she didn't feel that I loved her enough. I was baffled...I put my entire life on hold and never did anything with friends or coworkers over hanging out with her. She told me in a very serious tone that I should treat her like a princess. She told me on more than one occasion that she was my boss.

"Sometimes she'd accuse me of being insecure and it was hurting our relationship. I agree that it was but it was impossible not to feel insecure with what we had.

"In actuality, she was also extremely insecure. She told her sister that if I even looked at another girl at work she would kill me (exaggeration, not a real threat). She questioned me about taking a girl I took out to lunch years before we dated. We had sex probably 100 times and she never took her shirt off. She was embarrassed by the size of her breasts."

"I also noticed how she treated her father and it amazed me. I was sitting in their living room with her father watching a game on TV and she screamed from her bedroom, 'PA...BRING ME A SODA WITH ICE.' I was shocked that she could be that demanding of her father.

"So as I started to notice these things along with her obsession with how she looked, it started me trying to figure out if there was something more than just attitude going on. She would check the mirror and check her hair about twice every hour. Never let me see her without makeup but tell me that I should think she's beautiful without makeup on. How would I ever know that???"

3. "In 2005, my sisters secretly took my mother to an elder law attorney and obtained a Durable Power of Attorney, Health care proxy, living will with them as agents. They put the family home in a trust and had my mother make her will. They had her transfer all her money to accounts in their names.

"On Christmas Eve in 2006, my mother was abducted from the only home she has known for half a century. She was taken away from the people and things she loves under false pretenses by my sisters. They told her she was going to get physical therapy to strengthen her weak legs, and to do everything the facility said, otherwise Medicaid would not pay for the therapy.

"At first they took her to the hospital and then kept transferring her to different nursing facilities where they were drugging her with so many drugs that she could not lift up her own head and became so weak that she was unable to walk and talk and is now permanently in a wheelchair.

"I filed a Writ of Habeas Corpus to get her out of the nursing facility but my sisters filed a guardianship Petition, and instead of bringing her home, the judge appointed a temporary guardian to put her at my sister's house because my sisters said in the petition that I abused my mother (we lived in the same house for 27 years).

These allegations are false and at first devastated me. However, I later found that such accusations are a common pattern in guardianships because the goal in such a proceeding is not the person's best interest, but rather it is about how unscrupulous people get the most money out of the estate. I was never given the opportunity to present any evidence or cross examine my sisters.

"Instead, my mother is still being held incommunicado at my sister's home in Brooklyn in a wheel chair, with no phone in her room, no money to call a cab or cry out for help. And what can she do about it?

"It is more evil and sad than you could ever imagine. It is emotional torture for both me and my mother who told everyone she wants to go home to see her dog, and to die in familiar surroundings. I have not seen or talked to her for almost a year and cry myself to sleep wondering how she must be feeling about the daughters she trusted who have betrayed her. And I wonder if she thinks I let her down.

"My sisters filed the guardianship Petition asking to be able to put my mother into a nursing facility for good, and to be able to evict me from the family home and sell it. All of this is against my mother's verbal and written wishes."

4. "My horror story takes place in California and involves my aunt and the person taking advantage of her is her own son and daughter-in-law. I am sickened by what they have done to her and how she is being treated. She fought as hard as she could, on her own and by herself to try and fight off the Conservatorship they were seeking. The judge granted the conservatorship before the paperwork had even been submitted to the court showing the detail of what had happened to her money and home. It is sad when a stranger takes advantage of an elder but it should be criminal when a child does it to a parent. I am trying to help her but I do not know where to go or what to do. She now has no money and the court appointed attorney who represented her was totally not affective in representing her."

5. A COURT CASE: **Facing jail, 'dying millionairess' who cheated her lovers out of £100,000**

Last updated at 08:52am on 10.01.07

To the men she seduced, Emma Golightly was a wealthy business-woman who liked nothing more than to shower her lovers with top-of-the-range cars and exotic holidays.

When soon afterwards she told them she was suffering from terminal cancer, they invariably agreed to marry her.

One man, company director Chris Williams, walked down the aisle with the 22-year-old weeks after she told him she 'didn't want to die without being a bride'.

The truth, however, was that Golightly had no illness of the sort. Neither was she the millionairess she claimed to be.

All the gifts the men had been receiving – as well as many she had indulged in herself – had been paid for with their own credit cards.

The fantasist and serial bride was facing jail after admitting conning at least three men out of more than £100,000. She asked for 60 offences of deception into consideration.

Golightly, of Wallsend, North Tyneside, used lonely hearts columns to meet wealthy men and plunder their credit cards.

She even ripped off her own mother and grandmother to fund a lavish lifestyle.

Her deceit was uncovered after her victims were confronted with huge bills and called police.

Golightly had been due to be sentenced at Newcastle Crown Court this week but the case was adjourned until January 30 after the sudden death of her 19-year-old brother from a suspected heart attack. Her victims spoke of their ordeals.

The husband

The heartfelt plea from his 'dying' girlfriend was something company director Chris Williams could not resist and two days before Christmas 2004, the couple tied the knot at Register Office at the end of a whirlwind seven month affair.

She lied about her age on the wedding certificate, claiming she was 23 when she was 20, and a solicitor's daughter.

But it was the cancer ruse that was the cruelest of a string of lies Golightly told the new husband she met via a lonely hearts newspaper advert.

She told him they had been given a £500 wedding gift from her father but in fact she had taken it from Mr. Williams's bank account behind his back.

Golightly insisted she would foot the £8,600 bill for their week-long luxury honeymoon in Jamaica, which she put on his credit cards without his knowledge – as was the £200 train tickets to get the couple to Heathrow.

When later confronted by her new husband she admitted her deceit and promised to pay him back but the £12,000 cheque she gave him later bounced.

When she insisted on buying expensive Land Rover 4x4s for her husband and mother three months after their marriage Golightly said she could afford to pay for the vehicles out of savings and an inheritance.

The couple visited the car showroom and plumped for a £42,000 Land Rover Discovery for Mr. Williams, 33, and he agreed to put down a £1,000 deposit.

Golightly brazenly told sales staff the balance would be paid by electronic transfer and asked for a second £13,000 vehicle to be kept in the showroom until Mothering Sunday as a surprise for her parent.

Once she got her hand on both cars the electronic transfers never happened and Golightly's cheques invariably bounced.

In April 2005 Mr. Williams ordered his wife out of his home. 'It was a bad time in my life and I'd rather not talk about it,' he said.

The Bridegroom

Undaunted, Golightly turned her attentions on to a broadcasting executive from Heaton, once again callously playing the cancer card.

Despite legally still being Mrs. Williams, she even arranged to 'marry' her unsuspecting boyfriend – who she met on the internet – at Newcastle's Copthorne Hotel in October 2005, a month later.

She was calling herself Chelsea Taylor this time and his friends were already trying to ring alarm bells.

One said: 'She told him she only had six months to live. He said he would rather have that short time with her than not at all and so they were bringing the wedding forward.'

Golightly claimed she was part-owner of a Gateshead club and running her own successful wedding dress company but, unknown to her boyfriend, it was his credit card she was using to pay for their big day.

After the happy couple posed on the banks of the River Tyne it soon became obvious that things were not going to plan. The chauffeur refused to leave until he had been paid and the registrar failed to appear.

One guest said: 'My friend was stressed beyond belief and just wanted to marry the woman he was in love with and for her to be happy.'

'To everyone's relief, one of the guests, who was a lay preacher, offered to do a "blessing".' Golightly's 'cancer' drugs were later tested and turned out to be antihistamine tablets and an anti-depressant.

Her 'husband-to-be' threw her out when he realised the extent of her lies – and called the police when credit cards bills began to arrive.

The business partner

A third victim was duped into believing he was part-owner of a Newcastle bar with Golightly, who he met on the internet .

Half was in his name, Golightly told the man she had bombarded with gifts, before confiding that she was suffering from cancer which, if terminal, meant the whole business was his.

The couple arranged a romantic trip together in Egypt which she said she had paid for but when they turned up at Newcastle Airport there were no tickets – and no holiday.

Within a short time the man realised he had been hoodwinked , and his credit cards plundered.

The date

Another Tyneside man had a date with Golightly through a website called Dating Direct but decided she was as 'nutty as a fruitcake' and never saw her again.

A 'Chelsea' on the website describes herself as a 28 year old, divorced 'light blonde attractive' designer with a Masters degree and a wide range of interests – but posts no photograph.

Her date said: "When we met she wasn't what I expected but she certainly had the gift of the gab. She told me about her work as a leading oncologist. She talked about her great house and car, her horses. She had great imagination, she was never stumped for an answer or lost for words."

The Psychopath

1. "I married a psychopath; and believe me, it is not gender-specific. She kicked me repeatedly in the head with her boots on and otherwise displayed all the symptoms of psychopathy. I never

touched her yet she assaulted me repeatedly. Yes it really happens. In 9 years of marriage she kissed me briefly 4 times and rarely had sex with me but did with others. I am ashamed to play the victim – I don't like it. This woman was cunning, ruthless, unfaithful, thieving and a pathological liar. I have a wonderful wife now who actually smiles, kisses me and acts like a human being. She snapped me out of the shocking dependency and gullibility and took me far away. Believe me psychopathic females are very capable of committing atrocities akin to brutal wife beating and spouse abuse. More men than women statistically are psychopathic (3% against 1% of women). Let's not make it a gender issue. Females are quite capable of having this severe mental illness."

2. "Soon, she who could make me the happiest person could also make me feel like unlovable scum. So, when I was hit, as she told me, I deserved it. If only I could not be so tired and stay awake all night with her and do the shopping, cleaning, DIY, cooking, and earn more and spend more time with her and drive her everywhere but not drive so badly, and tell her something interesting and listen to her more and be like her ex (who had left one day without saying bye after four months) and always be there for her and get out when she told me, she wouldn't get angry with me. Soon the eggshells were so scattered that it was difficult to walk anywhere.

"When the boundaries of verbal abuse had been nudged, those of physical abuse kicked in, but always behind her closed door. It didn't matter what the 'reason' was in the end. Once it was for telling a joke she didn't find funny. Again, I must stress the blurred anger I saw, more like a starving, rabid dog ravaging some raw meat than a human being. Why didn't I leave? Because most of the time our love affair was gorgeous.

"She was kind, shy and vulnerable, or at least portrayed herself that way. I thought she'd been a victim, and I'd be the hero to save her. I was also chasing the high that we'd had, had nowhere to go, and felt really alone: I could talk to some male mates about it, but most couldn't relate to what I was saying. Even when I went to casualty about my ribs, I lied about how it had happened.

"I never hit back and the only marks she suffered were bruises on her arms from where she'd hit me so hard. I had to get away because I was going to kill myself, or kill her. When she threatened me with a baseball bat, I grabbed it and for a split second I was going to strike her. I believe we would have both been in institutions of one kind or another if I hadn't dropped it and walked away."

3. "Oh dear, this reminds me of my soon to be husband. He too was getting abused in every form or fashion. He was getting hit for just breathing. ...His wife would absolutely beat the crap out of him if he didn't walk the right way in public or hold her hand at a certain time. She was also having several affairs; the only reason she kept him around and wouldn't leave was because he had allowed himself to be controlled by her. She knew she could control him, but not the affairs. That's why she stayed. When he stopped letting her control him, she couldn't take it and left."

4. "I met her when she was hired part-time in the building where I work. I immediately found her very charming and funny. She began pursuing me by leaving notes under my office door, and e-mailing me. Eventually, she began calling me at home. I was somehow not convinced by her pursuit, but I could not ignore her charm, and since I had been out of the dating market for some time, I figured it would be all right to take her out; what did I have to lose?

"So, we began to date. She really came on like a freight train; calling me a lot, terrific sex every day... She adored me and I was flattered. She told me I was the perfect person, that I had won her over, and I was really enjoying myself, and her.

"She did, however, seem somewhat insecure, which I figured was OK since we've all been there before, so it was no problem for me to give her a little reassurance; she'd relax soon enough. But it never really happened.

"It was becoming frustrating in some ways for me. When the phone rang, she'd say, 'Who was that? Your other girlfriend?' Of course, I'd tell her I had no other girlfriends, but it never seemed to be enough reassurance. And I was falling deeply in love. She literally OD'd me on everything I ever wanted.

"Compliments, praise, sex, comfort, and just plain old fun. The little quirks didn't bother me at all; no one's perfect...but some of these quirks stayed in the back of my mind: We'd spend a whole day together, but after I took her home, she'd call as soon as I got in the door. I would ask if she forgot something, but she would just say no. I figured she wanted to talk more, but something seemed odd. She would call and e-mail me quite often when I was at work, but if I ever called her, she'd seem suspicious or wonder why I was calling. She would seem jealous or suspicious if I talked to another woman, yet she thought nothing of talking to a myriad of men on her cell phone when we were out on dates. Of course, I brought up the double standard, and got accused of being jealous. Hmmmmm.

"One day though, she suddenly turned cold. She said I wasn't giving enough to her, I wasn't committed enough to her. I tried to tell her that while I certainly wasn't dating anyone else, nor did I wish to, I had to grow into things with her, and that as much as I wanted to be married, we would have to approach it realistically. She cut off the sex, and I wrote her a letter explaining that I was all hers, that I wanted to work on the relationship with her, and that I loved her very much. Things righted themselves again, and she began talking constantly about our future, encouraging me to make plans for us, and that someday we would be married. She told me over and over she wanted to have children with me, and this really rang my dinner bell. Sex now seemed like 'baby practice' to me, and it felt very close and loving.

"A blissful summer led to her having to go to Europe for six weeks to gain a credential, and I spent a month going everywhere with her while she prepared for her trip. By this time, I had met and become friends with her family and relatives, and I saw our future together, and it was a dream I was 100% committed to. One day, I took her to the airport and she vanished on a plane. I was so excited; tired from helping her get ready to leave, and so in love that I sat down and cried like a child.

"But my tears were for other things: a deep, buried sense of worry. I began to recall her comments to me over the past month; things which now were causing me to feel insecure. 'I love you and I want to spend the rest of my life with you...if I don't change my mind.' Ouchhh!

"Upon her arrival in Europe, she called several times, sounding like she missed me. I gave her reassurance, told her I loved her, and was waiting home for her; everything would be fine. Sensing that she missed me, I wanted her to feel comfortable. I sent her letters, some pictures, and a tape of our favorite songs, thinking they would keep her company until we were reunited. Oddly enough, she seemed to respond negatively; though she would thank me and encourage me to send more, somehow it didn't seem genuine. After two weeks of her being there, something changed drastically.

"Her voice was no longer light and sing-songy, it was a dull, flat monotone. When I would try to speak our private language of love with her, she would respond sarcastically. I asked if things were OK, and she assured me they were, but things got worse. I was receiving letters that expressed love, but her emails began to express doubts about the relationship: 'I don't know … sometimes I feel like I'm missing out on something...things are going so well I feel I have to question why … sometimes I feel nauseous when I think of us being together forever … I miss you but I don't miss you.' I was shocked, and called her. She assured me that nothing was wrong, that things would be normal when she returned, and that she just was going a little crazy over there. I bit my tongue, gave her some space, and hoped for the best.

"Going to the airport to pick her up upon her return, I was so excited I forgot to take clothes for the night we'd spend at her parent's house. Finally, she came through the gate. No hug, no kiss, no warm greeting. She dropped her bags and said, 'I hardly recognized you.' That night we fell into bed; she turned her back on me. She said she wasn't sure how much she loved me anymore. I was fighting back tears, and I was very close to getting up, getting dressed, and driving home, but of course I had promised to help her move the next day, and I felt I should keep my obligation. Maybe she'd feel better in the morning.

"After I had moved her into her new place the next day, nothing had changed. She wanted to sleep together, but no sex. She wanted to be with me constantly, but little affection was offered. If I offered it to her, she'd turn her head, or push me away. I was very hurt and upset and I tried to talk to her about it, but she kept insisting there was nothing wrong, that she needed to adjust to being back in the states, and things would be fine if I just shut up and stopped pressuring her."

"Things got worse.

"The verbal abuse began, hard. Insults, name-calling, accusations that I had cheated on her while she was away, and then the sex games began.

"She knew I was dying for any scrap of affection she'd offer, yet she would act incredibly seductive until I responded, and then turn to stone and tell me to get my hands off of her. She would call me and invite me over to have sex, yet when I arrived, she'd be mean and rude, and tell me, 'You don't get anything. I changed my mind.' I'd be furious, and though I kept my cool and didn't yell, I would say I did not like being treated this way. She would tell me I was too sensitive, that this was supposed to be funny, and it was proof that I wasn't her type. Remember, this was the woman who only two months ago was telling me over and over that she wanted to have children with me, and was encouraging me to make long-term plans and life changes for us. My confusion was so deep, I had no idea of what was happening, and I hid my tears from her; since when she saw them. I would be yelled at for 'feeling too much'.

"I tried to back away, but she would only pursue me more. Yet when I was with her, she was cold as ice. Her rages began. Another botched attempt at intimacy from me led to her rolling on the bed in her underwear screaming 'I hate you!!! I hate you!!!' I would leave the house...and she would call acting as if nothing had happened, asking me to go out for coffee. My mind was reeling, and I had no idea what was real and what was not. I could not trust my own perceptions, and though I was hurting, she would insist I had nothing to feel hurt about. One night, as we were going to dinner, she came up from behind me, grabbed my private parts, and said 'Just ... because ... I ... can't. It took a few minutes to get my bearings from the shock of this violation. She said she didn't care. She laughed when I was crying. She'd blame me for being angry at her insults.

"After three months of this, I had to make my exit. I pursued my own interests, kept to my own schedule (instead of hers), and concentrated on protecting myself, but it was very difficult to keep away from her; I missed her terribly, and her still calling me non-stop gave me a false sense of hope. Little did I know that at the time, she had rekindled an old romance with someone who never knew she and I were ever dating. She refused to let me go or tell me the truth. I even took her on a vacation where she spent the whole weekend making excuses as to why she was 'untouchable'.

"Things dwindled away to nothing; she slowly took away things until the relationship died of attrition. My dreams of having children with her were dead and gone, and when I saw her once I grabbed and held her and told her how much I wanted to have a baby with her. She stood there like a statue and said nothing. I cried and cried for months.

"She continued to call me constantly and pursue me for over a year, but anytime things began to get close, she'd turn to stone, or blame me for being 'too mushy'. The entire time she was in a relationship with someone else, and pursuing other relationships as well. She would tell me she missed me and wanted to get back together, but I told her that was not possible unless she could own up and make amends for the past ... but she never would. I never received a single verbal apology from her for anything. If I didn't give in, she'd try the sexual route, sending me X-rated emails until we made plans to get together, then she'd cancel at the last second ... and then she'd blame me for being angry about it. Why didn't I just come over and 'make her do it'??? One night she called and wanted me to insult her and make her feel helpless. But I refused.

"The last time I heard from her, she wrote to make small talk. I told her I was not interested in talking about the weather, and she responded by telling me she had a new, 'perfect' boyfriend. How insensitive. I was livid at this response. Then I later found out from a mutual friend about the cheating she did, how she insisted I be 100% devoted to her, while she always explored other options. This girl cared about no one but herself."

"I know she is poison, and she has not changed at all. How could she fall out of love so fast? I will never know. That's easy. This person has no clue about love. She was never there...This lady can't handle the 'pressure' of attachments. She feels like she's being choked, even though at one level, she does want a commitment. I am still angry at her, but I never take that anger out on anyone else. I have dated others, but have not been in another love relationship since, and I wonder if I ever will. I was betrayed by the only person who said she wanted to have children with me. I know intime, things will be better. But I am still haunted by many horrifying incidents, and the memory of the sweetest person I'd ever known, whom I loved more than anyone I'd ever know, who turned on me...just when things were going well.

"As a 'P.S.', I should add that I found an interesting dovetail between my story and the story you posted, my ex, after she changed, only seemed to show interest when she feared losing me. Sort of a didn't-want-me-but-didn't-want-anyone-else-to-have-me situation."

"I also wanted to say that one of the reasons I felt it was OK to venture into things was that early on she was very vulnerable and feared me hurting her; in turn, I figured that anyone who was so fearful of being hurt would not do the same to someone. I didn't know that all her accusations of me cheating were her projection. She was a compulsive liar, plain and simple. I loved her and trusted her, and believed what she was telling me.

"I left out a large section of my story where after she changed, she tried to manipulate me into beating her (by hitting me and challenging me to 'show her who's the boss'), but I refused to do it. Unfortunately, this made me a wimp in her eyes."

5. "Nobody believed me ... She got away with legally abusing my daughter physically and emotionally... I got sole custody but only after I had been completely investigated and scapegoat/-stereotyped. One of the case workers wept openly at realizing her failure. They realized my daughter and I were telling the truth much too late."

6. "My mother engaged in constant nit-picking, put downs, petty criticism, withholding of affection, insinuations, spleen venting, complaining and complaining about me to others, occasional silent treatment and frequent negative comparisons with other girls my own age; 'Why can't you be more like so and so.' To the world she presented the image of the perfect mother and hostess and I would be confused and angry when my school friends would say to me, 'Your mother is so nice, she's such a good person, you are so mean about her.' I was frequently punished, often physically, for 'being bad'. Sometimes I was not aware of what I was supposed to have done and other times my older brother pointed the finger at me for 'bad things' he had done and I was punished for those. Protesting only increased the punishment.

"Day in day out my life at home consisted of my older brother 'sledging' me; that is, whispering insults and verbal abuse to me when no-one else could hear, and my mother constantly marginalizing me within the family. If I ever cried as a result of punishment I was told that I was weak and unable to control myself, could not be trusted to tell the truth and was therefore guilty and deserving of punishment. My mother frequently told me that I was undeserving both of material gifts and friendship from others. This adversely affected me in adulthood for a long time. My father suffered from high-blood pressure and had a short temper. My mother often used this to her advantage to provoke him into turning on me. If I displayed any insolence or resistance towards her (which I did often!) she would go and get my father and manipulate him into anger. I grew to become frightened of my father (especially since he doled out the physical punish- ments) and this process detrimentally affected my relationship with him (and other authority figures) from adolescence until his death when I was 29.

"I am not a weak person. I naively never learned to back down for my own good and always stood up for myself but I was no match for my mother. She could reduce me to tears in seconds which was something I became increasingly ashamed of as I approached adulthood. I left home for good when I was 20 and went to live overseas exhausted and struggling terribly to find my feet in the adult world."

7. "Below is a brief description I wrote for myself about my life with my mother growing up. It has taken a long time for me to gain any clarity about this relationship. It is crazy-making.

"THE RULE

Every house has its unspoken rules. In my house growing up the unspoken rule was that I would never acknowledge my mother's bad behavior toward me and in return she would buy me something after she had acted-out, a dress or a pair of shoes. I never agreed to this rule. For a long time I didn't even realize there was a rule.

"My input into this matter was never solicited or even desired. This was the rule, accept it or pay the consequences. The consequences could be very unpleasant. One did not break this rule even by defending one's basic rights of dignity. This was viewed as criticism, and criticism was never tolerated. The consequences for breaking the rule or, God forbid, mentioning that she was out of control ranged from physical punishment, to screaming, to grounding and always they included shunning. Groveling was expected to regain her good graces.

"Anything could set her off. Of course, misbehavior always worked, but sometimes it could be walking into a room at the wrong time or saying something or making noise, or laughing. Sometimes my dad and I talking would set her off. One never knew. This went on for years. I, of course, was powerless about any of this – her behavior or the consequences I paid.

"Over time it became clear that my dad was pretty powerless himself. Sometimes he could calm things down, but not often. My mother would rage until she stopped. Her moods controlled the house- hold.

"Sometimes her moods were good and she was fun. She was like The Girl With The Curl, When she was good she was very, very good, but when she was bad she was horrid.

"The most interesting, difficult, ironic and unsettling aspect of all this is that outside the home my mother was very much a milktoast. She was two different people. I didn't realize this or understand it for a very long time. My mother would do anything for anyone. She would walk on broken glass for her friends. She was deferential to people she perceived as her betters to the point that as I got older it embarrassed me. She saved all her anger, frustration, fears and God knows what else for her daughter and her husband. The rest of the world viewed her as some kind of saint or at the least a pussycat. At home she was more like a caged lion.

"This was the rule and I played by it as best I could. As a child you are not aware of how things are affecting you. In my case, I was an only, which made this even more pronounced. I didn't think about my situation. I reacted to it. I coped as best I could. It wasn't until I was a teenager that I began to really get an inkling of what was happening.

"It was then, I believe, that the ambivalence that I feel toward my mother to this day was born. There is nothing worse than this kind of ambivalence. It wreaks havoc with your emotions. It is the classic love/hate syndrome. It is a no-win situation, a double bind laced with knotty knots. It is mucky, murky, inky. It can drive you stark raving mad. It has almost done me in several times.

"I don't think there is ever a good resolution to ambivalent feelings toward a parent. Emotions run too deep. The best one can hope for is an emotional distance that keeps the seesaw of emotions at bay. I am 56 and still working on the appropriate distance. I have noticed that in recent years it is harder for me to maintain real closeness. I am fairly certain that whatever it is I feel for my mother, it isn't love. I suspect that what I do feel is gratitude for what she has done for me. I also feel a lot of anger. I am particularly angry that she, in my opinion, has never been accountable for her behavior toward me. I don't think my father ever experienced accountability either, but since he is long dead, only she knows the answer to that. Truthfully, I wish I didn't feel the gratitude – the old ambivalence again, receding but still present.

"What about forgiveness? Ah, so much easier said than done. How does one forgive a person whose actions resulted in years of depression, suicidal tendencies and feelings of failure. If I live two lifetimes I will never be able to sort out how my childhood environment affected my life. Therapy has helped, but the answers are an intertwining of my personality and my environment, destined I believe never to be fully understood. The best I can hope for is a good life going forward and a reasonable comfort level with the dreaded ambivalence. I continue to work on it."

8. "My mother always used to beat me with a razor strap and tell me how ashamed of me she was. She was ashamed of my Southern accent; she was ashamed of my grades. ... When I was thirteen, I started messing around with boys. When my mother found out, she started freaking whenever I'd get near my stepfather. Nobody ever hugged in my house, so I never touched him, but she'd still accuse me of trying to turn him on when all I'd be doing was sitting around in my gym clothes or asking him to help me put on a necklace. When I got pregnant at fourteen, she called me a whore and whipped me with an extension cord so bad that I still have the scars. But I kept running around because at least it was a little affection. All a guy would have to do is walk me home from church and I'd fall in love. When you don't get love at home, you look for it anywhere you can."

9. "I was married to a female sociopath for almost 18 yrs. the things we found out about her and her double life! The saying 'Love is blind,' is true. She showed no feelings even while watching a tear jerker of a movie. In a 7-hour trial over custody, she was made to read out loud a 3-page love letter she wrote to one of her boyfriends 22 yrs younger than her! – showed no feelings or emotions! My oldest son testified against her. It seems the only way to hurt a sociopath is through money. I feel so bad for my sons, they lived all this and they didn't deserve it! I had to put a restraining order on her when she attacked me in front of my sons. My oldest said to me later, 'Dad, I don't know how you didn't just beat the hell out of her!' I said, 'I can't raise you from a jail cell, can I?

"I feel like the whole thing was like a damn soap opera! When I got custody, and she had to pay me child support, she lost it; she destroyed my motorcycle with a hammer and threw paint all over my javelin. I didn't care; all I wanted was my sons.

"She is with a ex-con now who is 13 years younger than her, and I thank god every day we are away from her!

"The sociopath will lie to your face without blinking an eye! It is scary as hell! There has to be something missing in the genes or something.

"It's been almost 10 years since all that happened; and sometimes the pain comes back when you try to understand it all. But these people will destroy themselves. My sons want nothing to do with her at all; and haven't seen her in almost ten years. She has missed out on so much and doesn't even know she will be a grandmother! In a way, you have to feel sorry for her. Even these people have a choice; they are adults, not little kids."

10. COURT CASE: from "The Guardian," Steven Morris / Fri, 20 Apr 2007

Psychopath Training! Women laughed as they forced toddlers to take part in 'dog fight'

A mother and her three daughters who forced two toddlers to take part in a "dog fight" and filmed it walked free from court yesterday.

The women, including the children's mother, goaded the tearful brother and sister to punch each other and even use a magazine and hairbrush as weapons. When the boy, who was in a nappy, stopped fighting they called him a "wimp" and "bloody faggot".

Passing sentence at Plymouth crown court, Judge Francis Gilbert said the video taken of the fight was "shocking". He said: "You laughed at them, you mocked them, you swore at them. You compelled them to hit each other even though they clearly did not want to. You were cruel, callous, clearly causing the children to hurt each other for your own pleasure."

He singled out the children's grandmother, who had told police that she saw nothing wrong with what they had done as it would "toughen them up".

But the judge was persuaded not to jail them immediately, instead giving the four a one-year suspended sentence and ordering them to do 100 hours of community work.

The court was told how the mother of the children, Zara Care, 21, and her sisters, Serenza Olver, 29, and Danielle Olver, 19, had met at the home of their mother, Carole Olver, 48.

They formed a circle in the living room around the children, a three-year-old girl and a boy of two, and urged them to fight while Zara Care capturing the whole episode on video.

In the film up to six adults, including a man, are seen chatting and smoking. As the two children run around the room, one of the women can be heard to say to them, "Do you want to play?" before pushing the boy towards the girl.

The children start circling and slapping each other – goaded by four women, who can be seen and heard laughing.

The boy, who is wearing just a nappy and a T-shirt, is then floored by a blow from his sister and lies on the floor crying.

After clambering on to an armchair to escape, he buries his head under a cushion but a woman in the room tells him: "Get up – don't be a wimp all your life."

He staggers to his feet and punches his sister in the mouth, and, as she falls to the ground, is encouraged to kick her.

A female voice says: "And again, whilst she's down, boot her."

He then tries to leave the room but an older child blocks his path and the girl again runs over and pummels his back with her fists.

The boy is then told by a female voice: "Get up and punch her, you bloody faggot."

He tries to refuse, but then grabs a large black hairbrush and begins to beat his sister, while a woman is heard to say: "He needs weapons, she just has a fist."

The girl is caught in the mouth by the brush and begins to scream and lifts her arm in the air, appealing for help from an unseen adult – but is turned away.

At this point, an older child in the room can be heard to say: "Is it our turn yet?" The film ends with the two toddlers screaming and crying, and an adult saying: "That's enough."

During the video the women hurl a stream of orders, such as "jump on him", "kick her" and "hit his face".

The word "punch" is heard more than 20 times. The video came to light after the children's father, a serving soldier, returned from Iraq and decided to show his parents footage from the video camera the women used.

He had expected it to feature the children playing but he was horrified to come upon the eight-minute film of them fighting.

David Gittins, prosecuting, said that the father compared what he saw to a "dog fight" and was reduced to tears. He subsequently went to social services, who called in the police.

The children's grandmother, a mother of eight, showed no remorse when she was interviewed, insisting it would "harden" them up, it was stated.

The judge criticized her for still seeming defiant. The three other defendants wept as the offence was described.

Defending the women, who admitted child cruelty offences, Rupert Taylor said they were not wicked.

The three daughters had never been in trouble with the police before. But they were ill-educated, had few advantages in life, and did not realise what they were doing was abhorrent.

Mr. Taylor said that although they had treated the infants so badly, family was important for them and they were all very close. "They are ashamed and frightened," he said.

The judge said the "horror" of what they did meant it was tempting to jail them.

But the judge added that he took into account the fact that two of the women, Serenza and Danielle, had children of their own to look after – and also said that Zara's biggest punishment was that her children had been taken out of her care and were now being looked after by other relatives.

11. COURT CASE: "news.com.au", Liza Kappelle / Mon, 23 Apr 2007

Into the mind of the psychopath: Girls 'just felt right' murdering friend

TWO teenagers who wanted to experience murder told police it "felt right" to strangle a friend and bury her body in a shallow grave beneath her West Australian home.

The 17-year-old girls, who cannot be named due to their age, today faced a sentencing hearing in Perth Children's Court after pleading guilty to murdering Eliza Jane Davis in the small coal mining town of Collie on June 18, 2006.

As the girls sat stony-faced in court today, Prosecutor Simon Stone said they had confessed that after partying with Eliza on the Saturday night they decided to kill her.

"Sunday morning me and (her) woke up, and we were just talking, and for some reason we just decided to kill her," one of the girls told police in her interview.

"We just did it because we felt like it; it is hard to explain," the other girl said.

"I knew we had wanted to kill someone before.

"We knew it was wrong, but it didn't feel wrong at all; it just felt right."

The girls planned their attack and changed into old clothes.

One of them snuck up behind Eliza as she was reading, wrapped speaker wire twice around her throat and quickly tightened it as the other held her down, trying to press a chemical soaked cloth into her mouth.

"She started not being able to get her breath, and we just kept going," one of the girls said. "She was just yelling at us, 'What the f**k, what are you doing' ... 'Oh you freaks, what's wrong with you psychos.'"

Mr. Stone said they chose to strangle Eliza because one of them had to return to Perth that afternoon and they wanted a quick and "non-messy" killing.

"As our friend, we did not really want her to suffer," one told police.

"We didn't really expect to get away with it. We were willing to take the risk."

The girls regretted the fuss the killing caused but neither felt remorse for their dead friend, Mr. Stone said.

"If she had died another way it probably would have bothered me ... but it just did not," one girl said.

The girls reported Eliza missing after they buried her and pretended to help her family look for the dead girl.

The girls turned themselves in several days later, walking into separate police stations and directing authorities to where they buried her body.

Mr. Stone told the court the girls had no remorse and were holding back on the reason behind their cold-blooded, premeditated, sadistic killing.

"It is a mystery, your honour, what happened."

He said the girls had discussed killing someone else and one had prepared for homicide by killing two kittens.

"Whilst together (they) will continue to pose some risk to others in custody."

Mr. Stone called for sentences of life in prison.

III: CHILDREN

BOYS

1. "Eddie only loves me when he wants to – on his own terms. Once I was stooping over the oven and he ran up behind me full tilt and threw his arms around my legs. He was great at wanting to hug me at very inconvenient times. Well, I practically shot right into the oven. I told my husband, 'This is like Hansel and Gretel and guess who I am! And I don't like the part of being a witch even a little bit!'"

2. "The detective confronted me... 'You'd con your own father, Frank.'

I already had. My father was the mark for the first score I ever made. Dad possessed the one trait necessary in the perfect pigeon, blind trust, and I plucked him for $3,400. I was 15 at the time."

3. "My son could walk up to perfect strangers and within 5 minutes have them wishing that he was their son."

4. "The only way I could hold and rock Jim when he was small was if I clutched him desperately to my breast. And he had to be in one of those baby blankets, so tightly wrapped that his arms and legs couldn't get free. If I didn't do that, he would grab the arms of the chair and try to pull himself free from me! This was when he was only about four months old!"

5. "Do you know hard it is to hug a board? That is exactly how it felt when you tried to hug Danny. He stiffened and pulled away from you. I guess he just didn't know what it was to love."

6. "One parent told of her son's repeated fights at school. Whenever the child got an opportunity he would bully someone, usually smaller than he, into a fight. He was a better fighter (he had a lot of experience) and inevitably would send the other child home with a bloody nose or black eye. Teachers said he enjoyed hurting other children, humiliating them."

7. "I feel guilty for bringing one into this world to prey on others.

And there isn't a thing I can say or do to help him. I don't want to sit by and watch him lie and manipulate his way into someone's life."

8. "My son had zero attachment to me as a baby. He never acknowledged me, never once called me mommy, no eye contact, bizarre behaviour. I remained single until he was 9. Then I made another horrible mistake. I got involved with yet another one of 'them.' This one being much smarter than the last. [From him], I have beautiful twin daughters. They are quite normal!"

9. "I also have a son 18 years of age. He has exhibited problems since childhood. He also has rages, lies, manipulates. He is now off to a very good college and is extremely bright which actually makes it more lethal. He just hasn't been right since birth. He is no longer living with me and I pray he does well in life. My therapist said I did everything I possibly could for him including therapy since age 3."

10. "My son will be 4 in January. He has had an aggressive temperament since he was around 2 years. He was in full-time daycare until I quit work recently in July with the birth of our daughter. Even in daycare we had constant visits with the director about his behavior (biting, hitting, etc. of other kids his age). He has just started preschool this year and has been exhibiting similar behavior. He throws toys, pushes and hits his other classmates. His teachers do a good job of keeping me informed of his behavior on a day to day basis and he has had some good days. They do place in him in time-out in the classroom for bad behavior, talk to him, and he has also been sent to the preschool director's office. Recently though, he is back to his terrible behavior both at home and at school. We set limits at home and use discipline techniques such as time-out and spanking, but he just doesn't seem to care. He laughs when he is spanked and sits in time-out until we tell him to come out (usually 3-4 minutes). He is fine but then starts right back to the bad behavior. I always have to keep a very watchful eye on him because he will run off (yesterday towards the road with a car coming.) I dread birthday parties because they always end with us hauling him out of there for bad behavior."

11. "I have a son who just turned 4 in November. He is very bad lot;

he doesn't listen, he has a smart mouth; and he does what he wants whenever he wants, and pitches a fit because I won't allow it. I don't know what to do, he is very smart on other terms he knows all his colors and shapes and what everything is around the house he isn't in school yet because he is still not potty trained I have tried everything he will not poopoo in the potty, I have tried sitting him on there, telling him he can get candy or a toy after he goes to the potty like a big boy. Am I doing something wrong here? He will pee in the potty every now and then; but I don't understand why he won't do the other? He was behind with everything else he learned to do also: like crawling, walking, talking, and now potty training. I feel like this is all my fault. What should I do?"

12. "My 6-year-old son has had a problem with authority, following directions, doing what is asked of him, meltdowns, and back talking since he was 4 or 5 yrs old. It started in preschool, got worse in kindergarten; and now that he is in 1st, it seems to get worse. He knows better. Now he is stealing from school. He is very bright, but hates to TRY to do anything. He would rather throw a fit, or say he's too tired, or thirsty, or he can't. He puts more effort into manipulation, and lies than anything. On the flip side, he can be the most loving, kind kid ever. Everyone tends to like him. He smiles and it's all ok. We often refer to him as our bipolar son, but honestly I think that's just an excuse. We have two other kids, 3 & 8. The 8-yr-old has had some behavior problems, larger than his peers, but each year he seems to get better. This is not the case with the 6-yr-old. Attention at all cost is his motto. The 3-yr-old is the only girl and does seem to get a lot of attention, and his problems seemed to start when she was 1-year-old. Before that he was one of the best kids ever. We need some help. We have tried all the rewards, charts, time outs, gutting the room, I even had him wear a I AM A THIEF sign because he won't stop stealing. He even takes karate; I heard the discipline in that helps. He has sooooo much potential, but with all the problems it doesn't shine through. I'm sure we could be more consistent, and we are trying. Sometimes my husband works out of town. He has everything a kid could want, and more. Please give us some insight on what to do.

Thank you. At wit's end."

13. "He hurts his brother constantly, hitting, scratching, biting and worse. He is supervised, but does this in front of me. He does the same thing to me when I try to give him a time-out or discipline him."

14. "Anything he gets a hold of is broken almost immediately. When we tell them to go to bed, they strip the bedclothes off the beds and physically take their mattresses off the beds. He repeatedly does things he has been told not to. He coerces his brother to do things, so he can say he didn't do it. 'Connor did it,' is the phrase I hear most often. Even when I see my 3-year-old do something, he denies it, blames his brother or starts hitting, kicking and spitting on me. He lies constantly and this concerns me because he has a clear understanding of the difference between reality and make-believe and dreams. We've had to remove everything from their room except their beds because he would not stay out of their dressers and played with their toys in the middle of the night. We were afraid they would get hurt. No matter what I say or do, he refuses to listen to or obey me. He fights me at every turn.

15. "Our 10- year-old son fits traits of ODD perfectly and began showing those signs almost from day 1. Extremely bright, imaginative and verbal. The usual behavior mod. 'systems' (time out, credits, withdrawal of privileges) not effective. He has been increasingly violent/destructive at home, though not at school or elsewhere. Tried Risperdol but discontinued since improvement seemed minor in proportion to risks. Tried NHA (Howard Glasser), again only moderate and short-lived improvement. Am now exploring possible food triggers (wheat, sugar, dairy, chemical additives) but it's hard to get compliance with elimination of foods when he's at school (we send a good lunch, but he trades, gets treats, etc.).

"He once gleefully spit over the balcony onto people's heads at the museum, right in front of his friends! We left immediately. As always, no remorse. Just sort of this calm satisfaction.

"Son has exceptionally loving 5-year-old sister whom he takes great satisfaction in tormenting. We have taken pains to avoid showing anything that could be construed as preferential treatment toward her, but still he HATES her and has the verbal skills to tell her so in very illustrative terms, constantly, from the time he wakes up. Classically, he shows no remorse, never accepts blame, lies naturally, is selfish, 'lazy' and is unmoved by the anguish or misfortunes of others. He sometimes remarks that he doesn't like his appearance, and is unwilling to try new things for fear he won't instantly be good at it. (Of course he won't admit to these feelings of insecurity.)

"All along, I have take some consolation in the fact that his behavior is usually fine (or at least age-appropriate) at school and when at friends' homes. He seems to reserve all the horror for his parents. Also, I take some consolation in the fact that he seems genuinely sorry and loving when he accidentally bumps his pet bunny (as opposed to torturing animals, I mean). And I HAVE seen him be kind to his sister when he doesn't realize we are listening, although he still never DOES anything for someone else unless there's something in it for him.

"So, here's the question: now that he's approaching adolescence (he's only 10 but shows some early signs of puberty), and he seems to also fit the characteristics of sociopathic personality disorder (TOTAL lack of conscience, NO empathy), what are our prospects for this child?

16. "My four-year-old got into my son's room yesterday, when I thought he was in his bed a sleep, but he wasn't. He killed my son's hamster with an antenna. There is no abuse in the home. Why would he do something like this? He just turned 4."

17. "My son is 17 months old. If he does not get whatever he wants, he will scream and hit his head against the wall or his mother or brother whoever is next to him, or hurt himself. He will scream and cry when he is put in his bed in the evening. He seems too violent. We pay all the attentions he wants. In contrast, his 5-year-old brother is well behaved and very gentle. We are loving, professional parents. There is no history of violence of children in our family. Are these passing behaviours, and will growing up overcome this type of behaviour?"

18. "My 2 stepsons are in the house 24/7. The oldest is our worst problem. He is 13, very angry and antisocial. He is loud, rude, and disrespectful to everyone in the home. He irritates his 10-year-old brother all day. He has no friends and when not in school, just watches TV. He insists on being the center of attention and argues everything anyone ever says to him (I realize this may be due to being 13) but it is excessive. When he speaks; it's either to criticize others, complain about anything that's not his idea or about him, or compliment himself. When disciplined, he throws temper tantrums just like a 3 year old. Yelling, screaming, face turns red, his eyeballs begin to wobble. If we continue to discipline him he will 'disconnect' close his eyes, fall to the floor in a fetal-like position and stay that way until he passes out/falls asleep...and it is impossible to wake him up. He is constantly 'buzzing', always tapping, making noises, loud squeals, animal-like noises. He has to be corrected everyday for the same poor behaviors, he never learns. My wife tries to stand behind me, but is unaccustomed to strict behavior and eventually her soft-heart allows her to give-in which completely ruins any progress we make. I insist on only 4 rules and they are

non-negotiable: Be kind, nice, polite, and respectful to everyone. I lead by example, but it is ignored and mocked. Her boys will only come to me when they need something, and I am always there to help and support them, every time without fail, but they never show any gratitude, just take what I give them and carry on the rudeness. Of course, I am now getting resentful. Because our marriage is falling apart, my wife now thinks we should give up and send the oldest boy back to where they moved from (1200 miles away) to live with his grandparents, which is what he wants. Their dad lives nearby us but is a horrible role model, and my wife has been keeping him out of their lives. Now here's an interesting point: The oldest boy does great in school, gets 'A's in Honors Classes, and 'A's in conduct. Always has been a great student. But when he walks through the door, all hell breaks loose. Is sending him away going to help him, us, our family? I'm at the point now, where I actually think this is best. The middle child is having trouble, too. But he internalizes his anger. He basically ignores anything I say to him and clings to his mom. We are down to one child left. Now what?"

19. "My child is 3 years old and his behavior scares me at times. His behavior has been getting worse and worse no matter what I do to discipline him he won't get the message and he does it again. For example, my son has a short temper I already know that since he was very little but he has become violent towards me and anyone who tries to tell him to stop being bad. My son fights with his cousins like he was a 10-year-old. He is also aggressive violent towards other kids too. My son knows that he's behavior will get him punished and doesn't seem to care that's what bothers me the most. I have tried to talk to him about it and he seems to understand but he does it again. Time- out is like a game to him and mean or nice just doesn't work. I really feel like he has issues but I don't know what kind or how serious. I thought of sending him to pre-school programs or summer activities but I'm truly scared how he will act with other kids and people and how bad he will embarrass me by being bad in public. He really loses it when he doesn't get his way, like a new toy or something other kids have, he acts like everything should be only his. Doesn't like to share anything and he overreacts when I try to discipline him. How worse can it get?"

20. "I haven't seen or heard from my son in 2 years. From the night I 'unmasked' him it has been both a mixture of never-ending grief and profound relief. The grief never goes away because, after all, he is my son and I will always love him. I wish I could say the grief gets better. I can't. There are times when the pain is just a little duller and there is some respite; and there are times when the pain is as acute as an open wound. Birthdays (his) and holidays are the hardest.

"I live with the knowledge that the day will more than likely come that I will get the phone call that every parent dreads, and I will in all probability have to bury my son. His choice of lifestyle almost guarantees this. I agonize over this and wonder ahead of time if I will ever be able to forgive myself for walking away from him. I worry if he's cold. I worry if he's hungry or sick. Sometimes the not knowing is worse than knowing. It's a catch-22 situation. If I do know that he is sick or in trouble my mother instincts are to contact him and try once again to help or somehow make it better. Common sense tells me that I cannot. I cannot open myself up to him ever again. He knows my weaknesses and as you all know would not hesitate to use them against me.

"For years I lived with the verbal and emotional abuse. I have listened to him rant and rave against me saying things to me that no mother should ever have to hear from her child. He has told me that he can't wait for the day that I die. That he will spit on my grave. He has called me unspeakable names and physically threatened me. He has also written me heartbreaking letters of apology, promising that he was going to get his life together and make me proud of him. I have watched him cry real (or so I thought) tears because his life was so messed up. I have comforted him and I have loved him and I have forgiven him time and time again only to have him turn around and stab me in the heart when he didn't get the thing he wanted from me or hear the words he wanted to hear. He has cost me thousands of dollars. He has laughed in my face at my tears of hurt and mocked my sadness.

"In the two years since he has been out of my life there has been so much sadness in my heart and a hole that will never completely close; but there has also been a certain amount of peace as well. For the first time I can hear the phone ring and not dread answering it for fear that it will be him with another traumatic tale of how he's in trouble again and it's not his fault – How he quit his job because he was the only one doing any work and everybody was out to get him; how the current love of his life has broken up with him; how the car is broken down and he doesn't have the money to fix it, and how can he work if he doesn't have a car. The list goes on and on. For the first time I can live my life without the utter chaos that he

221

brings with him wherever he goes. I can try to enjoy a Christmas without the underlying tension that he brings into a room with him. Speaking of Christmas, he managed to spoil the last Christmas I had with my father before he died. I can only remember one Christmas that he didn't create a scene before the day was over.

"I have said many times that in a way his death would be easier to accept. It would at least be a cleaner kind of grief because death is final. When you have a psychopath in your life as long as they are alive they manage to taint your life either up close and personal or from a distance through other family members or friends. Even though he is physically distant he is never out of my thoughts."

21. "Another subject, serving time for fraud, told us that as a child he would put a noose around the neck of a cat, tie the other end of the string to the top of a pole, and bat the cat around the pole with a tennis racket. He said that his sister raised puppies and he would kill the ones she didn't want to keep. 'I'd tie them to a rail and use their heads for baseball practice,' he said, smiling slightly.

"Cruelty to other children – including siblings – is often part of the young psychopath's inability to experience the sort of empathy that checks normal people's impulses to inflict pain, even when enraged. 'The shocking things he did to his baby sister's doll felt like warnings, but we brushed them aside,' one mother told me. 'But when he actually tried to smother his sister in her crib and snipped the skin of her neck with a pair of scissors, we realized with horror that we should have trusted our worst intuitions from the start.'"

22. "The difference between being married or dating a psychopath and parenting a psychopath is both the same and so very different. The difference lies in your ability to divorce a spouse or break up with a lover. How do you divorce a child? How do you divorce a person you gave birth to and nurtured and loved with all your heart? How do you make other people understand why you can no longer see or keep in touch with that child? It goes against everything anyone has ever believed about being a parent. Your child is your child and that is a bond like no other. ...I'm not saying my pain is worse than yours. Pain is pain. I'm just saying that the pain a mother feels when she knows that there is nothing she can do for her child is excruciating. I was once told by a psychiatrist that the best way I could deal with my son was to very lovingly, very gently and very firmly walk away. I have done this. It hurts.

"If I can be of help to just one mother or father to feel that they are not alone and they are not the only parent who has a 'love/hate' relationship with their child then maybe this whole situation I found myself in will be easier to bear. It would be my wish to help parents understand that they are not responsible for what their child has become. It would also be my wish to help them on the road to forgiving themselves because there is so much guilt involved. Our children see to that. I would like to help another parent understand that it's alright to dislike their child to the point that it sometimes borders on hate even as you continue to love that child with every fiber in your body. I think that just by letting other parents know that they are not alone would go a long way toward accomplishing this. Sometimes just knowing that you're not alone is enough but I also understand that some people need more. They need a place to express their anger as well as their hurt and not be judged for their feelings. It's hard for the average parent to understand our feelings because after all, this is your child you're talking about, and it just isn't natural to feel that way about your child. What I have had to learn to accept is that no, it isn't natural but we're not talking about an ordinary child either. I have had to learn that my child isn't normal and never will be and there is nothing I can do to fix it.

"There's no medicine he can take. There's no therapy to make him better. He is a predator and that will never change. Finally and most importantly, to me anyway, I have learned that while I can never fix my child I can fix me. I can truly understand what a psychopath is and through understanding I can better protect myself from this familiar stranger that I gave birth to. I can't change who he is or what he is but I can change how I react to him. I also understand that what works for me doesn't necessarily work for everyone. We all have to find our own way of dealing with these children.

"There is no right way or wrong way but there is a way. We just have to find it and hopefully with each other's help we will."

23. "We have learned to deal with him unemotionally as ASPD find emotional people scary. We have learned to be tough and to not allow others to malign us for our 'harsh attitudes'. We have learned to deal with him with our own best interest at heart because nothing we do will change him or his behavior. We have learned to never show any real depth of feelings for him because he interprets this as weakness and will exploit it. We only deal with him matter-of-factly. We have learned that, although this is not his fault and he is mentally ill, he is also dangerous to those around him and their protection must come first. We have learned the definition of true powerlessness. We have learned that to love a child with ASPD can be deadly both to them and to yourself. We have had to learn to start trying to kill that emotion as much as possible for our own survival. We have had to accept he will, most likely, end up in prison or dead and can only hope he doesn't hurt too many along the way. We have learned we can only do the best we can because there will be very little help for us along the way and probably none for him."

24. "What can be done with a 17-yr-old with this situation? My son fits a lot of this description...it took us probably 4 years when he was little to get him to brush his teeth without an argument every night about it. That pattern remains. He isn't interested in anything but TV, computer games, and his cell phone. Well, he has a new girlfriend, but she's not a positive influence. He's become more secretive, more withdrawn from our family, and he's become a liar, which is something new...even when he was at his worst, he was honest with us. Now, not so much. I took away his cellphone last night. He won't follow the rules on bedtime, and texting (we just don't allow it because of cost, and he has no job, so he can't pay for it). We got him a phone so we could keep in touch as a family...but for him, it's a right, I guess. He sits us down like he's the parent, and tells us what we need to think about...plays games with us. Wants us to tell him what we think we should do about the situation we have at home, so he can then figure out a 'solution'. Last night, I had enough, and took his phone, which in anger he threw on the floor. I just don't know how to address this whole thing. Adding structure? It's never worked in the past...and any structure we have added has always ended up being just TOO much to maintain. It lasts for a month, or maybe 2, but after that amount of daily arguing...and I mean daily, how can you keep on at that level? Every day...the same issues. If we were to ground him for every offence, he'd never leave the home. I am convinced that he'd just never have an opportunity to see anything but our 4 walls...because he just never stops. I'm at a loss. I don't see hope anywhere."

25. "H. sounds like my son (who's half his age: 8 years old) right down to the 'getting in the tub and falling asleep with the water running over him' bit. The comment above by a teacher that these are just kids behaving badly who need better parenting, is also a typical reaction to my boy. We have reached the point of virtual social isolation. Even he prefers to bury himself in one or two preferred solitary activities than having to deal with the constant scolding. He longs for friends but seems unwilling to learn the social skills we try to teach. One of his hobbies has become pretty much an obsession and is the source of most of our conflicts because he doesn't want to stop to do anything else. Homework and bedtime are the biggest battles. Mornings I've kind of mastered, because I just lead him around from one thing to the next; awake or asleep – it doesn't much matter to me! Many days we don't get to do anything fun because all the time is taken up fighting over basics such as meals, homework, showers etc. I have no idea how a schedule helps ODD [oppositional defiance disorder] parents because it has never helped mine other than to serve as a focus of conflict. Family meetings do help but the effect of the rewards/consequences we discuss is limited. That's simply because the most meaningful reward/consequence for this little boy is getting/not getting his own way. Nothing else even seems to come close to being meaningful and that makes parenting a nearly-impossible task. I could take away or grant every coveted possession or every beloved activity – all that would do is make him happier or angrier; it just doesn't seem to translate into actual positive behavior changes. Praise affects his mood, but also has little effect on actual behavior. It sometimes seems to me that when he achieves something positive, it must have taken some Herculean effort, because once he gets praised he seems to relax his guard and fall right back into the cycle of 'resist-fight-fight some more'. Strangely enough, some days he'll be an absolute angel. I still haven't figured out why or what other than God's grace is responsible for the occasional perfect day (usually either at school or at home, rarely both places on the same day). For those who think ODD is simply a label for kids who lack good parenting: all I can say is, I used to think that too until my son came along to teach me otherwise."

26. "My 15-year-old stepson has Anti-Social Personality Disorder (ASPD). However, until he is 18 years old he cannot be 'officially' diagnosed nor treated as such. Consequently, he is not being treated at all. Not that that makes much difference. There does not seem to be any hope for him. Everything I read says it is basically incurable and untreatable.

"I was the first one to realize the truth when he was about 12. Having been, in the past, a practicing psychotherapist, certain behaviors caught my attention; lack of appropriate emotional response, unwillingness to take on any responsibility, ability to manipulate, lack of social skills and immaturity, lying and blaming. I hoped it was something else. But, as time passed, it became undeniable. Finally, we took him for intensive testing. Off the record, our suspicions were confirmed. On the record he was diagnosed with 'conduct disorder'. Over time, his behavior has worsened.

"He is now textbook ASPD with the exception of displaying cruelty to animals (although he cannot be left alone with my small grand- children, even for a few minutes, because he will hurt them if he is). Since they cannot make an official diagnosis of ASPD until he is 18 they refuse to 'officially' treat him as such. He smokes pot, fails every subject in school and refuses to do schoolwork, steals anything we don't lock down, lies constantly, blames everyone else, displays strange sexual behaviors, cons anyone who will buy it, refuses to obey any rules at school or at home, and has already been arrested 3 times. He honestly does not believe rules of any kind apply to him. He sees any attempt to place limitations on his behavior as a challenge to prove he cannot be controlled. He has no real emotions (doesn't even grasp the concept) and seems to truly not comprehend there is a problem. As long as no one crosses him or requires anything from him he is charming, witty and pleasant. Otherwise, he is either acting like we are the problem children he must tolerate or he becomes angry and verbally aggressive. We feel like his prisoners most of the time.

"There are other less threatening associated problems; poor memory, poor planning skills, inability to project consequences to behavior, boredom due to bland emotional life, leading to thrill seeking. He does not comprehend the connection between work and reward and believes he will succeed in life simply because he wants to. He believes anything he wants is 'owed' to him. He is incapable of comprehending others as separate from himself and is oblivious to their wants or needs. He knows no boundaries and does not recognize the rights of others nor respect them. He doesn't understand why others find his behavior intolerable. The hardest thing we had to accept is that this child is incapable of loving. He does not love us. Not in any true sense.

"Initially, no one wants to accept he is ASPD. We have been through numerous therapists. They waste a great deal of our money and time while we wait for them to finally come to the same conclusion everyone else eventually comes to. Then they refuse to attempt to treat him. We have gone through the same thing with his schools. He is the master at identifying and latching on to a co-dependant teacher of counselor and exploiting them most of the school year before we finally get the call of resignation and agreement that he is indeed ASPD. We have repeated this over and over. We begin every school year and every first counseling session the same way; begging for them to address this for what it is as opposed to trying everything else that has already been tried unsuccessfully. We usually have put up with the attitude that they know better. We have been told they are sure he does have emotions, he just suppresses them. We have been assured they can get to the bottom of it all. Most of the time they are a little arrogant about it. Most of the time they treat us as if we are horrible for believing such a thing about our son. But, eventually, they admit defeat. Then they act like something must be wrong with us to have birthed such a twisted kid. (In fact, he is adopted).

"We have managed to learn a few things that may be helpful to other parents of ASPD kids. We have learned:

- the definition of true powerlessness. We cannot 'fix' him or help him.
- it is not our fault or a failure in our parenting abilities.
- to deal with him unemotionally. ASPDs find emotional people scary. We also refrain from using 'feeling' words in our conversation as these words mean nothing to him.
- to never show any real depth of feelings for him beyond being pleasant because he interprets this as weakness and will exploit it. We only deal with him matter-of-factly.
- to not try to project our own feelings or those we believe he should have in him. The best he can do is to imitate those emotions for the purpose of exploitation.
- to be absolutely consistent. He sees inconsistency as weakness and will exploit it. Consequences must be swift, immediate and without emotion and without fail.
- to describe possible consequences only in what he has to gain or lose. He has no concept of right or wrong except in relationship to his own discomfort or pleasure. Guilt is beyond his abilities. Shaming him only annoys him.
- to not waste our time explaining why we must say 'no'. Our explanations only provide him an opportunity to look for a loop-hole or argue in an attempt to wear us down.
- not to expect him to learn much from experience. He won't.
- to act the same toward him when he is being charming as when he is not. We try to maintain a consistently even response at all

228

times.

- to acknowledge but not reward good behavior. If we reward it, he sees it as a new method of scamming.
- to suspect underlying motives to sudden charm or helpfulness. There always is one.
- to avoid feeling sorry for him. It makes us weak and he exploits it.
- to be tough and to not allow others to malign us for our 'harsh attitudes'.
- to remember we cannot 'hurt his feelings.' Sometimes harsh words are what will get his attention, at least temporarily, to deal with him with our own best interest at heart because nothing we do will change him or his behavior. We can only protect ourselves and others.
- Although this is not his fault and he is mentally ill, he is also dangerous to those around him, and their protection must come first; to accept that this child is a predator. He will use and abuse anyone to get what he wants without any concern for the victim. To understand that, although he appears to be, he is not evil. He is only concerned with doing and getting what he wants. He is oblivious to the harm it is causing others.
- to love a child with ASPD can be deadly both to them and to us.

"We have to disassociate from love for him as much as possible for our own survival. We have had to accept he will, most likely, end up in prison or dead and can only hope he doesn't hurt too many along the way.

"We can only do the best we can because there will be very little help for us along the way and probably none for him. We cannot possibly expect others to understand. Unless you have been there, it's almost impossible to comprehend. More than once we have had to deal with others who see us as the monsters. More than once we have had to defend what little sanity our methods provide against 'caring' people who want to come to our son's 'defense', projecting their own emotions on to him.

"We are sure he will leave us as soon as he can. We stand very much in his way of what he wants to do and refuse to cater to him. We won't try to stop him. Sociopaths rarely maintain a relationship with anyone they cannot use. He will move on to the next 'sucker' who will support him. It seems the best we can hope for is he will end up as a con-man as opposed to a rapist or murderer. We have grave concerns that he will be released on society and probably do much damage to others before (if ever) he is stopped. We also fear what will happen if he marries and/or has children. We feel helpless to protect whatever future victims he may encounter. We can only protect our family and ourselves.

"I know this isn't what you want to hear. I know you would rather hear that something you could do would make a difference. I wish I could say that is the case. But, so far, it has not proven to be so. I have not tried to give you hope. I have tried to give you strength and courage and to let you know you are not the bad one and you are not alone. Most of all, I have tried to share the tools that have helped make our lives with a sociopath more manageable; a way to survive until he is old enough to go. A day we are looking forward to."

GIRLS

27. "Laurie entered the room and immediately took control, but it was so subtle the doctor didn't recognize it. At first, she hung her head and acted frightened, so when he attempted to coax her out, she pretended to be resistant, bashful, and shy (which she isn't at all).

"Then, after a few minutes, she said that it was easy to talk to him: 'Much better than those doctors at school' While the doctor was taking this in, she commented on how pretty the designs on his tie were, and asked to sit on his lap. Then she proceeded to tell him what he wanted to hear, about how she had gotten into some trouble in school, but it was because no one understood her and how it felt real good to be with him ... in fact, she asked him if he would be her new daddy! She said all her father ever did was yell at her.

"Afterward, the doctor told me that he had established a perfect rapport with Laurie and that she was a loving child who was just misunderstood! He said we should be giving her more love. I couldn't believe it. Our 8-year-old daughter had conned a psychiatrist.

"[Just three weeks before this 'loving child' had poked another little girl's eye out with a pencil at school after she hadn't gotten her way.]"

28. "I tried to kiss Katie when she was small, but even when she was very little she moved her face away. You can't kiss a baby who is jerking away from you all the time. It got worse as she got older. Sometimes I just broke down and cried because my beautiful little girl seemed to hate me. I'll tell you, I told my baby doctor about it and I know he thought I was going crazy."

29. "It was so hard for me to feel warm toward this child. I felt cold. I felt so bad feeling that way. I wondered what on earth was wrong with me. But … inside … I felt so uncomfortable, so strange. I knew this child wasn't like our other children. She had this plastic, phony smile. It wasn't like a real smile at all."

30. "At times, Nancy is good but it's only when she wants something or she's being threatened. And she does such weird things to be the center of attraction. Once, we had a group of relative strangers over and John (Nancy's foster brother) had been sharing one of the things that he had done that really pleased him. Well, this group of strangers was talking and laughing about John's experience, and Nancy marches into the middle of the room. Clear as a bell she says, 'Last week Kenny took me down into the basement and pulled my pants down and played with me.' Well, you can imagine the conversation just came to a sudden, embarrassed, violent halt!"

31. "By two [years old] we wondered why she was so sad and nasty. We were so blind and always made excuses, just knowing that she would outgrow it or would get better with each stage of her life. Instead, it almost seems to have gotten worse. What a hard time it is to have people with this disorder in our lives!"

32. "I have had to work so very hard to distance myself emotionally from my own daughter. I would do anything to make it 'right.' My husband and I have done everything in our power to help her. We can do no more. I still love her, but I know that she is who she is, and that just about kills me."

33. "She made comments of her 7-year-old daughter as being pure evil and how there was absolutely no mother/child bonding no matter how hard she tried. She did bring her daughter to work once, and at 7 years old, she was not a very likable little girl. There was some very distant weirdness with her, but I felt sorry for her thinking it was her mother's lack of love. Fast forward to where I am now, I do understand what she was trying to say. I wonder how things turned out."

34. "My 6-year-old daughter is exceptionally bright and a year ahead of her peers with her studies at school. However, she is emotionally very immature. I am becoming increasingly concerned with her behaviour. She will do what she is told most of the time and sanctions or consistent discipline tend to work when she doesn't. The real problem is that she must be in control of every situation and she will get incredibly upset if she can't. She has a 3-year-old sister who is emotionally mature (or right for her age), a 7-year-old step-sister who is very mature for her age and a 4-year-old step brother. She sees her step-siblings every other weekend. If the others are happily playing a game, my daughter will wade in and insist they play it her way. This upsets everyone, but mostly my daughter who simply cannot cope with their refusal and will vent her frustration by screaming and crying. It's the same story at school or on occasions when there are friends or similar aged children at home. She is intensely competitive and must win or be the best at everything – she cannot cope when she is not first, the best or the brightest. She is a perfectionist who will not begin her school work until she has completely understood the task, often holding up the class with her endless questions. Her teachers say this is unnecessary as she is the only one who really gets it first time! Their view is that although she is bright, she has some emotional and social problems. She does not make friends easily – I believe other children are very wary of her and her outbursts when things don't go her way. She gets frustrated by simple things very easily. I know beyond a shadow of a doubt she does not and possibly cannot listen or hear what I say, regardless of how I approach her. She talks over me and when she is quiet, her eyes are completely glazed over. This does concern me. She idolizes her father (she stays with him every other weekend) who is himself a deeply competitive man. I should say that I have a very positive relationship with him – no animosity – we split when she was three, but the children have all adjusted very well on the whole. She is a very confident girl, often putting on shows for the family, will perform with absolutely no sense of fear or embarrassment that I see naturally in other children her age. It is almost as though this social connection – that and the inability to see how her actions affect people around her – is completely missing. She is also extremely generous and will make gifts and draw pictures for anyone in the house on a daily basis. She has a significant amount of my time after school and I always try and ensure I spend a good hour just with her. I am becoming sad for her that I think she is not very happy and am keen to find a way of under-standing why she is like this and why she simply does not understand the effect of her actions or can't hear me when I talk to her."

35. "I am concerned about my daughter. She is 5 years old, only child in a middle class family. She is happy, bright, out-going and by all accounts a serious student (for a 5-year-old).

"What concerns me is this...In the play ground and after school care she prefers to play (tag, chase) with boys 3-4 years older than herself. I often find her talking to them in somewhat private situations (as private as a school yard can be). I discovered she chases them around pretending to kiss them. She follows the older boys around although often times they seem to ignore her.

"I also discovered she undresses dolls with them and points out female anatomy (breasts). She is not embarrassed about this nor does she try to hide it, it seems on the surface in the spirit of play and fun.

"She does have girlfriends her own age but does prefer the older boys.

"Should I be concerned about this?"

36. "This is my niece [10 years old]. She is very sweet, and very smart, but she exhibits certain behaviors that concern her mother and me. Her mother is her adoptive mother, as her real mother left her when she was 6ms old, and has shown up sporadically, and has also had 5 more children after my niece, and has given up all of them, as well. Abandonment issues are there, but she doesn't show much feeling, either way...happy or sad.

"Ok...she lies, she exaggerates, she shows off, she tells stories to me about her parents that are wrong and when she is confronted she swears it was a miscommunication. She is on 2 different meds for ADHD ...Strattera & Aderal. She is showing signs of sexual behavior. Teaching the young boys next door how to play spin the bottle, and she gets upset when boys don't like her. When we have gone swimming, my baby boys who are almost 2 didn't have swim suits on, and she would duck underwater to look at their penis. She is very annoying to the other children she befriends. Her mother found an email she wrote saying she wanted to have sex with a certain boy. My mother caught her with her pants down in someone else's bed. She doesn't listen to instruction and has a hard time using manners. I made her write 20 times 'I will say please.' She turned it into a game and wrote 30x's, 'because that's what I wanted to do...how old are you auntie? Ok than I will write it 33x's.' So her punishment didn't work. She didn't care. She doesn't cry for anything, she shows no emotions while getting punished, and her consequences do not affect her and they do no good. When she is told to do something, she finds 30 things to do in the middle of her task to procrastinate, making the adults repeat 30x's for her to continue to task. When she thinks the task is done, it actually isn't. Then when she is getting in trouble she whines and says 'I'm always getting yelled at,' and acts like she is starting to feel bad about herself. She has been to therapists & child psychologists who she manipulates and the doctor tells her mom & dad that they are the ones that need counseling. She is not verbally abusive, nor does she swear or use foul language. She throws away her homework, and hides notes from the teachers getting close to failing some classes, but she has excelled in Lacrosse. Her parents as well as I, because I watch her during the summer vacation, have tried every punishment, have tried to talk to her, have asked her to create her own punishment, have made lists...if we can think of it we do it. Without success. She also has a 19-yr-old male cousin that we have found alone with her one several occasions. She may have provoked it.

"What could possibly be the problem, and what unconventional ways should we take to help her. Both her mom & I have done research, and some things point to ODD...She is a great liar, and it is hard to distinguish the truth from her stories. Her lack of compassion for consequences, and her sexual exploration are probably the biggest concerns.

"...May I also add, that she has childish behavior where she is LOUD and interrupts, when you tell her to lower her voice she can't or just decides to continue to be loud. I will tell her to please not scream because the babies are sleeping, and 15 minutes later she will holler for me across the house. Sometimes she laughs instantly in a made up 'stupid' way. She also uses silly language like calling the computer the 'Compooper'. When we are out she purposely talks loud so other people around will hear what she is saying and she is usually making something up, or talking about her boyfriend, which she doesn't have one. Also, she will ask a question to which she already knows the answer to, and when I do not acknowledge the question and just give her a look, she'll ask it again and insist she doesn't know. I also took her to the library last week, and she walked up and down the aisles farting, then giggling, and at one point said 'AUNTIE!' and blamed it on me. I kept telling her to BE QUIET, and to stop farting, and she didn't.

"I love my niece, and I want to help her; and I am tired of trying to punish her, and feeling like I am always yelling at her. I know that her mother has 1000 more incidents, and is tired as well. We are advocates for her, but she is constantly testing and pushing and defying and disrespecting. May I add that her mother and I are the most hard on her as well. We 'expect' things from her, where her grandparents & father are more relaxed and feel more 'pity' for her because of her ADHD and her real mother splitting on her. They tend to let most things slide."

37. "I strongly believe, after some research and years of experience with my adoptive child (I am actually the grandparent who adopted her) that she is sociopathic. She has no remorse, intentionally gets in trouble whether she gets attention for it or not, drives me to the brink as everything is a competition that she must win regardless of her punishment. Rewards and punishments do not work! The more exciting the better. She looks me straight in the eye and lies profusely. She tears up her toys into pieces when angry, and boy can she get angry ... to the point of shaking or as cool and calm and collect as can be.

"The worst part is her charm. It is so sickeningly sweet and scary at times. Right in the middle of being in trouble she switches it on, smiles and laughs. It's very odd. The worst part is she reminds me so much of that little girl in "The Bad Seed". She commits an offense then sings and plays with glee after having been punished. It is a daily event and I now realize that to feed into anything that gets her adrenaline pumping is the worst thing I can do. She is no way a hyper child. She has a great attention span. She is not add/adhd. She was neglected and abused by my daughter and those she was left with at a very early age. My daughter, the biological mother of this child, is a drug addict and most likely sociopathic herself. She had 3 children, basically sold the other 2 before I could get to them. In addition, my biological mother is 'insane' and alcoholic and was institutionalized when I was 9. She also was adopted at birth. She, to this day, also has no conscience or remorse and is also very manipulative just as this 5 year-old child of mine. I am no doctor, but I am certain that my child is a sociopath.

"In addition, she is very mature and intelligent, can stand in a corner for up an entire day without moving (this was not done by me). She can take any punishment, lose any toys or rights without a bat of an eye, but gets you back later. I read where biologically, the problem may be a need for them to higher their adrenaline (thrill seeking) and dopamine does this ... how do I lower her dopamine level while increasing the serotonin and norepinephrine levels? I don't want her on meds, that day will surely come soon enough;

but for now she is 5 and I need to be able to teach her how to cope in society regardless of this condition. And, I need to be able to cope myself. Any leads to diet help, support groups, information, treatment and parenting skills for parents of sociopathic/antisocial disordered children would be greatly appreciated."

38. "I have a daughter that was diagnosed with Oppositional defiance disorder and she has been leaping into psychopath personality without developing full fledge Conduct Disorder. Here is a list I observe: She is a girl and I believe that girls manifest different behaviors than do boys because there are so few of them to be observed:

- Is glib and superficial (her emotion feels fake everyone tells me this)
- Becomes easily annoyed and then becomes violent (manipulating friends to hurt or go after someone and either physically harm or verbally abuse)
- Has utilized a weapon to scare a family member and said it was a joke
- Shows no remorse (very cold demeanor when challenged about behavior)
- Has two different personalities (excessively nice, and hostile, aggressive and cold.
- Most people who don't know her believe she is very sweet and can't believe you when you tell them things she has done. (Dr Jekyll and Mr. Hyde Syndrome)
- Manipulates people to get what she wants (makes up stories about people to get attention away from herself when she is in trouble)
- Starts fights with people that she is close to by lying and telling stories
- Is highly sexually precocious and sexually inappropriate but will tell you she does not like boys at all and most boyfriends are just friends even with there is sexual encounters
- Is somewhat aggressive sexually with boys, men
- stares coldly when challenged

- Makes people believe she agrees with them about rules and then later does what she wants that goes against them
- She is very shallow and superficial in emotion
- States she loves animals but has little to do with them (sometimes holds her cat but very little)
- Tells lies and can't remember them
- Has very limited memory capabilities unless she has been hurt Then remembers to get even and harbors for a long time
- Is always complaining about somatic pain and exaggerates for attention
- Constantly denies things she has done or said and is convincing to the point that you actually question yourself
- Believes her lies
- Engages in attention-seeking behavior that is often destructive
- Highly impulsive with no regard for consequences
- Irresponsible to the point of almost stealing (keeping books from library, school, friends CDs, clothing, etc)
- Copies bizarre lyrics with high sexual and violent overtones with very little understanding of the meanings (can recite the lyrics but if you ask her what that music means she states no understanding of it)
- Treats people more like objects rather that human beings and when threatened will become aggressive
- Her since of reality is not most peoples' reality and often scares people
- Has no real connection with anyone and complains of it
- States that she does not care about hurting people
- Does not recognize most societal norms and rules. Will break the smallest rules without regard for it
- Has unrealistic optimism
- Has very short term relationships (makes friends easily and the loses after a few months)
- Seems to be highly rejected from her peers

- Seems to have been sexually assaulted more that most girls her age (15)
- Several boys have been accused of sexually assaulting her with little consequences directed toward her false accusations
- Any form of punishment does not affect her at all and she states she does not care"

39. "Hi! Just to say that I recognise many of the signs mentioned in the first post re rad/fledgling. Oh if only I had realised when my adopted daughter was younger. She is now full grown and an adult.

- The lack of enjoyment of music and dancing
- No interest in pets or animals like the other children
- Only laughed when someone got hurt or embarrassed
- Liked one to one relationships and could not share easily
- Does not express emotions or feelings for anyone
- The hyper vigilance to others' business
- No memories from past
- Never praises anyone

"And also some I noticed like:

- No tears if she cried just dry silent heaving
- Hiding important things around the house so the owner would panic and watching them search
- Going into trances/strange expressions
- Materialistic

"She would find out what you did not like and make sure you had an encounter. For instance, one of her brothers hated coffee creams and she even at young age of six went to the trouble of getting one out of the box and taking it to him. She had this way of acting so sweetly and gaining your confidence. I remember seeing her give it to him and thinking oh how sweet, and hearing him ask what flavour it was and she saying innocently it is strawberry I think. He reacted violently on finding it was coffee and pushed her so she fell to the floor. I don't remember thinking too much of it at the time and told my son off for pushing her believing I guess it was a honest mistake on her part. The trouble is looking back there were too many 'honest' mistakes. The problem was who would think a small child is capable of cold and calculating manipulation. And what started as small things like teasing her brothers with sweets grew into much more dangerous stuff.

"I also agree with the stirring of emotions in people so the child can feel. Our daughter loved hiding things and watching us get distraught trying to find them. This could range from a brother's important homework book to once even my wheeled suitcase at a station. I remember turning my back and her and the suitcase were gone. Then after a search she turned up but no case. She was 17 at the time so no baby. She knew that inside that case were our passports and laptop. For a minute or so she denied having the suitcase but eventually gave the sly smile which we knew was as close to admitting it she ever came. Luckily a station employee had found the case and we were able to go on with the journey but our lives have been full of similar dramas that no other child ever came close to doing. All the negative energy she whirled up in us. I mean why try and ruin your own family's holiday. But then I remember the look in her face when she saw us racing around trying to fix whatever she had interfered with; and I know she got a thrill out of it. Not the normal naughty child thing but a real evil buzz.

"Once, too, she scratched a teacher's car from front to back with her keys because the teacher had taken her large hoop earrings away. That took some time to prove and she was caught out only by chance.

"I remember sitting in the principal's office and they confronted her and she said after realising the game was up, 'Well, at least she is insured isn't she' (referring to the damage)!!!

"The school was always trying to tell us that something was not right but for the most part I believed my daughter that they had got it wrong. I wish I had listened now. You cannot believe how good these children are though at soothing your worries. The really clever ones could make you believe white is black! Teenage years are hell; they seem to get a hormonal boost above and beyond the norm!"

Chapter10
CODEPENDENTS

This provocative topic raises the question whether codependents are in fact pathics themselves, either natural or conditioned; or whether their pathic counterparts (spouse, parents) draw out the worst in them so that they can experience this "worst" if not actively (sadistically) then passively (masochistically);or whether their natural temperament is simply so passive and impressionable that they gravitate to the strong-arm, pathic, type, whether it be male or female; or whether their childhood hard-cased family and/or social environment had conditioned them to be ruled by pathics.

---

1. "There are some very few of us who actually seek out relationships with narcissists. We do this with the full knowledge that we are not wanted, despised even. We persist and pursue no matter the consequences, no matter the cost.

"I am an 'inverted narcissist'. It is because as a child I was 'imprinted/fixated' with a particular pattern involving relationships. I was engulfed so completely by my father's personality and repressed so severely by various other factors in my childhood that I simply didn't develop a recognizable personality. I existed purely as an extension of my father. I was his genius Wunderkind. He ignored my mother and poured all his energy and effort into me. I did not develop full-blown secondary narcissism...I developed into the perfect 'other half' of the narcissist molding me. I became the perfect, eager co-dependent. And this is an imprint, a pattern in my psyche, a way of (not) relating to the world of relationships by only being able to truly relate to one person (my father) and then one kind of person – the narcissist.

"He is my perfect lover, my perfect mate, a fit that is so slick and smooth, so comfortable and effortless, so filled with meaning and actual feelings – that's the other thing. I cannot feel on my own. I am incomplete. I can only feel when I am engulfed by another (first it was my father) and now – well now it has to be a narcissist. Not just any narcissist either. He must be exceedingly smart, good

242

looking, have adequate reproductive equipment and some knowledge on how to use it and that's about it.

"When I am engulfed by someone like this I feel completed, I can actually FEEL. I am whole again. I function as a sibyl, an oracle, an extension of the narcissist. His fiercest protector, his purveyor/-procurer of [attention, admiration, etc.]; the secretary, organizer, manager, etc.. I think you get the picture and this gives me INTENSE PLEASURE.

"So the answer to your question: 'Why would anyone want to be with someone who doesn't want them back?' The short answer is, 'Because there is no one else remotely worth looking at.'"

2. "I am BUILT this way. I may have overstated it by saying that I have 'no choice' because, in fact I do."

"The choice is – live in an emotionally deadened monochrome world where I can reasonably interact with normal people OR I can choose to be with a narcissist in which case my world is Technicolor, emotionally satisfying, alive and wondrous (also can be turbulent and a real roller coaster ride for the unprepared, not to mention incredibly damaging for people who are not inverted narcissists and who fall into relationships with narcissists). As I have walked on both sides of the street, and because I have developed coping mechanisms that protect me really quite well, I can reasonably safely engage in a primary, intimate relationship with a narcissist without getting hurt by it."

"The real WHY of it all is that I learned, as a young child, that being 'eaten alive' by a narcissist parent, to the point where your existence is but an extension of his own, was how all relationships ought to work. It is a psychological imprint – my 'love map', it is what feels right to me intrinsically. A pattern of living – I don't know how else to describe it so you and others will understand how very natural and normal this is for me. It is not the torturous existence that most of the survivors of narcissism are recounting on this list."

"My experiences with narcissists, to me, ARE NORMAL for me. Comfortable like an old pair of slippers that fit perfectly. I don't expect many people to attempt to do this, to 'make themselves into' this kind of person. I don't think anyone could, if they tried.

"It is my need to be engulfed and merged that drives me to these relationships; and when I get those needs met I feel more normal, better about myself. I am the outer extension of the narcissist. In many ways I am a vanguard, a public two-way warning system, fiercely defending my narcissist from harm, and fiercely loyal to him, catering to his every need in order to protect his fragile existence. These are the dynamics of my particular version of engulfment. I don't need anyone to take care of me. I need only to be needed in this very particular way, by a narcissist who inevitably possesses the ability to engulf in a way that normal, fully realized adults cannot. It is somewhat paradoxical – I feel freer and more independent with a narcissist than without one. I achieve more in my life when I am in this form of relationship. I try harder, work harder, am more creative, think better of myself, excel in most every aspect of my life."

3. "It depends on the non-narcissist, really. Narcissism is a RIGID, systemic pattern of responses. It is so all-pervasive and all-encompassing that it is a PERSONALITY disorder. If the non-narcissist is co-dependent, for instance, then the narcissist is a perfect match for him and the union will last..."

4. "I go ahead and cater to him and pretend that his words don't hurt; and later, I engage in an internal fight with myself for being so damned submissive. It's a constant battle and I can't seem to decide which voice in my head I should listen to...I feel like a fool, yet, I would rather be a fool with him than a lonely, well-rounded woman without him. I've often said that the only way that we can stay together is because we feed off of each other. I give him everything he needs and he takes it. Seeing him happy and pleased is what gives me pleasure. I feel very successful then."

5. "The thing is, I am at my best when I feel secure in a relationship with a NPD. I seem to thrive on it even when things go bad. When left alone I can't function. It took me 2 years just to be able to keep my home and my personal appearance presentable. Now I'm back to square one. I loathe myself, I am terribly depressed and struggle just to get out of bed, let alone take care of myself. I do only the absolute minimum and am convinced that a normal guy will never want me. I am attractive, financially secure, intelligent and in good shape, I look much younger than I am and still, I feel like I have the plague. I have no social skills without a mate next to me, and I cannot find anyone that is remotely interested in me. I see myself getting older and less attractive and that is the only thing I had to offer men."

6. "If I displayed behaviour that made my X look good to others, I was insipidly overvalued. When I dared be something other than who she wanted me to be, the sarcastic criticism and total devaluation was unbelievable. So, I learned to be all things to all people. I get a heavenly high from surrendering my power to a narcissist, to catering to them, in having them overvalue and need me, and it is the only time that I truly feel alive …"

7. "Ok why do we stay. Seriously I have friends who are willing to help me and let me live with them and all I want to do is stay with Mike. … Ummm am I psycho or what? The past four nights he has hit me left bruises on me, slapped me across the face, pushed me while I was holding my child, and threw me on the ground. And I don't leave because of what reason???? He's not even nice to me after he hurts me, he just says it's my fault that we were fighting and I need to stop being a b*tch. And I'm not even a b*tch to him you know I just try to talk to him about things and he just loses his temper. I feel ugly, worthless, like no one else Is going to want me even though everyone cannot believe that I would stay with him and they tell me that I'm pretty and nice and lovable but I just don't believe them. I stay there and I'm sooooo unhappy and depressed all the time I'm never ever happy, I'm always crying or sleeping because I'm too depressed to even get out of bed. I hate this. Why am I so afraid of leaving this a**h*le? It shouldn't be hard when someone hits you and talks to you the way he does. So what do I have to do to get out of there knowing it's the right thing to do. I'm staying the night with my mom me and the baby are and all I'm obsessing about is I wonder If he'll miss me, I wonder if he'll call me, I wonder I wonder I wonder. Instead of relaxing and just being

happy I'm away from the abuse for awhile. It's almost like I want to go back and be abused I feel sick to my stomach because of the way I'm thinking. I should be glad I'm away from it for the night, and I should be enjoying it. Instead, I'm even more depressed and I want him to call and I want him to miss us being there. WHY DOES THIS HAPPEN? Am I crazy or is this what all people have been abused go through??? How do I forget about him and think about my baby and myself? I feel horrible for my child that his mother is this way, you know? Instead of doing what's right and being worried about things I should be worried about, I'm worrying about the worthless piece of sh*t a**h*le who I have a baby with."

8. "It used to be that when I went out, I'd often find myself attracted to one particular guy (and not necessarily the best looking one in the room) where all we had to do was make eye contact and it was INSTANT SPARKS...almost like some invisible magnetic energy was drawing us to each other...

"Every time this happened, I thought what I was feeling was PAS-SION...or love at first sight... little did I know that I was deeply attracted to sociopathic personality types because of MY OWN dysfunctional psychology.

"You see, although I've never really had any trouble meeting attractive, successful, sweet guys...I usually didn't feel attracted to them. I always found myself saying there's 'no passion'... or they were too nice or boring.

"I now know that my concept of passion was really my addiction to the wrong type of guys...It turns out I was addicted to emotional highs and lows that sociopaths bombarded me with that keep me hooked ... in 'normal healthy relationships', there tends to be a more steady emotional ride and you don't feel the intensity of the highs and lows you're used to, and therefore, think there's something wrong or missing.

"I was amazed to learn that our brains actually become physically addicted to emotional intensity and the more we subject ourselves to roller coaster relationships of hot and cold intensity, the more addicted we get (just like a drug). This happens especially to those of us who grew up with a lot of 'dysfunction' in the home.

"And, of course, that's why these encounters always led to unfulfilling relationships where I constantly felt anxious, got manipulated and strung along ...

"I didn't understand why this was happening to me and a friend of mine recommended I go see a therapist, so I did. Well, it didn't take my therapist long to reach a very common conclusion – I had a codependent personality (which apparently explained everything) ...

"It turns out that because codependents like to live through or for others, have a strong need to 'fix' people and tend to seek out relationships where we can play a victim role ... and because sociopaths are so full of themselves and thrive on controlling and manipulating others, when us codependents and a sociopath get together, it's like nitro and glycerin – BOOM!

"Bottom line: I knew if I didn't do something about this immediately, I would continue downward on the destructive spiral that I was already on.

"Can you guess what I did? I actually made a vow <u>not</u> to get involved with anyone until I got myself figured out and it was probably the most difficult part of my healing process (Seriously, you have no idea how codependent you really are until you try to *not* be involved with anyone romantically for a while!).

"Now you may be wondering how a nice girl like me developed a codependent personality ...

Well, I figured this out too ...

"It turns out that it's extremely common for children of alcoholics and addicts to be diagnosed as codependent because codependency stems from being abandoned (or abused) as a child and alcoholics and addicts essentially abandon their kids for their addictions. Although I'm not an alcoholic or drug addict, my father did have a drinking problem and that was the likely source for my codependency issues."

9. "We have very little choice in all of this. We are as vacant and warped as the narcissist. X is wont to say, 'I don't HAVE a personality disorder, I AM a personality disorder.' It defines who we are and how we will respond. You will always and ONLY have real

feelings when you are with a narcissist. It is your love map, it is the programming within your psyche. Does it need to control your behaviour? Not necessarily. Knowing what you are can at least give you the opportunity to forecast the effect of an action before you take it. So, loveless black and white may be the very healthiest thing for you for the foreseeable future. I tend to think of these episodes with narcissists as being cyclic. You will likely need to cut loose for a while when your child is older."

10. "In my case, I realise that while I can't stop loving my current narcissist, it isn't necessary for me to avoid as long as I can understand [his abuse]. In my way of looking at it, he is deserving of love, and since I can give him love without it hurting me, then as long as he needs it, he shall have it."

11. "There's another difficulty: the love we have to our family. I have also a family full of narcissistic and perverts (i.e. they not only ignore you as a person but also like to make you suffer), and even they did terrible things to me and continue doing so, I can't leave. It's so difficult for me to imagine a life without them. I don't like being treated that way and I know that they will not change, but they're my family, my mom, dad and siblings, it's really too hard. The problem with these kind of people is that it's never enough for them. Although I know my mother well, for example, so I know what to expect from her so that she doesn't make me suffer; she would do whatever she can to succeed. For instance, I know that in all our of conversations, she will make subtle comments to make me feel bad or react, and I feel now prepared to survive those situations (many years ago I couldn't, so I tried to avoid the dinners and lunch with my family, producing reactions against my antisocial behavior); and as she knows that, she's trying to affect me in other ways, like saying lies about me to other members of the family, establishing relationships with people near to my friends and boyfriend so that she could manipulate them against me or know what I'm doing, even speaking about me as if I was the greatest person in the world in front of other people in order to make them compete with me or to convince them that I'm a liar when I speak of the ways she treats me. All what she does is for hurting me or other people. She functions that way; she is that, that's her structure. And even knowing that she will never stop, I can't go. Perhaps my behavior is pathologic, but what can I do with all the love I feel for them. Well, I am now trying to convince myself that they are not indispensable. It's a difficult task.

12. "You have to pimp for the narcissist, intellectually, and sexually. If your narcissist is somatic, you are much better off lining up the sex partners than leaving it to him. Intellectual pimping is more varied. You can think of wonderful things and then subtly string out the idea, in the most delicate of packages and watch the narcissist cogitate their way to 'their' brilliant discovery whilst you bask in the glow of their perfection and success. ... The point of this entire exercise is to assure YOUR supply, which is the narcissist himself, not to punish yourself by giving away a great idea or abase yourself because, of course, YOU are not worthy of having such a great idea on your own – but who knows, it may seem that way to the inverted narcissist. It really depends on how self-aware the inverted is."

13. "I think I am an inverted N as I match a lot of the descriptions and now I wonder if I should go back to my new N and beg his forgiveness and ask him to try again with me. I just can't get him out of my mind. We dated exclusively for about 5 months (though I found out he went on a blind date out of town after three months and he denies it was a date, he was just meeting a coworker's kid at their request, he wasn't sure why they insisted he meet her and felt weird about it). After the first two months, he became very distant and we rarely saw each other, but he continued to call a couple times a week. I told myself if he was interested in someone else he would break things off, why complicate his life with hanging on to someone he didn't want to be with, right? Instead, he kept showing me that he cared by making real efforts; I could tell it was difficult for him.

"He told me he would call me and he wouldn't. I would end up calling him; he would tell me that he found that attractive. This last straw was when I couldn't get a hold of him on New Years and he didn't call; so I sent him a beautiful poem and told him how much I loved all of him, but that it hurt too much and I needed to move on. I wished him happiness and asked him not to call.

"He did, two weeks later to apologize and ask if we could be friends and that he'd call from time to time to get together. I said yes! Ughh! I emailed him a couple of weeks after that and he emailed lightheartedly back. I responded and then nothing. It's been over a week now and I know I am a fool but don't know how to be anything else. I am too old and have a history of physical, emotional and sexual abuse by my family since I was a baby. I have been through years of counseling and look at the good it's done. Not for the lack of trying, I thought I was doing better, I thought I was stronger and smarter. I thought I could avoid this. And even now after knowing all I do, I cannot change my behavior and my responses to an N.

"...I think I'm doing well to not have contacted him in the last week, and I intend on not contacting him ...I have said that a hundred times before. Every day is torture without him. I couldn't go to work today because I felt so bad about myself."

"Is this as good as it gets? Should I go to him now and offer myself to him again, beg him to take me back? I don't think I'd be good for anyone else, really, I'm just as messed up as he is, only I feel my short- comings way too much."

14. "Should a physically handicapped person feel ashamed of her handicap? No and neither should we. The trouble with us is that we are fooled into thinking that these relationships are 'guilty pleasures'. They feel so very good for a time but they are more akin to addiction satisfaction rather than being the 'right match' or an 'appropriate relationship'. I am still very conflicted myself about this. I wrote a few months ago that it was like having a caged very dangerous animal inside of me. When I get near narcissists, the animal smells its own kind and it wants out. I very carefully 'micro-manage' my life. This means that I daily do fairly regular reality checks and keep a very tight rein on myself and my behaviour. I am also obsessive-compulsive."

15. "I feel as though I'm constantly on an emotional roller coaster. I may wake up in a good mood, but if my N partner does or says something, which is hurtful to me, my mood changes immediately. I now feel sad, empty, afraid. All I want to do at this point is anything that will make him say something NICE to me.

"Once he does, I'm back on top of the world. This pattern of mood changes, or whatever you may call them, can take place several times a day. Each and every day. I've gotten to the point where I'm not sure that I can trust myself to feel any one way, because I know that I have no control over myself. He has the control. It's scary, yet I've sort of come to depend on him determining how I am going to feel."

16. "I have both a therapist and psychiatrist, and they helped me see how I gravitate toward men without consciences because that is what I was raised around – criminals, con artists, and my mother's third husband who is a genuine psychopath. In fact, I was willing to look the other way for this guy precisely because I grew up looking the other way."

17. "I was in an abusive relationship for over 5 years. Mostly verbal at first, then physical ... sometimes, I had wished he would just hit me instead of speaking the things he said to me. He had major issues and I felt sorry for him, so I stayed. I wanted to be loved, didn't think any- one else would love him like I did, or that anyone else would love me ... he gave me herpes to mark his territory so no one would want me. I got pregnant, but miscarried...and was relieved because the thought of bringing up a child around him made me sick. It was a hard road to get free from him; every time I would leave or try to get him to leave it would turn into a threatening conversation. Or, crazy as it sounds, he would threaten to leave and I would beg him to stay...the thought of being alone at the time was worse to me. At times, I couldn't figure out why I couldn't leave; it was like I was tied to him or something...I had opportunity to leave but didn't. ... Why? But let me tell you...things have changed and I am free. Not only free from this relationship and others like it, but free from the words and worthlessness I felt from all the horrible things he said to me. After 5 years of hearing how stupid, ugly, fat and worthless I was, I begin to believe those things. After I was out of this relationship with this man, I seemed to attract this kind of man – they all seemed sweet at first but turned into another abusive relationship...why? I went through countless relationships where I was treated like dirt. I was a good person with a kind heart. All I wanted was someone to love me ... why were men so mean to me? Why would God let this happen to me? I believed the lies that I didn't deserve to be treated well by a man...and being treated like garbage became 'normal' for me. But the real question is ... not 'Why are all these men treating me so bad and abusing me?' but 'Why do I allow it????' Why did I stay in a relationship for 5 years with someone who obviously beat the snot out of me and treated me like dirt? It has nothing to do with the men ... it has everything to do with how I look at myself. I had worth issues ... most women do. Our worth is connected in how we look, how much money we have, how many men we sleep with, how skinny we are, etc ... a lot of men put that value on us; but we allow it, and submit totally to it, by allowing destructive behavior into our lives. ... Whether it be abuse, drugs, eating disorders, needless and obsessive cosmetic surgery, etc. the list goes on."

18. "Some honesty here.

"When my partner was hitting me, as much as I hated it, I knew I was, at that moment in time, the centre of his universe. As sick as this sounds, it was one of the reasons why I stayed as long as I did. We were also doing drugs together, and that was a real pull to keep getting back together.

"I realized that in order for things to change, (I was always waiting for him to make the changes), that I would have to make the first step away.

"I went to a 12-step program to get off the drugs. It was only then I was properly prepared with clear thinking to make changes in my life.

"It was hard, scary, but worth it.

"I went back to school, got my B.A., and am now a free-lance writer/journalist.

"I have come far, yet I know that I have to be on guard to keep myself safe.

"I have an affinity to 'bad boys'. I think this is a commonality amongst women who are in abusive relationships.

"However, this is not the case across the board, not by any means."

19. "I must say I have been out of my abusive marriage going on 5 years...first I thought love kept me there but just now I realize it was fear ... fear of rejection, fear of not having anyone love me because I know have to wear false teeth, fear that I might black out again and not remember how I got where I was standing at. I must say that I still live in fear.

"I recall several times during a 'fight' or a break-up, I would go to my Mom and tell her, 'I just can't see myself without him.' (Mom didn't have a clue what was going on behind closed doors). I was madly in love with this guy, well; I was madly in love with the guy he 'pretended' to be in the beginning of the relationship. I hated the man he 'actually' was, but like all of us, I thought it was my fault, because he was like he was. I think I was the one who wasn't 'perfect'. He was trying to make me perfect, make me a better person ... help me get a grip on my temper & my 'mouth'. I ran it a lot. I look back now and see that ... it was all about control. I didn't have a temper problem. He would push my buttons and I would react like any normal person. He just wanted to use me as a door mat and telling me I was imperfect, was his way of making feel as if something was wrong with me.

"But I was finally able to get away from this guy. When I was done, I was done. He lived with me ... and that's the funny, part. It was my house but yet, I never thought about kicking him out until after 3 years of pure hell. I tried to find the answer as to why I put up with it for so long ... and I realized, that even if I told this guy it was over, that he wasn't treating me or my daughter very well, he would have manipulated his way back into our lives. I couldn't just say, 'I feel this or that.' After all, he controlled my feelings. He could be so charming when he wanted too. But in the end, when I had finally had enough, within 2 days I had EVERYTHING of his packed and out of my house ... even down to the magnets on my refrigerator that were his ... everything was gone. And let me tell you, even though my heart hurt, because I was honestly and truly in love with this guy, a peace of mind came over me. It felt as if 200 lbs were lifted off my shoulders. My daughter was happy but yet scared at the same time. She was afraid he was coming back. But he never did! Oh, yea, he tried calling & coming down to the house, being all Mr. Nice-Nice, but I pretty much figured out his tactics and his ways. I knew he was just blowing smoke up my ... well, you know. I had smoke coming out of my ears, he was blowing smoke so bad. I didn't fall for his lines anymore. It was over."

20. "This girl from work heard yelling. She and her sister went racing down the hall to see what was going on. And the drunk, stupid ex-N had his girlfriend down on the floor (in this scuzzy bathroom), wouldn't let her up, slapping at her, yelling and cussing in her face, and she was curled up in a fetal position, crying. I told her 'That's what he does best.' She and her sister talked to the girlfriend for two and a half hours, trying to tell her to get away, leave the bas****, etc. And she couldn't see it, or understand it. She kept saying, 'But I love him!' And 'I can make it all better. I just have to work at this relationship more.'

"I have to tell you something. I am at work at this very moment. I am in the courtroom. In the past 15 minutes I have had three different women come in and try to get their 'loves' out of jail for battering them. The last woman, was very badly bruised and not all there. Yet she cried and cried that she had to be able to see him (there is a no contact order with him and he's in jail) How does this happen? I had to explain to her that it was like if he burnt her house down ... maybe she didn't mind it but it was against the law and no amount of love is going help this time. I really feel sorry for these women who honestly believe that they can help them or change them. And yet ... I – other than the physical abuse – let a man do it to me. It seems for every 'P' that is out there, there is at least 3 women wanting to save him!"

"When he raped his ex-girlfriend his mother spent $50,000 to keep him out of jail. And he looks like one of these guys you see in a magazine. So, his family always laugh and say, 'Why would he have to rape anybody, he's got all kinds of women throwing themselves at him.' All the evidence was there. He always had the victim's deposition laying around the house, but I never read it until after the second break-up. Needless to say, I was astounded. The same things he had said to her when beating her up, he said to me."

21. "I have wrestled with this question for a long time. While with him, I sometimes wondered, 'What on earth am I doing here?' I refused to believe my life was such a mess, that he was lying – and in my refusal to accept reality, I trapped myself in my disbelief. Since gaining my freedom, I have looked back on those 4 years 9 months and wondered, 'What on earth was wrong with me that I stayed so long?' In my acceptance of reality, I let go of my disbelief and accept I was a victim, long before I met him.

"I know there are the physiological/psychological factors that compounded my convoluted thinking causing me to accept my belief that I was incapable of leaving him and would be lost without him. I know these factors contributed to my inertia and the resultant trauma bonding that held me pinioned in his unholy embrace. But none of these factors explain why an intelligent, well-educated, articulate woman did what I did.

"Why did I stay?

"I stayed because in the process of burying my truth beneath his lies, I turned off my inner voice of reason. I quit listening to myself telling me that regardless of what he was saying, what he was doing wasn't adding up. I gave into despair, helplessness and confusion and gave up on me. I wanted the rosy sunrise of his promises, the gilded cage of his castle in the air and gave into the magical thinking so that he could make my dreams come true.

"I stayed because I didn't want to take responsibility for what was happening in my life, my daughters' lives and to me.

"I stayed because it was easier to stay than to leave. It was easier to take the coward's way out by staying locked into his machinations than to take the leap into the unknown by leaving him and his lies behind.

"I stayed even though I knew he was lying. I knew he was deceiving me. I knew he was manipulating me. I knew all of this but I refused to look at the truth because to look at the truth meant having to look at me – and I was too frightened to do that.

"I stayed because I was a victim and I didn't want to admit it.

"As I write this I think about those who might say, 'But you can't blame yourself. You didn't know who he was when you first met him. You went into that relationship with your arms wide open in love and expected to have your love reciprocated in equal measure.'

"And all of that is true.

"None of it matters though when I look at the reasons for why I stayed.

"I could walk into a hundred relationships with my arms wide open and still find them empty – because my arms wide-open were filled with my own empty promises that I would treat myself with love and respect, truth and honesty. My lack of clarity in my beliefs, my values, my principles trapped me in his lies because I didn't know what I stood for.

"I stayed, not because of him, but because of me. My weaknesses brought me to my knees. My weaknesses kept me locked inside the web he wove around me.

"Two and a half years after gaining my freedom, I am willing to stand in the naked light and state, unequivocally, I stayed because of me.

"He abused me. He lied. He deceived. He used terrifying stories to hold me silent. He manipulated my mind and smothered me with his untruths.

"But I am the one who chose to believe him. To let go of reason so that I could accept his unreasonable words and actions. Accept his unacceptable behaviour and compromise on myself – not because of who he was, but because of who I was and who I refused to be : independent, strong, uncompromising in my belief in me and what I deserved from love and life.

"I stayed because I did not have the courage and strength of character to stand up for me without fear.

"In my world, post P, I am 100% accountable for me. Post P I cannot hold him accountable for what happens to me today. Just as he is ac- countable for what he did, I am accountable for what I did, and what I do today.

"Today, I let him go, in peace, without shame, blame or pain. Holding onto resentment, bitterness, anger keep me from living the beautiful life I deserve. I let him go because I have the courage to take charge of my life today, to be 100% accountable for me today and to make choices that love and support me every step of the way.

"I leave him behind because I know that the past is gone, today is alive and tomorrow is just a dream away. A dream that will come true as long as I walk my path with dignity, grace and ease, 100% accountable for me."

Chapter 11
SEX

The following selections, under heading 1, clearly point out the allure of sexual attraction and the seductive vulnerability that it arouses in the victims of pathic manhood – I should say, *male*hood; since pathics perform sex mainly as the male animal of dominance and control and ejaculation. On the other side of the sexes, men, of course, succumb to the "femme fatale" of pathic *female*-hood just as easily as women do to men pathics; which is a phenomenon far more pervasive than family affairs (Samson and Delilah, Cleopatra and Antony, for two examples).

The selections under heading 2, challenges the reader's side of the issue of whether women in general, or a type of woman, are attracted to "bad guys" for the thrill of it, temporarily in their early youth until they find a "good guy" to marry and have children with; or habitually throughout their lives; and of whether this attraction is inborn or conditioned, or both.

---

1. "The psychopath is a vessel of hate masquerading as a vessel of love. Sex, to him, is a weapon of destruction, a hateful act, a means of penetrating to the victim's innermost being, and doing violence to her soul.

"The victim cannot protect herself because the very nature of sex is surrender, opening the self, and surrendering it to the other."

2. "All too soon I began to hear about all his past relationships with other women, especially his ex-wife. I never could quite measure up to her. I had to hear about their sex life and how great it was and how good she could cook and how wonderful her children (not his) were and on and on and on. The first really cruel thing he did to me was one afternoon he was going to bed (he worked odd hours) I thought I would slip in beside him thinking it would be nice time for intimacy. Just as I touched him he turned his back and snarled at me to leave him alone. That's pretty much how it was for ten years. He refused to have sex, only when he wanted and that was far and few between."

3. "While having sex (never did make love) he was rough and abusive."

4. "P used to close his eyes when he was making love to me which basically made me feel like a 'thing' and not even there. There was no tender look, tender caresses or soul connection. There was a deafening quiet and absence of intimate pillow talk that connects souls as well as bodies. No compliments, no discussion, no playful interaction, just the act itself. In some ways I thought it was a comfortable silence of two people sharing deeply; but that was just my projection. He felt nothing emotional while I was deeply in love with him. To him, it was a skin thing, further evidenced by his penchant for wanting to do it with the lights out. No need for eye contact or connection. Can only say this in retrospect. At the time I was pleased as can be that he was interested in pleasuring me but that became less important to him as the months rolled on. And then after I had the baby and weeks had passed he was disinterested. I know now because he was getting it somewhere else."

5. "I remember the first passionate kiss so many years ago, just like it was yesterday. Halfway through, he took a deep breath almost like a big sigh. I will never forget it and I asked him about it because my gut was telling me that he was bored or something. He said that he just needed some more air. Red flag. I ignored it. Then during our intimate times, he seemed to know so much about a woman's anatomy and told me all about it. Slowly over time, I was not allowed to face him anymore, had to be face down. If on the rare times I did get to face him, he always stared straight ahead at the wall or covered my face with a piece of clothing. The kissing, hugging and foreplay no longer exist either."

6. "Your post evoked a memory of yet another conversation I had with my ex-N. I had referred to sex as making love. She looked at me very inquisitively and said: 'I noticed you say that a lot – why do you call it 'making love?' So, I replied: 'Why, what would you call it?' Her response was: 'I would just call it SEX. I'm not really sure what LOVE is!' Looking back, it was yet another obvious NPD zinger that zinged right by me."

7. "THE FIRST GIANT RED FLAG ... needed instant gratification. It felt like he was needy. Had to spend every moment together. Pushed the sex so insistently. The relationship did not form naturally, it was rushed and he dictated the pace ... totally controlled and manipulated things in spite of all my efforts to slow it down."

8. "I need to tell you that the children my N professed to love, he was abusing sexually. I stayed with him for 16 years – and he abused my elementary school age daughter for 4 years. She repressed everything."

9. "I know that if my husband had been like yours, he'd have had a true believer in me. That kind of focused sexual attention makes a woman feel so claimed, so wanted, needed, bonded. I had almost forgotten because of what life with my husband was like, but he was like that, in our beginning. Before we lived together, we spent entire weekends in bed. I remember him taking me back to his cabin for a weekend, driving over a bridge at 100 mph, then once in his house, turning me upside down and shaking me out of my hip hugger jeans because he couldn't get the zipper down fast enough. Having sex for literally hours at a time, rest briefly, start over. I had never had a relationship like that. I felt like he was starving and I was the only food on the planet.

"His sexual humiliation of me began before we married. But the moment we were married, something else changed, too: his hunger for me. Suddenly, it was as if he'd always just finished a big meal, and I was cold spinach left on the plate.

"I know what you mean about feeling raped after your husband expressed such need for you, and then abandoned you just 24 hours later. I felt some version of that, after being the tantalizing steak in a hungry man's eyes, and then reverting to cold porridge overnight. I well remember the feelings of confusion and rejection. What happened to you, in an instant, happened to me over 30 years. I gradually realized that the focused sexual attention had not been passion born of love. You realized it the moment you realized he had left just after expressing such need and passion. And it does feel a lot like rape."

10. "I am relating my experience and opinion below:

"For the p, sex is a stimulating obsession with him. Women in his life are just for his amusement and pleasure. The sex, at first, is all consuming and very passionate. Later on, he seemed to have gotten bored, like the thrill is in the getting and it is on to the next victim or else he cannot contain the beast in him or most likely at little of both.

"If you look closely enough, you will notice the p has an obsession with a certain part of the female anatomy, not really the person after the initial thrill as worn off for the p. Then, the physical part gets more and more bizarre.

"He related his fantasy is about women covering their faces and being tied up. So, the mask slipped in his quest for a bizarre fantasy.

"In the beginning though, while he is wooing you and the sex is great, he is still out there looking for his next victim – in the bars and on adult personal sites or in chatrooms, creating a persona of

Prince Charming.

"At first I thought I wasn't pretty or perfect enough for him, but then with the help of this forum, I now believe it isn't about me. It is about him. His wife can't satisfy him, nor could I satisfy him, nor can any single women – a bottomless pit of a sexual pervert always on the prowl for the next one. So, the more women know that he's out there, they can save themselves the emotional toll as it has been taken on his previous victims."

11. "EVERYTHING was about sex to my p. Any issue over which I struggled for some control was about sex to him. He told me, in later years, that he really viewed me as always attempting to control HIM. In his twisted view, if I squirmed for any control over my own life, I was controlling him. I understand, now, that the p believes he has the right to control everyone, and when his victim attempts to gain any control over her own life, she is wresting that control away from him. She has no rights. She does not actually exist, in his view. She is an extension of him. I believe that, for psychopaths, sex and control are all bound up together."

12. "I was basically with a guy who was very, very emotionally, verbally, sexually, and somewhat physically abusive. He is, has, narcissistic personality disorder (NPD) and so he criticized everything I did. (Even the way I looked at him) He would joke about killing me and he's always been in some sort of trouble. He was obsessive about me at first. He displayed all of the Red Flags of an emotional abuser. He would call me like 6 or 7 times of day and text-message me in between; very protective; jealous; told me I was perfect for him; asked me if I thought I could marry a guy like him; asked me to come with him to meet his family; used me – this was all within a few weeks. He wouldn't attend my graduation from college nor my graduation party (He was around the corner at a bar). And only talked about himself. He still doesn't know much about me! He also raped, sexually coerced (complained), sexually intimidated (held me down and pushed even harder) me several times. He called me a nympho in the beginning when I asked him for sex like once or twice. So after that I stopped asking. Then the

first time he raped me he pinned me down and made me have anal sex with him. I didn't realize until later that the week before I told him that I didn't want to do it, and he said, 'Oh you will' – I guess he kept that promise!! So, after that I became numb and sort of blocked it out. Anyway, eventually I broke up with him."

13. "After 23 years in a relationship with a kind person, but sexually dysfunctional, I was starved for sexual attention, to feel like a woman who was desired. I immediately attracted someone who I know now is a psychopath. I just ended the relationship after 2 months of abuse, which began almost right after the affair began. At first, I thought it was a matter of PTSD with BPD (bad enough), as his last wife committed suicide and he was severely traumatized (this was 4 years ago). But now I'm sure he drove her to suicide.

"The pattern fits so exactly, from sympathy for my starved sexual life, giving incredible great sex lasting for hours at the beginning (but little or no foreplay), hints about his group marriage 'hippie' friends, just hang and enjoy playing, then learning about daily pot smoking, other substance abuse, no visible signs of income, lying about other relationships, hysterical jealousy if I talk even about a male friend, walking away from me or changing the subject if I talked about myself, making up illnesses so I would take care of him (and of course, not up for sex), miraculous recoveries only to ditch our date and make sure I knew he was going to spend the time with another woman.

"...Thank God it was only a short time. But the intense psychological/ emotional brutality shut me down sexually for good it feels like...I'm seeking therapy to understand my vulnerabilities and to close these 'holes' in my personality. I went from passive abuse to active abuse. It was like taking candy from a baby."

14. "The sex with P was very mechanical, cold, unfeeling, gymnastic. He was all into 'Point your toes, arch your back'. Do this, do that. Very little, if any kissing. He was only into genitals touching. I can't remember having sex with him and our chests touching. I'd ask him to kiss me more, more foreplay and he did try once, but I could tell his heart wasn't in it. He also always wanted to give me a massage.

When we broke up I found out that he had put a hidden camera in the bedroom the first time we had sex and put the pictures on a porn website he had. I am still trying to get over that by going to a therapist. My mind couldn't understand how he could do something so vile like that until I found a website on psychopaths."

15. "I know one woman who told me her brother raped her and her sister after he returned from World War 2. She and her sister confronted their brother about his abuse and asked to go into therapy with him. He said basically 'So what? I raped you, get over it.' One sister went insane. The other has lived a life of deprivation with a N-husband. When the brother died, the deprived sister told me that 1200 people came to his funeral, most of whom went to the same church as the brother and held him in the highest esteem. He got away with it. Ns get away with, and have gotten away with murder, all the time."

16. "I never thought my X-N/P was sadistic, but now I remember days where I cried my eyes out, and while the tears were streaming down my cheeks, he would become sexually aroused and start looking at my chest and touching me, then try to have sex with me."

17. "P used sex, from our beginning, to take away my autonomy. He violated me sexually by having sex with all my friends, neighbors, associates, so that I could not turn anywhere without being confronted by the sickening awareness of p's sexual betrayals. He had sex with other women in my bed. He humiliated me, in all social settings by having sexually charged conversations with other women, in my presence; often stranding me somewhere with our babies, while he disappeared for hours, with one of these women.

"I did not have a jealous or suspicious bone in my body when I met the p. But, OF COURSE, I developed those traits. It actually took a long time, and tremendous effort on p's part. I did not understand that behavior. Because it ran contrary to the wisdom of my heart, I remained innocent for a ridiculously long time. While p was setting me up to become his invention, he constantly planted the concept, in my mind, and the minds of all observers, that our problems were the result of my irrational jealousy and suspicion. This worked perfectly in later years when he had perfected his act so that he did not behave, in obvious ways, in front of others, but seduced women by pretending to be suffering from my irrational jealousy and control of him.

"P turned every issue, in later years, into one about sex (and MY mental sickness about it). It did not matter if we argued over who was to get the water softener salt, p turned the argument into one about my torture of him over sexual issues. This thing he had done to me became HIS absolute out.

"When we went through a horrible time, while he was working for a mental health agency (a problem-ridden time which had NOTHING to do with sex), he was befriended by 2 female therapists on the staff. I asked him how he characterized our problems to them. He said, 'I told them I made a few mistakes years ago, and that you have never been able to let it go.'

"P was the sole creator of this fiction. No matter how hard I tried to stay away from the subject, He invariably brought it up within seconds of any conflict, 'Now you're going to start telling me how I slept with all your friends. I can't take it anymore. I'm going to kill myself.'

"This speaks of two things to me, now. One is that p contracted a reality in which he tortured me, sexually, while creating an illusion of the opposite, that I tortured HIM sexually. The other is that sex was his ultimate soul-destroying weapon. I have read that sexual abuse is absolutely the most damaging, that it destroys the souls of children (and I think it has the potential of doing that to adults, too). This makes sense because, when you think of sex, as an expression of love, in order for it to work, the person who loves has to surrender her being, her separateness, for a moment, and allow herself to fall backward, over something that feels like a waterfall. She has to relinquish control, abandon her boundaries. This can be a spiritual experience, and in its truest, purest expression, it IS a spiritual experience. Thus, sex can be a vehicle of ultimate healing power, or a vehicle of ultimate destructive power. It is a question of WHO and WHAT is in control in the moment that the woman (in this case) relinquishes control. I have no doubt that the psychopath recognizes (perhaps not consciously) the exploitative potential of sex as a weapon to destroy at the deepest level. Mine used it to breathtaking perfection.

"Now, I want to expand on the effects of p's sexual torture. Because of his many affairs, and the way they were stuffed in my face, and his incessant fantasizing in my ear about sex with other women during sex with me, I became unable to have sexual feelings as myself. As myself, I was so bloody wounded by p's betrayals that I could not experience erotic feeling without hellish pain so overwhelming it shut me down.

"I was so, so, so determined to overcome 'my problem' and continue to satisfy p's 'needs' that I never once allowed 'my problem' to get in his way. Instead, I dissociated and became whatever woman p was fantasizing about. In other words, I became the woman p was cheating on me with, in my inner identity, my sexual identity. Inevitably, as I approached and crossed the threshold, that place where you let go of all control, and fall backwards (body falling, spirit rising), I ascended, not into paradise, but I descended into hell. That moment was rich with all of Kris's agony, the recognition that I had just participated in another annihilation of myself, another soul murder, another debasement to the bottom of the world.

"Sometimes, when we were not being sexual, I talked to p about 'my problem,' very gently, hoping 'we' could work on solving it together. P's most usual reaction was extreme self-pity. 'Wow, that really hurts me to know that something that is so special to me actually hurts you. I don't know if I can get past that.' (Poor thing to be so burdened by my problems.)

"So, in sexual situations, I was careful to keep 'my problem' to myself. P never noticed that I suffered a descent into hell at the big moment. And he might stop the fantasizing for a week, after a discussion, but he never stopped it for long. So I guess he was able to transcend my thoughtless burdening of him with my problems.

"This speaks to what I was describing, in my previous post, that the p is able to cause almost limitless destruction to his victim, to her soul, to actually take her soul to hell, repeatedly, through the weapon of sexual torture. And all the while he is doing it, he paints her as HIS abuser. She is always hurting HIM, not the other way around. The psychopath has all the exits covered.

"I absolutely see this sexual abuse as the most vile, pernicious abuse in the psychopath's repertoire. I suffered every kind of abuse, emotion- al, physical, psychological, but the sexual abuse was, without question, the most agonizing and deeply, deeply damaging. Sexual abuse is abuse to every level of a person's being. It reaches into one's core humanity and poisons and destroys.

"Sex, 'intercourse,' is a physical metaphor for spiritual intercourse. It is one of 2 acts in physical human life in which the boundaries of human separateness are penetrated, and it mirrors the spiritual concept of love. The other act is violence and murder, and this mirrors the spiritual concept of hate."

18. "My brother raped me the first time when I was eight. He was fourteen and really strong for his age. After that he forced himself on me at least three or four times a week. The pain was so unbearable that I sort of went away from myself. I realize now that he must have been pretty crazy, because he'd tie me up and torture me with knives. Scissors, razor blades, screwdrivers, anything he could find. The only way I could survive was to pretend that this was happening to someone else.

"I never told my parents anything about what Tommy was doing to me because he threatened to kill me if I did, and I believed him. My dad was a lawyer who put in sixteen-hour days including weekends, and my mom was a pill junkie. Neither one of them ever protected me. The few hours that Dad was home, he wanted peace and quiet, and he expected me to look after Mom. My whole childhood seems like one big blur of nothing but pain."

19. "She lied because she knew I would throw her out of the house if I found out. She likes to have two or more men going at the same time, knows that other people find this wrong, so she covers it up. The lying also adds drama, which makes the affair more titillating and exciting, and the other man more desirable. She often referred to 'illicit' sex as the most exciting. She is about drama, and lying helps create and maintain drama. It is an aphrodisiac for her. The lies are automatic; she is so good at it. It has become habitual, part of her normal behavior. I think she is so psychopathic that she would lie even when she doesn't need to."

2

SEXUAL SELECTION
[Good Guys vs. Bad Guys]

The passages in this section are responses to an internet forum which express various individuals' thoughts regarding the thesis put forth in the following article.

Bad Guys Really Do Get The Most Girls
18 June 2008, NewScientist.com news service, Mason Inman

NICE guys knew it; now two studies have confirmed it: bad boys get the most girls. The finding may help explain why a nasty suite of antisocial personality traits known as the "dark triad" persists in the human population, despite their potentially grave cultural costs.

The traits are the self-obsession of narcissism; the impulsive, thrill-seeking and callous behaviour of psychopaths; and the deceitful and exploitative nature of Machiavellianism. At their extreme, these traits would be highly detrimental for life in traditional human societies. People with these personalities risk being shunned by others and shut out of relationships, leaving them without a mate, hungry and vulnerable to predators.

But being just slightly evil could have an upside: a prolific sex life, says Peter Jonason at New Mexico State University in Las Cruces. "We have some evidence that the three traits are really the same thing and may represent a successful evolutionary strategy."

Jonason and his colleagues subjected 200 college students to personality tests designed to rank them for each of the dark triad traits. They also asked about their attitudes to sexual relationships and about their sex lives, including how many partners they'd had and whether they were seeking brief affairs.

"High 'dark triad'" scorers are more likely to try to poach other people's partners for a brief affair."

The study found that those who scored higher on the dark triad personality traits tended to have more partners and more desire for short-term relationships, Jonason reported at the Human Behavior and Evolution Society meeting in Kyoto, Japan, earlier this month. But the correlation only held in males.

James Bond epitomizes this set of traits, Jonason says. "He's clearly disagreeable, very extroverted and likes trying new things — killing people, new women." Just as Bond seduces woman after woman, people with dark triad traits may be more successful with a quantity-style or shotgun approach to reproduction, even if they don't stick around for parenting. "The strategy seems to have worked. We still have these traits," Jonason says.

This observation seems to hold across cultures. David Schmitt of Bradley University in Peoria, Illinois, presented preliminary results at the same meeting from a survey of more than 35,000 people in 57 countries. He found a similar link between the dark triad and reproductive success in men. "It is universal across cultures for high dark triad scorers to be more active in short-term mating," Schmitt says. "They are more likely to try and poach other people's partners for a brief affair."

Barbara Oakley of Oakland University in Rochester, Michigan, says that the studies "verify something a lot of people have conjectured about."

Christopher von Rueden of the University of California at Santa Barbara says that the studies are important because they confirm that personality variation has direct fitness consequences.

"They still have to explain why it hasn't spread to everyone," says Matthew Keller of the University of Colorado in Boulder. "There must be some cost of the traits." One possibility, both Keller and Jonason suggest, is that the strategy is most successful when dark triad nationallities are rare. Otherwise, others would become more wary and guarded.

Men's Views on the Above Article

1. "The dark triad behaviors may hold as attractors because in times of severe risk from outside dangers, men who indicated a bawdy self-confidence – instead of an overarching fear of the world – at least 'looked' as if they could handle anything (and maybe they could). This is an evolutionary holdover, with the great irony being that offspring from these types have less an opportunity to flourish, because they're not nurtured for modernity. Evolution, in this case, is still at work. ..."

2. "Being one of those sociopathic/narcissistic men I have to admit: I hate you emotionally healthy women with high self-esteem. I hope your numbers don't increase. Nothing like a self-assertive, confident woman to screw up a perfect opportunity. What about gals who feign weakness to attract a man? It's a mixed-up, jumbled-up world. I like mine hot, thank you. My girlfriend disdains the nice guys. Does this say more about her or the nice guys? Hmmm, I wonder. I take my hat off to you, my common sense lady. Do you have any sisters that are a little off-kilter?"

3. "Those men that I have known who claim to score often are, in fact, predators. I don't, and we don't, know whether they are as successful as claimed. Assume they are. Why, then, would they be so successful? They tell me, and I believe that it is because, they ask for sex much more often and of many more women than the rest of us. They expect to be turned down most of the time, get slapped and get cursed, quite often. Even though the turndown rate is high, the sheer volume of attempts yields a lot of successes. (kind of like WALMART with a low profit margin but huge sales.)"

"Perhaps more of us would do the same thing if it were not for the pain of rejection that doesn't seem to bother these hunters. Perhaps the tolerance of rejection arises from the narcissism and psychopathy that the author of the article seems to have found. The other quality of the triad, scheming, seems only to be a matter of finding the way to ask that has the best chance of success.

"Bottom line is that these guys may be successful more often than others, not because women find them more attractive, but because they try harder and more often."

4. "Bad boys do get laid more: FACT. Good guys will, by nature pass up many opportunities because they exercise moral restraint. They respect women and defer to their wishes. The woman is grateful. Everybody is happy. The naughty lil girl inside her is aching to have the bad lil boy in him jimmy the lock and let her out of her cage. Just for the night, and just between them. It's sweeter when you're a cheater. It is shallow and short-sighted, but it's HOT HOT HOT. And it avoids the harsh light of reality and responsibility. Like a diamond, we all have many facets. Indulge your wild side, boys AND girls. Get down, get funky. If you are a BAD boy, that gives her permission to be a BAD girl. It's so simple, children. Just don't make any in the process (i.e.: harsh reality and responsibility)."

5. "After 6+ (+++..!) decades depressing experience of the wicked ways of the world, being one of the GGs who come last (or more usually not at all), it grieves me to admit it but I have to say that ET is right on the button with this analysis of the psychology involved. He has put it in the proverbial nutshell. And, contrary to some of the earlier posts from defenders of the myth that 'nice girls don't', there are in fact very few nice (straight) girls (and fewer still mature women) so strong-minded that they haven't been vulnerable to the depredations of some smooth-operating bastard at some time in their lives. And often only too delighted to be able to salve any guilty conscience by blaming the 'naughty' boy that led them 'astray'. (And again, and again. . . and again.)

"In any analysis of sexual behaviour it needs to be kept firmly in mind that females are just as driven by their genes and hormones to reproduce as are men, and can be just as ready to delude themselves by grasping at any weak 'excuse' to switch off their inhibitions, let their hair down and kick over the traces.

"Since the 'sexual revolution' of the 1960s, and more especially since the arrival of the anonymity of the web, there are now, thankfully, far more women around who are prepared to be honest and up-front about these issues. Readers who have UNRESTRICTED ACCESS to the web can learn much from doing a search (these sexual topics are mostly blocked by the majority of firewalls, set up to 'protect the innocent'). As perhaps could the people who did this 'world shattering original research'! The only new thing it has revealed to me is that maybe not so many participants lie on these surveys as we'd previously suspected.

"I just wish someone had been honest enough to explain all this to me when I was a confused innocent teenager back in the 50s: when girls were brought up to be devious and dishonest (to defend their reputations) WITHOUT the safety valve of being able to ease their consciences by telling the truth anonymously on the web."

6. "You've obviously never spent any time in a bar in Texas. The majority of women there are single mothers looking for more bad boy hookups or a nice guy to raise their bad boy's offspring and the motherless aren't exactly looking for nice guys either.

"Generalizing of course and I'm aware that the Texas bar scene isn't necessarily representative of the world. But then I don't suppose you saw the recent news report about the high school girls who made pacts to have children. Doubt very much they selected nice guys by choice or accident.

"Like the other replies to this, I don't believe we can presume that the bad boy traits are either being deselected or selected for. Time and evolution will determine that.

"I would not call being an oversexed loon an evolutionary pro. Nobody who has ever thought objectively about life would. It is aberrant. Sure, it increases your chances of having children, but is evolution always right? There's ample proof that many species have evolved into simpler organisms. Most often in the case of parasites. Devolution in other words. Might this not be the case here? Is it not generally these types who parasitically prey on the rest of society? I rest my case.

"And what about the evolution of society itself? Any benefit to society is an automatic benefit to everybody's progeny."

7. "Of course nice guys might complain about the bad guys 'getting all the girls' but really, all most nice guys want is a stable relationship, with a nice girl (so I might suppose), so an interesting study for researchers interested in the existence of these traits might be of females as well. Perhaps the assertions of some posters, that women with similar qualities are involved with 'dark triad' men, is true, or perhaps it's a mix, with 'good girls' and 'bad girls' falling for the 'bad guys' (I use the quotes not in a degrading manner but because these are colloquial expressions)."

8. "I've often wondered why women are attracted to the 'rascal-type'. Could it be that in a self-less abandonment of their own happiness (in line with the selfish gene theory), they seek mates who they know will give them sons who, through similar behaviour to their fathers, will spread the mother's genes too?"

9. "The implication here seems to be that having 'dark triad' traits makes you more 'successful' with women – which is further implied to be getting laid a lot with different people.

"Would it be at least as believable and valid to say that if you are not heavy on these traits you'd be far less inclined to seek casual sex... And if you are not looking, you aren't going to get it, are you!"

10. "These days the bad guys only get some of the girls. The same loose girls are also spending their time with the other bad guys. They frequently end up bringing up the children on their own at considerable disadvantage. Even if they do land the bad guy in a long term relationship he is probably a useless father."

11. "I was a member of a rock group that toured internationally and there was a new pool of people every night. I don't recall ever engaging in activity that I would classify as dishonest. There was no trickery. There was just women who wanted to have some fun with a young guy who wasn't going to be around long enough to disappoint them.

"I guess one could argue the perception of the 'rock star' is in of itself a lie, but there are plenty of women out there who want the 'bad' guy, but that doesn't make all the 'bad' guys dishonest. I certainly saw a lot of guys (and a few women!) abuse their status and situation and do things I personally found unacceptable. But some of the assessments of this article (which has dubious source data indeed) seem to me to be extremely self-righteous and prudish. People (especially young people) like to get down. And if wool is being pulled over the sexes' collective eyes that is almost always in my experience, because it's part of the dance that is done, and not some evil manipulation at the hand of James Bond. (Who by the way is an icon desired by plenty of women and envied by plenty of men in spite of what some commentators here would have you believe.) Especially Connery & Craig.)

"Oh, and I'm now very happily married to an absolutely amazing woman. I've always been of the opinion that monogamy is the most rewarding sexual lifestyle, even though it is plain to me that I personally am not built for it. It's a damn good thing I have a brain to counteract the peeps otherwise I'd be doomed to never enjoy the true satisfaction of long-term intimacy and enlightenment of an ever building love.

"Love is all you need, indeed, but sometimes casual sex will do just fine. And it's not nearly as steeped in manipulation and dishonesty that some would suggest and when it is it is quite often part of the fun for the two (or more!) that decide to tango."

12. "I never had as many women in my life as when I was dealing drugs. Once I went 'clean' I had to go out and compete against these bad boys. Another thought, ever notice gangbangers, rock stars, and guys in jail seem to always have a smoking hot chick? Now we know why."

13. "It would be more informative if the investigators start with the proposition: it takes two to mate. This way, the female side of the equation could be understood. It (the black triad traits) can't be alluring to ALL females. So the question becomes what type of females are drawn to such traits? What proportion does this

represent in the female population? The study could also address whether there are any correlation between the black triad traits and other contributors towards being considered (by females) as potential mates such as social status, financial resources, physical attributes (height, weight etc. etc.)? In short, a better study is needed on this fascinating topic."

14. "I love women and have always felt a moral and ethical responsibility to do my part to improve the gene pool. I have often made myself available for sex with the multitudes of women who have pursued me, many of whom have committed relationships with other men. After these many years I've yet to hear any complaints. It occurs to me that women are more likely to be the aggressors for these kinds of affairs for their own reasons, and I suspect there are other good men who have raised my offspring. I don't know whether this makes me a good guy or a bad buy, but I appreciate all the good sex."

15. "No matter how many studies are done that prove this fact, women will continue to deny they are attracted to bad boys because it makes it seem like they are not in control of their own faculties. In fact they aren't. Women claim to know what's good for them since they gained rights on the back of civil rights movement but they still don't. Women think with their hearts, not their heads. They love power and influence and bad boys exhibit those traits to some extent. Women cannot resist them no matter how much they try because it's not something that can be resisted by effort alone. Women are not in control of themselves emotionally most of the time. This just adds more proof to the heaping pile of evidence."

16. "I learned to disrespect girls because they respond by wanting to have sex with you. I was the really nice guy who never got laid. Now I am 45, with a lot of experience and a child. I can say with little reservation that you are looking at a masochistic streak in women not attraction to bad boys. If a good boy is willing to smack that ass, she's gonna go for him too. I would posit that this has more to do with aggressive behaviour than the triad. Some good guys are aggressive and they get laid more. Women want to be wanted and how do they know unless you tell them. Also, the media's idea of what a bad boy is, seems to be what girls go for. Not the actual bad boy. The actual bad boy generally speaking has too many emotional problems to focus on girls much. I have known a few."

17. "Face it; nice guys aren't fun. They're not a challenge and they're not a thrill. The minute you give in and play to the pampering, attention, and I-love-yous, it goes down the drain. Now you're boring, same old, same old; no longer fun and your woman's looking at the next fun challenging man.

"I hardly call my 'girlfriend' back. I make her wait on me all the time. I only smile when I hear 'I-love-you'. I don't buy her much. She knows I flirt. She knows I like the attention too. I'm so terrible. I make her jealous ALL the time.

"Yet a year later she still puts up with me. She loves me to the bone and everything about me, and my life. From the way I dress or the way I act, to how I do my hair.

"I just moved into a new neighborhood. My second day there, the neighbor lady came over and introduced herself. All dressed up for a Saturday night out. Told me to stop by and have a couple beers with her any time. And told me we should go out together sometime.

"I love being bad."

18. "This article does not mention anything about 'the bad *girls*': the shrills, the scolds, the self centered Paris Hilton [an international celebrity] twits, and the total harridans.

"No mention at all, about the shrewish Leona Helmslys and Cruela DeVilles of this world, figures into the article – and none of the commentary.

"People tend to buy into the 'sugar and spice and everything nice' ruse. I saw through it by the time I was 3. But then, I had the 'advantage' of having been surrounded by a pack of catty shrews."

19. "I have heard from a poet friend of mine who spent her college years going to places where the local 'boys', who weren't exactly academic, the factory hands, when there were factories, the rough exteriors and the 'availability' of someone who wasn't as inhibited."

20. "I recently had a girl dump her date in the middle of a party to go skinny dipping with me and some other people in the pool. He, of course, got mad and left. She later told me that she thought he was a 'stick in the mud'. Maybe it's not a question of nice guy vs. bad guy, but exciting vs. dull."

21. "Why Women Prefer Bad Boys. Women say they want a nice guy, yet usually end up dating bad boys. Here's why:

"Not real: Nice guys are too nice. No one can always be that nice unless they're a saint. They are busy being nice instead of being real and women instinctually don't trust that. Bad boys keep it real. Nice guys don't want to upset the apple cart.

"Respect: No one respects a doormat. Nice guys don't set boundaries or make any real demands. A bad boy doesn't let a woman walk all over him or control him. Women can't respect a man they can control. No respect = No attraction.

"Predictable: Most people lead boring, predictable lives, so they're attracted to people who are exciting and unpredictable. Bad boys are always a challenge. Nice guys are never a challenge. Predictable = No excitement = No challenge = I prefer a bad boy.

"Mother Nature: Women are designed to nurture. However, instead of doing this with children, they often end up doing it with bad boys. They think their love will save them. Nice guys rarely need to be saved. Fixer-Upper: Nice guys don't usually need to be fixed. Bad boys usually do, so they become a project. Women think if they can recreate the perfect man, he will never leave them. Also, if they're busy fixing someone else, they don't have to look at what needs to be fixed in their own lives.

"Sperm wars: Women are designed to procreate with the strongest possible genes. Bad boys are sending an unconscious message that they have great genes, so they're not afraid of losing the woman by misbehaving. Nice guys are sending a message that they don't think their genes are good enough, so they won't misbehave.

"Fear of intimacy: If a woman is afraid of intimacy, she subconsciously knows she can avoid it with a bad boy, since she can never get close enough to him to have to go there. A nice guy will eventually want a commitment, and that's scary.

"Low self-esteem: We don't feel comfortable with people who treat us better than we treat ourselves. If you don't think much of yourself, the bad boy is simply reinforcing your negative belief. A nice guy is treating you in a way you're unfamiliar with.

"Sex: Women feel a nice guy won't be good in bed. They like to be manhandled sometimes and think a nice guy won't be able to take control and get the job done. A bad boy comes across as being able to get the job done, even though that may not always be the case.

"Hot: Have you ever seen a bad boy who wasn't hot? I'm sure there are a few, but they wouldn't be able to get away with half the stuff they did if they didn't look so good. Meanwhile, when a woman describes someone as a nice guy, she means, He's not hot.

"Charm: Nice guys don't always know what to say, and are sometimes at a loss for words. Bad boys can be very charming and know exactly what women want to hear. However, they eventually switch over to being selfish. By the time they reveal their true colors, the woman has fallen for them and has a hard time letting go.

"Protection: Historically, men have protected women physically and otherwise. Bad boys give the illusion of being able to protect women, while with nice guys, women aren't so sure.

"Life is about balance. Most men fall into either the bad boy or the nice guy category. The ideal man is neither, but walks that fine line between the two. Until men learn how to do this, more often than not, women will choose the bad boy. Remember: Love inspires, empowers, uplifts and enlightens."

22. "The dark triad behaviors may hold as attractors because in times of severe risk from outside dangers, men who indicated a bawdy self-confidence – instead of an overarching fear of the world – at least 'looked' as if they could handle anything (and maybe they could). This is an evolutionary holdover, with the great irony being

that offspring from these types have less an opportunity to flourish, because they're not nurtured for modernity. Evolution, in this case, is still at work. ..."

23. "My educated guess is that without the proper care of a parent the 'bad guys' could ultimately die off. If not the human race is in jeopardy because they will be more vulnerable without male figures in their lives. For instance, the wolf is an animal that stays with its mate. Now would the children be more likely to survive? Also, the evolution of these 'bad guy' children depends on a care taker. In nature females nurse the child but the males bring back food and protect them. Without this I should think that we would be digressing in evolution not progressing. It is really up to the 'nice guy' to refuse to care for a 'bad guy' child in order to prevent a world of degenerates and immature men and dare I say worthless males. I find this study not only biased but also ultimately sexist...Who's to say women will not 'evolve' in a way to know what is better for them. Here's another proven study which may argue the contrary. In nature, human beings like wolves need to feel security in packs and clans and tribes. Degenerates are not helpful to the pack and ultimately will be scrapped...especially in times of little resources such as food. Cannibalism will seem awfully tempting. If this is the inevitable truth [along with] the future of the human in evolution, [then] to the 'bad guys' I say, 'For the good of the species, grow up...or take your medication.'"

24. "Another aspect of this [sexual selection] in modern times is that many women choose to use birth control with men like these (when it's made available to them), and so generally it's likely that birth control could impact the number of kids that these dark triad men will be able to have."

25. "My opinion, girls tend to have a primal attraction to bad guys, 'cus no nice dude is gonna beat down a wolf, or spear and elephant, or even kill a rival tribe member..."

26. "In evolutionary terms, men need to have a bad side."

27. "I would have to agree with you that many nice guys are passed over for the suave sophisticated and confident man. Women never see it's a ploy to sweep them off of their feet before they catch on there's nothing there but suave and possibly a lot of money to help the suaveness. I'm fortunate to be able to retire soon at 52. I'm not the suave guy but some call me nice looking. I've never shown a lot of confidence with dating. I'm not shy just not so secure [with my feelings]. In business I'm very successful and always finish first. That power is a turn on to many women when they're younger; but anyone in the mid forties kind of gets over that. I do think I'll find the one for me; but that will be after she's so mistreated that she's messed up."

28. "I'm a nice guy and I will get the woman for me. I believe in playing honest, fair, caring, and loving. I am very secure and stable and can handle another family added to my financial situation. I believe in sharing that wealth and my time. I feel like I'm writing an ad. I have to believe that women will learn the value in what I have to offer"

29. "Nice guys with money often get taken such as women who swear they are on birth control and I'm talking about 30 to early 40 years old; women with kids. No prenup 'cause you're not married, so you're stuck."

30. "Most nice guys can't wait to meet and marry the woman who loves them; [but] that woman usually doesn't seem to know what she wants and keeps one eye roaming."

31. "Women habitually date not nice guys. It's just the way of the world."

32. "I certainly have been in situations where a woman I was with lost interest and went to, or returned to, a 'bad boy'. Was it passion, was I too 'boring' in comparison. I never really know. How could someone return to a man that had cheated on her? I don't really know. But men can do the same thing...go after the Ferrari instead of the reliable Camry. It happens...we're human. I realized after my divorce that I had a propensity to be attracted to women who were a little more impulsive, and 'exciting' than me. I would later find these traits to be uncomfortable. I've had to work pretty hard to keep from being impulsive myself and letting this happen again, and I've been pretty successful. One irritating thing I find is the friends who keep telling me I'm a 'good guy' (thanks!), and you just have to find the right girl and she's out there somewhere for you...when I'm not really sure that's what I want. I know they're just trying to cheer me up, but I don't think they know me as well as they think they do...I digress. Do nice guys finish last? I don't think so, and I certainly hope not. I'm having fun being a dad and raising my children, being with my family. I socialize when I can, maybe I meet the love of my life; maybe I don't. We'll see what the cards hold. I'm happy with my life and don't feel like I'm in last place. If 'she' wants the bad boy, she's going to have to look somewhere else."

Women's Views on the Article

33. "These types of men keep being born in the population obviously because they spread their seed more successfully. But also, I proffer, because their female partners, the women who fall for these men, are also passing on their genes in the process. Mating is a two-way street. I never cease to be exasperated at the stupidity and shallowness of women who are attracted to the 'bad boy' types.

"I also believe that this dark triad is a type of genetic parasitism. I had a flatmate once who fit this triad rather well, and he was an adopted child. He had a marauding, psychopathic and self-centered approach to women and he had no shortage of them. I knew one of his partners too, who was a wild type and very manipulative towards the decent people. Once I pondered what his off-spring would be like, probably without him even being around to see their birth, and how would their genes show through in their behaviour. He turned out the way he did despite being brought up in a decent family, which got me wondering about genetically-endowed behaviour. Then it dawned on me that his offspring would be just like him if they were male, and like his female 'partner' if they were female. And I realized that his parents must have been the same way too (hence him being given up for adoption by a single mother). He was already an offspring of this 'dark triad' lineage that had been going on for some time, probably for many generations.

"Since those days whenever I'm around a 'bad boy' type I try to find out about his parentage. Very often they come from a line of dark triad types."

34. "Dude, it's not that other types of guys aren't fun; it's that badasses are more fun. They are sexually attractive by virtue of their dominant nature. We need not debate biology on that fact.

"So let's talk about why a normal girl might want to hook up with an a-hole.

"Consider: a 'bad boy' is unlikely to feel nervous in bed — they'll do what they want, and in all likelihood they'll seek to please their partner with that same undivided attitude, if only because they see an advantage in doing so, or because it makes things [more arousing]."

35. "Sociopathic/narcissistic men have more sex because they are sexual predators, treating sex like a recreational sport and women as 'game'. They only manage to pull the wool over women's eyes temporarily, and it's because they're skilled actors lacking a conscience. Let's not forget that women who do fall prey to these men are generally naifs with low self-esteem. Let's feel sorry for their prey and stop putting 'bad guys' up on pedestals. Emotionally healthy women want genuinely nice guys for partners."

36. "As a woman, I can vouch for the attractiveness of the 'dark' male. I have fallen for it and I probably will again.

"But I am not a typical woman. I had myself sterilized so I could enjoy my sex life more. There's already enough people.

"I'm not interested in marriage either, and at 36 don't see it changing.

"Nice guys can be associated with a lack of backbone. Not saying all nice guys are like this.

"And 'dark' guys can be nice too.

"Men of strong mind, strong body, strong character and full of wit are my favorite — rarity in the America, especially in South

Carolina (in fact the women here have raised a bunch of inept men).

"I'm a natural at flirting. Always have been. Monogamy doesn't fit in my head and I dream of having the male version of a harem – (like Madeline Kahn's role in, 'History of the World,' Mel Brooks)

"I also liken my sexual conquests like the good old days of war. Need something that a smaller country has? Invade them; take it and leave; maybe establish some sort of relationship.

"Aristippus (c. 435-356 BC) said it best: 'The art of life lies in taking pleasures as they pass, and the keenest pleasures are not intellectual, nor are they always moral.'"

37. "I hate nice guys, they make me sick, they make my skin crawl."

38. "Guys: I offer my personal experience for your enlightenment. For what it's worth, I 'chose' one once. (Rather, allowed him to seduce me.) Why? I am a seemingly intelligent professional woman with a mind of my own. Why did I get involved with DT [Dark Triad]? Here are some reasons:

"1) Forbidden fruit (Psychopaths tend toward relationships that are in some way, illicit: an affair with a married person, old man with young chick, a boss with an employee, a student with a teacher, a relative, etc. – forbidden. That is often a source of the excitement. For me that translated into someone twenty years older, blue collar (cop) – I was working on my dissertation (no boring briefcase with him), and one of us was married. He slept with five guns under his pillow. You never knew when one of them would go off. That was exciting, too.

"2) White hot sex (Psychopaths are often mechanically proficient. They have the gift of touch. They know what works, what to do. Sex with him was a religious experience. Eventually it became an addiction. I wasn't the only one. Women would leave messages on his voicemail asking him out or begging him to call them. If you wanted a foot massage, he knew just how to hold it, where to put pressure, etc.. Same with holding your hand. He was firm, possessive, never let you slide away. No fish grip there.)

"3) Physical perfection (Psychopaths are often physically gorgeous, well-built, prime specimens with lots of testosterone – square jaw, good shape, manly features, nothing grackle about them. This one was a former athlete. Built like a god. Outran twenty-somethings.)

"4) Aura (I can't explain it. Just standing next to him for a few minutes was enough to make me rip his clothes off. He smelled divine. Woodsy, sweaty, natural.)

"He was like the finest chocolate. You couldn't get enough. But you ended up paying the price later. He invited me over one day. My replacement walked out of his bedroom wearing his shirt. She was 40 years younger than he was, his "new model".

"Was it worth it? To the contrary. It cost so much more than it was worth, but I learned my lesson. I have no one to blame but myself."

39. "I was married to Mr. Slightly Dark Triad for 18 years, and he did get laid a lot, and lied about it and got away with it. So what constitutes a successful relationship? Being extra clever that the woman you marry is highly tolerant, has low self-esteem, loves unconditionally and is quite gullible? Um.....definitely, yes."

40. "Homes that are filled with noise and confusion: Children who come from homes that are loud and aggressive will often times steer away from a good quiet boy and find them boring."

41. "A lot of us girls don't actually want children. A lot of us (particularly from my age group) cringe at the idea of childbirth, and most of us aren't leaping for joy at the idea of sacrificing the best years of our lives for some whinny little toddler. 'Bad boys' for us are more attractive to us because unlike 'nice' guys, they are on the same page as us as far as kids are concerned. I personally hate most children, even as a child I hated other children, I have no desire to be a mother, so 'stability' and 'family-raising' abilities are not at the top of my priority list, and since white picket fences and snot nosed children tend to be at the top of 'nice guys' to do list, I try to stay clear of them."

42. "I understand the psychology behind this belief, and yes, it appears on the surface that it's true: nice girls love bad boys. I've wondered about it myself, and I suppose that one of the main reasons behind it is this: bad boys give good girls permission to be bad themselves, and perhaps the good girls live out their own fantasies through the actions of the bad boys. It's almost like being bad by proxy. I've learned a few things about relationships over the years, however, and I'm convinced that the saying is limited in its scope and vision. Nice guys do get the girl. The hero in the white hat does ride off into the sunset with the nice girl curled around him, hugging him 'round the neck. How does this work? Two things have to fall into place; first: the nice girl has to love the nice guy; and, second, the nice guy has to love the nice girl."

43. "The DTs I know are NOT the leaders!!! They are womanizing Lotharios, antisocial jackasses, who live on the fringe of society, not at the top of it, or at the bottom of society, shunned by the acknowledged pillars of society: the professionals, doctors, lawyers, scientist.

"All you guys out there on this blog – how many DT dudes do you associate with? Surely you all know some. Do you respect them? Would you vote for one? Would you hire one as an employee for your company? Would you invite one to an important meeting you were hosting?

"Even the ones who make it to the top as world leaders are shunned by the majority of the free world and they are considered rogues, renegades, and evil power mongers. I do not see them as successful alpha males.

"My husband – the ultimate nice guy – and his colleagues are the true alpha males. The ones who get real power and get things done in the world by being cooperative, socially concerned, actively involved, and responsible.

"Someone who works hard and does the right thing 24/7, trying to make the place a better world for his family and the rest of the world...THAT is an alpha male! – not some fast-talking Svengali who targets vulnerable women as easy prey. That is truly pathetic, not an object of admiration."

44. "Nice guys can be highly attractive to women – I've been married to the nicest guy out for five years and he's just gorgeous. So keep hoping that most girls out there still want to be happy and settle down with a nice guy. What the nice guy needs to find out is 'What does this woman really need or really want?' Once he gives her that, she's putty in his hands."

45. "A few factors are absent from consideration here – the article is all about passing along of genes, but what about memes [cultural information]? If nice guys are fathering and raising their children over the long term, then they are much more successful in passing along their traits in this realm. The study also further underscores the need for education and empowerment of women. Who are the most likely to have short-term affairs with men like this, and bear their children? Not educated and empowered women who value their futures and the quality of their lives and that of their children, that's for sure (and I'd venture to guess they'd be more likely to abort unintended pregnancies from brief encounters, underlying another need, which is to protect women's right to choose). Uneducated women who have little concern for their future are more likely to bear the babies of guys like these, since they have not been taught or empowered to seek better for themselves and their children."

46. "When you think about bad boys, one tends to picture a hot, dark-haired suave guy in leathers on a bike. You shouldn't judge a book by its cover but as far as bad boys are concerned, if you dwell into their pasts, they tend to move around a lot, they are bad because of their upbringing, lack of education and learned habits. The unknown and mysterious always attracts. I haven't met too many rebels that have a good education, if even a complete one, and let's not talk about social etiquette and acceptable behaviour. Would you really want that kind of father/role model for your children?"

47. "I agree with you that they can't sustain a relationship for long and this is just my opinion without real research but the difference between the bad boy and a player is that a player goes from woman to woman basically playing with their emotions, but usually a woman can spot those men and may even willingly engage knowing it's for the short term. A bad boy however, keeps stringing the woman along and nice guy can't get through. The relationship is rocky and goes up and down but still continues. I know so many women who like the nice guy but don't like how he's so nice that it makes them uncomfortable. I often wonder why these women aren't comfortable being treated kindly? I think that's something someone should look into. I've been through enough bad boys to have a true appreciation for a nice guy!"

48. "Dealing with the dark side – everyone probably does have a dark side. My question is how dark and in what area? Do they leave their socks on the floor, do they gamble, drink alone too much, do they cheat on you? In other words, there's a difference and each woman knows her limits. I can't handle a cheater or someone who lies to be with or bait other women. I also make that clear in the relationship that those are deal-breakers for me. Nice men and women do have a dark side but to what degree and at what cost to you is what makes the difference. A genuinely true nice guy's dark side isn't as dark or manipulating as a sheep's in wolf's clothing.

"… I can't argue with some of what you said, but I will argue that the woman won't need to be messed up by the time she seeks you out. In fact she might have dusted herself off and found a whole new person inside that still believes in the fairytale. I've been through some tough times and I've met wonderful people in my life. The ones that lost my trust didn't scar me for life, but they have made me look more closely at the guys who are steady-tempered, predictable, caring, and who put my needs before their own, or right up there with them. They are consistent and loyal regardless of the situation. I don't think I went out thinking, 'Oh, I'm with a bad boy; lucky me.' But, when the nice guy turned jerk shows his true colors, a woman like me starts to learn the value in a nice guy."

49. "The 'nice guy' has to generate the same kind of excitement that the 'bad boy' produces. He has to sweep her off her feet. He has to be courtly, attentive, and kind, and yet not be afraid to gather her in his arms and kiss her as she needs to be kissed, until her knees grow weak and her head is spinning."

"He can't be afraid of her, as so many nice guys seem to be. I've dated a few nice guys who were so tentative about making a move on me that I finally just gave up on them. Most girls don't want to be the one who pursues, at least not in the beginning. (We're usually fine with it later, but remember, 'nice girls' are raised to let the men make the first move.) So, while the nice guy is sitting beside us on the couch, his pulse racing, wondering if he should just go for it and ending up not doing a thing, the bad boy would have already made his move. He's not afraid of being told 'no'. He understands that there are a certain number of 'no's' he has to go through before he gets what he wants, and he is determined.

"Nice guys, on the other hand, are afraid of being told 'no', so they never risk it. What they don't seem to realize, though, is if we let you get close enough to us to take us out, we expect you to make a move. We also expect you to back off if we signal that it's too much too soon, but trust me ... We think you don't like us if you don't try. And if we say 'yes' to another date, we want you to try again.

"The 'nice girl' has to also be a 'good woman'. Good women understand what's important in a guy. We want someone who will respect us, who will care about our feelings, who will slay our dragons and protect us, who will fight to keep us, and remind us quite often that he's lucky to have us. It doesn't hurt if he can make us laugh (one of the most powerful aphrodisiacs around, by the way).

"I want to know that he adores me, he can't live without me (even if he really can), and he would move mountains to be with me. That's the kind of nice guy who will win my heart. That's the kind of nice guy a grown woman searches for. That's the kind of nice guy a 'good woman' treasures, and he's someone she will care for and love with everything she's got. That's the kind of nice guy with whom she wants to ride off into the sunset, fully secure in the fact that she's got a man who truly places her at the top of his desires, wants, and needs – and lets her know it.

"So don't give up, nice guys. There are lots of women out there who are looking for you. When you find one, don't be afraid of her. Don't be afraid to show her what she means to you, and don't be afraid to kiss her until she can't remember her own name. That's what she wants. While 'The Love Song of J. Alfred Prufrock' may be my favorite poem, I'd certainly never want to date poor old J. Alfred. In the poem, T.S. Eliot's protagonist asks himself, 'Do I dare? Do I dare?' He wonders, 'Should I, after tea and cakes and ices, have the strength to force the moment to its crisis?'

"A bad boy would. And I've known enough 'nice guys' to know that there's a 'bad boy' in every one of them. We want you to be the nice guy who allows the bad boy to come out once in a while.

"Perhaps it sounds complicated, all that I've written, above. Maybe it is. But who ever said anything worthwhile was easy? Don't live out your lives as Prufrock did. Unlike J. Alfred, you should 'dare to eat a peach.'"

50. "There's good news and bad news for all you nice guys out there. Your day will come. It just may not be today.

"Nearly all women go through some period in their lives when they're swept up by a bad boy. The Navy Seal with the amazing bod and the mental prowess of a fruit plate. The Harley guy with mean beard stubble and an attitude to match. The Josh Hartnett look-alike who makes us feel like the center of the universe, and then puts the moves on our roommate the minute we leave for the ladies' room. We can see these guys coming a mile away, and yet we fall for it every time.

"Why?

"Part of us actually likes to believe we can be the one girl to turn this wild man into a pussycat. Part of us just like that down-to-our-toes thrill, the excitement of something we KNOW is bad for us. (Like chocolate cheesecake, and Jimmy Choo shoes.) Part of us are just gluttons for misery.

"Most women actually grow out of the bad-boy phase once we hit our mid-twenties. Our girlfriends start to couple off, and we start wondering if we used up our nice guy quota in college when we were still torturing men for sport. That's where you come in,

Mr. Sweet Guy. Because you're the guy we really want.

"Here's my advice for all the nice guys:

"Remember what we were wearing on our first date. Give romantic gifts on birthdays and anniversaries (and remember flower-mandatory holidays such as Valentine's Day.) Get what we're all about. Let us know what you're all about. Kill any bugs that sneak into the kitchen. Give us your coat when it gets chilly outside. And remember there's a fine line between being a nice guy and being a doormat — don't take any crap from us. After all, you don't want to be a good boy in love with a bad girl."

Chapter 12
RELIGION

What a perfect guise for the pathics of theatrical talent! Who, of the congregation, would ever guess it that these "men of God" are in fact men of "Satan" with their families, and when it comes to fleecing and seducing their flock.

---

1. "Did you know that many evangelical pastors are Ns? It's actually a great place to get the N-supply. The members love you, think that you actually are superior to them because of the misconception that a pastor is greater than any other member of the body of Christ. This misconception would never be revealed by an N pastor. Then there is the money issue which actually steals from widows, lies about 'the more you give the more you will receive,' cons people about legality of tithing which is not a new covenant teaching. Convincing others how to dress, how to wear your hair and other insidious teachings (does this sound Taliban-ish?), that are not biblical. It's a prime place, a breeding ground for NS."

2. "The pastor is ok, but at times I felt odd when I did Bible study with him. I can't explain it. I never told my ex about it because he would not have believed it. He thinks that his church and the pastor are perfect. The entire time that I attended his church (about 4 months) I felt strange. Maybe it is because I am Catholic. It's like they wanted me there but I did not have long hair and I wore makeup and pants. They did not. They tried to tell me that the Bible

says women need to dress like them. My ex was always saying that I did not read the Bible right or go to church enough, etc.. I think that he uses his strict religious beliefs to make him feel superior to others. He also would treat people mean, have sex with me, take items from work (supplies), and con people. That to me is not Christian. Reading the Bible is great, but if you're acting like an ass in your daily life, what's that about?"

3. "She has been in trouble with the law; well, hasn't gotten caught is more like it; and the threat of that looms over her constantly which I like to remind her of on occasion. She has tried to rip me off of money before, stolen half my possessions; as a kid, she set a fire in my cousin's bedroom and blamed their older brother for it and only showed remorse when she got caught. All of us who watched this were dumbfounded. She likes to pretend she is my younger brother's mother (she has 14 years on him and I am somewhere smack in the middle). If she doesn't get exactly what SHE wants on the pizza, when there are 14 other people to consider, she will scream and cry on the floor literally. She is a religious zealot but doesn't even OWN a bible! She wants kids and can't have any and openly admits she would 'probably abuse them.' She only wants them for the attention they can bring her among family and whatnot."

4. "This jerk was just a boyfriend of 1.5 years. He had a criminal past, used heroin, and then got RELIGION to abuse people with. I should have known better."

5. "Well I am Jewish. And both of my parents have used the religion to the best of their abilities to make me feel guilty. I have been threatened with all sorts of things like phone calls from the Rabbi, etc., telling me I should honor my parents. I always offer them a discussion of what the religion says about honoring people who sexually abused you. That ends it pretty quick. I'm never phased by the 'religious talk' although I am pretty religious myself. I've just seen so many 'practicing people' who are criminals and abusers. ... Sadly they have got my brother (who is a rabbi himself) hooked on the honoring your parents' thing. That has served as an excellent splitting device between us. As everyone here has said it's all about guilt and power; just another tool for them to use."

6. "I am doing well. It has been one month without my ex. I wanted to ask if anyone has had an N. that used church as a weapon. When I met him he preached that the Bible was The Word; no room for interpretations. But we had sex and he would say: 'WELL I AM ONLY HUMAN.' I asked him if it was wrong for him to engage in sex, and he said, yes; but he will confess it. Don't get me wrong I think the Bible is a great document but why do so many people say one thing and do another. He goes to church four times a week and if I would ever suggest that we did something on his church day I was EVIL. (I couldn't suggest something to do on his hunting days either). I did try his church and it was not for me. He became so angry with me. Saying, 'You rejected my church.' In his mind his church is the one and only. I wrote before that towards the end of our relationship he withheld sex, among other things; and if we did have sex (not much) he would immediately strip the bed and get a shower. I wondered what this was about."

7. "My husband ... uses God as a weapon in our marriage. He isn't interested in how men are told to honor and respect their wife, but he will go into Proverbs and pull out a couple of verses that say not to live under the roof with a quarrelsome wife (that would be the wife that begs him to stop being verbally and emotionally abusive). That little word 'submission' gave him the 'Power' to treat me any way he wants. He read the Bible once...and now he is an expert. He lives one way and expects everyone else to live another ... We were all put on this earth to endure his wrath."

8. "About the religion thing. My N-brother 'found God' during one of his flare-ups. (His N-ism seems to go through really awful periods, then he's tolerable for a few months, then the N-ism flares-up again). He beats us with his newfound 'faith' and his very strange idea of what God is and does. It just seems to give him more ugly things to say.

Some of his favorites being: 'May God have mercy on your ugly soul.' 'How do you face your Higher Power?' And about the Golden

Rule, 'Well, that's YOUR opinion.' *ad nausea*. One year, soon after finding God, he announced that he was worshipping some form of nature god; pantheism, (?) I think it's called. So, being a good little sister, I sent him a note on the equinox. He didn't get it. 'What's an equinox?' So much for the depth of that faith of his, huh! He doesn't attend a church, admits to never having read the Bible or any other religious book or book about religion, but currently every other word out of his mouth is God this and Higher Power that. It just gives him one more way to judge everyone else as inferior or less than him. It's not faith; it's another weapon for him to use to belittle people."

9. "I am going to church now and teaching Sunday all because my ex N boyfriend said he went to church on a regular basis and invited me to join him. We went to about 3 churches and listened to the ministers before picking one that we felt comfortable with. Later we officially became members. It was something I wanted to do anyway because I had grown up attending church and being active in youth groups. I had stopped many years ago because my ex-husband was of a different faith (Catholic vs. Protestant), worked shifts and wouldn't go with me. I had 3 children 18 months apart and was working part-time; so I decided that it was more important to be relaxed and stay home with my children. That is one good thing that came out of this last relationship. At first, he was gung-ho about attending church. Eventually he joined the choir, and was invited to join some committees ... but he decided that he couldn't help with the committees because they would infringe on his time too much and he was busy at work. And in the meantime, he was cheating on me and pulling disappearing acts and spewing verbal abuse at me whenever he got angry! He was what I call a 'Christian in name only.' In other words, he had the act down, but he wasn't living his faith in his daily life. He looked good because he showed up for choir practice every Thursday evening and was up front for everyone to see on Sunday mornings; but he didn't treat his family and friends with much love or respect. Whenever he pulled a disappearing act on weekends, I went to church alone, for comfort and strength. I didn't know that other people had noticed this until well after we had broken up. I was talking to a friend's husband (someone who joined the church at the same time I did, but I already knew her because we had previously worked together at the same place), and said that the only reason I had joined the church was because he had wanted to join a church. My friend's husband said, 'Well, it doesn't matter because you attended church more than he did anyway!' I decided to help teach Sunday school when they asked for volunteers since he was already singing with the choir. My point is that for the N in my life it was an act. It made him look good; he used it on his resume when job-hunting. He knew all the right words, but not the feelings that were supposed to accompany his faith. Where I don't make a big deal of teaching Sunday school; and only close friends know about it, he had to volunteer to sing a solo on Christmas Eve. But I spent the night alone wrapping my family's and his gifts until 11:30. Then he went to bed and he refused to spend Christmas day with my family and me. I went alone. I firmly believe that being Christian means that you love your neighbor at all times and treat them with courtesy and respect no matter what their faith (or not) is. It is about how you treat everyone that crosses your path no matter what the circumstances are. Being human and having sex with someone you love is the physical expression of love...something to share and enjoy... but here again mine also withheld sex when he was angry with me, my kids, his job, stuff that was going on in his life ... he didn't have the feelings that go with true love."

10. "Mine liked to use religion as a club to beat people with. One of the first things he demanded when I married him was that my three children by a previous marriage, all teenagers, 14, 16, and 19, join in family prayers. Since he and his family never had family prayers, and since it was not a tradition with my children and myself, I knew it wouldn't fly. I did ask the children, who looked at me as if I had gone out of my mind, since they resented mandatory Sunday mass, which I did insist on. N knew the mind of God totally and God always agreed with N even though I had asked a few priests I knew if not having family prayers was an indicator of my failure as a Catholic mother. They thought it was enough that the kids went to

Sunday mass. Ex-N was enraged at my 'failure' and called me a bad mother, bad Catholic, and horrible wife. Since he pretty much stopped going to mass after we were married, I was confused and off balance. Being married or in love with an N is a constant round of confusion and pain, though. I think Ns use God to their own advantage to get their way. Your N found God rather suddenly when you fled, finally Free; but I'm willing to bet my N and your N both serve a God who is going to punish us for not doing what the N wants us to."

11. "My ex-N was very vocal about not believing in God. He thought religion was stupid and 'Every war in history has been fought over religion...it must be evil.' He had no respect for spirituality. I was shocked the first time I met his parents. His parents are Orthodox Jews. His parents' home is FULL of Jewish books and artifacts. In fact, a rabbi joined us for dinner. It was clear that religion was an extremely important part of their lives. I later asked N when he lost his faith. He said he never really had it. He said that even as a child he thought the whole thing was BS. He said he has never had the courage to tell his family; and asked that I keep it quiet. He continues to go to temple and participate in religious ceremonies just to make an appearance to the family. I was left not really knowing what to believe. I've read that many Ns are atheists because they want NOTHING to be better than them. They are threatened by the power of God. N wants to be omnipotent. I was puzzled why he was hiding this from his family. I think he is ashamed. Or maybe being an atheist is part of his False Self and not his Real Self. Additionally, after I left him, he called me once and begged me to marry him. He said that he'd been praying to God to forgive him and to bring me back to him. Hummm...I thought he didn't believe in God."

12. My N was born Jewish. He lied to every girlfriend he had and said he was Protestant. His last name could, strangely, be either Jewish or Irish; so he got away with it, with me too. It was only after I met his mother....no way can you miss a Jewish mother!! So he admits she was, but his father was Protestant. After we married

and mother was moving, we cleaned out her attic and I found his father's temple papers and other evidence he too was Jewish. And the brothers all married Jewish women; their kids all had Bar Mitzvahs (all boys). I asked N at one if he had had one and he said NO. Then his mother told me he had a huge one in a big city with a 16-piece band! He decided he was 'southern Baptist' about 7-8 years ago when all that Southern Baptist Convention" stuff was big in the news. He liked their controlling views of women. Then he found a local Baptist church and insisted I go with him. I said no, and he said I was stopping HIM from going because a lone man in church 'looks bad'...does he think it makes him look gay? I wonder. Anyway, I never went...so was a bad wife too. All he does is preach to people, pontificate; and he is the most dishonest person I have ever met. He walks around 'Bible MIS-quoting' from his bad memory, and always twisted to his needs. But the end result of it is that he MAKES people believe he is 100% honest because they buy that he is RELIGIOUS and really into GOD! What a CON MAN!"

13. "You wrote about the trance-like state he went into when you discussed religion. I saw [my] P in a trance-like state a couple of times during our relationship. Once it occurred when his 'worlds' collided. He was trying to keep his estranged wife from dating (while he dated me and – it turned out – several other women). The ex got furious at his double standard and crashed into his apartment one evening when I was over there. He went into a trance – it was completely bizarre."

14. "And while talking about religion, one time he became hysterical and burst into tears. He said he had to make his peace with God. I'm not sure what he meant except that he has destroyed every important relationship in his life (which I suspect has its roots in sexual abuse as a child)."

15. "He appears to the outside world to be loving, considerate, helpful, charming, knowledgeable and hardworking. They think he's boy wonder. He tells everyone of his deep religious commitment, attends church, and has little old ladies bringing him religious writings. His business is a source of NS for him (big time) and puts him in contact with many people where he is able to garner much NS. It works beautifully. And, I have never met a more evil, cunning, ruthless predator in my life."

16. "At first it started with just verbal intimidation. Then it went to slaps. Then it went to fits of rage where he'd try to choke me or ram me in the face with large objects. Then it went to slamming me up against walls. Of course, I knew something was terribly wrong; but in the 'church' the 'holiness church,' you don't leave. You stay. You pray. You 'submit' to your husband. You come to church, and you speak in tongues, and you run around the building, and you NEVER let down the 'mask.' Well, the last straw was when his male lover threatened to kill me; and he came home to confirm that threat. I was gone that night, and never looked back."

17.   "Everything was so unreal. My stepfather was this popular minister with a real big congregation. The people who came to church on Sunday just loved him. I remember sitting in church and listening to him sermonize about mortal sin. I just wanted to scream out that this man is a hypocrite. I wanted to stand up and testify in front of the whole church that this wonderful man of God is screwing his thirteen-year-old stepdaughter!"

18. "Manipulation of spiritual truth is one of the psychopath's most insidious tools. Mine (who was in a Master of Divinity program at the local seminary) used this tool to talk me into *ménage a trois*, 30 years ago. This was to help me free my soul of possessiveness, and to stretch my capacity for love to encompass more than one person. He also pulled the celibacy thing "The psychopath is a vessel – you know, him being evolved beyond sexuality. The reality was, he was used beyond doing it, again, when he got home to me."

19. "My p told me initially that he felt I had been 'sent to him from God.' One of the first things he did was bring me a small South American nativity from his mother's native country to place upon my mantle. All the while, he was being unmasked and ejected on every front. He lost his job for getting aggressive verbally with a superior. His roommate almost beat his ass, he said for borrowing a video (these guys are notorious for having no respect for other's property!), his landlord evicted him (Something I should have done a dozen times for the incense burns, ink stains, etc. that he created). Yet those words about God softened me, I thought he was a lost lamb, poor thing. In time he brought into my home morning, noon and night pot-smoking, pornography, and admiration for the life of the swingers. Still, I looked at that nativity. How ironic."

20. "The P I was involved with was a 'good' Muslim. He professed to pray 5 times a day and never drank alcohol. This myth was portrayed not just by himself but by the OW (other woman), and they fooled many people. What I did not know at the time was that he slept around with anything that moved and sold drugs.

"Not being a religious person myself and not familiar with Shariah law I didn't realise just how ridiculous his behaviour was – he was having an affair with a married woman (me). When I did eventually question him about it, he covered it up by saying it was his 'destiny' to fall in love with me even though it was against his religion. In the honeymoon phase, that was very believable; and of course, if I had known about the OW, I would have smelled a rat much sooner.

"As so many have said – if I had not been blinded by his flattery and charm and looked at his actions, I may not have been sucked into the whirlpool."

21. "My S (sociopath) got up on the witness stand and pretended to be pious and holy and a regular church attender. The judge believed him. All lies. He would attend only on special occasions. He had repeatedly made disparaging comments about my faith, and the people at my church. He also made many remarks about how religion was a useful tool to keep other people (the gullible fools, in his opinion) from things that he didn't like. He had his own set of rules to live by. He basically had the attitude that he wanted to 'look' like a moral person, but whenever morality was incon-venient to him, he would find some exception about why he should be exempt from the rules."

22. "The truth around sociopaths and religion needs to be kept center stage. I have long maintained that religious sociopaths are particularly dangerous. Why? Because religion is a powerful means of control over others with the same religious convictions. Religious sociopaths are amazingly good at 'talking the (religious) talk' and getting others to let their guard down and trust them. Their charming front makes them great preachers. It's easy to be fooled by these con artists. How easy? I met my ex on a Christian dating site. He had been a pastor of various churches and has a Bible site on the web. He had told me that he had hit his wife once or twice and regretted it, but I later learned that he battered her repeatedly throughout their marriage, kicking, punching, and even choking her. He told me that his kids would not talk to him because of his 'evil witch' wife. The truth was (I later found out), he had hit and threatened his kids and there was a protective order in place that I never knew about! Shortly after we married, he began to threaten me also. And this is only the tip of the iceberg with him. He continues to lie about all of it to others, saying he is a 'victim', and continues to publish Christian newsletters and get a following for himself."

23. "You are so right about that, and the 'forgiveness' aspect of religion is so twisted to mean 'pretend none of this happened', but that is NOT the definition of 'forgiveness' that is appropriate or right or good. The Ps are so good at taking some scripture out of context and twisting the meaning to mean something entirely perverted, to help them maintain their power and their control.

"Even within families this perverted view of religion is used as a club to emotionally and spiritually BATTER members of the family. I was a victim of this emotional and spiritual religious abuse by being told by my mother that if I didn't 'forgive' (her definition of 'pretend the abuse never happened') that I was going to hell and burn forever. It is only NOW at 61 years old that I have finally said NO MORE to this guilt and fear battering.

"Unfortunately, many people who are religiously abused turn their backs on not only their twisted abusers but on the very spiritual support that TRUE religion and belief can give. This abuse robs these people not only of their happiness it deprives them of their spiritual support as well. What twisted, wicked evil people these predators are."

24. "My NH always has one foot on the Pulpit and the other in the Gutter."

Chapter 13

IN THE WORKPLACE

The workplace is a hotbed for pathics to manipulate their way to the "top". All that is needed to secure their position "in the firm" is their particular expertise that contributes to profits. Once entrenched in their position, they can let loose their pathic ways over subordinates with practically full impunity. At bottom they are not so much concerned with the firm as they are with their own self-aggrandizement, or with manipulating and dominating, or with abuse. The emotional devastation they cause their victims is more than one can imagine.

---

1. "There are wolverines in organizations who are critical and negative about everything. But they are not in any way trying to improve the organization. Their motive is not even to advance some agenda for personal gain. Their only apparent motive is to destroy what others have/do/achieve.

"They like to tear down, not build. They're more like organizational vandals than anything else. Whatever someone proposes, reports, or achieves, they pick it apart and torpedo it — sometimes very tactfully."

"To an outsider it can look at first like the need for additional information in order to be convinced or a preliminary analysis prior to giving support. Or it may just seem like being picky about the details. That's the case with some people, but not wolverines.

"Wolverines always find fault, pick things apart, nay-say and

302

criticize without finding anything positive or proposing an alternative. The game is that others hold up ideas, and they shoot them down. And the pattern never really changes. When you see that pattern, you know you're probably dealing with a wolverine.

"Such folks are largely guided by their own chronic envy. They deeply resent others' positive ideas and achievements because, in their pathological narcissism, they see those as assaults on their own fragile self-esteem. They gain stature in their own eyes only by reducing the stature of others. What they don't have, others can't either."

2. "He [His former boss] was replaced by a notorious bully who was humourless, inflexible, a workaholic, a perfectionist and a grudge-bearer. Because of this, he had not had any direct management of staff but even those he came into contact with indirectly complained of his manner. However, he was the only person who was able to take on the top job immediately and he relished it. For one thing he had hated my previous boss with a vengeance and had taken every opportunity to denigrate him professionally and personally. For another reason, it gave him a power base he had craved for, with control of hundreds of thousands of pounds. To control that, he felt that he had to control me – I was an obvious target and I knew this."

3. "My last boss was a psychopath. We all knew it. We watched our backs. Several of us who had been with the company many years with outstanding performance lost our jobs. She'd been in her management position just five months at that time. She is still there. I'm still unemployed, almost ten months later."

4. "I had a job I loved for six months, got a substantial raise after three months, and then a management change. I was assigned to a woman who had a reputation for not keeping assistants. I went in with an open mind the first week of June. She never gave me a chance – gave me assignments and then told me she never told me to do it; talked about me within earshot; consistently set me up to fail. I finally resigned after seven weeks. I have never ever worked for a more manipulative person.

However, anyone who did not work for her would say she was the nicest person – always remembering birthdays, etc. Yes, a definite psychopath."

5. "This problem is not limited to the corporate world. As a former teacher and current non-profit worker, I have encountered quite a few supervisors over the years that would not do well on the psychopath test. The scariest part is that these people were spending donors and/or taxpayers' money to carry out their schemes and demean their employees! Thankfully, now I'm in an environment where people are more open and pleasant to work with."

6. "My boss is a psychopath. He is the most ruthless, selfish person I've ever met. It is so difficult working for him. He takes credit for everything others do. He sounds so elegant when he talks in public, he would fool you all. Gosh, now that I know he is actually a psychopath, kind of scares me."

7. "I've worked for a few of these [sociopaths], but none as bad as my last one. Certain employees get the shaft from him, and then he gets the president of the company to lay me off because I have the nerve to demand some respect. Other employees have told me that I was treated worse than any others who have ever been there, and I believe it. One lady even had a heart attack because of a demeaning outburst in front of employees and customers one day. The owner refused to do anything, saying that it was just the way things were going to be – don't like it, you can leave. One thing I want to know: how does one get another job when these evil people are getting called for references on us? I've been unemployed for almost 4 months, and I think I'm running out of possibilities at this point."

8. "Psychopaths all get away with it and it is LEGAL. Some articles call them bullies, and there is nothing we can do about it. My boss, the psychopath, bullied me in front of customers, auditors and co-workers, funny, never in front of the owner of the business. Everyone knew it and no one said a thing. Inclusive [the boss] kept giving more and more responsibility until one day, the owner fired me due to performance. Never once did the owner allow a meeting I requested many times to advise him of this situation; so here I am without a job. I believe the owner has fallen into this psychopath grasp and all of the employees are unhappy and being released one by one by the psycho; and the owner just lays back and enjoys the show."

9. "The reason these psychopaths exist is because their bosses allow it. They get the results they want and do not care about the damage inflected on us. These people are obviously not blind or stupid. They know what's going on."

10. "I joined the 'managed by a psycho boss' society years ago – assumed a new position with a new manager who spent the first 6 months trying to get me fired. In my case, I beat him at his own game – developed strong one-on-one relationships with his clients who praised my work and 'his obvious good management'. It fed the ego need and he backed off. But I watched the charm and venom pattern – co-workers and even management really didn't know how to respond to it, which kept him on the payroll for years. But happily, time wounds all heels and his maniacal need to skirt chase resulted in eventual HR [human relations] actions and dismissal."

11. "Wow! I too have been the victim of psycho supervisors. One actu- ally told me to 'Think again about carpooling with her." Duh? Why would carpooling with a co-worker be detrimental to me? I did get laid off but after she left on medical leave for cancer treatment – sometimes there is a universal debt to pay when you live your life in hopes of destroying others."

"But my favorite psycho was the one who told me that I could not move into a new position because I did not have the necessary experience – the new position was tasks and responsibilities that were split from my job because there was not enough time to finish all my work without overtime. I couldn't believe it! Work I had been doing for years but I was not experienced enough! I took that one over her head and won. I wasn't the only victim and eventually she was demoted and was so embarrassed by it, she retired. She also told me that I should move to Arizona because I suffered from allergies and when I said that was not an option because I wanted to stay near my family, she threatened to put me in for a medical lay off. I stopped that one by having my doctor write a letter stating my allergies did not interfere in my job. When she found out, she tried to force me to sign a release she wrote so she could speak directly to my doctor!! NOT!"

12. "First off, my understanding is that psychopath IS a derogatory term! I worked (as a supervisor) for a psychopathic organization – and this was a contractor to a US government agency. From the head mucky muck, who seemed to be half in the bag most times, to the HR manager who thought we couldn't discipline people for sticking their fingers in my chest and challenging a supervisory directive (because they didn't know they couldn't do that – I am SERIOUS!!) to the 'manager' who was previously a truck driver and undermined everything I did by going to my clerks without involving me in directives, etc., and talked out of both sides of his mouth. The last straw was when I attempted to handle a disciplinary matter and got a 2-day suspension out of it because they thought I didn't handle it properly. I had been there all of 10 months.

"I handed in my resignation in the same meeting they gave me my suspension days and the HR manager had the audacity to say 'May I ask why you're resigning?'"

13. "I have worked in the medical field in Health Information Management for 30 years. I can state that almost all of the managers I have worked for fit the psychopath profile. The horrible things that I have seen perpetrated on other employees and myself are worthy of a book. My most recent supervisor (I quit) admitted to someone that she was going to keep her job no matter who she had to hurt along the way.

"The story is too long to relate here but I went from being a favored employee to *persona* non *grate* in a matter of a couple of weeks after having been hospitalized briefly for a cardiac problem.

"She and her system drove out at least three predecessors in my position that I am aware of. One quit in one day, another in a week and another survived about four months as I did. The woman who replaced me was there about a month and she has quit as well. Had I not been desperate for a paycheck I would have quit the first week myself.

"The sad reality is that if these psychos don't have a legitimate cause to terminate an employee, they find all manner of other ways to make their lives miserable and force them out; and we can't call it discrimination under any law."

14. "When we had meetings, he would use cuss words and break objects over the floor. Everyone in the facility would be scared of him. I worked there for years and had perfect attendance and always had excellent job evaluations, had never been written up. I got terminated over something that was not even my job responsibility. The ones the blame fell on walked scot-free. This manager has been there for about five months. He has no respect for anyone. He talks over the top of everyone who is trying to inform and let him know something. I am not there now; but feel sorry for the ones that still have to deal with him. He is so unprofessional. This man truly did not fit in as a manager."

15. "Two years ago I worked at a place with not one but several psychopaths. One of them was the attorney, and even though she was not my boss, she acted like one all the time. She was absolutely irrational, maniacally crazy, intentionally mean, and pretty stupid since she was driving everybody who came on board for that position away; and the turnover was so high, that productivity was extremely low...My suggestion – try to get out of such places as soon as possible. The fact that the crazy maniac had been there for more than 6 years, and 27 people have changed on the position that had to work with her for those 6 years, tells that even though she's a psychopath and has a record at HR, she must be well connected with someone in the organization that helps her being kept there!!! Management of that place was just as crazy and irrational, with no skills and vision; so there you go!"

16. "One 47-year-old manager has taken a shine to me for reasons unknown to me, and has not stopped harassing me. He even went so far as to try and stick his hand up my skirt. I brought this to the attention of the store owner, and the first thing he said was, 'Are you sure this happened?'... No, I just had a bad dream and I thought I'd share it with you...OF COURSE IT HAPPENED! And to make matters worse, he delegated the matter to the second most powerful person in the store...our general manager...WHO HAPPENS TO BE MY CREEPY MANAGER'S LIVE IN GIRLFRIEND!! Whose side do you think she's taking. Man, every time I turn around I have another knife to pull out of my back."

17. "I worked for a man whom I'm sure was a sociopath. He ruined me financially and has left many an emotional scar on me. I'm not over it yet. Sometimes I wonder if I'll ever get over it. It has made me question who I am, what I accomplished professionally during the years I worked for him; and, most of all, how I let this man play me for the fool. What's more, I'm an artist, and I haven't been able to move forward with my career after the blow I received from this man.

"He came on with sweet talk and charm, making it seem like he was more interested in my work and in me than anyone had ever been in my whole life (In truth, he thought he could profit off of my unique artistic style and for a long time he did.). He offered me a high-dollar contract that was to take place over a period of years and he made me feel so important. Constantly, he fed me compliments. He even sent me gifts – flowers, credit cards for meals, etc..

"Everything seemed like a dream come true. I bought a new car and my dream house in a nice area of town. I thought the bad days were behind me...that I'd be financially secure for the rest of my life. He promised me time and again that that was so. And I overlooked the strange quirks and the way he manipulated me – making me work 80 hours plus a week and always wanting to know where I was. He'd call for several hour phone meetings – among other things. Believe me this is only the tip of the iceberg.

"I even began to think that this man had my house bugged, because he strangely seemed to know what my family and I talked about in private. We could never find any evidence of that, however.

"And then, he started getting behind on the payments he owed me and always had an excuse as to why, but I let it slide, believing that he'd come through.

"He didn't. When company profits declined, he broke the contract and became downright cruel to me. When threatened with a lawsuit over the back pay and breach of contract, he tried to throw me over the edge with fear tactics. I believe he did this in hopes that I'd commit suicide – I nearly did.

"In short, my family and I lost our home and just about everything we had. Even then, we were deeply in debt – even owing money to the IRS. He didn't care. We had to move into an old dilapidated house that we'd owned that was fit to be red tagged (this is where we live now, and we may even lose it before this is all over.). When I told my boss about the house, he arrogantly said that I didn't know better but to live in a house like that. Forget that I had no choice.

"As for the financial ruin, in his eyes, he had nothing to do with that. It was all my fault, because I hadn't managed my money well. Forget that he hadn't fulfilled his monetary obligations to me and owed me several hundred thousand dollars in back pay (on top of cutting my pay 70% suddenly). He told me once that after I finally got my money problems in order (which I could do, according to him, by living frugally and investing) that maybe then I'd be as good of a person as he was and that he'd respect me again.

"I realize now that he'd set me up from the start – gave me that big contract (which he had never intended to fulfill) so that I'd become financially dependent on him. Then he could 'own' me.

"This becomes absolutely clear when he wanted me to stay on with the company in 2005 – at yet another huge pay cut. He thought that I was so desperate that I'd have no choice but to accept.

"I surprised him. I walked away from him and his company at the first of the year."

"But, like I said, the scars remain, and I'm struggling to understand how all of this happened."

18. "I'd worked in this small charity for 11 years, and most of my colleagues had been there for over 5 years. We worked well as a team, the salary was minimal, but we enjoyed the work and often worked more than our contracted hours because we believed in what we were doing."

19. "At the end of 1999, a new female director was appointed. The previous director, a kindly gentleman with plenty of managerial experience, had reluctantly retired having reached the age of 70. The management committee, made up of good but inexperienced people, appointed a 35-year-old woman who seemed to have a glowing record of achievement in the charity sector. However, it was clear from day one that there was something odd about this woman.

"She swanned around the premises as if she owned the place, and whilst she made many of the right noises, something wasn't right. With hindsight I now realise she was appraising all the staff, seeing who she could con and who was likely to see through her. The former, mostly the younger and less experienced workers, fell for her charm. However, four of us, all older and more experienced than her, she identified as a threat. She immediately set about making our lives difficult; mainly, I think, to encourage us to leave.

"When that didn't work, she started reorganising everything. It was clear, though, that she didn't have the faintest idea how to run a small charitable organisation like ours. We knew she didn't, and she knew we knew she didn't. After about a month, she seemed to make it her life's ambition to get rid of the four older more experienced staff. I realise now that it was a question of control; those she could control kept their jobs, those she couldn't, she wanted to get rid of.

"She would give orders one day, then contradict them the next. When we queried her, she became aggressive and accused us of having poor memories and distorting the facts. She was in charge and what she said went. If anybody didn't like it they could leave.

"Everything had to change. We'd been doing this work for too long, she claimed, and it was time to get up to date and up to speed. The fact we had honed our work routine from years of

310

experience cut no ice with this woman. In fact, nothing cut any ice with her – it was like talking to a brick wall.

"Within a month, three new committees had been established. The Witch, as she had become known, chaired two of them and her protégé, a young immature man whom she had bewitched, was appointed chairman of the third committee. All three had grand names but to this day no-one can identify any achievement or result from these meetings. The word 'policy' was bandied about at every opportunity though. The committees seemed to be way for The Witch to get her name mentioned in influential circles within the city.

"After four months, dissent was rife and what was formerly a happy co-operative atmosphere had become poisoned. People were suspicious of each other and refused to talk. In fact the director had banned talking in some parts of the premises 'so that people could concentrate on their work and get it done faster and with fewer mistakes.' What mistakes there were was never defined.

"The breakthrough came when a colleague found Tim Field's web site, 'Bully Online'. She brought in a copy of his profile of the serial bully and highlighted everything that applied to The Witch. Almost everything applied. Charming, narcissistic, arrogant, Jekyll & Hyde, liar – suddenly everything made sense. She was disordered, dysfunctional, aggressive, paranoid and more besides – in short, somebody with all the hallmarks of a personality disorder. I remember a colleague had jokingly referred to her as a psycho; and this off-the-cuff remark turned out to be uncannily accurate.

"The realisation that she was not a normal person like the rest of us was just the start of a long bruising battle. It would have been so much easier just to leave but we four oldies decided we had to do something otherwise she'd carry on doing this to other people. We established quickly that legal action would be difficult but nevertheless we started down that route with a grievance procedure. The Witch outmaneuvered the management committee at every stage, and was able to deflect every allegation whilst blaming just about everyone, except herself, for the failings of the charity, which by this time were apparent and mounting.

"After eighteen months of hell, with two early retirements, a near-suicide, a dismissal and a court case, the management committee finally admitted that The Witch might not have been a wise choice after all. Although no-one knows the precise details, it was rumoured that she got a good reference and a promise not to take further action against her. I think the management committee was scared of her and had no idea what to do.

"To cut a long story short, the glowing record that she arrived with turned out to be grossly embroidered. The previous charity had told her to leave and given her a reference to expedite her departure and to avoid legal action and bad publicity. It turned out this had happened several times in her career; in fact it appears she's careered from job to job, amassing an impressive CV of names, but always leaving under a cloud, although nothing was ever recorded on paper.

"We've lost many good people because of The Witch, but the saddest part is that the charitable work we've achieved in the last two years is a fraction of what we used to do. A new director is in the process of being appointed; but most of the staff have become disaffected and many are planning to leave. It's a great shame, and a great waste, especially as this is all down to one person – who, we hear on the grapevine, already has another charity lined up to take her on."

20. "I don't know how my boss from my last job would be categorized. He terrorized nearly everybody in the department. Of course, his boss was the same way and I suspect the company president was likewise. He was the head of another department when the company decided to combine his and my department into one. He walked around for the first two weeks threatening to fire everybody who didn't follow his new guidelines. One day in particular, he had a young woman coming in for an interview. He instructed me to 'check her out and tell me if she's a fox'. Eventually, this type of behavior caught up with him, after we had a female employee, who had resigned shortly after giving birth to her first daughter, write a letter to the company. The HR department verbally reprimanded him. He then had the gall to call a

department meeting and tell everybody that WE had to watch our language and behavior. Typical management type; hell goes far in life."

21. "Organizations attract them [sociopaths] and tolerate their destructiveness because they impart the illusion to their superiors that their mischief results in more added value than the bad behavior subtracts. Plus, many of the higher level managers don't really see the chaos they cause, only the additional half-percent of net revenue added this quarter. 'High water covers a lot of stumps' to quote an old southern expression. One thing the sociopathic bosses know how to do – achieve the current organizational objectives and they are safe as long as they do."

"I worked for a sociopath for several years that was a management disaster in-the-flesh, but his division performed in a stellar fashion financially – ultimately the only criteria for success. He finally experienced a bad quarter and posted a significant loss. Had he not carried the baggage and reputation of being a totally ruthless and abusive senior manager, I believe he would have been extended some forgiveness for the atypical quarterly results. Instead, he was summarily fired on the spot. What goes around comes around – unfortunately many of us don't get to witness the execution."

23. "My best friend and I worked for her until she fired us (at different times), although she tries to make everyone believe we quit. During that year and a half or so, we became very clear of the seriousness of her hateful and destructive nature. I couldn't take any more of her rages and just plain negative energy. When I left her employ I was a wreck for 2 weeks, couldn't find peace, couldn't think straight, or clean the house, or anything. It takes time to recover. I later learned that other employees had to heal in time after quitting. She is only down to a handful of people now and I hear they are looking around. I have cut her completely out of my life now and have found this is the only way to never be her victim again. She has tried and succeeded in turning some of my siblings against me. It makes me sick to think that they will sell their souls to

the devil for what she can monetarily offer them."

24. "I was employed as a specialist Art and Special Needs teacher, part time, at a state primary school. I worked there, happily for nine years. In that time, I participated fully in the life of the school, working on costumes and sets for plays and concerts as well as the teaching duties for which I was employed. I often went in on my days off to put up displays etc.. My Headteacher appeared to appreciate the work I did and my level of commitment. Parents, governors, fellow members of staff and the children often said that the school looked wonderful. Ofsted came and I was the only member of staff to be given Grade 1. The inspector suggested that I be made a member of the senior management team and be given a pay rise and be made full time teaching Art across the school and 1/1 special needs.

"I soon found, that as part of the senior team I was expected to agree with everything the head-teacher wanted to do without question.

"I knew that this man had a history of bullying female teachers out of their jobs. There was a string of evidence to support this. He never did anything that technically he was not allowed to do. His bullying methods were subtle and insidious. He would isolate his victim and tell them that they were failing or that their classroom practice needed a lot to be desired. He would send in other members of staff to observe and report. He would phone the unfortunate at home and tell them that they were going to be inspected. He would bring in the attached inspector to observe. He would hound and demoralize the individual until they left. Once isolated thus, other teachers at the school were so afraid that his attentions would land on them, that there was no support to be expected. He knew that I was unhappy with this sort of practice and when I made it known that as a senior manager I would not take part in gratuitous moderation the tables turned on me."

"I experienced all of his techniques, including him changing the nature of my job and forcing me to become a class teacher or lose my job. I resigned and went to work in a private school where I am extremely happy.

"I applied for Threshold just before I left. It came as no surprise to me that he recommended that I should not pass.

"I think he took pleasure in writing to me personally to let me know. I still have contacts with the school and have heard that he continues to behave in this way and indeed has an inner circle of favoured teachers who assist him.

"One teacher he bullied is now deputy head of a private school and all the others are employed and highly valued in their current schools. Not one of them is a failing teacher. My students get A's and A*'s for their GCSE's. I now teach 11-year-olds to 17-year-olds. While head- teachers in the state sector have powers that they can legally abuse I, as a teacher who has proof of being an excellent practitioner will never work in a state school."

25. "I have had a psycho boss who called his two employees in to yell at them for hours at a time...insane. What a waste of time, creating negative feelings and perpetually feeling like you are walking on egg-shells. I have also worked for people who were extremely negative behind my back...not even giving me a chance to tell them what was going on. Out of the blue, they made plans with me for later in the week, then fired me that day! Documenting everything is a great idea. I wasn't even given a reason for being 'let go' but suspect it was on the word of a person who suffered from extreme paranoia...for a place that prided itself on communication, this was a prime example of a massive break-down in communication. Cover your tracks or you may be hunted down by a stealthy predator and the 'groupthink' phenomenon. Psycho. Now I'm unemployed with no unemployment [insurance] (I was going to school and working part time before this). Men, beware women who are man-haters!!! They are more common than you think!"

26. "I worked as community fundraiser for a large local branch of a national charity. Over the years I took on more and varied responsibilities, to include PR and Marketing, thereby lightening the load of management and also raising the profile of the agency. I formed warm and productive working relationships with all those with whom I came into contact. I had been a loyal, hard-working and conscientious member of the team for six years, and I know that my work was recognized and valued by my colleagues as well as all three previous Directors and the Deputy Director with whom I had worked closely.

"In September 1998 a new Director, who had previously managed another, much smaller, local branch, took over in the run-up to a merger of the two centers. She was immediately recognized by all the staff as a control freak, constantly comparing us unfavourably to the other branch, changing individual and office methods and systems just for the sake of it, rummaging through staff's desk drawers in their absence, butting in on conversations and talking loudly in the office even when staff were in the midst of telephone calls with distressed clients.

"At first she was very friendly towards me, taking me out on shopping expeditions for the office, assuring me that my position would never be under-valued, and that she knew I had a very heavy work-load for the limited number of hours I worked. However, from late February 1999 onwards, after she had been exposed in the first of many lies, I became aware of a shift in her attitude. She began to check up on my work, telling me that she had been told to do so by the Chair of the Trustees, although I subsequently learned that this was another lie. Despite my agreeing to work an extra day, she then told me I couldn't, but increased my workload anyway. I never received thanks or even acknowledgement. I was subjected to nit-picking, unfounded criticism, and specious comments. She kept making criticisms that I couldn't relate to, and to which my colleagues couldn't relate either. Instructions were changed, denied and contradicted. She pointedly ignored all the positive aspects of my work and made only trivial and negative observations which also demonstrated her lack of understanding about my job. She spoke to me on more than one occasion as if she were a tyrannical headmistress reprimanding a naughty child. Her tone was intimidating and more than once I was left shaking and close to tears.

"My work was constantly undermined and de-valued. For example, after much time and energy, and with her knowledge, I produced detailed Fundraising and Marketing Strategy documents for the benefit of the centre. She finally asked to see the completed documents nearly 3 months after I had told her they were ready. She said we would discuss them further at a future date. They were never referred to again. A successful grant application which I made was reported on with no reference to me, either directly or indirectly. She attempted to sabotage a project which I undertook with some local university students, and then lied to the management committee that their final presentation had not taken place.

"She told me I had 'taken too much on myself', and when I asked in what way, she could only say that certain items of post came addressed to me instead of her. She ignored or belittled all my ideas and suggestions, set me frivolous tasks and made it impossible for me to carry out my work. The very nature of my job was changing. After I politely asked to be treated with respect and spoken to courteously, her bullying behaviour escalated in frequency and intensity.

"I continued to lose confidence in her ability to manage me and to make balanced decisions. She would not trust me to get on with any of the jobs I had been used to doing. Often, I would find notes from her asking why I hadn't done this or that. During regular supervision with her, she would patronise and belittle me, and no record of these sessions was ever given to me. As I tried to organise a fundraising event, she interfered constantly with my work, insulting my knowledge and experience by giving me menial tasks to do at every stage. In June, I was invited to attend a meeting to report on my progress on the event so far. Throughout this meeting, she glared at me, complained I hadn't done things that I patently had, and made unreasonable and illogical demands. She also laughed as she encouraged dishonestly obtaining money from supporters.

"During this very busy period when I had other major tasks to do as well as organizing this event, she continued to give me time-wasting exercises, which resulted in me frequently having to stay late in order to complete unnecessary work. We learned of people who had left because of her, that the branch where she had come from were delighted to get rid of her. Her behaviour was upsetting everyone; there was a palpable sense of relief in the office on her days away. But I was clearly the prime target. I always found I could relate very well to all my other colleagues, as well as to my previous bosses, but she didn't seem able to relate to anyone without playing the heavy 'boss lady'.

"One Friday in mid-1999 she stood over me in a threatening manner and addressed me with such hostility that I had to ask her not to speak to me that way. This took place in front of a witness, who was shocked by her facial expressions and body language. Early on the following Monday morning, a non-working day for me, The Witch (as she had come to be known) telephoned me at my home. The content of this call was completely ridiculous and her tone was highly aggressive. She continued to abuse me until I became so distressed that I told her I resigned.

"When I later visited my GP [General Practitioner], she diagnosed me with acute stress and depression, and told me had I not left my job, she would have had to sign me off. Not receiving any apology from The Witch, I then wrote to the Chairman telling him of my reluctant decision to resign. Some days later, I received a vitriolic letter from her which was clearly intended to intimidate me and resulted in me breaking down in fear and hysterics. This led to me consulting a solicitor and I took action for constructive dismissal.

"The next four months were sheer hell. I had other pressures going on in my life at the time, I was out of work, and I had to write a detailed account of everything that had taken place. I was exhausted, I kept crying uncontrollably, and my blood counts were severely affected (I suffer with a serious blood condition which, until then, had been kept fairly stable). Without the loving support of family and friends, and constant telephone calls from ex-colleagues, I don't know what I would have done. This, and anti-depressants, helped me through until I was fortunate enough to find another job. Had I not been helped towards this by a friend within the organisation, I would possibly still believe that I was incapable of finding new employment.

"Why did I stick it out as long as I did? Because for ages I refused

318

to allow one individual to force me out of a job I loved. I had felt I was doing something of value, and was worried, as my health doesn't permit me to work full-time, that I wouldn't find anything else. Eventually I realised I had already lost the job I loved – she had taken it from me as soon as she started her campaign. Now, eighteen months into the far better job which I found, still in the voluntary sector, my self-esteem is finally more or less restored, though it doesn't take much of a trigger to bring the memories flooding back. My understanding, supportive boss tells me that when I started there I appeared terrified all the time and my body was turned in on itself. I have wonderful colleagues, I meet amazing people all the time and, perhaps best of all, I am in a position to make some inroads into raising awareness of the scourge of workplace bullying, particularly in the voluntary sector. There is life after bullying, and together we can tackle it."

27. "Just three years after becoming a police officer, I was promoted to sergeant – the first (and so far only) woman to be promoted to rank in this department. Accepting that promotion was perhaps the worst mistake I've ever made.

"The very first shift that I worked as a sergeant, one lieutenant began to belittle and correct me in front of the officers. For about a year, I tried to deal with the Lt. by myself, assuming that he was just inept with people and didn't know how to supervise. But it only got worse. For another year, I went to the captain – who did nothing. Finally, I went to the chief. He said that he already knew that the Lt. was 'harassing' me because other co-workers had told him so. He said that he had had a talk with the Lt. that very morning – and the problem would stop.

"I felt incredibly relieved and hopeful. I shouldn't have.

"Over the next two years, I went to the chief eight times. Each time, the Lt. would stop talking to me for a while then the bullying would start up again, getting worse and worse until I went to the chief – again. Another Lt. joined in, then another, then one of the captains.

"I finally went outside the department for help. I got an attorney, went through the personnel system... The chief retired rather than deal with the Lt. When the new chief was hired (from outside the department and outside the state), he quickly won my trust. In order to let him get on with the task of cleaning up all the former chief's other messes, I settled with the city. I should have sued them then. Too much of a team player, I guess.

"It took him another three and a half years to break me down, but the new chief finally succeeded – with 'kindness' and 'friendship' – where the obvious bullying by the others had not. Naiveté is, indeed, the worst enemy. I believed. I 'had' to believe that the new chief was my champion. That he was there to make things right.

"Of course, he wasn't. With 20/20 hindsight, I know that he was hired very specifically to deal with me. Hindsight has finally let me see that the man is a sociopath – a very intelligent, experienced, *professional* sociopath. I never stood a chance.

"In 1997, after eleven years with the department, I went through a stress breakdown. I never went back to work. I tried to get the Equal Employment Opportunity Commission to investigate my case and represent me. They told me to go sue the department on my own. No attorney would take my case because there was no money to be made in it. (In the USA no governmental agency – even on the local level – can be assessed for punitive damages; and, until very recently, there was a $300,000 cap on sexual harassment litigation.) I went through vocational rehabilitation; they told me I was very smart and could do al- most anything – and sent me on my way. I'm still dealing with Workers' Compensation and the State Public Employees' Retirement System (PERS) – still on my own.

"The city's lawyer is fighting me tooth and nail over my Workers' Comp claim. PERS has sent me to two different psychiatrists, both of whom determined that I was 'totally, permanently disabled'. The first shrink said that my job had caused it. PERS didn't like that determination so they sent me to another shrink – who said that what had happened to me had 'no' appreciable effect on me! Never mind that he never read my documentation of what had happened...

"I only stumbled onto Tim Field's web site a few months ago. It has made a tremendous difference to me, giving me hope and validation and information with which to fight onward. I've stood up for myself so well that PERS demanded a continuance because the State of Alaska 'Law Department can't deal with so many witnesses' and so much documentation.

"(With Tim's permission, I included a lot of the information from his web site in my evidence 'packet' - almost 1400 pages total.)"

"So, I fight on. My husband is still supportive and encouraging – and as patient with me as he can possibly be. (Without him, I would long ago have ended up living on the street...) I have given up any hope of making any difference in my (former) department.

"I've finally figured out that PERS is trying to stall long enough that we sink into poverty and I have to withdraw the money from my retirement account. If I did that, they would be through with me – forever! I would get no pension, much less any disability pension! Which just makes me want to fight them even harder!"

28. "In April 2000 I opened a shop with an original concept: a bookstore cafe. For the area in North London it is unique. From day one, it was exceedingly successful. Single-handedly, I lifted the value of the street, I brought more customers to the area and therefore more business to everyone – everyone but my neighbour, who owns a sandwich bar next door to me.

"Throughout the first six months of opening, I had a few problems with deliveries not arriving, delivery items being stolen, being reported to the Council by my neighbours claiming that I was doing things I hadn't the permission to do. For the first six months I felt like there was always a fire that had to be put out. As a first time business owner, I thought all of this was normal so I would deal with each issue as it arose.

"Finally, one day I got a call from one of my suppliers telling me they had received a call from my neighbour who was trying to discredit me and get them to supply her instead. I started putting two and two together finally, and realised that a lot of the start-up problems I experienced was due to her manipulative meddling (she has only been there one year longer than I).

"When I blocked all of her efforts towards my suppliers, it got worse. She became threatening and violent. On several occasions she has threatened my life. She will walk up and down outside my windows giving me and my employees a psychopathic grin. She has intimidated some of my customers so much so that they feel they have to go around the block in order to avoid her shop just to come into mine, or they have to cross the street and pretend they are not coming in. She has even attacked a customer of mine! She has verbally abused my employees, my mother and myself. She has accused me of being violent towards her when no such thing has ever happened.

"I have called the police so many times now due to the violence of it all. They did warn her, but it's not working. Instead, she has 'recruited' my surrounding neighbours in her campaign of terror, by playing on their sympathy: telling them that I have thrown her to the ground while she was pregnant! So, now I have the other neighbours to deal with as well – seems like I am now surrounded by a bunch of hooligans.

"She has also 'recruited' children and friends now to do her dirty work. I have had my windows smashed twice in less than a month. I have had eggs and firecrackers thrown at us. I have reported everything to the police who I seem to think have their hands tied without clear hard evidence. They also give me the impression that egg throwing isn't such a big deal and that I shouldn't be calling 999 for such a minor incident.

"I have written to EVERYONE (councilor of the area, chief of police, CID etc.) and have received very little support. I went to a barrister / solicitor who fear that if I press harassment charges that she will lie her way into getting me in trouble as well – which is most certainly the case. I have installed a camera and have two recordings of the children – but the school (Acland Burghley in Tufnell Park) claim not to be able to tell who it is. I have identified the kids as well in a photo – but nothing is being done.

"Meanwhile, business is doing exceedingly well, despite this terror. My customers are the ones who support me and the cafe. Many of them are gay, Jewish or generally artistically inclined and so what seems like persecution by a bunch of hooligans makes 'our kind' stronger. But, I am the one who must hold it all together and lead by example. Only in my solitary moments I wonder if I am strong enough to carry on."

29. "I've worked in the care of disabled people for 15 years. For the last six years I've been part of a small team providing care for a group of adults in their own home. About 18 months ago, a married couple joined the team, and since then I've watched most of the original team members being picked off, one by one, by them. Over the last few months, I too have become a 'victim', and I am now off sick and unable to see a time when I will ever feel comfortable and safe working in my usual job again.

"I've experienced malicious gossip, about fellow staff and myself; I've seen the people we provide care for treated in a totally unacceptable manner; I've been on the receiving end of insulting, derogatory remarks about myself and women in general; fed the wrong information about tasks involved in my job, leading to mistakes; I've had a fellow professional wagged her finger at me and shout extremely abusive comments on my work in front of the bullies and others – even though I'd only met her a short while before – I later found out that this couple had spent a considerable amount of time telling her what an awful person I was, prior to her even meeting me; I've been isolated and ignored – I could go on, and fill pages with the incidents and ...

"To make matters worse, my new line manager is obviously very friendly with, and supports, these bullies, and the one or two other new staff who are now part of their gang. Since making a formal complaint, my line manager has threatened me with disciplinary action if I dare to meet or speak to my former workmates even socially. She has spent a lot of time warning me of all the nasty repercussions that await me if I proceed with my complaint; and worse still, has kept the bullies informed of everything I have said and done, despite my being assured that confidentiality would be maintained, resulting in one of the 'gang' actually making threats and leaving me terrified not just for my own safety, but that of my family.

"The impression I've had from the reaction of senior managers is that to act on this now would be an admission of their failure to deal with this situation when others first reported it, and rather than risk it becoming known that they have failed miserably in upholding their own policy on bullying, they are going to try and sweep it all under the carpet.

"Like most of my workmates, I have a family and can't afford to leave my job. Also, like all my workmates, I am now on the sick with work related stress, which is hardly going to enhance my prospects of finding alternative work. Nor can I ever imagine feeling confident or safe in my usual work place again. For the first time in my life I am receiving counseling and on medication to help me cope. We are looking into legal steps that we can perhaps take, but in reality all of us are so shaken in confidence and so weary and sick of the whole business, that we don't really know where to go from here.

"My employers are supposedly investigating the situation, but have already told me I will be expected to go back to work in the same environment, with the same people, when its 'sorted', telling me in advance that they will take no action. I've got together with five other staff who have had the same experience as myself – they have also made complaints – and we are seeking legal advice – though whether we can get our union's support in that, we don't yet know. I can't believe, that at the age of 37, with years of experience in my work, that I am in this situation. I have now found out that at least five others, who have raised the same complaints/concerns as myself, have been subjected to the same treatment from this manager.

"I wish there was some sort of independent body to support the victims of bullying in the workplace, something that could put pressure on employers to uphold their own policies in dealing with this sort of situation."

30. "I worked in a legal services company in the City of London. Prior to that I had run single-handed a company offering similar services, and left with a sheaf of testimonials from satisfied clients.

"I was the General Manager, overseeing most of the day to day work of the company, giving advice on Company Law, setting up companies, supervising staff. The workload was onerous in the extreme but I preferred to be working to listening to the Directors who, I shortly discovered, were a pair of abusive drunks.

"M, a failed lawyer, was an hysterical oaf who would scream, swear and break wind wildly in the open plan office when he came back with a bellyful after lunch. I could deal with almost everything but the smell. The other one, B, a failed banker (although that could be Cockney Rhyming Slang) was a far more slimy underhand vicious type altogether. He appeared charming and very much a father figure at first. He would call the staff in for little paternal chats. I was disgusted to find him telling me details of another member of staff's recent abortion which had obviously been told to him in confidence. There were many instances of this. He would listen in on the odd personal phone calls I got and comment on them if a male rang me. He did this to everyone and one day came and asked me to confront the Accounts Clerk. He'd listened in to her calls and surmised that she was a prostitute in the evenings. I told him to confront her himself – the girl obviously couldn't live on the wages he paid!!

"The atmosphere at that place was rancid, and not just because of M's wind.

"M started picking on one of the support staff, a Jamaican girl with a strong island accent. He accused her of being illiterate because she could not pronounce her aitches. This was complete rubbish. She was by far the best qualified of our support staff, with an A level in Law. He also encouraged others of the support staff to ridicule her. I got on very well with this person and tried to stand up for her. That made me one of the enemies. I found myself working without a lunch hour most days. I would be left to deal with irate customers when the directors made mistakes: I remember seeing both of them laughing one day when I had to apologize on the company's behalf for a tremendous cock up they'd made.

"My workload was such that I couldn't help but make the odd mistake. My mistakes were trivial. I was called in for a meeting one day and berated in front of an associate of the Directors – it was an exercise in humiliation. I had made minor spelling mistakes on a legal document. I had B shouting at me for 10 minutes. He failed to mention that he had in recent weeks: sold the same company twice, changed the name of a company that we had no connection with, and given the shares of yet another company to the wrong people. In the grand scale of things my mistakes were minute. But I'm convinced to this day that he got some sort of sexual kick from humiliating women.

"Things got worse for the Jamaican girl. I urged her to leave. By now I had developed such tension in my neck that I couldn't move it. I was taking driving lessons at the time and had to learn to reverse without looking over my shoulder. I broke out in eczema on my face – it was so bad that a client who imported T-tree products gave me several bottles of his preparations to try and cure it.

"I couldn't sleep. I tried massage, I tried an isolation tank. But still I had to go back to the mad house on a Monday morning and listen to the effing, blinding and farting all day, and the random acts of verbal vileness. I was beyond thinking straight. I just couldn't see a way out.

"Then I booked a holiday. I went to Ireland. And within days I realised that I wasn't a prisoner and I didn't have to go back. So I never did. My Jamaican friend stayed there: the directors found it very amusing when the office junior threw a chair at her one day. When she showed signs of standing up for herself she was made redundant. Still, she has another job now and she's happy.

"And M eventually had a nervous breakdown and B had a heart attack – which couldn't have happened to a nicer pair of blokes."

31. "In September of last year, I began doctoral-track studies at a national-level university in a southern USA state, majoring in French Linguistics. I was also employed by the department as a Teaching Assistant. By random assignment, my work supervisor was a French exchange student hired to lecture for one year, on a temporary basis, for two basic French grammar classes – a girl only 22 years old (significantly younger than me), with no prior teaching experience.

"I'm not sure if I can adequately explain the sequence of inter-personal dynamics. Briefly, in the fall of 2002, my supervisor got it into her head that she wanted a romantic relationship with me.

This, I did not particularly want from her, having already watched her have a brief fling with one of my then-friends, in what was a small and gossip-filled graduate department.

"After excusing myself from advances several times, all Hell broke loose. Within weeks, this girl had spoken falsely of me to the professors in charge of my program, to my co-workers, and to a woman with whom I had started to like very much and had started to develop a relationship. Although I never could get my co-workers to repeat the exact words said about me, it was clear that my work supervisor had made ethnically derogatory remarks about me and my family, had mischaracterized the working relationship, and had attributed very anti-social opinions to me that I know I had never voiced, because I don't hold them! Opinions that would pass for hostility to minorities, to the professors in charge of my academic progress, and similar.

"I think this might have been bullying, instead of ordinary moaning and complaining, because the results were severe.

"From my professors – I was denied needed teaching opportunities that had been promised to me, and I was denied the chance to study abroad for a year in Paris (which was one of the main reasons I had joined the department!). A male professor, who became very close to my female supervisor, began making derogatory remarks about me inside the classroom, in front of other students, while also showering only these other students with academic favors that he had previously shown no sign of giving to anyone.

"From co-workers – my personal life was dissected negatively in the gossip mill, and I was belittled in conversation, sometimes falsely accused of being a 'dirty playboy', 'the lowest common denominator', etc., and deliberately excluded from departmental socializing events. The growing relationship mentioned before simply died in the water without explanation, until my supervisor's talk came out weeks later.

"On top of it all – this supervisor, again who was a 22 year old girl from an obscure hamlet in the north of France, while in Texas turned out to live with a much older American man that nobody knew much about, except that he was very large, physically, and intimidating in demeanor. This is significant because she persuaded this man to follow me around my routine on the university campus, to take notes, attempt to gain secret access to my e-mail account, possibly question my co-workers about me. As before, I learned of this piecemeal, much later.

"My attempts to resolve the situation with my supervisor peacefully and calmly only made the attacks worse. She began to call me a 'dog', on account of what she perceived to be my ethnicity (a grandmother from Spain), to my face during working hours and in front of my co-workers. And attempts to ask the faculty to help me resolve the problem were either ignored, or resulted in certain faculty worsening their interactions with me. To the level of artificially low semester grades and hostile suggestions that I was somehow not suited for graduate-level study, after prior evaluations had established very good performance, and after the same professors had previously given praise and encouragement for my academic progress.

"The end result? I became sick for eight weeks with a serious lung virus, which the doctor confirmed was made worse by occupational stress. By December of last year, the outlook for my future in the department was so bleak, that I was strongly 'encouraged' (read: 'forced') to resign my job and to quit the doctoral program – two weeks before Christmas!

"None of my co-workers expressed any sympathy for what I went through, or responded to my suggestions to file a grievance for their own negative experiences.

"And my former supervisor remains in the department to this day. No disciplinary action was taken against her, despite proven violations of university policy and Federal civil rights law."

32. "I ran a halfway house for ex-cons, and split my time between counseling these guys, finding them jobs, and raising money to keep the thing going. One guy acted like my best friend – I really liked him; he could come on like a pussycat. And then he just upped and cleaned us out. Not once but twice he completely emptied the place: type- writers, furniture, food, office supplies, everything.

After the first time, he somehow managed to convince me he was ashamed and sorry, and I can't believe I fell for that remorse bit; but I did. About a month later he forged a check and all but closed out our bank account. This time he disappeared, and that was the end of that venture. There I was standing in the bank clutching a bunch of overdraft notices..."

33. "I worked with many anti-social women who hated decent bosses that believed in God, believed in their wives and home life, believed in truth and justice ... that they did everything to ensure those bosses were out the doors and soon. These women detested working for decent bosses that they could not manipulate first sexually. After manipulating sexually, all the other tricks to their trades came out to play and everyone is fair game to them. Lies are told behind everyone's back to ensure they get their own way ... they worked all the years from 1988 on to nail me...which started the beginning and the end of my career in 1998 until I retired in 2004. Six years of enduring the wrath of all the anti-social personalities that booted all the decent managers out of their positions and installed their anti-social cronies in their places and all the checks and balances were gone. To run that place through CHAOS, anti-social CHAOS. To say or do anything they wanted, when they wanted. Many people lost their careers during this time, but those anti-social women are still there, still allowed to weave their dark evil magic on all the new comers, still collecting paychecks, still getting promotions, still destroying careers and personal lives, still sleeping with bosses, still running the show from behind the scenes ... and then some, still keeping the chaos growing."

IN THE CLASSROOM

From PARENTS

34. "My youngest son is very sensitive and he cannot cope at school at all, he is on Distant Education at the moment on psychological and medical grounds. It's not just when he is bullied and/or treated unfairly that is the problem, but also when other children are targeted – he cares so much. He found school so stressful and depressing, he became sick. He says that the teachers do nothing and many are psychological bullies especially to the students that they don't particularly like. There is a lot of favoritism and discrimination going on. Students with ADHD and the like are targeted as are those of certain ethnic backgrounds. Children like mine who stand up for themselves and publicly complain, even though they know that they will be victimized and bullied for it, and who cannot sit back and do nothing are also targeted. My children have been to 5 different schools and the younger one says that it isn't getting better – it is getting markedly worse."

35. "My 9-yr-old had a year from hell with his 3rd grade teacher. She called him names in front of the class, always singled him out; made him feel like he was worthless!! She is a teacher that doesn't belong with children, she belongs with PROZAC!! I tried speaking with her; is/was a waste of time. I went to the principal; that was waste of time as well. Finally, I just told my son, not to disrespect her, but just ignore her. Don't let her upset you. Needless to say, it really didn't work. She hurt him so much that by the end of the year, he has not one bit of self esteem left. I want to still knock her on her butt!! Some teachers just have no business being teachers; they don't understand that they are an example to these impressionable little minds, and that they could really do some heavy duty damage. I say take whatever action works; sue if you can. I spoke to many educators and lawyers, they say this is a definite case, but who has the time??"

36. "In 6th grade my son had a teacher who would call the LD kids 'baby', 'rug rat', 'rodent', and would have them beg on their hands and knees for papers if they forgot to put their name on it. In this class there were two Michaels and my son always only put his 1st name on the paper – if she only received an assignment from one of them she gave the credit to the other kid – this happened for half the year until she got an aide. The aide pointed out that my son was the only one who still reversed letters and that the papers where his. At my sons IEP meeting she told us the boy needed 'major

counseling and to be medicated.' She also said he was very lazy and refused to do work. Her complaints lead to some more testing that deter- mined he had a language disability and was only reading at a 3rd grade level and had fine motor issues. We and 4 other sets of parents submitted a formal complaint, the result was she had tenure and there was nothing we could do. They did monitor the class the rest of the year though causing her to 'behave' herself. My son to this day still has terrible memories of this class."

37. "My son is 10 years old, and has the most nasty teacher who did not take a liking to my other son [either]. For example, he was in an argument with another boy in the playground the way 10-year-olds argue. Nothing was done about the other boy; and in not saying mine is an angel; but to make him write a letter of apology to herself and the other boy; then rip it up in front of the class. Is there any need? He's a kid for God's sake. He kept asking me, 'Mum why did she make me write it, [and then] just to rip it up?' Then if he puts his hand up to answer a question, he gets told, in a very abrupt voice, 'Put your hand down; what would I want to ask you the answer for?' I could go on and on with a lot of nasty things, but the thing that makes me mad [is that] the school sides with the witch; and when I confront her, he doesn't say a word. I'm not the only mum who can see through her – put it that way. I'VE REALLY HAD ENOUGH. NOW, PLEASE HELP; OR COULD YOU GIVE ME ANY ADVICE. Thank you."

5. "Here is what my children say. 'It's the adults that are the problem as many of them are racist and bullies and if they don't like a kid they make it obvious.' My children are of Lebanese background and intellectually gifted and they have found that more often than not the teachers either ostracize them or publicly humiliate them. The other kids notice the fact that the teacher is treating them unfairly, so in order to be on the teacher's good side they take the teacher's cue as they know that the teacher and school will turn a blind eye; and that bullies are protected. Of course, there has been the odd occasion where they have had a teacher who is not like that, but it has been the minority."

38. "When my son was in sixth grade, he came home with a rip in his new sneakers. He told me the gym teacher did it during a sneaker check. It sounded like a fib, or at best, an accident on the teacher's part, but I needed to clarify things.

'You mean he tugged on your sneaker and it ripped?' I asked.

'No, he said. It ripped when he threw it across the floor and it hit the doorway.'

'He threw it across the floor?' I tried to keep my voice guarded. Yeah, if your sneaker comes off, he throws it. My sneaker ripped when it hit the doorway and flew into the hall. Then I had to go get it.'

"I couldn't believe what I was hearing, but I struggled to keep my emotions to myself. If this teacher was so concerned about safety, how does he explain forcing a child to run across the slippery gym floor in bare socks to fetch his sneakers? What about the embarrassment and humiliation? Isn't that a form of bullying? I thought my son was exaggerating. But what if he wasn't?

"I had a hard time accepting my son's explanation, but I couldn't let it go. Either he wasn't telling the truth, or this teacher was way out of line. Both scenarios needed to be addressed. I made an appointment to talk with the principal the next morning.

"The principal met my concerns with doubt. When she tried to dismiss me, I told her I wanted to speak to the gym teacher in person.

"The minute this man walked into her office, I could tell there was a problem. I knew my son had told the truth. The gym teacher barely said hello. He didn't reach out to shake my hand, nor did he return my smile. He had a cocky attitude, but he didn't even know why I was there yet.

"I bit my tongue, complementing him on his concern for safety. He shrugged his shoulders in response. Then I told him that my son came home with a rip in his new sneakers. Another shrug. Diplomacy wasn't working, so I asked him if he threw my son's sneaker across the room.

'Yeah, so?' was his reply.

"'Yeah, so?' My emotions kicked in. 'Who do you think you are? This isn't boot camp and my son is not a Marine. He is a sixth grade student. 'You mean to tell me you whipped his sneaker across the gym, and then made him fetch it like a dog?'

"'Hey, they weren't tied,' was all he said.

"'Don't you ever, I mean ever as much as touch my son again. If his sneakers aren't tied, make him sit out of class, give him demerits, or call me, but if you touch him again, I'll come into that gym and throw you across the room. Got it?'

"'Hey, whatever,' he said. 'I have rules. His sneakers weren't tied.'

"For a brief moment, I floundered. The principal's silence made me uncomfortable and the gym teacher's attitude was intimidating. I gathered my thoughts, took a deep breath and said, 'Don't you realize how damaging your actions are?'

"'Is that all?' he said, directing his question to the principal. Then he left the room.

"Two weeks later, the gym teacher was gone. I'm not certain what happened, but I believe his attitude aided in his demise. I wasn't looking for his dismissal; just common courtesy and respect for my son and his classmates. I guess that was more than he could offer."

39. "My ten-year-old son was bullied recently. He was told that he was an 'embarrassment.' He was told to 'Shut up.' He was yelled at and scolded in a tone of voice tinged with disgust and disdain. He was told he would be punished for any mistakes he or his peers made in the future. Surprisingly, this didn't happen at school. The bully wasn't even a peer of his. The bully was his swim coach, a young lady of perhaps 26 years of age. She was desperately trying to motivate her swimmers to swim fast in the big meet the next day. And this was her attempt at motivation.

In speaking to the lady in charge of the coaches on this swim team, it quickly became apparent that this type of "incentive" was not only okay with her, it was actually encouraged. She said that 9- and 10-year-old boys were 'squirrely' and 'needed to be taken down a notch'. She was in full support of her coaches yelling at, embarrassing and insulting young children to motivate them to swim faster. 'That's just the way swimming is,' she said. Had I not spent 12 years of my childhood swimming competitively, I may have believed her."

40. "When I was a [staff member at a school], I met a teacher that bullied kids... He was in his late fifties and he was physically unwell. He had a short fuse, which everybody sort of wrote off to the fact that he was diabetic... He was completely irrational actually and he couldn't get along with the other staff members either. He and I had to work together on a couple of very important projects for the school and he could only be nice until somebody made a mistake. The mistake could be really small, a minor infraction. Then, it was like he would just lose his mind. I always thought it funny for a person with that personality trait to become a teacher. People make mistakes, especially when they're learning.

...

"It was interesting because it was probably somewhere in-between the time that I had the problem with Jack's grade-two teacher and the grade-eight teacher. I think it was probably a really big learning curve for me. He went off on me in front of students. I had basically compiled a list for him of kids that could be considered for an award at graduation...and I left off a kid who, I guess, should have been on the list. At this point, we're only making the list. It's not a big deal, just add her and move on. This teacher came into my office and he was ranting and raving about me being incompetent and did it in front of students. When he left, the students started laughing and I just felt horrible. I wondered why they were laughing and they told me that he's like that all the time. That's just the way he is in class. He was a total joke among the students. He had such a bad temper and it was commonly known, too, that he would take a dislike to particular kids and ride them until they dropped the class. In high school, particularly an inner city high school, students just drop, they ditch, or they don't attend.

If they can, they go and see a guidance counselor and change to another section; they'll change their schedule.

"I started watching what the interactions were for this teacher. Because I was getting more education, the principal was giving me more responsibility ... This was an inner city school and we had pregnancies and drug use ... oh, we had all of it. [My job had evolved]. I [was given the responsibility] to change schedules and to help with scholarship applications. The school actually brought in another [staff person], so that half of the time I could work out of like a little office in the back. I met with kids and it was mostly about this person.

"Guidance already knew about this teacher. So, I went and spoke to the administrator about this teacher who basically said, "You know, he's a year and a half away from retirement. When he goes, he goes. He might even do his last year on sick leave. Let's not ... rock the boat because it's not going to help."

"I think that this teacher should have been removed from the classroom and receive counseling. Put him on a paid leave, who cares, but he should be out of the classroom and should have no student contact time until a counselor has agreed that he is fit to be put back into the classroom."

Solution

"Jack's teacher was in his mid-to-late fifties, also very close to retirement. It was commonly known that he was a very grumpy, angry man and that he had a very short fuse that he would go off at a moment's notice.

"The sexual and socially inappropriate language choices of the teacher were disturbing enough for Amy to take action without needing other evidence to support her conclusion.

"When I look back on it, I was quite shameful. I knew that he was an elderly man and I knew that there were obviously sex/gender issues simmering on the pot because otherwise it wouldn't be coming home in the form of all these comments. So, I decided to squeeze the pimple to see what comes out. So, I put on ammunition to go and visit the teacher. I do recall putting on a pencil thin black skirt and really tall black hooker boots, and a skinny black blouse. Of course, that was the day that I wore my long blonde hair down.

"This time I didn't make an appointment to talk to the teacher. I felt that last time I'd been usurped simply by doing what I felt was right, which was contacting administration. Last time [in grade 2], the administration became involved in the situation and they acted not as a mediator, but as an advocate for the teacher. They double tag teamed me and basically wrote me off. This time, I wasn't going to let that happen. This time, I decided to just go in unannounced. I went one day after school when I knew there was no cross country.

"I knew the teacher would be sitting at his desk in his classroom and I walked in and I may have slammed the door so that he would look up from his desk on the other side of the room and there I was standing there in all of my golden glory.

"The meeting was very confrontational, one-sided and riddled with emotion.

"It was very confrontational, but it was very one sided and I didn't let him get a word in. I basically told him, I bullied him and I remember that he tried to speak up a couple of times in a very meek and mousy mild way… 'Just a minute, if I can explain that comment'… and I shut him down. I wouldn't let him explain the comments at all because I was pissed and the comments are completely unacceptable, so there is no explanation that can wash them away.

"The first teacher that I encountered in the bullying situation was able to explain away some of her comments by rephrasing things and chalking it up to my misunderstanding, but here there was no misunderstanding. I said, 'If even half of what my child says is true, what you are saying is bullying, it's sexual harassment, it's completely inappropriate… it's inappropriate for your profession, for your age, for your station, for your situation of being in charge of children.'

"I propped my arms on the desk and I leaned over him and it was one of those days … when I've gotten so agitated and so frustrated about something and I've taken it out on one person in a sort of a stream of consciousness, a lightning bolt of verbs and adjectives and nouns that just get more and more and more riddled with intensity and I just took the guy out.

"My parting words were, 'If my child comes home with even one comment that you'd said this or that or the word homo or fairy or gay or faggot crosses your lips around my kid, even if he hears you talking about other kids, I will be having this conversation with the Director of Education." The way that I walked into this classroom and announced myself today is the way that I would go into his office and announce myself. By that time, I'd worked around enough schools that I could drop a few names and legitimate names because I knew these people … When I left the room, I'm pretty sure he was lying in the foetal position chewing on his hairpiece.

"The teacher just backed right down, but it was obvious to me that he needed to be told and he needed to be told in that way or it wasn't going to stop. I suspect that if I had gone to the administrator about the situation, it probably would've gone by the way of some sort of administrative shuffle and kind of been swept under the rug. [The type of bullying was] so loaded and it was borderline sexual harassment. [If I had gone to the administrator], I would never have had the opportunity to nip that in the bud, and I really do feel like I nipped that in the bud. I honestly [don't think he ever spoke to anyone like that again]. I think he was close to tears when I left the classroom that day. He was absolutely convinced that I was going to take it further and that it was just a simple matter of my whim, my mood. [I think he believed that] if he stepped out of line and I got wind of it, then his whole career would come crashing down."

41. "It must be an epidemic but I have had to complain about 3 different ones this year. I have never had to go to the principal and complain until my son moved up to Elementary this year in 3. He was illegally removed from an EIP class because he broke his leg in 3 places and his class was not accessible. The regular teacher had explosive temper tantrums and shook him in his wheel chair on one occasion, when he was using the crutches, she threw them across

the room yelling and screaming, she had thrown everything out of a desk (of another student) into the trash can and demanded to the boy that she was going to make his mother pay for the books and for her not to bring him back to school because he didn't learn anyway. Yes, this happened to someone else's child but traumatized my son as well as the whole class. This was 1 teacher in a period of 2 months. After I was called a liar and my son was a liar by the principal, the teacher openly admitted to doing these things to me and the principal. Of course, her version was a little softer and then I called five other parents to ask them what they knew. Open and shut, my son was removed. As far as that teacher goes, I don't think any of the other parents had any more related problems of that nature which is good. As for my son, he was placed back into his EIP class against their wishes and the teacher has harassed me as well as my son the rest of this year. I think if I knew for sure the other teacher could and would remain calm, I should have left him in her class. Same school, different teacher, my son was sent to another room because he would not get on task. That teacher taking for granted that he had behavior problems, immediately put him in the floor, refuse him a book or desk 'You will probably tear up my books or write on my desk' ??? He has never done such a thing. She continued by calling him 'PEST' repeatedly and then got her class to call him a pest. She took a wooden pointer stick and waved in his face, slamming it against the carpet and against the desk beside him and he was really afraid she was going to hit him. In shock when he told me this and not wanting to be called a liar again, I called some other parents of children in that class, (this is a small town) and ask them to ask their children what happen today while I stayed on the phone. Not only was I horrified and the other parents, but the children all felt shamed (the ones who did name calling) and they were also put into a position they did not ask to be in. I am glad my son comes home and tells me what happens during his day. A lot of kids don't mention a word until you ask them directly. It is really scary to me who the people really are teaching the kids in schools nowadays. When I brought this to the principal's attention, he immediately told me that he had never had a complaint on that particular teacher but he was saying he didn't believe me or my son and that he would make sure he was never sent to her room again and he would talk to her. I feel sorry for all the good teachers out there. I know there has to be some, somewhere. I hope 'we' get one soon."

From STUDENTS

42. "Okay, I have this teacher who is a cocky idiot. He regularly picks on me and today's bully time was when I couldn't explain what I was doing and he said, 'It's people like you who start world wars, you can't communicate properly!' Hello! I have a job in customer services and have plenty of friends. Next, I was nervous because I had to leave the room early. He let me, but then he started imitating my nervous twitch and mentioned it to the whole class. Thank God none of them laughed; they've got my back. Next there was an Asian girl in the class who complained that it was hot and the teacher said, 'How the hell do you manage in Pakistan?' or something similar. That was racist right? What should I do?"

43. "My younger sister now goes to the same school I used to. She, also, is having trouble with a teacher I had trouble with when I was at school. This particular male teacher is a complete bully, and several times I was physically and verbally abused by him through-out my time at that school. By 'physically', I mean he had grabbed me roughly; and once grabbed my hand which was wrapped in a bandage after I got burnt. It makes me so angry looking back, that he was able to get away with that behavior. It wasn't just me; it was many students who suffered this kind of treatment: often shouting at pupils telling them they were morons etc. Now my sister is getting the same treatment, but the school is siding with the teacher. She is very shy and can't stick up for herself very well. What can be done??? Is there a council or an organisation who can help? Please help."

44. "I am talking about teachers bullying students and denying them an education, like what is happening to me, I demand my rights! My English teacher, who is a control freak with a rage control problem, and I had a huge confrontation the week before last and ever since she refuses to let me in the class and makes me go to ISS. I am not allowed back until my dad comes to school and he won't because he is too busy with work. I am being denied an education and am ready to sue with or without my dad's support."

45. "My new school was supposed to be run on 'Christian' lines, but was a hot-bed of bullying, snobbery and class distinction. I was the youngest and smallest boy in the class and was also a poor kid at a rich kids' school. Physical bullying was rife and was frequently done openly in front of the teachers. It was considered 'good form' to accept the bullying and unacceptable to 'sneak', i.e. report it to the teachers. Some of the teachers joined in with psychological bullying. I honestly believe that, despite their high academic qualifications, some of the teachers were too stupid to understand the implications of their actions."

46. "I still have a bully. He happens to be my English teacher. I swear the man is Satan in the flesh. He insults everyone, He's like a Nazi (he doesn't laugh, smile or joke), and he thinks he's better than everyone because he has a bigger vocabulary than the rest of us. Well, being from a rural area, you're not going to have that. I really can't do anything about it except walk out because the administration takes the teacher's word over the student; which is BS. And to make matters worse, he isn't qualified to teach English. He's qualified to teach Political Science. He is the worst English teacher I've ever had. Oh, and 90% of the seniors he has this year are failing for either the marking period or the year. He's doing that deliberately. (no one believes me)"

47 "My English teacher actually bullies kids (no, I'm not just being a 9-year-old complaining; she actually bullies them). She 'picks on' certain people, and gives a huge amount of criticism and gives a detention whenever she gets the chance. Not everyone is treated like this, some kids NEVER get a detention no matter how much homework they don't do, and how badly they behave. She also insults people by saying 'You're dumb, aren't you', 'THAT WORKS LIKE THE DOGS BREAKFAST' and 'KEEP WITH THE TIMES' in a harsh,

mean voice. Should I lodge a complaint about this woman, or should I just let her get away with it."

48. I had a teacher in Grade 4 throw my report in my face and call me stupid in front of my class. She also dumped out my desk in front of my class and made me pick it up because it was so disorganised.

49. All I got from my dad was 'Did you punch him in the mouth'. The teachers would turn it around and ask me what I did to provoke them. When I would fight back I would get in trouble and the kid that was bullying me wouldn't or we got the same punishment. I even had a teacher allow a student to bully me right in front of them telling me I deserved it."

50. I have had two of these teachers [tenured] in my life. One of them was so mean, and brutal, that she should have been fired before I ever became a student of hers. Now, she is still teaching at the middle school that I attended and I heard that she is still, and mean as she used to be; and that the students in her class are learning nothing from her. I remember all of the horrible things she said to me and all of the horrible names she called me in class. I should have gotten her fired. I regret it not having done it. This teacher made my life, and the lives of others students a living Hell.

51. "Bullies are cowards who look to others of a similar nature in order to validate their cruel treatment. There are those who will back up a bully to save their own neck or because, in their souls, they too enjoy this cruel 'sport.' To this day I cannot stand to see cruel treatment, whether it be in the movies or on a newscast. I especially cannot tolerate it if I see an adult encouraging and joining in the bullying. A lot of this has to do with the torture I went through as a child at the hands of a cruel and vicious teacher. I was nine years old and for two years I was her victim. She allowed and encouraged other students to torment me. What she did was un-forgivable.

"Miss Florence Pons was a heavy smoking, muscular, woman in her forties with short, iron-grey hair. You could see her in her shorts, sweatshirt, and high-top sneakers, walking up and down the schoolyard puffing hard at a cigarette before gym class. A compact, tough woman, her passion was volleyball in the winter and softball in the spring. She came to my elementary school on Tuesdays and Thursdays and those were days of hellish torture for me.

"I was nine years old, short and chubby and wore glasses. I was near-sighted as hell but I hated wearing my glasses at school; most especially I hated bringing them to gym class. Because of my eyesight, my lack of co-ordination or a combination of both, I was lousy at sports. In softball, I couldn't hit the ball, couldn't run fast, couldn't catch worth a damn. As for volleyball, I was constantly getting hit in the face. Sports were never going to be something at which I excelled and the fact that we had to take phys. ed. twice weekly was, for me, a forced hell.

"Miss Pons liked kids who were athletic, who could run, hit a ball, play sports. She didn't like me. I was different, outside of her range of what a child should be. I was quiet because I was shy. I was shy because I was overweight and wore glasses. There was another reason I was shy. I was the only one in my neighborhood whose parents had gotten a divorce and that also made me different.

"The kids in the neighborhood called me 'four-eyed fatso,' 'fat-ass,' "fat-pig," and just about any other word combination they could make using the word fat. They were especially cruel when they said my father left me because I was fat. I was called names on my way to school, on my way home from school, and any other time I ventured out of my house. I became a 'book worm' because books were the only friends I had. My life was sad, I cried a lot, and I now know that, at the ripe old age of ten, I teetered on the edge of depression because of the unrelenting cruelty of kids.

"When I first met Miss Pons the second week of fourth grade, we were lined up in the gym waiting to be weighed. ...[When]I got on the scale. She looked at the number, raised her eyebrows and called out my weight number, 122 pounds. Then she looked me up and down. '122? Wow! Let's see if we can run some of that blubber off of you this year. What's your name?" When I mumbled my name, she put a red mark next to it. I heard the kids giggle and I saw the secretary smother a laugh. I got off the scale and was going to the back of the line when I heard her call my name and say, 'Hey, where are you going, chubs? I've got to get your height.'

"That was my introduction into hell with Miss Pons. It was to get much worse.

"The first time a kid called me fat in front of Miss Pons I thought she hadn't heard it but I was wrong. We were playing softball and, of course, I struck out. This incensed the other players and one girl said if I put all my fat behind my swing I might hit the ball once in a while. The other kids laughed and I walked back to the bench forgetting to give my helmet to the next batter. As I passed Miss Pons, I saw her look at the girl and smile.

'Hey, Minnesota Fats! [a fat character (Jackie Gleason) in the movie *The Hustler*] You forgetting something? The helmet!'

"It was Miss Pons talking to me! The kids just about rolled on the ground with laughter at that one even though none of us had any idea who Minnesota Fats was. I was devastated. I sat in the corner of the playground with my head down so no one could see the tears running down my face.

"My 'team' lost the game and as we were going inside one of the kids said, 'We lost because of Mini-Fats. God, I hope I'm never on a team with her again!' So, thanks to Miss Pons a new name was added to the already full arsenal of fat names they had for me.

"Miss Pons never let up on me, I was her target. I was told to run around the field an extra lap to see if I could "lose some of that fat." In our health class, which she also taught, she said that the human body can go without food for a week, longer if water is available.

"'Some of us can literally live off our fat for seven days at least.' Then she pointed at me and said, 'Of course this girl can live off hers for a much longer time!'

"The kids became her audience and she loved it. They also curried favor with her by following her example. She never stopped anyone from calling me names and she humiliated me if I cried. I tried not to cry in her presence, saving my tears for a stall in the girls' bathroom if she would let me go.

"Once I was taking a note to the office and as I passed the open door of the faculty lounge I heard my music teacher, my favorite teacher, Mrs. Weiss say, 'Why don't you ease up on Kristy? I think you're being unfair to her.' She was talking to Miss Pons!

'Oh, come on! Nobody likes a fatty. It's her own fault, anyway. She puts the fork to the plate, doesn't she? I'm just trying to help her lose weight.'

'I'm so glad you're not my teacher, Florence,' said Mrs. Weiss.

"It is a short distance from being emotionally abused to physical abuse and the name calling no longer seemed to satisfy my tormenters. Shoving began to be added to the regimen. It became a macabre sort of game to see who could knock me over. The person with the strength to make me fall was the winner. Suffice it to say I stood with my back braced against a wall whenever I could.

"My life was miserable because of the cruelty of those kids. Miss Pons added to the misery by allowing, and subtly encouraging, my tormenters. I hated all of them and I hated Miss Pons. Through the emotional and physical abuse, my health began to suffer. I had trouble breathing and the start of the panic attacks that were to haunt me throughout childhood began. At night I prayed that she would die. As a child, I had been told to pray only for good things to happen, but I didn't care. I wished her dead. Actually, I wished them all dead, but her most of all.

"My wish and my prayers didn't come true, of course. I survived my two years of Miss Pons and I grew up. I didn't become an anorexic or bulimic because of her but I did become fixated about my weight for a long time. The torture I endured in childhood had a major effect on me. I became a loner and a very private person. It has taken me a long time to become more outgoing at social events. When I meet new people, especially if there is a crowd around, my husband says I have a cat-like wariness to my demeanor. Few people see this because I make an effort to have a smile on my face and to be friendly. But the outside me is different than the inside me. Outside I'm smiling and confident; inside, I'm still the fat little girl with glasses who was bullied by kids and their accomplice, Miss Pons.

"In my writing career I have tried to see the humor in life situations but even with a good imagination I see nothing funny in bullying. It is done with cruel intent and the adults who participate in, or encourage it, are the cruelest of all.

"My story doesn't quite end here because I saw Miss Pons ten years ago at a college graduation in the state where I had lived as a child. She was still tough looking, but I had replaced my fear of her with anger a long time ago.

"At the reception on the campus grounds I saw her looking at me. I turned away from her stare. She walked over, tapped me on the shoulder, and asked if she knew me because I looked very familiar. She never forgot a face, she said. I could have said no, she didn't know me. I could have just walked away but I was surprised at the swell of anger I felt when she touched me. I turned completely to face her.

"'Yes, Miss Pons, you do know me. You made my life a living hell when I was nine years old by calling me names and letting other kids get away with doing the same thing. You were cruel to an innocent child. I hated you then and I have a feeling of disgust for you now. I have nothing more to say to you; get away from me.'

"She looked at me and smiled. Then she said something unbelievable.

"'Whatever I said to you, you probably deserved. What, were you one of those kids who became a sniveling little crybaby when you got hit by a ball or were you one of the lazy fatties I always got stuck with?'

"I didn't answer her; I couldn't. No words could describe what I was feeling. I just looked at her standing there, the horror of my childhood, defiant and still cruel. I had to get away from her before I did something to her. My thoughts were not those of a rational adult. All those times I wished her dead came flooding back to me. I clenched my teeth and my fists and began to walk away.

"She called after me, 'You know, year after year, I used to hope I would get good, tough athletic kids, but all I got were whiners like you. I guess I didn't get my wish.'

"Neither did I, Miss Pons; neither did I."

Chapter 14

TRAUMATIC EFFECTS ON PATHICS' VICTIMS

This chapter focuses in on the physical, mental, and emotional trauma that pathics cause their victims; which justify the stigma 'pathic' applied to their type. They are like a deadly virus infecting everyone vulnerable to their influence. At their worst, they cause the disease that breaks down the homeostasis of the mind-body causing grave suffering to the victim.

1

1. "I lost myself and my purpose in life, and I became a victim, and eventually as sick as the abuser, by allowing myself to be pulled into an elaborate manipulation."

2. "I'm constantly torn between bitterness-blame-anger and the desire to wrap my arms around her because I feel so sorry for her."

3. "I too got so sick that I finally had to go to the doctor. I have Chronic Fatigue Syndrome. My hair was falling out, I was throwing up after every meal; and I was forcing myself to exercise three times a day – since I was the oldest women he had been with he likes them young. I was killing myself, and it was never enough. Why do we hate ourselves so much?"

4. "I feel emotionally and physically drained."

5. "I have had to work so very hard to distance myself emotionally from my own daughter."

6. "These trite attempts at placating my jagged pain with clichéd BS really hurt me! It further quilted me! It kept me enmeshed, feeling guilty, trapped in the labyrinth, isolated from any self-protective clarity! It threw me emotionally back in the tank with the blood-thirsty shark!"

7. "I feel like a gerbil on an exercise wheel going round and round each day that I have to see him. The cycle of grief repeats itself daily – denial, grief, anger, and denial grief, anger. In some ways I think he knows of the torment he puts me through; and I believe he enjoys it."

8. "Living with Ns and Ps makes us feel crazy, disconnected, wrong, like we are missing something that would make their actions make sense."

9. "This is the first time in my life I'm not terrified of the dark or feel a sense of foreboding in my own home. It always seemed like everywhere I lived was full of a dark force I could never put my finger on. Now, I understand the power, the negative energy a P/N has on everything around them. Living with them is like living in a non-stop horror movie. I really mean this. It makes me sick to even admit this or to discuss it openly."

10. "I fell to my knees after three days battling suicidal thoughts and complete destruction of everything I had believed to be real, to be true, to be reciprocated."

11. "I have been totally consumed by this madness; and it is time to let go."

12. "My N/P had me so high, made me feel so special and loved, that when he emotionally abused me, it seemed to just throw me completely off; and I was always clinging to those false highs. He made me feel so high, then so low. Also, I discovered I had severe depression, and when you are in this state, you can't make rational decisions. I also had a self-esteem problem, and when he was doing and saying things that made me feel so special, it temporarily erased those bad feelings about myself; and it felt so good to be with him."

13. "I suppose you can tell I'm scared. I believe I will end up either dead or in a mental hospital very soon if something drastic doesn't happen."

14. "It was the losing of myself that caused me the most anguish. I could feel it, like a brain washing, like a vampire, and he claimed he didn't know anything was wrong, didn't know what I meant when I said I was sad all the time and couldn't trust a word he said."

15. "Towards the end of my relationship with N, he told me: 'Your father couldn't break your spirit, and as hard as I've tried, neither can I.' About sums it all up, wouldn't you say?"

16. "The uneasy was always there for me. It was just easy to ignore in the beginning. As I got to know him, the uneasiness shifted to a feeling of walking on eggshells, since I never knew what action or word I might do would trip over one of his innumerable emotional land- mines."

17. "I've only known grief, lies, distorted realities, schemes, police, chaos, courts. I often feel like they sit in the eye of a self-created tornado and watch their loved ones circling around in total chaos; and if the winds ever die down, they find a way to get them whirling again."

18. "When you are discarded overnight by a psychopath/narcissist type you are stunned and confused by the realization that it didn't matter how much time you spent with him or not, how nice you were or not, and how much you gave to him or not – that's what's so cold and mind-boggling."

19. "I forgave her lies for years and always tried to rationalize an answer for her. How could anyone who professed such undying love for me be covertly trying to destroy me financially, emotionally, reputation ally, and any other way she could devise. My head told me many, many

times to leave but my heart would always make me stay (so she could stomp on it some more)."

20. "This guy got to me, like no one else ever has. I guess this is what being hooked on heroin feels like, always looking for your next fix; and it's never enough."

21. "I am not surprised at your nausea, because our bodies often are much more aware than our minds of the situations we are in and the kind of people we are around. And these kinds of sensations are our bodies' ways of communicating with us. When we are around people that put us in physical or emotional danger, we feel that and sometimes get nauseated. It is the same when we are around really good people we feel calm and at peace physically. With the Ps, we may feel giddy and over-stimulated mentally and emotionally, but never fully at ease in the body. At least that has been my experience. Even when sleeping with my P, I always had the sensation in my body of wanting and needing to get away or be vigilant – even while sleeping. And this was the case even before there was any intimacy, even from the very first date before things got so very odd. Some people call this intuition.

"I haven't read anything about it recently, but somewhere I read that the 'subconscious' mind is actually the body's awareness, that it is centered in the neurological tissue of the heart (which is about 60-70% neurological tissue), that the heart has very large nerve connections to the brain but no connection to the language centers, and that this 'body awareness' never sleeps, never turns off, and records and remembers everything. I'll have to do some more research and see if I can come up with some links. I know this much – when the mind and the body disagree, the body is ALWAYS right, and you can trust that.

"Also what I have observed is the truly evil end of the spectrum both in human and animal is always displayed in those deep dark holes for eyes. Can that be the easiest clue to tune into?

"I have had a body reaction the couple of times I have seen an unmasked evil being.

"I would venture to guess the body reaction over a period of time would just about shoot away the nervous system giving a path to PTSD.

"I think evil runs through most of nature probably to some degree. Ever had a pit bull stare at you? I can still see a vivid image of the one who was next to me in their car at a stop sign several years ago, the memory is fresh."

22. "My parents don't have to attack me physically to hurt me. My whole life they have torn me down, especially my mom. She thinks she is the perfect person, and that everyone else's goal in life is to be exactly like her. The only opinion is her opinion. If she doesn't like what she hears, she will verbally attack you until you are too tired to fight or stand up for yourself. I have been dealing with this for 13 years; and now I have no opinion at all. I hate her so much because I can barely make my mind up for myself. I don't even know how to begin to think. I tried to get her help; but she said the only problem was me and went off on another one of her speeches. I have such low self esteem because my whole life I have been taught that I am imperfect and I must live up to her standards. Now I am sick of it; and I'm tired of hurting myself just because she thinks she's God. Is anyone else verbally abused; and can anyone help me?"

Post Trauma Of Coping With Withdrawal From Pathics

23. "It is coming to terms with the fact that you mean and meant absolutely nothing to that person that you loved so much. I left my N two months ago and I still cry myself to sleep every night ... he is still the first thing I think of in the mornings, weekends – especially Sunday nights are the worst. Then I think what am I missing? ... I am missing the hope and dreams of what I thought he was and not what he actually is ... and then I hurt all over again ... and even though the pain has not gone away ... it has dulled; and the waves of intense pain are less and less with every passing day."

24. "I wanted to talk to ex-N so much today. Yet the desire to N-dip made me very anxious. It's as though my need for him, for someone so very bad for me, is finally becoming ego-diatonic. The urge to be with him creates strong inner dissonance because I know if I contact him, it's emotional suicide. Still, I am in so much pain. I can hardly work. My job seems overwhelming."

25. "People call it 'N-Dipping'. It is like fighting an addiction. So, if you are tempted to slide, it's entirely understandable. At one time you felt great love and passion for this man, and there is some part of you that WISHES he wasn't what you know him to be, WISHES it wasn't all true, that it didn't happen the way it did, and that you could GET BACK that guy you thought he was. I was always tempted to think maybe this is some sort of aberration, something going on in his life, stress, mental illness, and that the OTHER GUY, the one I fell in love with was the REAL HIM. I hated having to finally face the fact that I fell in love with a Jekyll and Hyde facade."

26. "I was sitting here wondering why I can't mentally rid myself of my own creep. He's not even a part of my life anymore. I don't see him, hear from him, talk or communicate with him... but he's inside my head and driving me crazy. He goes everywhere with me. He's a leech, a soul-sucker. I want rid of his presence, rid of his power, and rid of his control over my mind. But yet I let him hang on inside my head sapping at the good person I used to be."

27. "It is not unusual to have anxiety and panic attacks in the wake of the N-experience. It is in fact, quite normal, and they can last for many months afterwards."

28. "One of the signs of the abuse inflicted on you is having fleeting murderous violent horrible thoughts. You are not losing your mind, it is just your natural self-preservation instinct because you are feeling so intensely trapped. You are mentally 'fighting back'. You know deep down inside you are incapable of really doing anything. But the thoughts can be frightening, especially if you have never had them before. A lot of it has to do with the fact that you are so angry that this person has you in such a position."

29. "Sometimes hiding out is all you can do until you reach a place inside you where your own mind has re-surfaced and the N's diabolical hold upon your psyche has waned."

30. "Let me let you in on my little secret that I am learning day by day we can get our dignity back when we cut them off. I don't claim to be over him I have my moments when I need to hear his voice as if he were a drug; but once I get passed it I feel so much better."

31. "I have to fight my urge to take him back when I see that fake sad, lonely little boy look."

32. "Hearing his voice (only one word) brought back a lot of emotions, after all when I met him, he lured me with his voice."

33. "I could SO relate to that, and, even with my advice to you, others and MYSELF: (NO CONTACT!), the other day I, too was 'lured' back into conversation with 'the voice'... he took me by surprise, calling me at work from a payphone (I didn't recognize the number) and his 'alluring, polite, warm, sexy voice' had me responding to him before I even knew what I was doing! I know that sounds weak and inexcusable, but it's the God's honest truth! At first I truly didn't know it was him ... it was just a very familiar, friendly, trusting, yet seductive voice; and before I realized it was him, I was 'hooked'... Once I realized it was him, I became 'curious' and asked questions and engaged in conversation with him to more or less confirm the fact that he truly IS a psychopath, AND NOT the sweet, responsible, caring, loving, trustworthy, handsome and terrific man he portrayed himself as. Well, once again, as always when I 'engage' in conversation with him .. he 'beats around the bush' and twists things until I am so baffled and confused I am speechless and worn out. So ... back to the 'drawing board' once again ... NO CONTACT. What's the point? I don't want him in my life AT ALL (he scares me) and he brings nothing to me but disharmony, distrust, confusion, aggravation, and frustration that there is NO way to get through to him that he and I have NOTHING in common!"

2

TWO AUTHORS' TRAUMATIC EXPERIENCES OF THE PATHIC CHARACTER

The following two excerpts from published books are from the step-daughter of a famous movie actress, and from a famous 19th century playwright, Oscar Wilde. The former excerpt relates how a pathic mother violently distorted the life of her step-daughter; and the second excerpt relates how a pathic friend/lover pathetically destroyed Oscar Wilde's life and career.

As a side note, the former excerpt highlights how all three pathic traits can run through one individual (self-aggrandizement, manipulative-control, and violent abuse); and the latter excerpt highlights how a sensitive soft-natured man of the highest caliber of intelligence and artistic genius can be so unremittingly captivated by another person despite knowing all the pitfalls – disastrous, as it turned out for him – involved in being with such a person.

No Safe Place
By
Cristina Crawford (daughter of former movie actress Joan Crawford)

No safe place. Nowhere to hide. No way to escape the terror. No one to tell. No one to go to for help.

Is this a war zone? A ghetto? A natural catastrophe? No, this is the violence of day-to-day family life in many American homes. It is how I myself lived as a child, a teenager, and even as a young adult.

I did not grow up in a poor or blighted environment. I was a blonde, white child, my adoptive parent was a Hollywood movie star, and we lived in what many believed were luxurious surroundings. Still I carry deep and permanent scars from the violence of my childhood and developing years.

This was not violence from the outside world, from strangers or the streets, from gangs or muggers, but violence from those I, as a child, had been taught to love and trust, violence from those who were supposed to be safe and warm and filled with kindness but were not.

Fear followed me like an invisible shadow, for violence could erupt anywhere. It ambushed me in hallways, awoke me from sleep, disrupted the dinner table, spoiled my play in the backyard. Later, the continuing fear stole my friendships, denied me employment, and coerced and shamed me. More than any other event or person from my childhood, I remember the fear. It alone was constant; it alone could be counted upon. Whether awake or asleep, I was never free from its presence.

My adoptive mother was an angry, alcoholic woman who had clawed her way out of her own history of abuse and violence without ever healing or learning how to be a person along the way. She had no success establishing positive relationships with other adults that she couldn't manipulate and absolutely no idea what to do with children, except to control or punish them.

Perhaps she was simply passing along to others the only relationship skills she knew.

Looking back on my life, I cannot recall when the fear started, because I have no memory of ever feeling safe or protected. My biological mother left me just after I was born. In the house where I was taken for adoption, I felt even less safe, for those people who were not actually violent towards me betrayed my confidence in order to please my mother or to stay employed by her. There was no safe place for me and not one soul I could trust.

Constant danger and betrayal created a life under siege. I never knew where the next disaster lay hidden, so every new circumstance held the threat of chaos. The least infraction of an extensive list of "rules of conduct" brought inappropriate, lengthy punishments, often lasting for months. Within this rigid, controlling atmosphere, I could not learn those skills acquired through trial-and-error because the risk of failure was too great. I learned only parental rules, how to imitate violence, and how to lie. To my amazement lying about anything had less than a fifty-fifty chance of negative consequences, but telling the truth about my thoughts or feelings almost always resulted in physical punishment, aban-donment, mistrust, shame, addiction, and belittlement. I did not learn how to value myself, how to form friendships, how to learn new skills, how to resolve interpersonal conflict, how to evaluate others for trustworthiness, how to be kind to myself and others, how to ask for help or assurance, or how to love and be loved.

I did and did not learn as a child has affected the rest of my life. I spent my early years just trying to stay alive, while all the messages from and within were telling me to give up and die. Eventually I shut down the feelings of abandonment, terror, and helplessness. While I felt less pain that way, it left a terribly empty place in me which later, as a young adult, I would try to fill with cigarettes, alcohol, and sexual contact. It took me years and years and years of my adulthood to unlearn the lying, the addictions, the mistrust, and the abandonment of self and to learn the basic skills of how to be a person in the real world, how to earn a living, and how to have a relationship that isn't destructive or violent.

I learned to withdraw into a tiny inner recess of self where nothing could enter. It wasn't the same as being safe from harm, but it was the only haven available to me. The self I showed to the world was no longer an authentic 1f, but one redesigned for the sole purpose of surviving violence on a day-to-day basis.

In time I began to perpetrate the violence I had experienced as victim against other children at school. By fourth grade I was engaging regularly in schoolyard fistfights, hurling swearwords I'd heard from adults at home, and lying even when there was no obvious reason to do so.

I was quite pretty and intellectually gifted, skipping grades in grammar school and eventually becoming the youngest student in my class. But I was also a highly emotional child, quick to anger, needing to have my own way, and slow to heal my wounds.

Many children learn quickly that they can get their personal needs for love and care met by their parents. Thus, bonds are formed, trust is created, and protection and guidance are offered until the small people can manage in the world by themselves.

This was not my personal experience of early life. My body was physically hurt, punished, and ridiculed. My mind was programmed for servitude and made susceptible to manipulation. I was never allowed to express a choice freely or say no. My spirit was humiliated, terrorized, and prohibited from spontaneously embracing life, health, and happiness.

Instead of being protected, guided, and loved, I was taught to be ashamed, alone, frightened, suspicious, enraged, and empty, that I didn't belong anywhere and that nothing belonged to me. If anyone in the house expressed particular affection for me, they were dismissed. If I showed special preference for a friend or a toy, it was taken away from me. I was not permitted to lock bathroom doors or to keep a private diary. There was no mine or separate me. I was intended only as an appendage to my adoptive mother. I survived at her pleasure and could easily be destroyed the same way. That particular lesson I learned very early.

As a small child, I was hit and beaten with objects, threatened, deprived of basic necessities such as food and sleep, ignored, abandoned, disrespected, sexualized, and manipulated. I was told that I was a "selfish girl, ungrateful, not to be trusted, and a bad influence" on my siblings. I was constantly in trouble, living out the misery of childhood on a second chance basis, convinced that I was a fundamentally flawed human being and that probably nothing would ever set me right.

I felt terror of my mother's erratic, totally unpredictable behavior toward me and others. No matter what I did or how hard I tried, there was never any truce, peace, or safety. Fear of her next outbreak was ever present. Yet I needed her. I was a child and I could not take care of myself. I didn't know the difference between real love and dependence. I believed that because I needed and depended on her for survival, I should also love her. The fact that in my secret heart I did not have those feelings was very confusing.

Recently, after I spoke at a women's conference, a woman introduced herself as having been a classmate of mine in fourth grade. She recounted an incident I'd long forgotten, but which had etched itself in her memory. Evidently I had brought a photo of my adoptive mother to school, probably because a classmate had requested it. When asked about it, I held out the picture and said flatly, "I hate my mother." This statement from an eight- year-old astonished my old school friend even then.

Until sixth grade, I went to public school and lived at home. During those years (1943-1950), my mother was struggling with her third stormy marriage and having major problems with her career.

Sometimes she would demand that all the other people in the house - the cook, secretary, gardener, and cleaning woman – not speak to me. Days would go by and no one except the governess would look at me or direct a single word my way. Other times she would try to make them treat me like a "bad girl," using unkind looks or a degrading tone of voice.

At night, from my bed, I would hear arguments, swearing, screaming, door slamming, and the resounding crash of thrown objects. In the dark I would pray that nobody remembered I was alive in the next room. I lay so still my body became stiff, as though frozen or dead. Sometimes I didn't dare breathe for fear someone would hear, as unlikely as that was, given all the other noise.

I would hear footsteps and the sounds of people running up or down the stairs. Sometimes dark figures would run right through my room out onto a balcony, where the fight continued. Still frozen with terror, I would pretend to be asleep. No matter how much I wanted to pull the covers over my head for protection, I dared not move a muscle. Later my mother would comment, "You sleep so soundly, a circus could go through your room and you'd never hear it."

When I was about ten years old and watching television in another room, I heard the sound of my mother being hit by a man. I ran to help her. I started punching the man, kicking at him and yelling. He left quickly. She allowed herself to be helped upstairs. A week or so later, the man was back, and, to my horror, I was forced to apologize to him for my intrusion and "bad manners."

Today I recognize that early message as very similar to the one we receive as a society: Do not interfere. Turn your back and go on about your own business.

Until I was sent to boarding school and lived away from home most of the time, I was forced to watch while my little brother was beaten. We shared a room and we tried to help each other whenever we could, secretly, without anyone else seeing. During those horrible times when he was being hurt, I was also scared for myself and enraged with my mother. I felt absolutely powerless to help him and prayed only for the strength to live through that day or night.

My physical punishments from the age of four to sixteen took many different forms. I was beaten, slapped repeatedly in the face, tied up and left in the shower, locked up and left in a dark closet, denied food for days at a time, deprived of sleep, and prevented from seeing friends or receiving phone calls and letters. When I was asked by the woman who took care of us how I ended up tied in the shower, I told her I didn't know. To this day, I still do not know; the memory has never returned.

Once I was playing on the swings with a girlfriend when suddenly I saw a lot of blood staining my underpants. I was only about seven or eight years old, so it was not the onset of my menstrual period. The sight of blood, particularly my own, upset me, so by the time I had run up to the house to get help, I was nearly hysterical. My vagina was cut and bleeding profusely, but no one called for the doctor or took me for medical treatment. I was washed off and told to lie down in bed until the bleeding stopped. Then I was not supposed to play in the yard, swing on the swings, or walk up and down the stairs for a week or more. Various people carried me upstairs for a while, and nothing more was said. The official explanation was that I had hurt myself on the swing, but my under-pants were not torn and I hadn't been playing very hard. And no one seemed upset besides me.

Life as a child was mysterious. Things happened for which there was no sensible explanation. People left without saying goodbye. Nobody knew where they were going, whether or not they were ever coming back, or what had happened to cause them to go.

I was programmed mentally and emotionally to expect and endure violence, cruelty, and intentional harm. Violence stripped me of trust and innocence. It does that to every child it touches. All my energy was used to cope with the violence. There was little time left with which to learn the skills and behaviors needed for successful adulthood.

If I made friends at school, my mother tried to co-opt them. If that didn't work, she would manipulate them into taking sides with her against me or create a horrible scene when they came over to play so that they would be sure never to return. This pattern of behavior continued through my freshman year in college, when I finally learned to keep anything or anyone precious to me away from her. She still managed, however, to take the best job I ever had, acting on a soap opera, and to try to keep me from working with any of her friends in Hollywood during my years as an actress. Finally, I gave up fighting such an uphill battle. I left the entertainment business and returned to college. After obtaining my master's degree, I began a career in communications that kept me out of her grasp and brought me some success. Even after all the years that have passed, I can't help wondering what I might have been able to make of my life if pain and chaos had not claimed so much of my thought, time, and energy.

It wasn't until about five years ago that I realized how deeply the violence of my childhood had permeated the whole of my life. It was the first time that anyone said out loud to me that my fear of my mother and of the house in which I lived as a child was not usual. My therapist told me that home for a child is supposed to feel safe, protected, and secure.

My first feelings of safety, after forty years of living in fear, did not come from alarm systems, locks, guns, or guard dogs - although

I had those, too. I won a feeling of safety against the constant anxiety and fear only when the terrors and demons of my childhood had been reckoned with enough that they no longer governed my reactions to every moment of every day. I began to feel safe when I began to feel worthwhile as a woman and connected to my community as an adult. Only then could my body begin to unfreeze, to uncurl itself from the fetal position in which I slept each night as the only protection I felt I had left. Only then could I sleep more than a few hours at a time without suffering terrifying night- mares that left me exhausted and lying in a pool of sweat and tears.

In my late teens and early twenties, when I felt most despondent and helpless, I would daydream about going to my adoptive parent's funeral. I would see her lying dead in her coffin and myself standing beside her body for a long time to make sure that there were no signs of life, that death was not a trick, that she would not suddenly arise and laugh derisively at the deception. Then I would see myself standing at the gravesite and watching the coffin being covered with dirt. Everyone else was crying, while I was thanking God for being merciful and ridding the world of an evil force that destroyed everything it touched.

It still amazes me that I didn't suffer a total nervous breakdown or act out my daydream in real life. I certainly felt the rage. Sometimes, sad to say, I still do.

It is clear to me now that we survivors often relive as adults our nightmarish childhood experiences. The violence of these relived experiences came close to killing me many times during the fifty and more years of my life.

The onset of adulthood for me, and for millions like me who were on their own in their teens without benefit of a real childhood, was one step forward, three backwards; marking time, not making progress; constantly making mistakes that I didn't even know were mistakes, so I couldn't do better next time; feeling as though I did not belong anywhere, except perhaps with a group of others who were similarly disadvantaged; not knowing how to ask for help and fearing that asking would give others ammunition against me; not taking very good care of myself, but being very concerned with my appearance.

No one had ever taught me how to care for or respect myself. Closeness with an adult meant either sex or violence or both. Because no one had had compassion for me or my needs, I didn't know what compassion toward others might feel like. Without compassion, there was no empathy or real contact with others, and so no sense of us all being joined together in this world. Without compassion, I felt alone and angry .

In order to stay alive in that unlivable reality, at a very young age I learned the technique of numbing, a technique used commonly by children living in traumatic circumstances. I retreated to an alternate reality, a world of imagination, a world without pain. This alternate reality had both constructive and destructive aspects to it. While it was a brave attempt to create balance and safety out of chaos, it also could have become life-threatening by evolving into psychosis and multiple personality, and it was highly vulnerable to failure. But whether this world of imagination was primarily a positive or negative force, I had to keep it a secret or risk being labeled crazy.

Abused children learn to keep two worlds a secret: the real world of terror and violence from which they are trying to flee and the imaginary world of safety to which they escape for comfort. In order to manage everyday life, they construct a third world behind which to hide the other two.

A giant myth has been perpetrated that children forget or fanta-size (i.e., make up) the abusive parental behavior they suffered or claim to have suffered, and that violence experienced in childhood has no lasting negative consequences. This myth is believed and supported by such diverse groups as Freudian psychoanalysts, the media, government, the courts, fundamentalist sects, and vast segments of the general public, none of whom want to know differently.

Children cannot make up behavior for which they have no previous language, image, or frame of reference. On the other hand, "forgetting" or burying the brutal experiences of childhood for periods of time is not at all uncommon when the experiences were perceived by the child as life-threatening, when the trauma was of such magnitude that remembering it is literally unbearable and comparable to dying.

Adults are sometimes viewed as springing forth from puberty, as chickens hatch out of eggs, carrying no trace of their childhoods; but the experiences of childhood are, along with genetic make-up, the major influences on the development of an adult.

For most adults who have experienced childhood trauma, life continues chaotically until a serious crisis hits. Then the entire house of cards built of defenses, lies, and charades comes tumbling down. At that point, these people either go for help or give up.

One evening, when I was home from boarding school for a rare weekend visit, my mother took me out to dinner with some of her friends. She'd been drinking. She told her friends I had been expelled from school. It was a total fabrication. I was a model student, on the honor role, a cheerleader, an athlete.

At home, I protested. She slapped me so hard it made my ears ring. "You just love to make me hit you, don't you?" she said. I was thirteen years old. We were nearly the same height.

As she did not want anyone else to hear more of our dispute, she called me into the bar area. There she hit me again, throwing me off balance. I fell to the floor, hitting the back of my head on an ice chest. She climbed on top of me and began to choke me, banging my head on the floor. I thought she was trying to kill me.

After someone separated us, I was taken upstairs and locked in a back bedroom. The juvenile authorities came, and the officer told me she had called them and asked them to take me away, declaring me "incorrigible."

Something inside me snapped. That night I understood that the world is an insane place. What else can you call it? A society that permits parents to attempt murder and then tries to lock up the victim has to be crazy.

The officer did not take me to juvenile hall that night. He advised me to try to get along until I was eighteen and could go out on my own, because there was no other help for me.

Those who have not lived through serious trauma during childhood and whose early years were relatively normal see the world differently from those of us who are survivors. When they refer to mother, father, and family, they have in mind images very different from mine for exactly the same words. I am now convinced that this one element of difference is responsible for a vast chasm of misunderstanding which, at least until now, has been exceedingly difficult to cross. I am equally convinced that we have never quite come to terms with this underlying misunderstanding that makes it so hard to discuss mother-father violence without creating more fear and greater misunderstanding.

Oscar Wilde

From *De Profundus* (selections from an epistle to Alfred Lord Dougles)

1
If I write to you now as I do it is because your own silence and conduct during my long imprisonment have made it necessary.

2
I cannot reconstruct my letter, or rewrite it. You must take it as it stands, blotted in many places with tears, in some with the signs of passion or pain, and make it out as best you can, blots, corrections and all. As for the corrections and *errata,* I have made them in order that my words should be an absolute expression of my

thoughts, and err neither through surplusage nor through being inadequate. Language requires to be tuned, like a violin: and just as too many or too few vibrations in the voice of the singer or the trembling of the string will make the note false, so too much or too little in words will spoil the message. As it stands, at any rate, my letter has its definite meaning behind every phrase. There is in it nothing of rhetoric. Wherever there is erasion or substitution, however slight, however elaborrate, it is because I am seeking to render my real impression, to find for my mood its exact equivalent. Whatever is first in feeling comes always last in form.

I will admit that it is a severe letter. I have not spared you. Indeed you may say that, after admitting that to weigh you against the smallest of my sorrows, the meanest of my losses, would be really unfair to you, I have actually done so, and made scruple by scruple the most careful assay of your nature. That is true. But you must remember that you put yourself into the scales.

3

I saw quite clearly that my position in the world of Art, the interest my personality had always excited, my money, the luxury in which I lived, the thousand and one things that went to make up a life so charmingly, so wonderfully improbable as mine was, were, each and all of them, elements that fascinated you and made you cling to me: yet besides all this there was something more, some strange attraction for you: you loved me far better than you loved anybody else.

4

It did not occur to me ... that you could have the supreme vice, shallowness.

5

You must see now that your incapacity of being alone: your nature so exigent in its persistent claim on the attention and time of others. ... Your interests were merely in your meals and moods. Your desires were simply for amusements, for ordinary or less ordinary pleasures. They were what your temperament needed, or thought it needed for the moment. I should have forbidden you my house and my chambers except when I specially invited you. I blame myself without reserve for my weakness. It was merely weakness. One half-hour with Art was always more to me than a cycle with you. Nothing really at any period of my life was ever of the smallest importance to me compared with Art. But in the case of an artist, weakness is nothing less than a crime, when it is a weakness that paralyses the imagination. I blame myself again for having allowed you to bring me to utter and discreditable financial ruin.

I remember one morning in the early October of '92 sitting in the yellowing woods at Bracknell with your mother. At that time I knew very little of your real nature. I had stayed from a Saturday to Monday with you at Oxford. You had stayed with me at Cromer for ten days and played golf. The conversation turned on you, and your mother began to speak to me about your character She told me of your two chief faults, your vanity, and your being, as she termed it, *"all wrong about money."* I have a distinct recollection of how I laughed. I had no idea that the first would bring me to prison, and the second to bankruptcy. I thought vanity a sort of graceful flower for a young man to wear; as for extravagance – for I thought she meant no more than extravagance – the virtues of prudence and thrift were not in my own nature or my own race. But before our friendship was one month older I began to see what your mother really meant. Your insistence on a life of reckless profusion: your incessant demands for money: your claim that all your pleasure should be paid for by me whether I was with you or not: brought me after some time into" serious monetary difficulties, and what made the extravagances to me at any rate so monotonously uninteresting, as your persistent grasp on my life grew stronger and stronger, was that the money was really spent on little more than the pleasures of eating, drinking, and the like. Now and then it is a joy to have one's table red with wine and roses, but you outstripped all taste and temperance. You demanded without grace and received without thanks. You grew to think that you had a sort of right to live at my expense and in a profuse luxury to which you had never been accustomed, and which for that reason made your appetites all the more keen, and at the end if you lost money gambling in some Algiers Casino you simply telegraphed next morning to me in London to lodge the amount of your losses to your account at your bank, and gave the matter no further thought of any kind.

There was on far too many occasions too little joy or privilege in being your host. You forgot — I will not say the formal courtesy of thanks, for formal courtesies will strain a close friendship - but simply the grace of sweet companionship, the charm of pleasant conversation...and all those gentle humanities that make life lovely, and are an accompaniment to life as music might be, keeping things in time and filling with melody the harsh or silent places.

[M]ost of all I blame myself for the entire ethical degradation I allowed you to bring on me. The basis of character is will-power, and my will-power became absolutely subject to yours. It sounds a grotesque thing to say, but it is none the less true. Those incessant scenes that seemed to be almost physically necessary to you, and in which your mind and body grew distorted and you became a thing as terrible to look at as to listen to: that dreadful mania you inherit from your father, the mania for writing revolting and loathsome letters: your entire lack of any control over your emotions as displayed in your long resentful moods of sullen silence, no less than in the sudden fits of almost epileptic rage: ...You wore one out. It was the triumph of the smaller over the bigger nature. It was the case of that tyranny of the weak over the strong which, somewhere in one of my plays I describe as being "the only tyranny that lasts."

6

The night we arrive [at the Grand Hotel at Brighton] you fall ill with — that dreadful low fever that is foolishly called the influenza, your second, if not third attack. I need not remind you how I waited on you, and tended you, not merely with every luxury of fruit, flowers, presents, books, and the like that money can produce, but with that affection, tenderness and Love that, whatever you may think, is not to be procured for money. Except for an hour's walk in the morning, an hour's drive in the afternoon, I never left the hotel. I got special grapes from London for you, as you did not care for those the hotel sup- plied, invented things to please you, remained either with you or in the room next to yours, sat with you every evening to quiet or amuse you.

After four or five days you recover, and I take lodgings in order to try and finish my play. You, of course, accompany me. The morning after the day on which we were installed I feel extremely ill. You have to go to London on business, but promise to return in the afternoon. In London you meet a friend, and do not come back to Brighton till late the next day, by which time I am in a terrible fever, and the doctor finds I have caught the influenza from you. Nothing could have been more uncomfortable for anyone ill than the lodgings turn out to be. My sitting-room is on the first floor, my bedroom on the third. There is no manservant to wait on one, not even anyone to send out on a message, or to get what the doctor orders. But you are there. I feel no alarm. The next two days you leave me entirely alone without care, without attendance, without anything. It was not a question of grapes, flowers, and charming gifts: it was a question of mere necessaries: I could not even get the milk the doctor had ordered for me: lemonade was pronounced an impossibility: and when I begged you to procure me a book at the bookseller's, or if they had not got whatever I had fixed on to choose something else, you never even take the trouble to go there. And when I was left all day without anything to read in consequence, you calmly tell me that you bought me the book and that they promised to send it down, a statement which I found out by chance afterwards to have been entirely untrue from beginning to end. All the while you are of course living at my expense, driving about, dining at the Grand Hotel, and indeed only appearing in my room for money. On the Saturday night, you having left me completely unattended and alone since the morning, I asked you to come back after dinner, and sit with me for a little. With irritable voice and ungracious manner you promise to do so. I wait till eleven o'clock and you never appear. I then left a note for you in your room just reminding you of the promise you had made me, and how you had kept it. At three in the morning, unable to sleep, and tortured with thirst, I made my way, in the dark and cold, down to the sitting-room in the hopes of finding water there. I found *you.* You fell on me with every hideous word an intemperate mood, an undisciplined and untutored nature could suggest. By the terrible alchemy of egotism you converted your remorse into rage. You accused me of selfishness in expecting you to be with me when I was ill; of standing between you and your amusements; of trying to deprive you of your pleasures. You told me, and I know it was quite true, that you had come back at midnight simply in order to change your dress-clothes, and go out again to where you hoped new pleasures were waiting for you, but that by leaving for you a letter in which I had reminded you that you had neglected me the whole day and the whole evening, I had really robbed you of your desire for more enjoyments, and diminished your actual capacity for fresh delights. I went back upstairs in disgust, and remained sleepless till dawn, nor till long after dawn was I able to get anything to quench the thirst of the fever that was on me. At eleven o'clock you came into my room. In the previous scene I could not help observing that by my letter I had, at any rate, checked you in a night of more than usual excess. In the morning you were quite your- self. I waited naturally to hear what excuses you had to make, and in what way you were going to ask for the forgiveness that you knew in your heart was invariably waiting for you, no matter what you did; your absolute trust that I would always forgive you being the thing in you that I always really liked the best, perhaps the best thing in you to like. So far from doing that, you began to repeat the same scene with renewed, emphasis and more violent assertion. I told you to leave the room: you pretended to do so, but when I lifted up my head from the pillow in which I had buried it, you were still there, and with a brutality of laughter and hysteria of rage, you moved suddenly toward me. A sense of horror came over me, for what exact reason I could not make out; but I got out of my bed at once, and bare-footed and just as I was, made my way down the two flights of stairs to the sitting-room, which I did not leave till the owner of the lodgings – whom I had rung for – had assured me that you had left my bedroom, and promised to remain within call, in case of necessity. After an interval of an hour, during which time the doctor had come and found me, of course, in a state of absolute nervous prostration, as well as in a worse condition of fever than I had been at the outset, you returned silently, for money: took what you could find on the dressing-table and mantelpiece, and left the house with your luggage. Need I tell you what I thought of you during the two wretched lonely days of illness that followed? Is it necessary for me to state that I saw clearly that it would be a dishonour to myself to continue even an acquaintance with such a one as you had showed yourself to be? That I recognised that the ultimate moment had come, and recognized it as being really a great relief? And that I knew that for the future my Art and Life would be freer and better and more beautiful in every possible way? Ill as I was, I felt at ease. The fact that the separation was irrevocable gave me peace. By Tuesday the fever had left me, and for the first time I dined downstairs. Wednesday was my birthday. Amongst the telegrams and communications on my table was a letter in your handwriting. I opened it with a sense of sadness over me. I knew that the time had gone by when a pretty phrase, an expression of affection, a word of sorrow would make me take you back. But I was entirely deceived. I had underrated you. The letter you sent to me on my birthday was an elaborate repetition of the two scenes, set cunningly and carefully down in black and white! You mocked me with common jests. Your one satisfaction in the whole affair was, you said, that you retired to the Grand Hotel, and entered your luncheon to my account before you left for town. You congratulated me on my prudence in leaving my sick-bed, on my sudden flight downstairs. *"It was an ugly moment for you,"* you said, *"uglier than you imagine."* Ah! I felt it but too well. What it had really meant I did not know: whether you had with you the pistol you had bought to try and frighten your father with, and that, thinking it to be unloaded, you had once fired off in a public restaurant in my company: whether your hand was moving towards a common dinner-knife that by chance was lying on the table between us: whether, forgetting in your rage your low stature and inferior strength, you had thought of some specially personal insult, or attack even, as I lay ill there: I could not tell. I do not know to the present moment. All I know is that a feeling of utter horror had come over me, and that I had felt that unless I left the room at once, and got away, you would have done, or tried to do, something that would have been, even to you, a source of lifelong shame. Only once before in my life had I experience such a feeling of horror at any human being. It was when in my library at Tite Street, waving his small hands in the air in epileptic fury, your father, with his bully or his friend, between us, had stood uttering every foul word his foul mind could think of, and screaming the loathsome threats he afterwards with such cunning carried out. In the latter case he, of course, was the one who had to leave the room first. I drove him out. In your case I went. It was not the first time I had been obliged to save you from yourself.

You concluded your letter by saying: *"When you are not on your pedestal you are not interesting. The next time you are ill I will go away at once."* Ah! What coarseness of fibre does that reveal! What an entire lack of imagination! How callous, how common had the temperament by that time become! *"When you are not on your pedestal you are not interesting. The next time you are ill I will go away at once."* How often have those words come back to me in the wretched solitary cell of the various prisons I have been sent to. I have said them to myself over and over again, and seen in them, I hope unjustly, some of the secret of your strange silence. For you to write this to me, when the very illness and fever from which I was suffering I had caught from tending you, was of course revolting' in its coarseness and crudity; but for any human being in the whole world to write thus to another would be a sin for which there is no pardon, were there any sin for which there is none.

I confess that when I had finished your letter I felt almost polluted, as if by associating with one of such a nature I had soiled and shamed my life irretrievably. I had, it is true, done so, but I was not to learn how fully till just six months later on in life. I settled with myself to go back to London on the Friday, and see Sir George Lewis personally and request him to write to your father to state that I had determined never under any circumstances to allow you to enter my house, to sit at my board, to talk to me, walk with me, or anywhere and at any time to be my companion at all. This done I would have written to you just to inform you of the course of action I had adopted; the reasons you would inevitably have realised for yourself. I had everything arranged on Thursday night, when on Friday morning, as I was sitting at breakfast before starting. I happened to open the newspaper and saw in it a telegram stating that your elder brother, the real head of the family, the heir to the title, the pillar of the house, had been found dead in a ditch with his gun lying discharged beside him. The horror of the circumstances of the tragedy, now known to have been an accident, but then stained with a darker suggestion; the pathos of the sudden death of one so loved by all who knew him, and almost on the eve, as it were, of his marriage; my idea of what your own sorrow would, or should be; my consciousness of the misery awaiting your mother at the loss of the one to whom she clung for comfort and joy in life, and who, as she told me once herself, had from the very day of his birth never caused her to shed a single tear; my consciousness of your isolation, both your other brothers being out of Europe, and you consequently the only one to whom your mother and sister could look, not merely for companionship in their sorrow, but also for those dreary responsibilities of dreadful detail that Death always brings with it; the mere sense of the *lacrimae rerum,* of the tears of which the world is made, and of the sadness of all human things. Out of the confluence of these thoughts and emotions crowding into my brain came infinite pity for you and your family. My own griefs and bitternesses against you I forgot. What you had been to me in my sickness, I could not be to you in your bereavement. I telegraphed at once to you my deepest sympathy, and in the letter that followed invited you to come to my house as soon as you were able. I felt that to abandon you at that particular moment, and formally through a solicitor, would have been too terrible for you.

On your return to town from the actual scene of the tragedy to which you had been summoned, you came at once to me very sweetly and very simply, in your suit of woe, and with your eyes dim with tears. You sought consolation and help, as a child might seek it. I opened to you my house, my home, my heart. I made your sorrow mine also, that you might have help in bearing it. Never, even by one word, did I allude to your conduct towards me, to the revolting scenes, and the revolting letter. Your grief, which was real, seemed to me to bring you nearer to me than you had ever been. The flowers you took from me to put on your brother's grave were to be a symbol not merely of the beauty of his life, but of the beauty that in all lives lies dormant and may be brought to light.

The gods are strange. It is not of our vices only they make instruments to scourge us. They bring us to ruin through what in us is good, gentle, humane, loving. But for my pity and affection for you and yours, I would not now be weeping in this terrible place.

Of course I discern in all our relations, not Destiny merely, but Doom: Doom that walks always swiftly, because she goes to the shedding of blood. Through your father you come of a race, marriage with whom is horrible, friendship fatal, and that lays violent hands either on its own life or on the lives of others. In every little circumstance in which the ways of our lives met; in every point of great, or seemingly trivial import in which you came to me for pleasure or for help; in the small chances, the slight accidents that look, in their relation to life, to be no more than the dust that dances in a beam, or the leaf that flutters from a tree, Ruin followed, like the echo of a bitter cry, or the shadow that hunts with the beast of prey.

7

In your case, one had either to give up to you or to give you up. There was no other alter- native. Through deep if misplaced affection for you: through great pity for your defects of temper and temperament: through my own proverbial good-nature and Celtic laziness: through an artistic aversion to coarse scenes and ugly words: through that incapacity to bear resentment of any kind which at that time characterised me: through my dislike of seeing life made bitter and uncomely by what to me, with my eyes really fixed on other things, seemed to be mere trifles too petty for more than a moment's thought or interest-through these reasons, simple as they may sound, I gave up to you always. As a natural result, your claims, your efforts at domination, your exactions grew more and more unreasonable. Your meanest motive, your lowest appetite, your most common passion, became to you laws by which the lives of others were to be guided always, and to which, if necessary, they were to be without scruple sacrificed. Knowing that by making a scene you could always have your way, it was but natural that you should proceed, almost unconsciously I have no doubt, to every excess of vulgar violence. At the end you did not know to what goal you were hurrying, or with what aim in view. Having made your own of my genius, my willpower, and my fortune, you required, in the blindness of an inexhaustible greed, my entire existence. You took it. At the one supremely and tragically critical moment of all my life, just before my lamentable step of beginning my absurd action, on the one side there was your father attacking me with hideous cards left at my club, on the other side there was you attacking me with no less loathsome letters. The letter I received from you on the morning of the day I let you take me down to the Police Court to apply for the ridiculous warrant for your father's arrest was one of the worst you ever wrote, and for the most shameful reason. Between you both I lost my head. My judgment forsook me. Terror took its place. I saw no possible escape, I may say frankly, from either of you. Blindly I staggered as an ox into the shambles. I had made a gigantic psychological error. I had) always thought that my giving up to you in small things meant nothing: that when a great moment arrived I could reassert my willpower in its natural superiority. It was not so. At the great moment my will-power completely failed me. In life there is really no small or great thing. All things are of equal value and equal size. My habit – due to indifference chiefly at first – of giving up to you in everything had become insensibly a real part of my nature. Without my knowing it, it had stereotyped my temperament to one permanent and fatal mood. ... I had allowed you to sap my strength of character, and to me the formation of a habit had proved to be not Failure merely but Ruin. Ethically you had been even still more destructive to me than you had been artistically.

8

The warrant once granted, your will of course directed everything. At a time when I should have been in London taking wise counsel, and calmly considering the hideous trap in which I had allowed myself to be caught – the booby-trap as your father calls it to the present day – you insisted on my taking you to Monte Carlo, of all revolting places on God's earth, that all day, and all night as well, you might gamble as long as the Casino remained open. As for me-baccarat having no charms for me – I was left alone outside to myself. You refused to discuss even for five minutes the position to which you and your father had brought me. My business was merely to pay your hotel expenses and your losses. The slightest allusion to the ordeal waiting me was regarded as a bore. A new brand of champagne that was recommended to us had more interest for you.

On our return to London those of my friends who really desired my welfare implored me to retire abroad, and not to face an impossible trial. You imputed mean motives to them for giving such advice, and cowardice to me for listening to it. You forced me to stay to brazen it out, if possible, in the box by absurd and silly perjuries. At the end, I was of course arrested and your father became the hero of the hour:

9

Of course I should have got rid of you. I should have shaken you out of my life as a man shakes from his raiment a thing that has stung him...But my fault was, not that I did not part from you, but that I parted from you far too often. As far as I can make out I ended my friendship with you every three months regularly, and each time that I did so you managed by means of entreaties, telegrams, letters, the interposition of your friends, the inter- position of mine, and the like to induce me to allow you back. When at the end of March '93 you left my house at Torquay I had determined never to speak to you again, or to allow you under any circumstances to be with me, so revolting had been the scene you had made the night before your departure. You wrote and telegraphed from Bristol to beg me to forgive you and meet you. Your tutor, who had stayed behind, told me that he thought that at times you were quite irresponsible for what you said and did, and that most, if not all, of the men at Magdalen were of the same opinion. I consented to meet you, and of course I forgave you. On the way up to town you begged me to take you to the Savoy. That was indeed a visit fatal to me.

Three months later, in June, we are at Goring. Some of your Oxford friends come to stay from a Saturday to Monday. The morning of the day they went away you made a scene so dreadful, so distressing that I told you that we must part.

10

[I]n one more than usually revolting, when you came one Monday evening to my rooms accompanied by two of your friends, I found myself actually flying abroad next morning to escape from you, giving my family some absurd reason for my sudden departure, and leaving a false address with my servant for fear you might follow me by the next train. And I remember that afternoon, as I was in the railway carriage whirling up to Paris, thinking what an impossible, terrible, utterly wrong state my life had got into, when I, a man of world-wide reputation, was actually forced to run away from England, in order to try and get rid of a friendship that was entirely destructive of everything fine in me either from the intellectual or ethical point of view; the person from whom I was flying being no terrible creature sprung from sewer or mire into modern life with whom I had entangled my days, but you yourself, a young man of my own social rank and position, who had been at my own college at Oxford, and was an incessant guest at my house.

11

On my return to London … I remember sitting in my room and sadly and seriously trying to make up my mind whether or not you really were what you seemed to me to be, so full of terrible defects, so utterly ruinous both to yourself and to others, so fatal a one to know even or to be with. For a whole week I thought about it, and wondered if after all I was not unjust and mistaken in my estimate of you.

12

Of course you had your illusions, lived in them indeed, and through their shifting mists and coloured veils saw all things changed. You thought, I remember quite well, that your devoting yourself to me, to the entire exclusion of your family and family life, was a proof of your wonderful appreciation of me, and your great affection. No doubt to you it seemed so. But recollect that with me was luxury, high living, unlimited pleasure, money without stint. Your family life bored you. The "cold cheap wine of Salisbury," to use a phrase of your own making, was distasteful to you. On my side, and along with my intellectual attractions, were the fleshpots of Egypt. When you could not find me to be with, the companions whom you chose as substitutes were not flattering.

You thought again that in sending a lawyer's letter to your father to say that, rather than sever your eternal friendship with me, you would give up the allowance of £250 a year which, with I believe deductions for your Oxford debts, he was then making you, you were realising the very chivalry of friendship, touching the noblest note of self-denial. But your surrender of your little allowance did not mean that you were ready to give up even one of your most superfluous luxuries, or most unnecessary extravagances. On the contrary. Your appetite for luxurious living was never so keen. My expense for eight days in Paris for myself, you, and your Italian servant were nearly £150: Paillard alone absorbing £85. At the rate at which you wished to live, your entire income for a whole year, if you had taken your meals alone, and been especially economical in your selection of the cheaper form of pleasures, would hardly have lasted you for three weeks. The fact that in what was merely a pretence of bravado you had surrendered your allowance, such as it was, gave you at last a plausible reason for your claim to live at my expense, or what you thought a plausible reason: and on many occasions you seriously availed yourself of it, and gave the very fullest expression to it: and the continued drain, principally of course on me, but also to a certain extent, I know, on your mother, was never so distressing, because in my case at any rate, never so completely unaccompanied by the smallest word of thanks, or sense of limit.

You thought again that in attacking your own father with dreadful letters, abusive telegrams, and insulting postcards you were really fighting your mother's battles, coming forward as her champion, and avenging the no doubt terrible wrongs and sufferings of her married life. It was quite an illusion on your part; one of your worst indeed. The way for you to have avenged your mother's wrongs on your father, if you considered it part of a son's duty to do so, was by being a better son to your mother than you had been: by not making her afraid to speak to you on serious things: by not signing bills the payment of which devolved on her: by being gentler to her, and not bringing sorrow into her days. Your brother Francis made great amends to her for what she had suffered, by his sweetness and goodness to her through the brief years of his flower-like life. You should have taken him as your model. You were wrong even in fancying that it would have been an absolute delight and joy to your mother if you *had* managed through me to get your father put into prison.

13

[Y]ou, like myself, have had a terrible tragedy in your life, though one of an entirely opposite character to mine. Do you want to learn what it was? It was this. In you Hate was always stronger than Love. Your hatred of your father was of such stature that it entirely outstripped, o'erthrew, and overshadowed your love of me. There was no struggle between them at all, or but little; of such dimensions was your Hatred and of such monstrous growth. You did not realise that there is no room for both passions in the same soul. They cannot live together in that fair carven house. Love is fed by the imagination, by which we become wiser than we know, better than we feel, nobler than we are: by which we can see Life as a whole: by which, and by which alone, we can understand others in their real as in their ideal relations. Only what is fine, and finely conceived, can feed Love. But anything will feed Hate. There was not a glass of champagne you drank, not a rich dish you ate of in all those years, that did not feed your Hate and make it fat. So to gratify it, you gambled with my life, as you gambled with my money, carelessly, recklessly, indifferent to the consequence. If you lost, the loss would not, you fancied, be yours. If you won, yours, you knew, would be the exultation, and the advantages of victory.

Hate blinds people. You were not aware of that. Love can read the writing on the remotest star, but Hate so blinded you that you could see no further than the narrow, walled-in, and already lust-withered garden of your common desires. Your terrible lack of imagination, the one really fatal defect of your character was entirely the result of the Hate that lived in you. Subtly, silently, and in secret, Hate gnawed at you ...

14

[T]he idea of your being the object of a terrible quarrel between your father and a man of my position seemed to delight you. It, I suppose very naturally, pleased your vanity, and flattered your self-importance. That your father might have had your body, which did not interest me, and left me your soul, which did not interest him, would I have been to you a distressing solution of the question.

You scented the chance of a public scandal [in the legal case of his father with Wilde] and flew to it. The prospect of a battle in which you would be safe delighted you. I never remember you in higher spirits than you were for the rest of that season. Your only disappointment seemed to be that nothing actually happened, and that no further meeting or fracas had taken place between us. You consoled yourself by sending him telegrams of such a character that at last the wretched mall wrote to you and said that he had given orders to his servants that no telegram was to be brought to him under any pretence whatsoever. That did not daunt you. You saw the immense opportunities afforded by the open postcard, and availed yourself of them to the full. You hounded him on in the chase still more. I do not suppose he would ever really have given it up. Family instincts were strong in him. His hatred of you was just as persistent as your hatred of him, and I was the stalking-horse for both of you, and a mode of attacks as well as a mode of shelter.

15

[T]hat it was not your father but you who had put me into prison, that from beginning to end you were the responsible person, that it was through you, for you, and by you that I was there, never for one instant dawned upon you. Even the spectacle of me behind the bars of a wooden cage could not quicken that dead unimaginative nature. You had the sympathy and the sentimentality of the spectator of a rather pathetic play. That you were the true author of the hideous tragedy did not occur to you. I saw that you realised nothing of what you had done. I did not desire to be the one to tell you what your own heart should have told you, what it indeed would have told you if you had not let Hate harden it and make it insensate. Every- thing must come to one out of one's own nature. There is no use in telling a person a thing that they don't feel and can't understand. Besides, as things had turned out, the blow had fallen upon me alone. That was a source of pleasure to me. I was content for many reasons to suffer, though there was always to my eyes, as I watched you, something not a little contemptible in your complete and willful blindness.

16

[Were you in my situation in jail] Do you think that I would have allowed you to eat your heart away in darkness and solitude without trying in some way, however slight, to help you to bear the bitter burden of your disgrace? Do you think that I would not have let you know that if you suffered, I was suffering too: that if you wept, there were tears in my eyes also ... I would have written to you in season and out of season in the hope that some mere phrase, some single word, some broken echo even of Love might reach you. If you had refused to receive my letters, I would have written none the less, so that you should have known that at any rate there were always letters waiting for you. Many have done so to me. Every three months people write to me, or propose to write to me. Their letters and communications are kept. They will be handed to me when I go out of prison. I know that they are there. I know the names of the people who have written them. I know that they are full of sympathy, and affection, and kindness. That is sufficient for me. I need to know no more. Your silence has been horrible. Nor has it been a silence of weeks and months merely, but of years; or years even as they have to count them who, like yourself, live swiftly in happiness, and can hardly catch the gilt feet of the days as they dance by, and are out of breath in the chase after pleasure. It is a silence without excuse; a silence without palliation. I knew you had feet of clay. Who knew it better? When I wrote, among my aphorisms, that it was simply the feet of clay that made the gold of the image precious, it was of you I was thinking. But it is no gold image with clay feet that you have made of yourself. Out of the very dust of the common highway that the hooves of horned things pass into mire you have moulded your perfect semblance for me to look at.

17

To write to me a loathsome letter at 2.30, and fly to me for help and sympathy at 7.15 the same afternoon, was a perfectly ordinary occurrence in your life. You went quite beyond your father in such habits, as you did in others.

18

What was a profession to him and his class was a pleasure to you, and a very evil one. Nor have you given up your horrible habit of writing offensive letters, after all that has happened to me through them and for them. You still regard it as one of your accomplishments, and you exercise it on my friends, on those who have been kind to me in prison like Robert Sherard and others. That is disgraceful of you.

19

The truth always made you angry. Truth, indeed, is a thing that is most painful to listen to and most painful to utter. But it did not make you alter your views or your mode of life. Every day I had to pay for every single thing you did all day long. Only a person of absurd good nature or of indescribable folly would have done so. I unfortunately was a complete combination of both.

20

What I must know from you is why you have never made any

attempt to write to me, since the August of the year before last, more especially after, in the May of last year, eleven months ago now, you knew, and admitted to others that you knew, how you had made me suffer, and how I realised it. I waited month after month to hear from you. Even if I had not been waiting but had shut the doors against you, you should have remembered that no one can possibly shut the doors against Love for ever.

PART FOUR

Against the Evil in Pathics

Chapter 15
AGAINST EVIL IN GENERAL

Yes, it is possible to surmount, to protect oneself from, the evils facing us in one way or another, but first we must understand them, then have the courage to face and challenge them. The former chapters in this book have contributed to the understanding of evil in general and in particular (the pathics); this chapter encourages the reader to face and challenge them through the thoughts of eminent and perceptive persons.

1

Eminent Persons

The Book of Sirach (Ecclesiasticus)

1. Bring not every man into your house, for many are the snares of the crafty one; though he seem like a bird confined in a cage, yet like a spy he will pick out the weak spots.

2. The talebearer turns good into evil; with a spark he sets many coals afire.

3. The evil man lies in wait for blood, and plots against your choicest possessions.

4. Avoid a wicked man, for he breeds only evil, lest you incur a lasting stain.

5. Lodge a stranger with you, and he will subvert your course, and make a stranger of you to your own household.

6. Never trust your enemy, for his wickedness is like corrosion in bronze. Even though he acts humbly and peaceably toward you, take care to be on your guard against him

7. Rub him as one polishes a brazen mirror, and you will find that there is still corrosion. Let him not stand near you, lest he oust you and take your place. Let him not sit at your right hand, lest he then demand your seat, And in the end you will appreciate my advice, when you groan with regret, as I warned you.

8. Who pities a snake charmer when he is bitten, or anyone who goes near a wild beast? So is it with the companion of the proud man, who is involved in his sins: While you stand firm, he makes no bold move; but if you slip he cannot hold back. With his lips an enemy speaks sweetly, but in his heart he schemes to plunge you into the abyss.

9. Though your enemy has tears in his eyes, if given the chance, he will never have enough of your blood. If evil comes upon you, you will find him at hand; feigning to help, he will trip you up, then he will nod his head and clap his hands and hiss repeatedly, and show his true face.

Homer
For never, never, wicked man was wise.

Sophocles
All concerns of men go wrong when they wish to cure evil with evil.

Herodotus
1. It is better by noble boldness to run the risk of being subject to half of the evils we anticipate than to remain in cowardly listlessness for fear of what might happen.

2. It is some compensation for great evils that they enforce great lessons.

Virgil
Yield not to evils, but attack all the more boldly.

Publlllus Syrus
1 It is good to see in another's evil the things that we should flee from.
2 The wise man avoids evil by anticipating it.

Plutarch
Zeno first started that doctrine, that knavery is the best defense against a knave.

William Blake
Active Evil is better than Passive Good.

Shakspeare
There is some soul of goodness in things evil,

Would men observingly distil it out.
For our bad neighbour makes us early stirrers,
Which is both healthful and good husbandry:
Besides, they are our outward consciences,
And preachers to us all, admonishing
That we should dress us fairly for our end.
Thus may we gather honey from the weed,
And make a moral of the devil himself.

Alexander Solzhenitsyn
If only there were evil people somewhere insidiously committing evil deeds, and it were necessary only to separate them from the rest of us and destroy them. But the line dividing good and evil cuts through the heart of every human being, and who is willing to destroy his own heart?

George Bernard Shaw
If a man cannot look evil in the face without illusion, he will never know what it really is, or combat it effectually.

Albert Camus
What's true of all the evils in the world is ... it helps men to rise above themselves.

Carlyle
Evil, once manfully fronted, ceases to be evil.

Edmund Burke
The only thing necessary for the triumph of evil is for good men to do nothing. Whilst men are linked together, they easily and speedily communicate the alarm of any evil design. They are enabled to fathom it with common counsel, and to oppose it with united strength. Whereas, when they lie dispersed, without concert, order, or discipline, communication is uncertain, counsel difficult, and resistance impracticable. Where men are not acquainted with each other's principles, nor experienced in each other's talents, nor at all practiced in their mutual habitudes and dispositions by joint efforts in business; no personal confidence, no friendship, no common interest, subsisting among them; it is evidently impossible that they can act a public part with uniformity,

perseverance, or efficacy. In a connection, the most inconsiderable man, by adding to the weight of the whole, has his value, and his use; out of it, the greatest talents are wholly unserviceable to the public. No man, who is not inflamed by vain-glory into enthusiasm, can flatter himself that his single, unsupported, desultory, unsystematic endeavours, are of power to defeat the subtle designs and united cabals of ambitious citizens. When bad men combine, the good must associate; else they will fall, one by one, an unpitied sacrifice in a contemptible struggle.

Darwin

Man may be excused for feeling some pride at having risen, though not through his own exertions, to the very summit of the organic scale; and the fact of his having thus risen, instead of having been aboriginally placed there, may give him hope for a still higher destiny in the distant future. But we are not here concerned with hopes or fears, only with the truth as far as our reason permits us to discover it; and I have given the evidence to the best of my ability. We must, however, acknowledge, as it seems to me, that man with all his noble qualities, with sympathy which feels for the most debased, with benevolence which extends not only to other men but to the humblest living creature, with his god-like intellect which has penetrated into the movements and constitution of the solar system-with all these exalted powers – Man still bears in his bodily frame the indelible stamp of his lowly origin.

William James

1. There can be no existence of evil as a force to the healthy-minded individual.

2. There is something wrong with the world. There is no full consolation. Evil is evil and pain is pain; and in bearing them valiantly I think the only thing we can do is to believe that the good power of the world does not appoint them of its own free will but works under some dark and inscrutable limitations, and that we by our own patience and good will, can somehow strengthen his hands.

3. It seems to me that all a man has to depend on in this world, is,

in the last resort, mere brute power of resistance. I can't bring myself, as so many men seem able to do, to blink the evil out of sight, and gloss it over. It's as real as the good, and if it is denied, good must be denied too. It must be accepted and hated, and resisted while there's breath in our bodies.

4. Much of what we call evil is due entirely to the way men take the phenomenon. It can so often be converted into a bracing and tonic good by a simple change of the sufferer's inner attitude from one of fear to one of fight; its sting so often departs and turns into a relish when, after vainly seeking to shun it, we agree to face about and bear it cheerfully, that a man is simply bound in honor, with reference to many of the facts that seem at first to disconcert his peace, to adopt this way of escape. Refuse to admit their badness; despite their power; ignore their presence; turn your attention the other way; and so far as you yourself are concerned at any rate, though the facts may still exist, their evil character exists no longer. Since you make them evil or good by your own thoughts about them, it is the ruling of your thoughts which proves to be your principal concern.

5. The devil, *quoad existentiam*, may be good. That is, although he be a *principle* of evil, yet the universe, with such a principle in it, may practically be a better universe than it could have been without. On every hand, in a small way, we find that a certain amount of evil is a condition by which a higher form of good is bought. ... Even cruelty and treachery may be among the absolutely blessed fruits of time, and to quarrel with any of their details may be blasphemy. The only real blasphemy, in short, may be that pessimistic temper of the soul which lets it give way to such things as regrets, remorse, and grief.

6. Not the absence of vice, but vice there, and virtue holding her by the throat, seems the ideal human state. And there seems no reason to suppose it not a permanent human state. There is a deep truth in what the school of Schopenhauer insists on, — the illusoriness of the notion of moral progress. The more brutal forms of evil that go are replaced by others more subtle and more

poisonous. Our moral horizon moves with us as we move, and never do we draw nearer to the far-off line where the black waves and the azure meet. The final purpose of our creation seems most plausibly to be the greatest possible enrichment of our ethical consciousness, through the intensest play of contrasts and the widest diversity of characters. This of course obliges some of us to be vessels of wrath, while it calls others to be vessels of honor. But the subjectivist point of view reduces all these outward distinctions to a common denominator. The wretch languishing in the felon's cell may be drinking draughts of the wine of truth that will never pass the lips of the so-called favorite of fortune. And the peculiar consciousness of each of them is an indispensable note in the great ethical concert which the centuries as they roll are grinding out of the living heart of man.

7. The world is all the richer for having a devil in it, so long as we keep our foot upon his neck.

Schopenhauer

1. That a man is lying, we should pretend to believe him; for then he becomes bold and assured, lies more vigorously, and is unmasked.

2. No one who has to live amongst men should absolutely discard any person who has his due place in the order of nature, even though he is very wicked, or contemptible, or ridiculous. He must accept him as an unalterable fact – unalterable, because the necessary outcome of an eternal, fundamental principle; ... there must be fools and rogues in the world. If he acts otherwise, he will be committing an injustice, and giving a challenge of life and death to the man he discards. No one can alter his peculiar individuality, his moral character, his intellectual capacity, his temperament, or physique; and if we go so far as to condemn a man from every point of view, there will be nothing left him but to engage us in deadly conflict; for we are practically allowing him to the right to exist only on condition that he becomes another man – which is impossible; his nature forbids it.

So if you have to live amongst men, you must allow everyone the right to exist in accordance with the character he has, whatever he turns out to be; and all you should strive to do is to make use of this character in such a way as its kind of nature permit, rather than hope for any alteration in it, or to condemn it offhand for what it is; This is the true sense of the maxim — *Live and let live*. That, however, is a task which is difficult in proportion as it is right; and he is a happy man who can once for all avoid having to do with a great many of his fellow creatures.

...

I [am] inclined to laying down the following rule: When you come into contact with a man, no matter whom, do not attempt an objective appreciation of him according to his worth and dignity. Do not consider his bad will, or his narrow understanding and perverse ideas; as the former may lead you to hate and the latter to despise him; but fix your attention only upon his sufferings, his needs, his anxieties, his pains. Then you will always feel your kinship with him; you will sympathize with him; and instead of hatred or contempt, you will experience the communication that alone is the peace to which the Gospel calls us. The way to keep down hatred and contempt is certainly not look for a man's alleged "dignity," but, on the contrary to regard him as an object of pity [or a better term, compassion]

Nietzsche

1. Man is a rope stretched between the animal and the Overman — a rope over an abyss.

2. Whoever fights monsters should see to it that in the process he does not become a monster. And when you look long into an abyss, the abyss also looks into you.

James Fenimore Cooper

We live in a world of transgressions and selfishness, and no pictures that represent us otherwise can be true, though, happily, for human nature, gleamings of that pure spirit in whose likeness man has been fashioned are to be seen, relieving its deformities, and mitigating if not excusing its crimes.

Malthus

Evil exists in the world not to create despair but activity. We are not patiently to submit to it, but to exert ourselves to avoid it. It is not only the interest but the duty of every individual to use his utmost efforts to remove evil from himself and from as large a circle as he can influence, and the more he exercises himself in this duty, the more wisely he directs his efforts, and the more successful these efforts are, the more he will probably improve and exalt his own mind, and the more completely does he appear to fulfill the will of his Creator.

Jung

1. To confront a person with his shadow is to show him his own light. Once one has experienced a few times what it is like to stand judgingly between the opposites, one begins to understand what is meant by the self. Anyone who perceives his shadow and his light simultaneously sees himself from two sides and thus gets in the middle.

2. Filling the conscious mind with ideal conceptions is a characteristic of Western theosophy, but not the confrontation with the shadow and the world of darkness. One does not become enlightened by imagining figures of light, but by making the darkness conscious.

3. A man who is unconscious of himself acts in a blind, instinctive way and is in addition fooled by all the illusions that arise when he sees everything that he is not conscious of in himself coming to meet him from outside as projections upon his neighbour.

4. In reality, the acceptance of the shadow-side of human nature verges on the impossible. Consider for a moment what it means to grant the right of existence to what is unreasonable, senseless, and evil! Yet it is just this that the modern man insists upon. He wants to live with every side of himself – to know what he is. That is why he casts history aside. He wants to break with tradition so that he can experiment with his life and determine what value and meaning things have in themselves, apart from traditional presuppositions.

391

John Milton

What wisdom can there be to choose, what continence to forbear without the knowledge of evil? He that can apprehend and consider vice with all her baits and seeming pleasures, and yet abstain, and yet distinguish, and yet prefer that which is truly better, he is the true wayfaring Christian.

Voltaire

As long as people believe in absurdities they will continue to commit atrocities.

Leonardo Da Vinci

He who does not punish evil, commands it to be done.

Blaise Pascal

Truly it is an evil to be full of faults; but it is a still greater evil to be full of them and to be unwilling to recognize them, since that is to add the further fault of a voluntary illusion.

Mohammed

To overcome evil with good is good, to resist evil with evil is evil.

Buddha

There has to be evil so that good can prove its purity above it.

Vivekananda

1. Fly from evil and terror and misery, and they will follow you. Face them, and they will flee.

Gandhi

1. Must I do all the evil I can before I learn to shun it? Is it not enough to know the evil to shun it? If not, we should be sincere enough to admit that we love evil too well to give it up.

2. Non-cooperation with evil is as much a duty as is cooperation with good

Aurobindo

1. When I knew nothing, then I abhorred the criminal, sinful and impure, being myself full of crime, sin and impurity; but when I was cleansed and my eyes unsealed, then I bowed down in my spirit before the thief and the murderer and adored the feet of the harlot; For I saw that these souls had accepted the terrible burden

of evil and drained for all of us the greater portion of the churned poison of the world-ocean.

2. Meanness and selfishness are the only sins that I find it difficult to pardon; yet they alone are almost universal. Therefore these also must not be hated in others, but in ourselves annihilated.

PERCEPTIVE PERSONS

Helen Keller
I can say with conviction that the struggle which evil necessitates is one of the greatest blessings. It makes us strong, patient, helpful men and women. It lets us into the soul of things and teaches us that although the world is full of suffering, it is full also of the overcoming of it. My optimism, then, does not rest on the absence of evil, but on a glad belief in the preponderance of good and a willing effort always to cooperate with the good, that it may prevail.

Martin Luther King, Jr.
To ignore evil is to become an accomplice to it.

Anna Sewell
My doctrine is this, that if we see cruelty or wrong that we have the power to stop, and do nothing, we make ourselves sharers in the guilt.

Maíread Maguire
We frail humans are at one time capable of the greatest good and, at the same time, capable of the greatest evil. Change will only come about when each of us takes up the daily struggle ourselves to be more forgiving, compassionate, loving, and above all joyful in the knowledge that, by some miracle of grace, we can change as those around us can change too.

Helen Keller
Life is either a daring adventure or nothing. To keep our faces toward change and behave like free spirits in the presence of fate is strength undefeatable.

Pearl S. Buck
When good people in any country cease their vigilance and struggle, then evil men prevail.

2

[In Particular: <u>Courage</u>]

Eminent Persons

Ernest Hemingway
Cowardice, as distinguished from panic, is almost always simply a lack of ability to suspend the functioning of the imagination.

C.S. Lewis
Courage is not simply one of the virtues, but the form of every virtue at the testing point.

Raymond Lindquist
Courage is the power to let go of the familiar.

Mark Twain
Courage is resistance to fear, mastery of fear – not absence of fear. Except a creature be part coward it is not a compliment to say it is brave.

E.E. Cummings
It takes courage to grow up and turn out to be who you really are.

Anais Nin
Life expands or contracts in direct proportion to one's courage.

Shakespeare
Cowards die many times before their deaths; The valiant never taste of death but once.

Virgil
Fortune favors the brave.

Plato
Courage is knowing what not to fear.

Perceptive Persons

Eleanor Roosevelt
You gain strength, courage and confidence by every experience in which you really stop to look fear in the face. You are able to say to yourself, "I've lived through this horror. I can take the next thing that comes along." You must do the thing you think you cannot do.

Diane de Poitiers
Courage is as often the outcome of despair as of hope; in the one case we have nothing to lose, in the other everything to gain.

Mary Tyler Moore
Pain nourishes courage. You can't be brave if you've only had wonderful things happen to you.

Mary Anne Radmacher
Courage doesn't always roar. Sometimes courage is the little voice at the end of the day that says I'll try again tomorrow.

John Wainwright
There is no such thing as bravery; only degrees of fear.

Charles Kennedy
Courage is a peculiar kind of fear.

David Ben-Gurion
Courage is ... the knowledge of how to fear what ought to be feared and how not to fear what ought not to be feared.

Nicholas Murray Butler
Optimism is the foundation of courage.

Eddie Rickenbacher
Courage is doing what you are afraid to do. There can be no courage unless you're scared.

Ambrose Redmoon
Courage is not the absence of fear, but rather the judgement that something else is more important than fear.

Robert Anthony
Courage is simply the willingness to be afraid and act anyway.

David Lloyd George
Don't be afraid to take a big step if one is indicated; you can't cross a chasm in two small jumps.

David S. Muzzey
Faith is courage; it is creative. Despair is always destructive.

Keshavan Nair
With courage you will dare to take risks, have the strength to be compassionate and the wisdom to be humble. Courage is the foundation of integrity.

Chapter 16
AGAINST PATHICS IN PARTICULAR

This chapter carries further the purpose set forth in Chapter 15 in facing and protecting oneself from evil; but the target here is the evil specific to pathics.

1

Protective Suggestions Against Pathics in the Household

1. "To anyone feeling emotional and vulnerable and self-reflective ... call a close friend. Visit a loved one you haven't seen in years. Write heart-felt letters to anyone who means anything to you...but don't give in and show remorse or regret over a narcissist. You'll only leave the encounter still hurting and they'll have their NS-fix for the week."

2. "I can only say to those with doubts, with ideas of 'fixing it' — just don't. Move away and try to cut your losses. Why sit down to the table again to be dealt another bum hand?"

3. "Then, fool that I was, I tried to become a crusading Pollyanna, armed with books, clinical data, case histories — I valiantly tried to cure him; [but it was just] magical thinking. I gave up. It's useless and a total waste of my time when I needed to concentrate on getting me better and getting on with my life."

4. "I have been with my N for 11 years and was completely disillusioned by him. I did everything I could to make things work and tried fixing the unfixable. He exploited me and other women for years. I'm done with him and have decided that I'm going to move forward with my life."

5. "If I absolutely WANT to stop the N, I have hundreds of ways; but if I, in the back of my head, continue playing his game, it means that I'm still denying his disease and still trying to control or heal it…I thought of the 3 'C's: I don't Cause it, I can't Control it, and I can't Cure it…"

6. "I have learned lots of stuff about myself that I never before had to bother looking at. There IS a reason you are so attached and fell hard for this type. Finding that reason doesn't make the sorrow completely go away, but it does help to make sense of things."

7. "I felt that emptiness also when I confronted him with the truth of his being personality disordered. Then all you think is … How could I have been so fooled? Self-reflection is not an easy thing to do. You then have to face all aspects of yourself, shadow and light. Being able to do this is what makes us different."

8. "I am a firm believer that most women who accept a bad relationship had no voice as a child and suffered emotional and sometimes physical abuse; I know I did."

9. "Both of my sons eventually saw their N-dad for what he truly is. I didn't have to tell them or talk to them about their dad. They figured it out. Now we (my sons and I) are very close and have wonderful times when we are together. N-Dad's name isn't even mentioned between us anymore."

10. "When the 'devaluation' phase began I was totally confused having been in denial for so long about the one-dimensional aspect of our relationship."

11. "I am in the process of moving on with my life … enrolled in college and also looking forward to a divorce, and the day I will be REALLY free. I didn't come to these decisions easily … I suffered for over 35 years of marriage. The greatest revelation to me has been that my marriage has been a 'figment of MY imagination'. Please don't think that he will ever change. They can't. What they are is their survival mechanism. If it wasn't for the information that I

learned here I would probably be looking for a pine box! As I have taken my 'baby steps' in recovery, I find that I have regained my self-esteem. I have realized that I did everything I could to make the marriage work and when it failed, I was not to blame. I am a worthwhile person and so are you. You have suffered enough. PLEASE move on with your life! There is just so much more than life with a self-centered, ego-maniac who cares nothing for anyone except how they can serve them. Stay here and get strong. The fine people who post here have been through it all."

12. "You will never unlearn what you now know about narcissism. If you go back to the N, you will look at him – and you will know; and this knowledge will come between you."

13. "I'd love to be able to pick up the phone and call him and scream and yell and cry for all of the heartache I went through (and still go through) for him … But I know that it wouldn't do any good. It's truly heartbreaking to know that someone you loved more than life itself has no way of understanding what it feels like."

14. "We are de-programming ourselves (at least I hope we are!) and it can only get better. When WE look in the mirror we know who is looking back at us. What does the N see when he looks for the millionth time in his mirror. Best not to dwell too much on what he sees."

15. "Take lots of care. Look in other directions. Take your mind to a quiet place. Do something you never did before."

16. "Don't let your mind be invaded, even by your own negative thoughts/memories, or even by what you might consider memories of the 'good' times. 'Good times' do not exist in N-land."

17. "To him, trust was just about sex, and fidelity and had nothing to do with emotional intimacy. If you push for intimacy with an N, there is no choice for them other than to flee or devalue. There is no love there … they don't know what it means. That's why, I liken it to talking to an alien … they just don't get it."

18. "Staying with an N, or making contact with an ex-N, is like putting your hands directly on a hot stovetop to warm them. It will 'work' for five seconds before it burns you."

19. "That feeling of not getting it all out with her will fade, and you'll be glad you didn't get it all out with her, because she'd just use the information to somehow abuse you even more either now or in the future."

20. "Of course, he didn't have a clue what I meant. Explaining the notion (that the issues I had with him were all about a lack of emotional intimacy) was just an opportunity to engage in the 'blame (me) game,' 'word-salad game,' 'pathologize (me) game,' 'spin reality game,' and 'lure and slam game,' 'rationalize it all away game,' etc.. In other words, I had my first brush with the devaluation cycle. Very painful and bewildering."

21. "Once you are crystal clear in your perception of the N's true personality, you lose respect for them. Then you can put up with a lot, because you no longer feel the need to take what they say with any seriousness."

22. "You're not crazy. No way. Your anger is your weapon right now. You need to be angry. You have a right to be angry."

23. "After sinking into a pit of despair, going into shock one night and shaking so badly, I could not stop that shaking, I literally could not stop it. It frightened me. Then, I became angry; I get my strength from anger. The angrier I get, the stronger I get. Here I was driven into mind-numbing terror, pain, confusion. The anger became an almost welcome relief from the pain. How could he treat me that way? I had done nothing but work for our marriage. I was dumped like a bag of trash."

24. "Happiness is the best revenge, because that's something we're capable of; but they're not. Get angry, feel the hurt, but please don't act out on revenge. Then you'd just have to feel your own shame for living outside of your own values."

25. "Maybe it's just good, old-fashioned aversion to pain. None of us like to be hurt, and when we perceive things or situations as hurtful, we tend to avoid them. I used to avoid things too, as a reaction to all the pain I had suffered as a child. Some things should be avoided, and others should be worked through, and the trick for me has been partly learning how to tell the difference."

26. "What helped me was learning that I don't have to be all things to all people, and learning that I can be myself, and that is good enough for most people."

27. "I needed real human contact so badly after my experience with my ex-N. I enjoyed such simple things in life as to sit and have a give-and-take conversation, mutual respect, a smile, a touch. All of this without what the narcissist overlays upon social interaction. I was awed by how nice people are, how understanding, and at the same time, many, truly don't understand, yet they were human, and MAN WAS IT GOOD TO SPEND SOME TIME WITH A HUMAN!!!"

28. "Once you've had some time with zero contact with him you will see how your thinking clears and changes. Read everything here as it really helps and please keep sharing here. You'll find lots of support and comfort. When you are tempted to call him, sit down here and read or write until it passes. Vent, vent, vent!"

29. "Why don't we go? For any combination of reasons. Take a look at the 'you' before or at the time you started going out with the N – and the 'you' later on. Never was anyone less equipped to get out by that stage – yourself worth is in the gutter, you feel a failure, a deep sense of being a nothing – the things the N said to you, the insidious drip-feed of negatives, their behaviour that says so much about how little they respect or care for you. Then of course we really do have to face some of the nastiest – the what-ifs, the depression, the self hatred (how COULD I have put up with this, how DARE he did this to me without a blink of the eye – what must he have thought of me knowing I allowed him to do these things), the loneliness, sense of failure."

30. "It is here that I really talked about it. This place has been a solace for me for almost one year. I have told no one of this place. It is my little secret place with secret friends that I come to and talk about the hell I have been through… and hopefully help others who are in this hell."

31. "I stopped contact with the N. I felt stronger again, but very lonely. I posted here often at all times of the day and night, and always received love and support."

32. "I can come up here onto the forum and share the 'laughing on the outside, crying on the inside' syndrome, and not get judged for feeling like this, which keeps me going. One day, I will laugh on the inside as well – and I'll have all of you, and the fun and tears we share, to thank for that. You are my lifelines. Thanks."

33. "The support I have received from everyone here has been what made me turn the corner away from my ex-N. I am amazed at how people who were strangers to me two months ago, and who I would not recognize on the street, have helped me walk through the worst part of it unscathed."

34. "But as much as we are responsible for our own life we are responsible for society around us."

35. "Learn as much as you can as fast as you can, protect yourself financially and emotionally."

36. "Do not let him get the impression that these calls are rattling you. Be brusque and impolite (nothing else will have any effect) next time he tries this."

37. "There are worse things than being lonely." (living with an N)

38. "I really just need to tell him once and for all: 'I am not interested in speaking with you. My personal life is my business. Please stop calling me.' Say it in an unemotional, matter-of-fact voice. Then STOP talking to him. If he manages to get you on the phone, hang up the INSTANT you realize it's him. He will call and call, but eventually will give up and go away."

39. "Before I cut my losses and left my husband, I tried valiantly to predict what he would do or say, and speak accordingly. But it didn't matter; whatever I did, he would twist it to his own advantage. I agree with what you say about simple, strict language with the N. It seems the best route is as few words as possible with clear meaning. Similar to dealing with a toddler."

40. "My Ns love to try verbal manipulation. They're very good at it and most people fall for it time and again. It takes Ns 20-40 minutes of running the gamut of all their whining, complaining, argumentative and other persuasive tactics. Then in the end they hit my 'NO' brick-wall they have nowhere left to go. It's a horrible way to live but sometimes it's not possible to get them out of your life in one swift stroke; so boundaries become essential survival techniques for non-Ns."

41. "You have a remedy in the courts: it's called PAS, Parental Alienation Syndrome. I believe that Ns practice alienating their victims from each other all the time – it's one of their mainstays. You can prove this and your child can help; when your child understands that your ex has purposely been trying to stop her from loving you – it will free her too. Fortunately, Ns are verbal and document their own crazy antics through e-mail, regular mail, answering machine messages, and their own court papers, your ability to prove PAS won't be difficult; you can use the N's own words against him. Getting counseling for yourself and your child also proves the point; that your ex is causing intentional emotional damage to you and your child. File a PAS lawsuit. That ought to scare the heck out of him and get him off your back. In the meantime keep collecting evidence – his own words and mean-spirited actions."

42. "Ns love spreading lies and rumours. That's one of the things they do best. When you hear about them, put up your hand, palm outward (the stop-sign position). Tell whoever it is firmly and with a chuckle 'I don't want to hear anything about N'."

43. "Please do help yourself set some firm boundaries. One thing that helps me is to ask myself 'Would I want someone to treat my daughter this way?' More often than not the answer is 'No.' If it's not good enough for her, then it's not good enough for her mother."

44. "Call him on it. 'No, that's what YOU do, not me.' I've read suggestions that a victim should accuse the N of outrageous things too, it really throws them. And when they rage at you, rage back! They are counting on you NOT doing this. They are counting on you remaining a doormat, they hope you'll keep trying to be under-standing, etc., so they can keep wiping their feet on you."

45. "Circle those dates on your calendar and make plans that can't

be changed. Get tickets to a show or concert, commit to help out a friend or organization. Edge him out. Remember, the worst thing you can do to N is ignore him or discount his importance. You are over him, you can even give him a Mona Lisa smile and keep walking."

46. "Using very simple assertiveness statements works with these folks, however don't expect them to like it. Trying to enlist their cooperation is useless. Only by having very firm boundaries, telling them what your decisions are, and never, ever explaining or defending your- self are you able to maintain any sanity."

47. "Why not just act uninterested and give him a flat out 'NO' with ABSOLUTELY NO EXPLANATION?"

48. "Indifference is absolutely your best tool in dealing with the N. They HATE indifference. Do not react in any way to anything he says or does. Any reaction, good or bad is supply for them. Any response you get will not be real, merely another attempt at manipulating the situation. Do not let him do that. It's what he wants. Somewhere to place the blame, and to make you feel as bad as possible. He is not 'expecting' any particular reaction. ANY reaction will do for him."

49. "You are going to have to be stronger than you've ever been to block him ... block e-mails, get caller ID. For your mental health and safety you have to do this to get rid of him. He will not give up easily but you know you can't afford to have him in your life. You don't owe him any explanations or even advice about NPD. His denials and excuses will only confuse you more. And you can't help him."

50. "After the worst of it was over, what I found to be key was to have no contact with him. None. Do not say, 'Go to hell.' Do not say, 'I love you.' Do not, above all, try to sit down and have a dialogue, to reason with him. No response of any kind is the answer."

51. "Please, please do whatever it takes to avoid the phone. With narcissism, I suggest procrastination. Tell yourself you'll wait until tomorrow... then tomorrow repeat that same phrase ... 'phrase'...

meaning that you never initiate contact. Put off until 'tomorrow', what you MUST NOT DO TODAY!"

52. "DON'T ANSWER HIS MESSAGES...

DON'T MAKE CONTACT...

DON'T WASTE YOUR PRECIOUS TIME...

DON'T TOY WITH YOUR FRAGILE EMOTIONS...

No matter how much we want to believe they're not seedy weasels ... WE KNOW THEY ARE! And you know HE is ..."

53. "The boundaries I found most successful are where I don't answer his 'statements presented as questions'. Never fall for his 'yes/no' response type of questions. Never ask an N a question; it's just inviting lies. Never answer a question, either, always respond, 'I'll have to think about that' to give yourself time to think about what he's really trying. Whenever he asks his beating-around-the-bush questions I use the tactics of salesmen and just repeat his last 3-4 words back to him, posed as a question. When I don't want him bugging me any more I'll say: 'This is becoming annoying N.' With any luck you'll have him walking on eggshells."

54. "Be fully self reliant and responsible so you never, ever have to ask him for anything. When you do say NO, the ABSOLUTE WORST thing you can do is to change your mind. Practice, practice, practice your boundary statement until you can pull it off without batting an eye. Oh, and try chuckling at his words. The humiliation alone can often cause them to disappear like a vampire at sunrise."

55. "Start documenting everything now! Save copies of his e-mails or copies of the web sites that he frequents. Document how he treats your children. You can't be too detailed. It may be a pain to do but you will be glad you did. Do you work? If you leave do you have a way to support your kids on your own? I think a broken home is much better than exposing your kids to an out-of-control freak. One tip which I wish I had known when I separated from my ex-N is make him think it is all his idea. As far as the kids, you don't want him to use them as a weapon against you. Make visitations sound as though they help you out tremendously. That way he won't want contact with them. I feel for you. I've been split from my ex-N for two years and still have to deal with his control issues because of our child. I wish I didn't have to deal with him at all."

56. "Instead of seeing yourself as one person, dealing with an unreasonable crazy person, imagine that all of us are standing right behind you, forming a group. Take strength from us, for as long as you need that, until you can fly with the eagles – on your own."

57. "If you want to end a relationship with a narcissist, the formula is very simple: The narcissist analyses (and internalizes) everything in terms of blame and guilt, superiority and inferiority, gain (victory) and loss (defeat) and the resulting matrix of narcissistic supply."

"Shift the blame to yourself (I don't know what happened to me, I've changed, it's my fault, I'm to blame for this, you're constant, reliable and consistent...).

"Tell him you feel guilty (excruciatingly so, in great and picturesque detail).

"Tell him how superior he is and how inferior you feel.

"Make this separation your loss and his absolute, unmitigated gain.

"Convince him that he is likely to gain more supply from others

(future women?) than he ever did or will from you.

"BUT, make clear that your decision – though evidently 'erroneous' and 'pathological' – is FINAL, irrevocable and that all contact is to be severed henceforth.

"And never leave ANYTHING in writing behind you."

58. "I have the dog, the alarm system, the caller ID, 2 police reports filed, the motion detector light on 2 sides of the house, changed e-mail addresses, changed phone numbers, asked his friends to co-operate with my requests to distance myself, returned all his priority mail to sender, but I haven't yet done what you suggested regarding forwarding his e-mails. I'll try that. I've avoided that mainly because of the hurt that it might cause others. I think that the only way for me to make this nightmare stop is to 'shine a brighter light' on the darkness that he creates. I have also returned everything that was his. I have tried to literally and figuratively erase all the symbols and remembrances of the pain and agony that he brought into my life and the lives of anyone close to me. I do not want to ever forget the very excruciating lessons that I hope I have ingrained in my brain through this experience. If the pain needs to stay with me for the rest of my life as a reminder of what was, then so be it."

59. "We need to (1) Identify the problem(s). (2) Decide what to accept and what to change. (3) Take action. (4) Stop feeling sorry for our- selves or rehashing our problems. Beyond a certain point, it stunts our growth and progress. That's the process. It's the only way. Therapy can become a substitute for action-based change, a danger to watch for."

60. "I have since learned to do the same to him. After a fight I appear unaffected. It jangled him the first time I did it. And mind you, I did some serious acting to appear unfazed. It worked. The reaction was not the normal giddy happy-go-lucky guy. He was confused ... worried even. His control was slipping. Not cool. Surely he could NOT be losing his touch, his magic ability to control my emotions – in essence, control me."

61. "There is only one way for you (and the rest of us) to go – and that is onwards, upwards and away."

62. "I wish I could tell you that there was a way to reason with this wo- man.

"My suggestion is to install video surveillance cameras (they make them small now and ones that even 'see' and record in the DARK. Point them in the direction that will best catch her at her mischief and then RECORD the action.

"I would also get a small pocket-sized voice recorder and keep in 'ON' and in my pocket if you ever have to talk to her, or if she starts screaming at you then you can push 'record'.

"With this EVIDENCE you should be able to prosecute her with the LAW which should get your neighbors off your case as well.

"This woman may be a psychopath or she may be mentally dis- ordered or ill, but the problem doesn't matter, it is causing you grief.

"PROOF beyond a shadow of a doubt is I think your only option.

"The price of the equipment to get PROOF is coming down and you can either install it yourself or get someone else to do so. It can even be disguised in light fixtures or other 'normal' things, so it doesn't look like cameras."

2

Protective Suggestions Against Pathics in the Workplace

1. "I also had psychopaths for bosses. I was struck by three excellent suggestions for dealing with them.

(1) Document, Document, Document! Find a way to use your PC to work for you so you don't get stuck doing double work. The witch I worked for tried to dump as much work as possible on me so I'd be too frazzled to contest her. I had the blessing of being trained in PC software and light programming and my home PC and laptop (never trust the PCs on the job!) were my workhorses. Keep the laptop or PDA that you are using a complete secret, even from your friends! Secure your work-space by keeping your desktop clear – lock your desk every time you leave it. Whenever I was distracted away from my desk, her stooge had the opportunity to ransack it so I bought one of those $1.00 plastic wrist coil key chains that made it possible to lock my desk in a hot minute. Remove ALL personal information from your desk. These creeps will search your desk after hours – managers DO have the right to search your desk, locker and PC! Get in the habit of maintaining some kind of daily journal that accounts for the jobs you're working on and the time you took to work on them – even if you're working for the best boss in the world.

(2) Network – Enlist friends inside and outside your department. Friends outside your department aren't known by your psycho manager so they can help you store info in desks, lockers, etc.

408

out of the reach of your spying saboteur of a boss. My working buddies let me use a desk on another floor to type my notes into my laptop on my lunch hour. They can keep you posted on job openings in other departments and serve as your eyes and ears. Your family and non-company friends can suggest and work on any legal avenues you may need in future. The suggestion to question your next employers about psychopaths is priceless!

(3) CALL ON FATHER GOD. Psychopath/Sociopath ain't nothing but a $10.00 word for DEVIL. You can't fight what you don't know and can't see. Often these minions are working for higher ups that know exactly what they're doing and have ordered them to eliminate you, especially if you are an older worker that they wish to deprive of vested benefits. You cannot defeat that kind of organized evil alone. God CAN see and defeat the tricks of the Devil.

"I would warn 'Dennis' not to use the same weapons and tactics psychopaths use. They are the masters of black-bagging/back alley tactics; they've used all their rotten lives to fine-tune dirty fighting. You'd be fighting them on their terms and territory – they would win – hands down!

"One suggestion from me: If your job is a union shop, JOIN YOUR LOCAL: They're another outside agency you can appeal to if your rights are violated. As a former union steward from a family of union stewards, Trust me; union dues are worth it!"

2. "The last job I had (before I started my own 'one-man business'), was at a company just outside of Cincinnati. I heard recently from an 'insider', it is a shell of its' former self! Ahhh, sweet revenge! Some- times, my friends, there IS justice in the Universe.

"I left the company many years ago, after giving the two owners of the company plenty of time and feedback, to correct (i.e., FIRE) the existing crazies they had in their employ. I held a 'key' production position, so one would think the owners would have listened to me, but they didn't. I suspect many business owners 'look the other way' on these psychos, because they are afraid of them, and have no inter-personal skills or even the cajones to deal with these creepazoids.

"Anyway, one of the psychos was my immediate supervisor (gosh, 'ain't that always the way'?). Fortunately, this psycho wasn't real bright, and ended up even driving one of the owners nearly 'up a wall', and got himself fired! HA! I LOVED IT!

"However, they still had another psychopath running amok around the place, and if they had fired that creep (a woman this time) along with the other one, I'd probably still be working there. But they failed to deal with the problem, so I gave 'em my 2 week notice (sweet again!) and, as I said, started my own business, which, thus far, has worked out great! Ironic, isn't it? I used to sit at my desk at that place, and dream of no longer being vulnerable to these unspeakable jerks; and I hoped that if I ever did get away, it would be as nice as I imagined. And baby, IT IS!!

"For those of you still dealing with these sacks of feces on a daily basis, I want you to know, I understand only too well what you're dealing with, and how it makes you feel. These types are like 'emotional terrorists'. They seem to know exactly where and how to 'hit' you. Their 'hits' are designed to cripple your self-confidence, self-esteem and make you angry. If they had grown up in Iraq, they'd have been one of Sadaam's 'elite' torturers. And for what reason do they do these things to you? Oh, don't worry. They were already inventing reasons the first moment they met you. These people are, and have always been, the scourge of the human race. They are in management of all the small businesses, corporations and governments of all the countries on our sad little planet, because they are attracted to power. I hope there are enough good guys also in these same places to save us, but I'm not optimistic, based on my actual life experiences."

3. "My advice – Act. Do not react. When you meet her, be effusive. Be 'over the top' in saying hello and keep moving. Do not stand in her sphere of influence unless it's absolutely imperative. Whenever possible, beat her at her own game. Keep talking. Keep moving. She will eventually (and rather quickly) figure out she has no influence

on you and will search for easier prey.

"If you're being subjected to her nastiness, go quickly to management and let them know that she's interfering with you being able to perform your duties. Have journaled details."

4. "Some suggestions for you 'good guys':

"Don't try to deal with this alone. Bond with others in your company who understand (if there are any left who are as courageous as you), and hopefully you have family outside this place that will listen to you and be there for you. And keep looking at other job options. And speaking of that, even if it risks blowing the interview, ask your prospective employers how they deal with these types. Are they strong enough to confront such individuals? Do they even understand that such people exist? Are they psychos themselves? Well, maybe you don't want to ask them THAT, but stay focused on how they answer your other questions, and the expressions on their face. That will tell you if you want to be working there or not. No point in making a 'lateral move'..."

PART FIVE

Toward the Ascendancy of Justice and Wisdom

Chapter 17
A PHILOSOPHY AGAINST MALICE:
AURORALISM

1

1. Philosophy in its etymological root, means "love of wisdom."

2. In which case, a philosophy against malice is "a love of wisdom" against malice; which in other words, means that the love of wisdom is for good to prevail over evil.

3. This good includes both wisdom and justice; this evil includes both injustice and ignorance. In which case, a philosophy against malice would direct the ascendancy of justice and wisdom to prevail over injustice and ignorance.

4. "Love of wisdom" has two main senses: love as being *attracted to* wisdom, and love as being the *source* of wisdom.

5. Wisdom is both practical and contemplative (Aristotle): *practical* in the sense that when we know what is right, we act accordingly

with appropriate judgment; *contemplative* in the sense of reflecting upon the nature of reality in both its human and transcendent aspects.

6. Philosophy, as the love of wisdom, deals with truth and right as a way of life.

7. As there are many categories of truth and of right, whether in matters of beliefs and values, sciences and arts, metaphysics and religion, human nature and relationships, so there are as many philosophies to cover those categories.

8. The category of truth and right that most concerns us in this book is that of human nature and relationships.

9. So far this study has fairly much inundated the reader with the dark, suffering side of human nature and relationships, which comprises the bulk of knowledge needed to grasp the reality of pathic evil. The remaining part of this book comprises the light, redeeming, side of human nature and relationships; which includes (1) introductory perspectives of human nature as both hard and soft – Chapter 18; (2) a human-transcendent wisdom, including its source: Love – Chapter 19; and (3) a tactic of *assertive-passive* resistance – Chapter 20. I say, "introductory perspectives" inasmuch as I only <u>introduce</u> these three concepts rather than follow them in detail; otherwise, I would have myself another book within this one – a book which, as it turns out, I do have regarding love and wisdom, but certainly not as part of this book.

10. These three forthcoming perspectives: hard and soft natures, a human-transcendent wisdom, and an assertive-passive resistance course of action – including (4) an understanding of pathic evil gleaned through chapters 1 to 16, and (5) a self-understanding of the evil within ourselves – all comprise what I term as a *philosophy against malice*.

11. This philosophy covers not only the dark side of our nature, but the light side as well; and it is the light side of our nature – our transcendence – that is our salvation, our hope, our redemption, our "resurrection," so to speak, our glow.

12. And speaking of "glow," this is where we arrive at the name, the meaning, of this philosophy not only *against* malice, but *for* justice and wisdom; and it is the case for justice and wisdom to gradually take the ascendancy over injustice and ignorance.

13. Light is the glow of this philosophy: the light out of the darkness of pathic evil: the *aurora* of our mind – the dawning of a new consciousness unto the ascendancy of justice and wisdom.

14. As for the appropriate name for this uplifting, forward moving philosophy let me borrow this word, "aurora". from Roman mythology and poetry:– meaning: 'goddess of the dawn' "who renews herself every morning and flies across the sky, announcing the arrival of the sun." Analogously, this philosophy announces the arrival of the dawn of a new day of beliefs and values to supplant the dark of injustice and ignorance. Hence, the name of this philosophy: *Auroralism*; and name of an adherent of this philosophy: an *Auroralist*.

13. Let the beauty of the word "aurora" immerse our minds as we strive to live by and for this philosophy of auroralism – auroralism: a way of life that shines down on us in wisdom and love.

15. This auroralistic philosophy presupposes a new awareness, a new consciousness, that will raise intuition to articulation; and this intuition abides not in our subconscious nor unconscious mind, but, figuratively speaking, in our *transconscious* mind. And it is our transconsciousness that will "rise from the depths" to speak for itself, and to usher in the dawn of day, of which I speak, and of which the great prophet-psychologist-philosopher, Nietzsche, wrote; and it is through our transconsciousness, that the

philosophy of auroralism will emerge as the dominant force against the malice of evil.

Chapter 18

HARD-NATURES IN CONTRAST TO SOFT-NATURES

"I have a spotted Bengal cat who was named Muscle Man by my daughter when she was a toddler, because even as a kitten he looked like a professional wrestler. Grown now, he is much larger than most other domestic cats. His formidable claws resemble those of his Asian leopard-cat ancestors, but by temperament, he is gentle and peace-loving. My neighbor has a little calico who visits. Evidently the calico's predatory charisma is huge, and she is brilliant at directing the evil eye at other cats. Whenever she is within fifty feet, Muscle Man, all fifteen pounds of him to her seven, cringes and crouches in fear and feline deference. Muscle Man is a splendid cat. He is warm and loving, and he is close to my heart. Nonetheless, I would like to believe that some of his reactions are more primitive than mine. I hope I do not mistake fear for respect, because to do so would be to ensure my own victimization. Let us use our big human brains to overpower our animal tendency to bow to predators, so we can disentangle the reflexive confusion of anxiety and awe. In a perfect world, human respect would be an automatic reaction only to those who are strong, kind, and morally courageous. The person who profits from frightening you is not likely to be any of these."

- Martha Stout, author of *The Sociopath Next Door*

This chapter, and the last two chapters that follow, take a positive upswing to the <u>good</u> in men and women in opposition to pathic evil. This good is delineated through the concepts of love and wisdom; and descriptive of the type of persons who are receptive to the ways of these two concepts; namely, the soft-natured persons. Section 1 of this chapter explores, in outline mostly, this type of person in contrast to his opponent, the hard-natured individual. Section 2 explores the soft-natures exclusively; again, in outline mainly. Some of the remarks may seem as generalities without current scientific backing; but they are meant as exploratory, though meaningful, thoughts that others can debate, refute, or expand on.

1

HARD AS DISTINGUISHED FROM *SOFT* NATURES

1. Two concepts that are crucial in understanding the pathic character, and especially one's own character, as well – which is the main purpose of this chapter – are "hard" and "soft" natures. I name them "natures" insofar as individuals, I believe, are born either predominantly hard or predominantly soft; it is their nature, their particular physiological-psychological make-up (disposition, temperament) to be one or the other, and all the variations thereof. These distinctions are crucial in understanding human nature inasmuch as hard-natured persons are disposed to pathic, predatory behavior in the extreme; whereas soft-natured individuals are disposed to neurotic, victimized behavior, in the extreme. And since this book has so far emphasized understanding pathic-predatory behavior against the victim, it is the purpose of this chapter, and the two following chapters, to emphasize the victims' (as either potential or actual victim) perspective so as to understand and ward off predation.

As for the nature vs. nurture distinction, I opt for nature being the predominate factor that determines an individual's natural temperament, much as is witnessed with the higher animals that we are familiar with, such as cats and dogs. There is no way, other than chemically, that a cat or a dog that is born aggressively mean-spirited (hard-natured) or passively-gentle-spirited (soft-natured) can be essentially modified to its opposite. Yes, it is true that by abusive force (environment) a naturally aggressive, mean-spirited dog can be forced into submissive behavior; but it is his behavior that has been modified, not his nature; fear has modified the chemistry of his brain and glands so that he acts submissively under certain conditions. But fear cannot modify his genetic network that was invariably patterned upon conception. Similarly with a naturally soft-natured dog. It's hardly imaginable that under normal living conditions, that such a dog can be transformed into its opposite temperament.

One other point in the fixed nature of animals, taking certain breeds of dogs as a species, do not breeders over the years breed certain dogs to be sheep dogs or guard dogs, or lap dogs, or whatever else? Does not this fact in itself provide conclusive proof of the fixed nature of animals not only individually but as a species?

Certainly, humans are far more complex than dogs or cats; but I'm sure that anyone who has observed brutish conditions facing a man or woman would recognize similar patterns in human beings. An innately soft-natured person who is mistreated in her childhood, or simply is not affectionately loved as her particular being needs to be, tends to become dysfunctional, excessive, extreme, in one way or another, that, from one perspective, is self-protective; yet on another perspective, is self-destructive, because she is not living according to her natural propensities to love and be loved moderately or immoderately. In such circumstances, her self-identity has been askewed, off-kiltered, unknown, to her, having been absorbed in others' expectations, values and beliefs.

I, of course, speak in the extreme, more or less; since no one can be loved nor express love consistently, continually, as one would prefer; since life situations and people can never come up to what we idealize them to be. I speak rather from the position of a <u>serious</u> lack of such love in a person's life that can throw, or tip, him over to abnormality or oddity, or self-destruction, and the like. Such love needed in a loving person's life includes expressions of affection, sympathy, compassion, understanding, concern, patience, helpfulness, consideration, togetherness, freedom to be oneself, guidance, and so forth. Such love I define as an *affectionate bond of compassionate unity.* Such love is an essential aspect of a *soft-natured* person, or simply a *soft-nature.* A person who significantly lacks these love expressions in his/her makeup can be considered as hard-natured, or simply, a hard-nature. In the extreme, at the point of being deliberately and consistently inclined to hurt others, such hard-natured persons are considered as <u>pathics</u>, as this book well describes them.

2. Put simply, a hard-natured person is less impressionable than a soft-natured person; which means that social values and rules, concern for other people's feelings and rights, do not make much of an imprint upon him/her as they do for soft-natures. figuratively, we might say that a soft-natured person is like warm wax in which a thumb impression goes deeply; whereas a hard-natured person is like cold wax in which little or no impression is possible. Of course, there are degrees of heat that make wax more or less impressionable; and the less heat applied to the wax the harder it is to make a thumb impression; in which case, we have t a hard-natured person in the extreme, as pathic; inasmuch as a narcipath (toxic narcissist) is not as hard-natured as a sociopath; nor a sociopath as hard-natured as a psychopath.

In other words, the more impressionable a person is psychologically, the softer natured he or she is; and conversely, the less impressionable a person is psychologically, the harder natured that person is.

3. *A further extension of this wax analogy*: An analogy with soft and hard natures could be seen with wax. The warmer wax becomes, the more impressions can be made with it; the harder it becomes, the less impressions can be made on it. A knife flakes a hard candle; that same knife, cuts through a soft candle. Soft = warm or hot; hard = cool or cold. The hotter wax becomes, the less pliable, impressionable, it becomes, so that it melts rather than receives an impression made upon it. Hence, analogously speaking, we have what I term, the neurotpath: the person who tends to be inwardly destructive, against himself, or simply *self*-destructive neurotically. The cooler, then colder, wax becomes, the less pliable, impressionable, it becomes. Again, analogously speaking, we have the pathic (psychopath, sociopath, narcipath), who tends to be outwardly destructive against others, or *other*-destructive.

4. Loosely speaking, a hard-nature is *hard wired* physiologically, temperamentally – that is, psychosomatically; and a soft-nature is *soft-wired* physiologically and temperamentally – that is, psychosomatically.

5. We tend to think that soft-natures are good only, loving only, considerate only, helpful only, compassionate only, and so forth, without considering that they too have their extremes as do hard-natures; and can be, and are, destructive in their own distinctive ways.

6. An excessively hard-natured person makes for the pathic type of person, whether as a narcipath, a sociopath, a psychopath, or a psychoticpath. An excessively soft-natured person makes for the *neurotic* type of person. Such neurotics can be typified as a neuropathic type of person, whether as *ego*-neurotic, *socio*-neurotic, or *psycho*-neurotic. *Self*-destruction is such a person's earmark.

An *ego-neurotic* (generally speaking) is a person whose ego, self-identity, is so extremely fragile that she/he turns *passively* in on herself self-destructively either consciously or unconsciously. Such a person tends toward such mental disorders as manic-depression, schizophrenia, delusional or eating disorders, paranoia, and the like, to escape, bypass, her particular psychic emptiness or vulnerability.

A *socio-neurotic* (generally speaking) is a person whose ego, self-identity, is so extremely fragile that he turns *actively* from himself self-destructively, either consciously or unconsciously. Such a person tends toward workaholism, or humanitarian or political activism, and the like, in order to escape, bypass, compensate for, his particular psychic emptiness or vulnerability – which is not to say that all such activities are peopled by only socio-neurotics.

A *psycho-neurotic* (generally speaking) is one whose ego, self-identity, is so extremely fragile that she turns *aggressively* against herself self-destructively. Such a person tends toward self-abnegation, self-laceration, death-defying risks, one or another addiction, and the like, to escape, bypass, her particular psychic emptiness or vulnerability.

7. Moderate hard-natures would have no problem hurting others' *feelings*; but they would stop short at hurting another's *well-being*. That is where the pathics go.

8. Pathics tend to be aggressive; neuropathics tend to be passive – the sadist/masochist contrast.

9. The softer natures right on through to the neuropathics are the ideal victims for pathics. These latter can spot their victims as surely as the stalking lion spots and pounces on the weaker prey.

10. The distinctions between the narcipath, sociopath, and psychopath, are, of course on the same continuum of hard-naturedness, from hard (narcissist) to harder (sociopath) to hardest (psychopath). They are hardened against affectionate, sympathetic, compassionate human feelings and sentiments. They act mainly on intensified, raw-edged *emotions,* such as, resentment, rage, hatred, envy, revengefulness, and the like, that have been conditioned to be kept in check where necessary by their pretenses of humanly engaging feelings. When it is said that these types of individuals have no feelings, this is partly right inasmuch as they have none of the *soft* feelings for others – only raw, intense emotions; but they do experience the softer feelings toward *themselves,* in that narcissists, I'm sure, *feel* affection ('aren't I the one!') toward themselves however excessive or distorted that affection may be; sociopaths no doubt *feel* pride ('Aren't I the one!') at their manipulation, and control over, others. Psychopaths surely *feel* glee at their diabolical doings ('Aren't I the one!').

11. Hard-natures – in the extreme (pathics) – intentionally break down the well-being of others; by contrast, soft natures – in the extreme (neurotics) – often enough impulsively break down the well-being within *themselves*; and in the process, indirectly break down the well-being of those close to them.

12. Pathically, hard-natures are mostly *in* control of their destructive actions toward others – they gauge surreptitiously their schemes and actions; whereas neurotically soft-natures are mostly *out of* control of their *self*-destructive behavior. Impulsiveness is their earmark, just as it is with pathically hard-natures .

13. Consider pathics, as a whole, as hard-natures, and realize that they are all capable of using and abusing others for their own gratification. The extent to which they will go regarding this abuse decides whether they are narcipaths, sociopaths, psychopaths, or psychoticpaths. Narcipaths need to shine and so put everyone else down as shadows of their light. Sociopaths need to control, manipulate, and dominate; and so will use and abuse anyone for this purpose. Psychopaths need to hurt and harm, and so will use and abuse everyone for that purpose. The common thread weaving through pathics' behavior, however they may differ in their respective behavioral patterns, is *harm*. Harm they will do to anyone without compunction if need be or want be. Aside from their blatant bullying or brutality, the basic pattern of pathics can be summed up in this simple couplet: First they charm you ... then they harm you.

14. The following continuums are rough – and I emphasize the word "rough" – approximations in an attempt to consolidate the variations and differences between hard and soft natures.

- If a person is 10% soft-natured, then he is 90% hard-natured
  If a person is 20% soft-natured, then he is 80% hard-natured
  If a person is 30% soft-natured, then he is 70% hard-natured

If a person is 40% soft-natured, then he is 60% hard-natured
If a person is 50% soft-natured, then he is 50% hard-natured
If a person is 60% soft-natured, then he is 40% hard-natured
If a person is 70% soft-natured, then he is 30% hard-natured
If a person is 80% soft-natured, then he is 20% hard-natured
If a person is 90% soft-natured, then he is 10% hard-natured

- moderate hard-natures (narcipaths)
  extreme hard-natures (sociopaths)
  vicious hard-natures (psychopaths)
  fiendish hard-natures (psychoticpaths)

- hard-natured tendencies are *moderately* pathic (narcipathic) at 60%; hard-natured tendencies are *extremely* pathic (sociopathic) at 70%; hard-natured tendencies are *viciously* pathic (psychopathic) at 80%; hard-natured tendencies are *fiendishly* pathic (psychoticpathic) at 90%

15. The further a person is from the median, either on the soft or hard natured side, the further from normalcy (the norm in human behavior) that person tends.

16. A narcipath acts abusively more from *egotistical* motives than does a sociopath or psychopath.

17. The terms: psychopath, narcipath, sociopath, psychoticpath are clinical terms that signify persons of a hard nature taken to such an extreme that they are implacably rigid emotionally, intellectually, feelingly. Sensitivity is absolutely beyond their human capacity. Harming others is as natural to them as benefiting others is as natural to persons of a soft nature.

18. A *hardened* person is not basically a hard-*nature*, but a soft-nature turned hard by various untoward circumstances, such as abuse or addictions.

19. Could it be that a person who is, say, 60% soft-natured would be unhealthily attracted to a person who is 60% hard-natured?

20. The terms "hard" and "soft" natures have at least three advantages over the pathic terms for our understanding – one, they are not clinical terms with all the accompanying scientific jargon;

two, are self-explanatory and simple, whereas pathic terms are more complicated and abstract, and so, more difficult to grasp; and three, are more readily applicable to children, or to those who questionably are or are not pathics, without offense or misapplication. You could call a child hard-natured without sounding accusatory as it would sound if you called him a psycopath, or sociopath, or narcipath; you would have to have strong evidence to back up your claim, which is normally hard to come by. Even if the child is clearly, let us say, a psychopath evident from his continuously destructive behavior, still a professional (counselor, school principal, etc) could not accuse such a child as being a psychopath to his parents. Only a professional psychologist or psychiatrist could do so, and with the maximum caution.

21. One final contrast between soft-natures and hard-natures to be made is that soft-natures need foremost to be *loved* and to love, which includes all the soft expressions of that love, such as, affection, care, warmth, understanding, gentleness, appreciation, consideration, understanding and the like; whereas, hard-natures need foremost to be *needed* more than to be *loved*: the need to be respected, honored, admired for one's acts and deeds and expertise, and accomplishments.

If a soft-nature is loved for himself, there is no desperate need for him to be needed first and foremost; that comes next in his or her hierarchy of personal fulfillments, either consciously or unconsciously. By contrast, a hard-nature, whose need to be needed is foremost, does not need, nor even want, to be loved — wants none of that affection, attachment, caring, "effusions".

A soft-nature whose need to be loved is not met, or is distorted, suffers various forms of worthlessness, and might very well be satisfied with being needed only — at least, in that case, he is recognized as a meaningful entity to someone, or to others. A hard-nature whose need to be needed is frustrated also suffers worthlessness, and might be satisfied with being loved so long as he is adored, or he is able to control, or instill fear into those who supposedly love him; or rather, are obsessed with him.

22. Notice in the matter of addictions, that it is more the soft-natures who become addicted to drugs and alcohol than the hard-natures. These latter are hardly not as impressionable, nor vulnerable, to the intense emotional, psychic, disturbances and tensions that can lead a soft-natured person to addictions, of one type or another, in order to survive, or get by.

23. The "meanness" of a soft-natured woman: – "I was kind of mean today with the kids [her fourth grade students] – my kind of mean, which is sharp and impatient. I told them I was going to rest and go to the doctor for my allergies; and I will come back, and I wouldn't be grouchy anymore."

2

SOFT NATURES IN PARTICULAR

1. Some basic inclinations – despite good or poor judgment – of the fairly balanced soft-natured person:

Is inclined toward moral idealism – right, goodness, integrity, and the like

Is inclined to consider the better of people rather than the worst

Is inclined to be more on the defensive than on the offensive

Is inclined to guilt, or remorse, when he or she hurts another's feelings

Is inclined to be affectionate

Is inclined to be compassionate

Is inclined to be passionate

Is inclined to shame

Is inclined to love intensely and / or deeply

Is inclined toward variable neuroses

Is inclined to forgive others both discriminately and

indiscriminately

Is inclined to become hardened by adverse environmental conditions

Is inclined to knowledge and understanding

Is inclined to spirituality, wisdom, philosophy, metaphysics, aesthetics (art, literature, poetry, film, dance, music, etc.)

Is inclined to the love of natural and sensuous beauty

Is inclined to self-reflection, introspection, contemplation, meditation, etc.)

Is inclined to monogamy

Is inclined to humility

Is inclined to self-improvement

Is inclined to help others

Is inclined to "save the world"

Soft-Natures And Conscience

2. *A guilty conscience*: – That we don't do right by another person or others, or ourselves. It preys on us; and because of it, hard-natures prey upon it.

2:1 My mind tells me that something is wrong, and if I do it – or not do it – I will feel ashamed or remorseful, or guilty, or blameworthy.

2:2 I prefer not to hurt another's feelings; but when I do because of my self-will gone astray, I try to make amends.

2.3 Or if I do something morally wrong, I feel guilty, and might try to rationalize or justify my act; but the very fact that I have to rationalize or justify my act indicates that my conscience bothers, or plagues, me.

2:4 Or if I don't do my duty, or what I ought to do, my conscience assails me; and again I try to make amends.

2:5 Or if I don't come up to my expectations, I feel guilty, and so suffer from my conscience.

2.6 Or if I don't fulfill my obligations or responsibilities, I feel guilty, and so suffer from my conscience.

2:7 My conscience dictates to me what I believe is right and proper.

2:8 Hard-natures play off a soft-natured person's conscience; and accordingly, control and dominate her/him.

2:9 One's conscience can be so dictatorial, so dominating, that one can become stifled emotionally (underlying depression, for example); and so, dysfunctional psychologically.

2:10 Conscience is essentially a strong, soft-natured trait. The soft-nature's (moral-loving) conscience inhibits, prohibits, one from doing harm to others overall; yet regarding themselves, they often enough go against their conscience, when they have only themselves to answer to.

2:11 To be free of this "nagging conscience" and its train of guilt, shame, embarrassment, anxiety, of the "abyss" of evil – is this not a sometimes secret impulsion in the soft natured ones, if only for "a walk on the wild side," an exercise in consciencelessness, to be as the hard-natured ones! Would that not be one of our three wishes from the genie of the lamp?

Soft-natures and Love

2:12 As soft-natured persons are deeply and intensely, impressionable to human feelings and relationships, it is understandable why they would be especially bonded to intimates (their spouses, lovers, children, parents, friends, extended family) as well as humanity as a whole. This bond can be considered the love that draws them to others; and so to do good for and by them, to alleviate their suffering, to embrace them. Love, then, in this human sense, can be considered *an affectionate bond of compassionate unity*.

2:13 Soft-natures are given to caring-love – often excessively – so that the hard-natures make sure that their partner – their "victim" – falls head-over-heels in love with him/her. Once that love is cemented, the bond remains so tight that it would take an equal or stronger bond to break it (a splitting of the atom, so to speak). That is why the hard-natured ones make sure no other such bond occurs (other than for him/herself) by his victim; hence, his victim's weakening and breaking ties with old friends, family members, God, Jesus, and whoever or whatever else that would threaten the hold, the grip, he has on her, or she has on him.

2:14 The softer one is, the more receptive to love he or she is and so the more intense and/or deep she loves, the more understanding of others and oneself, the more she identifies with others. Sensory, sensual, sensuous, stimuli, impress themselves deeply, intensely, into her being. Yet if she is bound obsessively, compulsively, to a hard nature, all her love energy would be focused into her "lord"; and so, she has little or nothing left for others or for her broader, transcendent, side. And this is what is meant when we say a hard-natured person, bordering on or settled in, pathic behavior, has broken a person's spirit.

Soft-natures and Neurosis (a continued extension, from section 1)

3. Neurosis: "any of various mental or emotional disorders, such as hypochondria, arising from no apparent organic lesion and involving symptoms such as anxiety and depression." (American Heritage Dictionary)

3:1 The softer one is, the more receptive he is to neurosis; and the more neurotic one is, the more receptive he is to destructive — mostly self-destructive — behavior. And why is this? because soft-natures are more impressionable emotionally, sensitively, intellectually, than hard-natures; and being more impressionable, they are more subject to, more sensitive to, and so, more vulnerable to, the aura of others' various states of mind; that is, their moods, their body language, their pretenses, and so forth. They somehow identify with these conditions, and so, by transference, are affected by them; they "pick up on the vibes," so to speak, and consequently, are intensely vulnerable to anxiety at the other person's negativity, or are favorably receptive to the other person's positivity. Sympathy, compassion, empathy, for others are as natural to them, as the lack of these qualities are as natural to pathics.

3:2 The neurotically soft-natures have had their self-identity so inhibited, devalued, to such an extent that their self-worth is minimized to the unwarranted control, expectations, and influence, of others.

3:3   The soft-natured neurotic, of a dysfunctional type, can hardly function in society without excessive anxiety and/or inhibition. The psychoneurotic, to a further extreme, withdraws into the fantastic chambers of psychic fragmentation or derangement.

3:4   Some extremes of the soft-nature type: hyperactivity, neurosis, paranoia, mania, split personalities, delusions, masochism, compulsion, obsessions, and the list goes on.

3:5   It is the neurotics (mainly soft-natures in the extreme) who are, or become, the odd, the dysfunctional, the "sick," individuals. Pathics, on the other hand, are quite healthy-minded, so long as they are acting relatively successfully according to their natural tendencies and traits. Neurotics are especially susceptible to extremes of emotion, self-abnegation, insecurity; they are not the healthy-minded, since they are *not* "acting successfully according to their natural tendencies and traits."

3:6   In general, soft-natures, when psychically out of balance, tend toward neurotic behavior, often beyond their natural tendencies – that is, *not to act so excessively* against themselves, and therefore against others; while hard-natures, when psychically out of balance, tend toward pathic behavior, often beyond their natural tendencies – not to harm others *to the excess* that they do.

3:7   The soft natures have to be careful that they don't fall into the guilt trap of thinking that when, justifiably or unjustifiably, they feel no remorse about a certain matter, or act irresponsibly, or pretend to feelings or sentiments that they really don't feel, or act selfishly, or do not feel conscience-ridden on doing something wrong, or act from spite, and the like – that that they themselves might very well be hard-natured, or worse, pathics. Yes, soft-natures certainly do have the array of pathic traits, being human; and so are bound to express them toward others at times, perhaps even more often than they would prefer. The point of departure between them and the hard-natures or pathics, is: malice intended to harm others not only now and then, but continuously as a way of life. And for those soft-natures who are wise in the way of pathics, acting hard, even pathicly, (without conscience or remorse, for instance) is proven to be necessary for their own protection.

4. Then there are those soft-natures who have hardened themselves for protection against the harsh reality of an adverse environment, such as, family, school, workplace, or otherwise. Yet whose soft side cannot help but come through when in the company of a recognizable trustworthy fellow soft-nature.

Basic Characteristics of Soft-natures

5. The following catalogue is a spectrum of characteristics natural and habitual to soft-natures, on the whole. These characteristics are diametrically opposed to the characteristics of hard-natures as shown in chapter three. Let these be a stronghold against those.

accommodating – affable – affectionate – agreeable – amorous – amenable – amicable – bashful – benevolent – broad-minded – brotherly – candid – caring – charitable – cheerful – childlike – companionable – compassionate – conciliatory – congenial – conscionable – considerate – convivial – courteous – decorous – devoted – docile – domestic – dutiful – easygoing – empathetic – fair-minded – faithful – forgiving – forthright – generous – gentle – genuine – good-hearted – good-natured – gracious – guileless – grateful – high-minded – honest – honorable – humble – impartial – incorruptible – ingenuous – just – kindhearted – loving – loyal – modest – moral – noble – nurturing – open-handed – openhearted – open-minded – optimistic – patient – peaceful – polite – principled – high-principled – remorseful – reserved – respectful – responsible – right-minded – scrupulous – self-controlled – sensitive – sentimental – shy – softhearted – sympathetic – sweet – thankful – thoughtful – timid – transcendent – truthful – trustworthy – understanding – upfront – upright – virtuous – warm-hearted – wise

Chapter 19
THAT GOOD MAY PREVAIL OVER EVIL

INTRODUCTORY NOTES

1. Having read the previous chapter, soft-natured readers are most likely more familiar with the range of their particular characteristics in contrast to those of the hard-natures. The next step is to apply that knowledge as a *wisdom* in defense of their psychological well-being when threatened by a pathic intrusion. A strategy is needed, a strategy in keeping with the integrity of one's character – soft-natured, in this case. Morality (doing the right, just, thing) must be part of this strategy; but not in a narrow sense of a situation being right or wrong, good or bad; but rather right *and* wrong, good *and* bad.

2. The moral side of our character sees a situation as right or wrong; the transcendent side of our character sees a situation as possibly right *and* wrong. Our moral character sees a situation within the field of good and evil; our transcendent side sees a situation within and *beyond* good and evil. It is our transcendent side, including our morality, but in extension, that has to deal with the pathics.

3. Morality is certainly part of our transcendence – beyond the particular to the universal, beyond the self to selflessness, beyond

431

self-love to selfless love, etc. – but not the totality of the transcendent field.

4. We cannot deal with pathics on moral grounds alone; they're
well aware of that side of us; after all, they have spent their lives
studying us against us. They know the buttons to press, the nerve to
touch, to get what they want from us. Shelley, the great English
poet, touches on this point effectively,

> Until the mind can love, and admire, and trust, and hope,
> and endure, reasoned principles of moral conduct are seeds
> cast upon the highway of life which the unconscious passen-
> ger tramples into dust.

Or consider Gandhi's 20 year struggle against British rule of his
country. At least the British were a fairly civilized country despite its
injustices; but do you think Gandhi would have lasted more than
one protest were he up against the barbaric Hitler regime. He
would have been done away at a moment's notice.

5. When dealing with pathics, we have to consider that we're
dealing with the Hitler prototype, more or less. And in dealing with
the Hitler (or worse Stalin) prototype, our only recourses are to get
him out of our life, or if not that, subdue him. But the possibility of
either alternative would seem overwhelmingly impossible. Yet it
could be done. But how? Certainly not by applying moral or spiritual
principles. It would have to be *on the sly*, so to speak. We would
have to persuade or convince him that we're on his side, at his
bidding, even his friend in complicity. Our objective is to rid us of
him, bring him to his knees and keep him there ever on the watch
that he doesn't rise again. And if so-doing means going contrary to
our normal moral standards, or society's mores, then so be it. The
issue in this case has added another dimension to its morality;
which is: by this particular lie we are serving the truth in a larger
perspective; namely good, justice. This larger, greater, truth is that
there are pathics who will infiltrate themselves into our lives and
destroy, break down, our well-being; and if our well-being is broken

down, then we become less a person than we normally are; and that in itself is an evil. As an analogy, the good of our eyes is eyesight; its evil is blindness. Now would we even consider living life blindly by not protecting ourselves from that which potentially will blind us?

6. With this in mind, then, our lie is done with the intention that good prevails over evil; which is the contrary to the pathics' intention that evil prevails over good. We soft-natures are on the side of good, simple as that; and we insist that any particular good prevails over any particular evil; otherwise we die physically or psychologically, otherwise we live on our knees.

In this case, yes, the end justifies the means, but with the qualification that this *end* is the good, is justice; and that the *means*, to be sure is evil, injustice, done to the evil, unjust. perpetrator. The evil we do to the pathics is to take away their power, to unarm them for good – it is either them or us. And yes, it is the "eye for an eye ..." psychology: but not blinding an eye against those who blinded our eye; but by making sure they will not blind our other eye, nor, if we can help it, blind any other person's eye.

7. This strategy, then turns the tables on the long-dated maxim: "Might is right" to the moral-transcendent maxim: "Right is might."

8. To repeat, we need a wisdom for this strategy to take effect consistently. This wisdom must be broad enough to include all facets of human nature, not only its soft but its hard aspects, not only its good but its evil; and, as a generality, not only our humanness but our transcendence. And it must balance these two sides of our nature according to each person's character (disposition, temperament) and proclivities.

9. This wisdom I introduce as a *human-transcendent* wisdom, or simply, *human-transcendence*.

10. And wisdom, we might say is the *word* of Love.

11. The following fictional dialogue introduces these two concepts, love and wisdom, into this realm of evil and pathics; which further prepares the receptive reader to apply this human-transcendent wisdom against the pathics in his life, as set forth in the next chapter.

THAT GOOD MAY PREVAIL OVER EVIL

Sharon. Having read all your material on wisdom and love and meaning and self-freedom, and on your human-transcendent wisdom in particular, I still fail to see how it all can successfully and consistently combat evil; or how it will ever take the ascendancy over it, as you have so confidently asserted elsewhere. As I see it, the cards are too stacked up against you.

Joseph. Maybe so, if it is just a matter of "combating" evil; but the wisdom of human-transcendence – that is, the balance between our transcendence and our humanness – is not about combating evil, but about surpassing it.

Sharon. What do you mean by "surpassing" evil?

Joseph. Human-transcendence leaves evil as it is; it simply goes beyond it; that is, it transcends, evil's limitations and propensities.

S. And how does human-transcendence propose to do that?

J. By beating evil at its own game, so to speak.

S. You mean learn to be evil so that you can be more evil than the evil one himself? Like a game? A play?

J. Not exactly; rather by good learning evil's ways; then disguising itself as evil intent – not evil in action – without suspicion, then infiltrating it; and finally flushing it out, exposing it, and having it slink away, tail between its legs, or eliminating it if necessary in the given situation. Good can no longer be on the defensive against evil if it is to surpass it; but has to take the offensive; but an offensive not obvious to evil.

S. And how would good take this offensive?

J. By being sly, in a word.

S. But, normally we associate "sly" with evil – that is, undermining with unjust intent – rather than good.

434

J. Right. And that's what I mean by playing and beating evil at its own game.

S. Well that sounds all very well in theory; but I think a person would have to be fairly wise to be sly for the sake of good; and you know how rare a person that is.

J. You might be wrong on that score. For consider this, is it difficult for an evil person to pretend to be good to attain his or her ends?

S. No; that's understood.

J. Then why would it be difficult for a good person to feign evil?

S. Somehow, it's different and much more complex. To feign evil one would have to come off as evil; and how could a good person be able to stomach that; his conscience would do havoc to him.

J. There are two matters we have to consider here on this topic. First, when we say an evil one pretends to be good, what exactly does that imply? And second, as has been firmly established about human nature, evil resides in us as does good; it is a matter of degree that we call one person evil and another good; in which case, in feigning evil a good person is only enacting the potential evil aspect in himself.

S. Well, let's start with the first matter: what does it imply to say that an evil person pretends to be good?

J. That a distinction has to be made between an *act* of goodness and the *intention* behind that act. In which case an evil person can very well do an *act* of goodness but with an evil *intention*; as in telling the truth to a person that unknown to him, will do him harm.

S. I'm reminded of William Blake's incisive couplet: "A truth told with bad intent / beats all the lies you can invent."

J. It's amazing how he captures truths so simply yet comprehensively. Or another situation is in which money is lent to help a person in need though knowing full well that that poor victim will use the money to his detriment. In both these cases, both acts are seemingly good for the other; yet the intent behind them is meant to harm him.

S. That's clear; and this device by the mean ones is known as one of their more masterful ploys. But how is even the wise, good person supposed to glean that intention to harm him; especially if his need is so great that all he can see is the appearance that the imposter means well by him?

J. The wise person recognizes the signs that underlie the *seeming* good of the imposter.

S. Such as?

J. The signs of character. All the subtle and not so subtle indications that reveal an imposter's character: his tone of voice, his facial expressions, his manner of speaking, his seeming too good to be true, his obsequiousness, his presumption, his flattery, his overall superficiality, his feigned charm, and so forth, through the network of his scenarios.

S. I see that; and recognizing these indications can help a person be wary of such individuals; but I can't help thinking that those traits are just a "drop in the bucket,"; there's so much more to their makeup.

J. I agree with you. We certainly can't detect all the ways of duplicity; we would have to be all-knowing for that. However, these basic traits are so patterned and ingrained in such person's character that they can no sooner modify them than a dog its manner of barking. They do give the culprit away; they do send out the signs that something is amiss with this caricature of good; and the perceptive man or woman picks up on these signs as an antenna does radio waves, and shies away from such posturing. So, though an evil one can feign goodness, he cannot *be* good because of his contrary intentions – which bastardize the good that he does. And furthermore, since he or she is not *naturally* good, the "put on" is readily detected by the sensitive, wise person.

S. Well, such wisdom and sensitivity certainly do throw a curve into those "dastardly" ones; that's for sure; but certainly not infallibly; that is just as sure.

J. Of course; but then what is infallible in the matter of human beings?

We are talking about *minimizing* evil's sway, not eliminating it.

S. In that case, I concede that wisdom, as you have laid it out in your writings, surely does contribute to that minimizing. Now as to your second point, regarding the good feigning evil; I'm not sure the same reasoning or psychological maneuvers hold in this case.

J. Why don't you think so?

S. Well, for one thing, the good, as soft-natures, are far more impressionable than the evil ones; and so, though they may feign evil all right; yet, there remains the peril of their *becoming* evil, and of thrilling to it, if only in a given situation.

J. I see that. Very well said. And for that reason, I'm sure that is why so many of the good natures dread to even consider evil in relation to themselves lest they themselves fall into its seductive traps. They can vicariously read about it, watch, and listen, to it through the various media; but would never think of it as a reality as close to themselves; or if it happens to them violently, they are rendered traumatized. So, what is comes down to is: that the good cannot so easily feign evil for the reasons we mentioned.

S. Where, then, does that leave us? How do the good ones protect themselves from the bad ones?

J. Well, they surely cannot commit evil with a good intention, as can the evil ones commit a good act but with a bad intent; nor can they feign evil in act or in intention, except in small matters, such as lying to them to protect themselves; but they can take on the mask of evil, as though they are one of them, or in favor of them, when in their company; and in that way the good can draw them out as to their intentions and designs. Much like a spy, or undercover agent. A spy, or undercover agent, does not have to be a sage in order to flush out his prey; he just has to understand his ways and means, and use well thought-out strategy. I'm reminded of the noted play/movie "Streetcar named Desire"; both Tennessee Williams, the playwright, and Marlon Brando, the actor, masterfully capture the core of the character, Stanley Kowalski, as hard natured; while both of them are really soft natured.

I know this may sound over-simplified; but just as the evil ones know what buttons to press to get their way with the unsuspected, so the good ones can do the same. They just have to be strong-willed enough to play their game to a certain extent, and not be concerned when dealing with them with their familiar moral ideals such as breaches of truthfulness or honesty, or sincerity. They have to relax them in order to follow the rules of the dark ones if they are going to win their game. You have to play their game, as I said in the beginning.

S. I see what you're saying. Yet how does your wisdom of human-transcendence teach you this game?

J. We've come full circle to your original question, and I think I'm better prepared to answer it now.

S. Good. I hope you can, because it's crucial that you do so <u>convincingly</u>.

J. I don't know about "convincingly", but, at least it will make sense. Now you know by now the full spectrum of the human-transcendent wisdom, and how it is a way of life that balances both our humanness and our transcendence according to each individual's temperament and natural proclivities.

S. Right.

J. As for the humanness aspect of this wisdom, the human-transcendent individual will be familiar with the various facets of our ego-sensuality – pride, lust, vanity, willfulness, greed, and the like; as well as the dark side of our nature – self-destructiveness, meanness, spite, jealousy, vengefulness, inordinate lusts; as well as our needs – to be loved, to be needed, as the two most basic needs, that often go contrary to, or have to contend with, our transcendence. With this package of understanding of human nature and human relationships, he is fairly well fortified against the ignorance of which the evil ones take advantage over our vulnerabilities and frailties.

S. Yes, I see that as the understanding aspect of grappling with evil.

J. Now remember, as I said in the beginning of our talk, it is not a matter of good combating evil as it is *surpassing* evil, getting the better of it psychologically, intellectually, transcendently. In which case good *deals with,* rather than combats or grapples it, as you just put it.

S. But aren't you just mincing words: combat, grapple, deal with, surpass; doesn't it still come down to conflict, strife, between the two? They are opponents, enemies, and so each fights for its supremacy its victory, in its own ways.

J. Not exactly. Yes, evil is the enemy of good; no question about that They both have opposing agendas: one aims for destruction, breaking down; and the other for creation, building up. But when you "deal with" your enemy rather than outright fighting him, you can do so with diplomacy rather than warfare. You deal peacefully, intellectually, willfully, wily, with your opponent rather than waringly.

S. But you're speaking of victory over evil, surpassing it. Do you think evil is going to sit back and allow that for long? Do you think it will be satisfied with diplomacy while it keeps losing its position and stature?

J. No, you're right; it wouldn't. I didn't say that good would surpass evil in all cases, for all times; but that through wisdom, it will take the upper hand – surpass – more than it ever has. It will be like a chess game between the two; except that in the future, good will be the better player than evil; it will usurp evil's historical reign. Not that good will win every game, or that evil will not continue to devise moves to frustrate good – Remember Nietzsche's statement: "The more good the more evil." So, it will be not so much an ongoing fight anymore, but as an ongoing competition – with however, the difference that good will be the new, ongoing champion.

S. Well, it sounds fine; but I'm not sure it will be as simple as all that.

J. Perhaps not; but at least that will be the emerging position of the good in regards to evil; and so long as evil does not recognize, nor admit, this emerging position, just so long will it continue to lose ground, lose its grip on good. And in getting this head start, it might happen that evil never again gains its reigning position in life situations and world events.

S. Perhaps. I hope so.

J. And the ruling factor that will clinch this emerging attitude is the transcendent aspect of the human-transcendent wisdom.

S. How so?

J. Do you recall how I identified transcendence with love – love, as the bond of unity?

S. I do.

J. Now this love, which binds all things into their particular unity, from an atom to a human being, to the universe, is what identifies all things as essentially one. It is this Love, this *bond* of unity, that is the good person's path to understanding the evil in human nature

S. In what way?

J. From this dictum: Good attracts, evil repels.

S. I see that. That's as true as it comes; yet, on the other hand, doesn't evil attract as well? Remember our point on the seduction of evil that the good person dreads?

J. That's true. Yet this point is relevant to the direction I was going into.

S. In what way?

J. I was about to say, that a good person, and his behavior and good deeds, attract favorable responses from others.

S. Others of his kind, to be more precise; because evil persons would tend to be repulsed by such persons and their acts.

J. True, but let's leave out the evil factor for now.

S. All right.

J. Now it is known and agreed upon historically that love is an attracting force. Do you agree?

S. Of course.

J. And what I have added to this meaning of love is that love is a *unifying* force, or more to the point, *bond*, that binds all things together in form, purpose, and function.

S. By "function and form" you mean what?

J. Very simply, take our hands. They are unified into their particular form in order to function in a certain way, as with all parts of our body. Now you can extend this perspective to anything that exists, whether we are aware of it or not.

S. You're making a sweeping generalization, but overall, I see that.

J. So, love, as I see it, is an attracting power that binds all things into unity. This binding, this bond, is the Oneness, the Meaning, that underlies everything.

S. God, you mean.

J. If you like. And good draws people together of like mind. Right?

S. Right.

J. And this drawing together, is another way of saying good attracts?

S. Yes.

J. And, so synonymously, we can say that good is a form, or aspect, of love?

S. I see that.

J. A good person then we might say is a loving person?

S. I can't deny that. But let me ask you: by a "loving person" do you mean loving toward others?

J. Toward others, of course, in our context. Why do you ask?

S. Well, there certainly is the all-too-familiar situation in which a person loves himself more than he does others, or he may love his work more than others, or God more than others; or, heaven forbid, he may even love evil more than others – the evil ones again! How do you respond to that?

J. I would have to live another lifetime, to answer that. Still, this I can say in general: If love is universal, inasmuch as it is the bond of *all* unity; then all that we are and all that we do is love-based, so to speak, whether we love ourselves, others, God, nature, evil. In which case, the distinction to be made is that whatever we are attracted to more strongly is what we love more strongly. We can't escape loving something or other, since essentially we are love. The differences are in our classifications and values of what is loved. A person who loves himself, sometimes to the exclusion or inconsideration, of others, we classify as *self-love*. Our attraction to sex and all its multiple ramifications (courtship, marriage, children, for three), we might call *erotic love*. Our attraction to the welfare of others we call *humanistic love*. Our attraction to another person as being, at the core, a human being, whether spouse, children, friend, we term *vital love*. Our attraction to God, we call *God love*, or *Divine Love*. Our attraction to evil, we call *nihilistic love*. And so forth. Each person is inclined, more or less, to all of these classifications of love, according to his individual character and temperament. In either case, we all have all the variations of love, both human and transcendent, inherent to our humanity; it is just a matter of what we are more drawn to, what we love more; or as D.H. Lawrence stated it, "what we thrill to"; and in the case of monumental evil, one can say that even Hitler loved his dog, or that even Stalin loved his wife, and only her.

S. Very enlightening.

J. So, returning again to our main course, when I refer to a loving person, I refer to the classification of *vital love*, in the sense that his or her relation to another person is at the core of that person's humanity; and so is an *affectionate bond of compassionate unity*; and the intensity of this love depends on the person so loved.

S. I see that now.

J. So, a loving person, in the sense that he or she is motivated by an affectionate bond of compassionate unity, is in touch with the transcendence of love, or Transcendent Love, inasmuch as affection and compassion are a strong drawing to, a strong attracting power, toward others for their welfare; and to the degree that without that person, a severely painful breach is experienced.

S. I believe it.

J. The good, loving, person because he or she is in constant touch with love that goes beyond self to other selves, creatively, he is especially in touch with Transcendent Love – the basis of all human love – and so is unconsciously, or more to the point, *transconsciously*, in accord with Its meaning and so is receptive to the truths of human nature in general.

Accordingly, in relation to our topic, such a person is able to intuit, identify with, the evil in human nature as well as the good. He recognizes, intuits, senses, feels, the signs of evil; though he may not be fully conscious of them, nor be able to articulate them, nor unfortunately, to protect himself from them. That is why he must understand both the good and evil in himself and others so that he can protect himself and others from the harm of the evil ones. Recognizing, intuiting, sensing, are the first steps toward this *self-understanding*. The next step is to study the psychology (our humanness, in particular) and transcendence of human nature and relationships so as to raise the truths of our humanity to the surface, to our consciousness; and so, to fruition. Self-understanding must prevail.

And for self-understanding to prevail, wisdom, *human-transcendent* wisdom, in particular in our sense of the word, is the guide, the path, the teacher, the guru. And the first prerequisite of this self-understanding is to shed the myth that everybody is basically good, and that it is mainly environment that turns one from their goodness to evil. Not that there is no truth to environmental influences, because environment certainly can and does corrupt good-natured persons by the numbers.

S. And where does the evil one stand in relation to this human-transcendent wisdom?

J. Very far in the distance; since his love focuses <u>more</u> on destruction (evil) than creation (good, love), it is very limited and myopic. He is not open to self-understanding, and so, to understanding of others beyond his one-sided limited scope; since that would only expose him as psychologically, intellectually, inferior, limited, to the fullness of the humanity in others, and in himself. He is anti-human, anti-life; and so, these traits curtail any out-going of human sentiments and understanding.

I speak of evil in the extreme, of course; but the lesser modifications of this extreme are nonetheless potentially in the predominant evil person; it is simply a matter of circumstances that would give rise to them, as in the case of a quiet little accountant, given to "little" evils, is raised to position of authority in a Hitleritetype of regime.

S. If all that you say is true, and I think mostly it is, then it is possible for evil to be at a disadvantage for the first time in our history. All that is needed is a "course," so to speak, in human-transcendence.

J. Well, not so much a "course" but a lifetime study, a lifetime awareness, a lifetime of human interaction. It is a lifelong struggle; no time to let one's guard down, to be bored. There is no short-cut to, no six-week seminar, no prescriptions, to this way of gaining the ascendancy over evil, or more particularly, over injustice and ignorance; It is a "long row to hoe," so to speak; but one that is replete with discovery and adventure, and advancement.

S. I realize that.

J. My closing words, then, are: Let us be warriors of love than of hate, of peace than of war, of good than of evil – our own evil as well as others' evils; and that is how we can *"Give peace a chance"*, to quote John Lennon.

S. Yes, let us. And you know what comes to me in this regard?

J. What?

S. We are to reverse the well-known dictum of the unjust: "Might is right" to "Right is might."

J. It couldn't be better stated. Onward to the conscious transformation in which wisdom and justice will take the ascendancy over ignorance and injustice!

S. And, again, how does one attain this wisdom of human-transcendence?

J. By putting its concepts, principles and precepts into practice. Simple – and complex – as that.

S. So we'd have to be very familiar with this wisdom.

J. Without question.

S. Well, I'll have to follow it up. ... Before we close, I'd like to add a thought that came to me as you were discussing love as an attractive force that the binds all unity. You said, and I believe it,

444

that we can't escape loving something or other, since essentially we are love.

J. That's right.

S. Well, it brings to mind a statement Thoreau made about evil, which is, if I remember correctly, "There are thousands hacking at the branches of evil to one who is striking at the root."

J. Yes, I've read that.

S. Well, I think you yourself have struck at the root of evil, perhaps without knowing it.

J. No, I never thought of it. How so?

S. Well, if a good person is attracted to good and an evil person is attracted to evil; and "attracted to" is another ways of saying "loves", then the good person loves good (behavior) and the evil person loves evil (behavior).

J. Yes, that makes logical and psychological sense.

S. Then if the source, or to use Thoreau's term, "root" of good is love – since a good person is attracted to (loves) good acts; so, the source, or again, to use Thoreau's term, "root" of *evil* is love, as well – since an evil person is attracted to (loves) evil acts. Do you see that?

J. I do.

S. And do you agree?

J. Well it would be hard to swallow for some people to agree to the notion that the concept "love" is applied to evil. Normally, it's thought of in light of good only. But, I certainly agree; since my own argument implicitly rested on that idea; though I may not have recognized it in the sense that you have. So, let me ask, what exactly is your point?

S. Simply that, as I see it, the *root of evil is love*.

J. Well, you may be right!

S. And further, if love is the source, or root, or essence, of everything, all reality, then certainly that includes both good and evil.

J. Yes, and even more mysteriously, *beyond* both good and evil.

S. Does this perspective then solve the historical "problem of evil"?

J. It seems to; yet it seems somewhat oversimplified.

S. Ah, but remember Occam's razor: the simpler, the better!

J. Well, there's that to consider. In any case, if your point is true, then where does that lead us?

S. Perfect question; and let's leave it open as that.

J. Good enough.

Chapter 20
THE PLAY'S THE THING

1

ASSERTIVE-PASSIVE RESISTANCE

1. Having determined that love (as the bond of unity) and wisdom (as human-transcendence) are inclusive of a philosophy against malice (*auroralism*), we have next to apply this Love / wisdom paradigm to the practical affairs of dealing effectively and consistently with the pathic individual. Accordingly, we must employ a tactic, a course of action, that works in our favor instead of in theirs.

2. This course of action requires that we relax our moral strictures that we normally live by so that good and justice prevail over pathics' abusive agenda. In which case, we must feign sincerity, feign concern, feign moods – as they do; we must lie, fabricate, manipulate – as they do. Our prime intention and goal, however, is not to use or abuse pathics, but to thwart them from using and abusing <u>us</u>. Better that they be hurt or harmed than we be; so long as it is a matter of either them or us with no other choice.

3. This course of action against malice I call, *assertive-passive resistance*; that is: <u>now</u> resist passively, then assertively, or <u>now</u> resist assertively then passively, depending upon what the pathic and/or situation calls for. In either case, we are asserting our rights and our integrity.

4. Adhering to this course of action, we know when to step forward and when to back off; when to act and when to wait; yet always

447

with the purpose of resisting pathic cunning.

5. With assertive-passive resistance, we do not act on impulse in matters of importance or urgency; we wait it out, with caution, and with judgment, planning when to make our move. As a matter of fact, is that not what the pathics themselves do : devise their schemes, act out their part, then wait for the opportune moment to strike. The same with us. Only, the difference is that pathics are not *resisting* anyone or anything, except perhaps their impulse to act on their urges inappropriately; their objective is not resistance, but *evading* resistance. They intimidate before they themselves are intimidated; they take the offensive so as not be on the defensive. They will act the sheep in order to attack the sheep. In our case, however, we will act the sheep in order to attack the wolf.

6. Patience is the <u>virtue</u> of assertive-passive resistance.

7. We handle the mean ones if not by being overtly assertive, then by being covertly assertive, that is, acting passively.

8. At times, we must be immediately, obviously, assertive on the moment in order to offset their schemes; and at other times, patiently, secretly, passively assertive. In either case, the maxim, "Intimidate them before they intimidate you" applies either aggressively or passively.

9. With assertive-passive resistance we take the *offensive* – either passively or assertively – against the enemy (pathics in our case) instead of being always on the *defensive* against them :– lest we hurt their feelings, lest we be mistaken about them, lest we "upset the applecart," lest we become one of them, lest we violate norms of behavior, lest we go against our moral integrity, and on and on. We are *to intimidate them before they intimidate us*, if not by being overtly assertive, then by being covertly assertive; that is, passively. As an image, we have to dive into the often freezing water of their dealings to save ourselves, to save our loved ones, to "save the day" – even politically speaking, "to save the world".

10. This course of action of assertive-passive resistance, then, is a resistance that is basically an offensive, either assertively on the moment or passively with patience, against evil in general and pathic evil in particular.

11. An adherent of assertive-passive resistance against malice asserts his rights by 'whatever means necessary' on the side of justice, fairness, and the integrity (moral and otherwise) of a given situation.

12. We frequently have to sublimate our ego in order to attain our short range goals; which on the surface of it, seems as though we are foregoing, or repressing, our ego. Nothing could be furthest from the case. With pathics, we sublimate our ego, *as part of our play, and its subplo*t, that we ourselves script, not the pathics; so that we win our case, so that we win the game, again and again — considering, of course, our losses as well; which, however will be few and far between. The point is, through assertive — in the guise of passive — resistance we aggressively upstage our enemy to *our* advantage, in *our* best interest, not his. In which case, we enact an assertive-aggressive resistance. We are passive in our assertiveness, or, which amounts to the same thing, we are assertive in our passivity. We are on the offensive in our defense. Actually, this is called *diplomacy* in social and political circles.

13. Assertive-passive resistance is the soft-nature's defense-mechanism against the hard-nature's offense-mechanism.

14. Play-acting and role-playing (make up the palette for the adherent of assertive-passive resistance.

15. We soft-natures, in our assertive-passive resistance, are not so much <u>resisting evil as we are asserting good</u>; and by so doing, are usurping evil unexpectedly. We do what we can and hope for the best; we do not give up, we do not cave in. We are turning the other cheek so that the second slap hurts the pathic's hand more than it does our other cheek.

———————————————

2

The following notes start off in the usual advice-to-the-reader pattern, but then unexpectedly (for the author) veers off into the concept of *playacting*; which in hindsight, proves to be the perfect platform in opposition to the pathics, since they themselves are the consummate play-actors among us. In which case, we soft-natured individuals learn to *play* their own game, if not as well as them, then surely as protective of us.

"Perhaps one never seems so much at ease as when one has to play a part."
- Oscar Wilde

THE PLAY'S THE THING

Assertive-Passive Resistance against the Pathics

by the Author

1. Be civil to them, but subtly remote.

2. Be polite to them, but in passing.

3. Be courteous to them, but busily.

4. No *looking* at them except momentarily to be civil, polite, or courteous.

5. No replies to them except what they want to hear.

6. No comments to them that reveal your true feelings, beliefs, or values.

7. Listen agreeably to what they say; like, "That's very interesting," etc..

8. Act as though you're ignorant of the topic they're discussing; like: "I'm not sure I understand what you mean; can you explain it." Etc..

9. Don't be concerned about being aloof – you're in your own thoughts; you're very busy, no time to talk ... and the like.

10. Hold your anger in check; they feed on it.

11. When you say No to a request from them, stand by it emphatically. Be wary of their "exceptions," or blandishments.

12. Keep in mind always that you are playing a part, playing their game of "being on the sly," so to speak.

13. Play it their way, but in *your* play.

14. Be indecisive, unpredictable: today you say this, tomorrow you say that; now you are nice, then you are mean; now upbeat, then downbeat. Keep them guessing! Keep them confused. Keep them suspended.

15. If they're moody; you be moody; if cheerful, you're cheerful. Match your mood with their mood. Act the part in *your* play; not theirs!

16. Give them the "silent treatment." Have nothing to say except what is absolutely necessary to "keep the peace," in order to be civil or polite or courteous.

17. Give them something now and then, what they might need or want. Don't expect gratitude from them. If it comes, fine; if not, then fine as well.

18. Should they insult you, or use you, play the Gandhi, or Martin Luther King, or Mother Teresa, role of passive resistance, or soul force; for that frame of mind keeps you to your ultimate objective: beating them at their game.

19. Act stupidly at times, as though you don't quite know what's going on; you don't "get it."

20. Notice the word "act" in these scenes that <u>you</u> have created. This is your play in which you are the leading character.

21. Go through the motions of being or doing what they would

451

expect of you once they have "pushed your buttons." Let them think that you have been "suckered in" again.

22. For your play acting to work, you do have to set aside your ego and its natural self-love responses. But that shouldn't be too difficult in relation to them, since they are used to deflating other people's egos – once they have *inflated* them for their purposes, that is. In which case, you should keep your ego out of the picture with them; since it's only a manipulative puppet for them.

23. Do "keep up appearances" with them, since they know no way other than appearances; that's their style; so, you'd be right up there with them with your appearances as this or that. Then at another time, *don't* keep up appearances, so that they don't know what you're up to, don't know what's on your mind, don't know what's going on.

24. You move from warm to sudden frost; so that she asks if you're all right – as if they really care; they want you to be all right so that you will remain at their behest; and then you answer enigmatically, "I'm not sure," or "I don't want to talk about it." You are to be at center stage of your play.

25. Be a little "crazy" at times, as though you're not quite "all there."

26. And then there's the acting of, as though you're "not very well," somewhat sick; not up to doing anything but to go to bed; or quickly rushing to the toilet to throw up.

27. Compliment him in passing – You're looking good today, etc.; and then as quickly be on your way.

28. Don't tarry with him; or you'll be sorry you did – again!

29. As she hugs you goodbye or hello, soften just enough to not out-and-out reject her, yet at the same time, to get across the point that things are not what they seem.

30. Don't respond in defense to his wry comments that "humorously" push your buttons, "get you going", so to speak. Ignore him or chuckle along with his game.

31. Always have something to do when in her presence; otherwise you're vulnerable to her "attacks."

32. And when he frightens, or threatens, you; endure it; but be up and at it again in your play – in your defense.

33. Having continuously to forego your ego for the sake of your well-being is not easy most of the time; unless, of course, doing so, is playing your role in *your* play.

34. Then he'll/she'll be all nicey-nice for a while – until his next move, the next step to his schemes. And all the while, you are observing his every move, giving in, giving to him, a little here, a little there, never quite thwarting him – until he makes his move. Then you say no to him; then "up in arms," enraged, he becomes – but you just don't have what he wants. You have no money to give him, simple as that. Show him your "falsified" bank account, your "falsified" expenses to prove your point. All this takes some planning, I grant you; but, after all, you're trying to save your resources, your well-being, if not your sanity. Remember Hamlet's lines: "The play's the thing / wherein I'll catch the conscience of the king."

35. Don't "rain on their parade," as it is put, if you don't want to fuel their anger-unto-wrath against you; which is to say, in a nutshell, if they're enthusiastic about something, you respond enthusiastically – in your way, of course.

36. "Tell him he's handsome,"– a generality for any comment that will please them – is as good advice as any when it comes to keeping them at arms distance from you – for the time being, that is.

37. By identifying with your "foe," you are taking on her characteristics as an actor.

38. Subtlety is the key to your role in your play of dissimulation. Not to appear obvious. But if he is on to you, then you plead guilty as to taking on his characteristics of dissimulation; that you have lost yourself in his personality and have become more like him than yourself. That is what they call reverse psychology: passive-aggressive. Where this position will lead you in your relationship with him, depends in large part on the circumstances of the relationship, and the type of pathic he/she is.

39. As for the "killer" (of mind, soul, and body) pathics – out-and-out psychopath or psychoticpath – I'm not sure your play will proceed very far; since with these types, you are dealing with the "Evil One" personified, so to speak. They are the masters of disguise and harm; and there's hardly a dirty trick they're not on to; and so, hardly a way out of their clutches short of a mental and physical breakdown on your part, or his/her demise on their part. With him or her, it is a matter of saving your life; and some way more drastic than play acting is required. But if you're receptive to this notion of play acting, then play-act your way out of his/her life <u>posthaste</u>!

40. And if he insults you – as is his usually way – you respond, pas-sively, to get across that he's right. Lose your self-respect to him, and to him only, and to him in that particular scene when he insults you; since that is part of your role, and since you're going to be back in the next scene with your passive-aggressive act to bewilder him to no end.

41. Be careful not to fall into the trap of "If I do or say this, it will rupture our relationship for good"; because isn't that what you're aiming for to eventually end the relationship for good – *you're* good.

42. Be fearless, intrepid, enduring, in your play-scheme. Don't falter; because if you do, you will be in his grip again, under his control, with you out of control.

43. What of your children? What will they think of your play? Are you to tell them? It would probably be best that you don't until the play is over; since they might wittingly or unwittingly, give you away; and then where will you be? If they side with the pathic parent, for whatever reason, then most likely it won't matter much how you respond, or what you do, right or wrong, wisely or foolishly, you will have lost your effectiveness; the play will be over.. Your goal is to save yourself, your well-being, your sanity, your children, as best you can. You know what you are doing; *they* don't. You must keep it that way.

44. Make no eye contact with them, except fleetingly except when necessary for strategic purposes.

45. Keep them guessing; never quite knowing what you will do or say next.

46. To never let your guard down with them. That is to be your mandate.

47. Be sure you don't have her thinking that you have some kind of agenda against her. Your act is to keep them thinking that you're just not quite "all there" anymore.

48. Be indecisively contradictory; as though you're not quite sure what you mean, who you are, what to do.

49. I repeat: that you're starring in your own play will marvelously keep your anger at bay; and with your anger in check, you are free to keep upstaging your opponent.

50. Let her know that the reason you're so "down" – not depressed – most of the time is because you feel yourself a failure, that your life is at a standstill, that you're going nowhere; and you don't know what to do about it. But reassure him that you'll pick up in a while; it's just a transitory state of mind.

51. When with him/her, be staring into space now and then, as though your life is at a standstill.

52. In you play, you are actually applying Jesus' saying of "turn the other cheek"; only, you're turning your other cheek for the following effect: "You can break my body, but not my mind, will, nor spirit. What is a blow, a slap, a punch, a push, an insult? Here, do it again, you brute-coward. My will over yours will triumph in the end." – if you don't land in jail first for your brutality.

53. As you gradually win over him, do not feel sorry for him whatever you do! When that thought-feeling arises, squelch it, transcend it, immediately. He'll manage; he always does. If it's not you he uses and abuses, it will be someone else. There is always the next victim around the corner.

54. Yes it can be pleasurable to be feigning this and that at times; but I'm sure, it's just as often painful to be pretending, feigning, dissimulating so much day in and day out. There has to be some hint, some indication, of closure along the way, some proof that it is working: this play of yours; otherwise, the pressure of your role will become too much for you. And that is because falsehood is natural to them; yet is only play-acting to you. That is the advantage they have over you; so it takes constant vigilance and effort to keep "one up" on them. And how long can you keep up the "show?' All the energy required can drain you; and so, you might tend to let down your guard at times. And perhaps that is all right to fall into their clutches once again. Think of such times – scenes – as an intermission of the play. And when you're replenished, begin the next scene or act. Remember always that the play is not over until *you* determine that it is. In fact, the play never ends so long as that person is in your life. When she's gone for good, your play is over.

55. *An open-ended analysis –*: Dissimulation is the *modus operandi* of your play: dissimulation against you, dissimulation against him. His part of the dissimulation is as he plans it, expects it, and you are not to have any idea of what he is about in his schemes; and, you probably don't most of the time; but you do know that something is always going on, always brewing, in his secret chambers, to your detriment as he plots his way through your life. Little does he know that not only are you on to his game, but that you are playing the same game, except the rules are of your making – rules that protect you from him, rules that want nothing from him except your personal freedom.

So, he dissimulates in his <u>sly</u> way, and you dissimulate in your <u>sly</u> way. After all, and I repeat, it is *your* play; you're writing the script. You are identifying with, and so taking on his characteristics *in the play*.

This answers a possible objection to the theme of your play: that in identifying with a pathic, are you not applying the ancient saying, "an eye for an eye, a tooth for a tooth," or "The end justifies the means," – which are frowned upon by many people of a type? These sayings can be summed up as "Evil is to prevail depending upon the circumstances"; which is as open-ended as such sayings as "It depends on the person," or everyone's entitled to his opinion."

In answer, it is a matter of inverse psychology. Yes, you will lie, cheat, pretend, dissimulate in any way, but not for the same purpose as hers that harms you; your <u>purpose</u> is not to harm her, but to reach your goal of winning over him, of freeing yourself from him. "But," you might say, "Are you not harming her by depriving her of *his* good: depriving him of being superior to you, or of manipulating and controlling you, or of being malicious to you." From one perspective yes; from another, no. Yes, inasmuch as her good is taken from him by you from his being the predator to being relatively speaking, the victim. No, inasmuch your good is *gained* by no longer being the victim to a predator. And in the moral order of things, your good is far superior to her good. Yet, on the other hand, in the immoral, or even amoral, world, her good is superior to your good. It is then a matter of relativeness, as to which side you're on: good or evil, justice or injustice. Another way of looking at it, though, is this: the predator needs her victim to get on in life; yet the victim certainly does not need the predator to get on in life; in fact, he needs to get her out of her life; unless of course the victim is willing to be the prey (codependents). Yet in this analysis, I am referring to the *unwilling* victim; in which case, he neither wants to be the victim nor the predator; he just wants his freedom from her. What is natural to her as predator is unnatural for him as "predator" in his play; and what is unnatural for the predator to be the victim is equally unnatural for *him* to be the victim.

So, what it comes down to is this: the unwilling victim is play-acting with his own script to free himself from a predator by "whatever means necessary" (a tooth for a tooth...). In doing so, his underlying purpose is not to harm her as he harms him – predator-to-victim; but to free himself. He is acting out this purpose unnaturally. On the other side, the predator is acting out her purpose of harming an unwilling victim *naturally*; it is her way. Both are doing what they consider right for them, one from the standpoint of "might is right" (the predator) and the other of "right is might" (the unwilling victim). It is a matter of who wins, or *what* wins: justice or injustice. And thus, the eternal life-conflict between opposites goes on and on; and thus, there is nothing more to say on the matter, except *stagnation* – the same old story but almost always with the predator on top. A quite tedious repetition by now in our times. Perhaps it is time for justice to gradually take the ascendancy over injustice, for wisdom to gradually take the ascendancy over ignorance for the first time in human history.

3

A SUBPLOT: THE PATHIC SIBLING IN THE FAMILY

The following note-like, "stream of conscience," thoughts fairly much answer my troubled concern for all the poor unfortunate soft-natured children who are subject to, victims of, their hard-natured siblings. That answer is mainly in the lap of parents: parents who fairly much understand the pathic character and their ways, and can articulate and deal with them in defense of both themselves and their other children.

The pathic in your life is in your household; he's your child against his/her sibling.

You live in the day-to-day proximity of his wretchedness.

But now you know his ways and means of hurting, harming, and disrupting.

Armed with this knowledge, how do you protect your child from his sibling out to hurt and harm him?

Forget the family "blood is thicker than water" cliché with the hard-natured child. She certainly uses it against you.

Such hard-natures may be family in <u>blood</u>, but they certainly are not family in <u>love</u>. And love, in all its variant, positive,expressions, is everything, is it not, that holds people together, families together.

No love comes from her except her love of hurting and harming and disrupting her sibling – Love to see you squirm! Love to see your feelings hurt! Love to see you cry! Love to see you caught!

Ask yourself: Could you trust this child not to betray you to the authorities if it came to that? If your answer is no, then take that as an indication of the worthlessess of this child being a family member other than a blood relation.

That's it: consider your hard child as a *blood relation*, not as a *family member*.

A blood-related relationship with a hard-natured child often enough turns into a hotbed for duplicity, dissembling, mendacity, all in the grab for the "family jewels," so to speak.

Remember Jesus' warning, in words to the effect: Your enemy will be in your own household.

They're not worth it.

Protect your daughter from your son, and vice versa. Priority first. Who is the better one? Is it not the good son, the good daughter. Choose him/her against the other less the conscience-bite that you are going against your own son or daughter. *He* is against you by being against your better child, and against the family in extension.

Let him be scared of *you*; not the other way around!

Grab her by the "shirttails" and put her in her place.

The family is sacred, yes; but not against the serpentine ones that through their actions poison this sacredness.

The family bond is not all-inclusively set in stone. It must remain always flexible: now tight, then loose, now close then distant, to account for the personality types in the family.

Yes, the maternal or paternal instinct is inborn into parents, more or less; but blindly, instinctively, irrationally. Nature does not make distinctions in this regard since life, preservation of the species, is its foremost objective. It must, however, be up to *human* nature to make the distinctions to keep the family viable. And this distinction is to root out the decay, the poison, in the family lest all members become infected.

Root out the weeds that tend to strangle the health of the family. By "root out," I mean not *necessarily* to physically discard the weeded one, but to psychologically weed him/her out of your well-being; without reservation of, "But, he's my son; how can I be so cold, so heartless, so ruthless!" Rather, turn it to yourself: "I'm his mother (sister, father); how can he be so cold, heartless, so ruthless!"

Yes, she's my daughter: I've tried everything loving and good for her; but in the end, she's nothing but a virus infecting the family with discord. So, I have no other choice but to protect my family from her destructive influence.

If we are convinced that we all, as humans, are made up of all hard and soft qualities, more or less individually, that we have our dark and light sides; then let us be soft naturally, and hard *conditionally*, with the wisdom to apply our hard side without guilt or remorse or anxiety.

With these hard-natures, it's as though your life is set on a "fight mode".

Can any good come out of this?

Perhaps.

Be stronger than the hard one; if not physically then psychologically.

But how?

Situation1: the hard-natured child is notably younger than the soft-natured child. Not much of a problem here in controlling and monitoring the younger child. The older child is more at an advantage than the younger one so long as the former child is made aware of her sibling's proclivities.

Situation 2: The soft-natured sibling is notably younger than the hard-natured sibling. Surely the latter will abuse the younger whenever and wherever he can – not harmfully so much as hurt-ingly: name-calling, snitching, pranks, insults, pushing and shoving, ignoring, remoteness, and the like. The young one must be protected from the older by the parents, by another older soft-natured sibling, by grandparents. Etc.

Ah, here's the answer! It's the parents mainly, day-by-day, that can protect the soft-natured child from the hard-natured one. "Good! Someone is on my side! Someone knows what's going on! Someone who can protect me! Someone I can talk to about him!" – My parent (or better still: my parent<u>s</u>)!"

Teach your good son or daughter the ways and wiles of her hard-natured sibling.

Once a soft-natured parent(s) recognizes the ways and wiles of the hard-natured sibling, and can articulate this recognition, then he/she can undertake the immense task of dealing with the hard-natured child with the proper perspective and judgment for the protection and well-being, of the soft-natured child.

It takes a constant vigilance and preparation and foresight to keep one-up on the "little imp".

Pretend, pretend, pretend! Don't let the mean one know you both are on to him. Keep it between the two of you.

He most likely will "catch on" sooner or later that you favor his sibling over him. Deny it in whatever way necessary; just as he denies his underhanded doings.

Be always one up on him. He has no chance against the both of you being armed with his trickery, his duplicity.

Anticipate his every move, his every mood.

No sooner do you let your guard down in protecting your good child, the mean one will be at his dirty tricks again.

Remember that she will not take likely to being frustrated at her every turn. You therefore, have to give way to his side of the picture now and then. Which is all right so long you reassure your good one that it is only a temporary lapse on their part for the better good.

And when he "repents," take it for what it's worth; but don't soften too much, otherwise, you know what will happen; as it does over and over again.

Both you and your good daughter have to realize that it is primarily her nature to be what she is, and to do what she is inclined to do. That can no sooner change than can you change your nature. What *can* change is her behavior toward her sibling so long as she fears the consequences. It's like, she may lose out with her sibling, but she can be assured that there are, oh so many other potential victims out there to aim for. Still, expect her to be always on the look-out for an opening to enforce her will against her sibling if she can get away with it.

What this comes down to is that the family has her beat, won, overall, keeps its heel on her neck, and she knows it and has been conditioned to accept – or else! She is only a vulnerable human being, after all, as we all are, no matter how forceful her personality and tendencies may be. She is to realize once and for all that it is the family unit that prevails, not her little mean individuality; just as with the case of a tribal group which suppresses any person's individuality that threatens its security or customs or norms.

Parents need not distance themselves psychologically from the hard one, but they certainly do need to distance themselves *emotionally*; otherwise, those emotions will be shredded without mercy. As a matter of fact, if they ignore or mistreat that one "unfairly," the family dynamics will surely "go to hell," to speak figuratively (literally: hell on earth).

Hug her, show her affection and concern; tell her now and then you love her, do your duty toward her so far as she is your child despite the drama and trauma she causes – even though these parental expressions may mean very little or nothing to her in both the long and short run. At least you'll keep her from "getting even" with you. She'll have to admit, however reluctantly, that her parents did their best considering her wretched behavior.

Parents do have to respect their child for what he is – even admire him in a way for ruthless cleverness. First, he didn't ask to be born hard and troublesome; it was given to him by nature's genetic configuration. Second, it certainly seems that his type of person has its disruptive role in human intercourse, by being a counterpoint to the orderly, law-abiding, rule-abiding day-to-day status quo. It is just unfortunate that one such person lands in *your* household as a family member. If anyone's to blame, blame nature as the "culprit".

Should you tell your daughter/son that you know her to be hard; and that, therefore, "Here's what we're going to do about it"? I don't think you'll get very far with that approach; since nothing is going to change his disposition or inclinations, and since he will use that knowledge to your disadvantage. Better you keep secretive to win your way against her just as she keeps secretive to win her way against you and her sibling.

What happens to the family dynamic in the 'one hard/one soft' sibling situation if both parents work, and there is no proper supervision?

What happens when one of the parents is also a pathic person siding with the hard-natured child? Then the soft-natured parent obviously is to side with the soft-natured child – but subtly, surreptitiously, slyly, if need be. Being more flexible, and understanding, the soft-natured parent can manipulate, steer, the more rigid ones into, if not submission, then *common decency*. It's almost as though this *just* manipulation is a form of passive resistance against unjust violence

What if both parents are hard-natured thereby siding with the hard-natured child? Then that poor, unfortunate soft one doesn't stand much of a chance against all three. His life is blighted, thoroughly. What is to be done? How can he be helped? They won't let it happen. Hopefully, someone on the outside will catch the issue and save him somehow. Otherwise, I don't think there is much that can be done considering the way the family imperative rules, and has always had the last word, so long as no physical harm is done to the child. As far as psychological harm is concerned; well, that's not as obvious – though it should be; and probably is obvious by outsiders who cannot do anything about it. And so, the child is usually too far gone before, and if, help comes along.

Yet with the ever-growing awareness of the pathic reality happening in our times, and will happen even more, further on in time, perhaps even in such seemingly hopeless cases, such unfortunates can be saved before it's too late.

We see how imperative it is that this pathic reality must be infused into our consciousness so fully that soft-natures can effectively deal with these hard-natures. Along with this awareness, and accepting of, the hardness in us, we have to recognize and to use it, in order to protect ourselves and our loved ones from them; and – here's the hard part: without harming the harmer. We might have to *hurt* them: hurt their feelings; hurt them by having to temporarily and continually deprive them of their wants and pleasures; hurt them by causing them emotional disturbance; hurt them by continually punishing them for their behavior; but we will not meanly *harm* them – say, by removing them from the house, placing them in a detention center, depriving them of their freedom, keeping them from their friends, restraining them physically – except for the seriousness of unjust betrayal and physical violence that they might perpetrate on us or others.

So what all these thoughts come down to is that once the subjects of pathics, hard and soft natures, evil, and their interconnectedness are ingrained into our minds, personally and collectively, we will be better able to deal with them, handle them, protect ourselves from the long-arm of their baleful influence and behavior – even if they're family.

In last analysis, so long as our child cannot love us filially, then we have little choice for our own well-being, but to treat him as the "Love your enemy" transcendent maxim; that is, love him but at an emotional, sentimental, distance; do him no harm, but do not allow him to do *you* harm; "turn your other cheek" – as you will have to often enough, his being your child – but make sure that his hand hurts more than your cheek; forgive him "seventy-times-seven" – as you will have to, his being your child – but never *forget* his transgressions against your well-being.

Never slip <u>totally</u> into your children's deceits – or you're lost! Accept them as natural; be even willing to be their victim now and then – Give them their due; but always at a cautionary distance. Save yourself!

ATERWORD

1

In closing this bleakly disturbing, yet hopefully encouraging, book, I have these few forward-looking words to add. But first: Yes, the pathics are with us for good; and yes, there will always be their victims to exploit; and yes, they will always add to the pool of sorrow and suffering upon mankind, and always pollute and infect the innocent and unwary. So much, then, for the "bleakly, disturbing" side of the human condition – its dark side. What of the "hopefully, encouraging" side of the human condition – its bright side?

A charge lodged against this book might be that it emphasizes the dark side almost to the exclusion of the bright side; which is true, except that the prime purpose of the book dictates the appropriate proportion of the book as it is – the very title, Of Pathics and Evil, and its subtitle, "A Philosophy against Malice" verify this proportion. Its first purpose is to immerse the receptive reader so fully into the reality of pathic evil that he/she will gain an ongoing awareness of its presence, and so, be ever after "on the alert" and against them. Its secondary purpose – as proposed in the last three chapters – is to get to the root of pathic evil (the *love* of evil) so that receptive readers will gain both a psychological and transcendent self-understanding of their own character (whether soft or hard natures) with the wisdom to *act* in conformity with this understanding.

2

The underlying theme of this book; that justice and wisdom take the ascendancy over injustice and ignorance, serves as a preface to the conscious transformation occurring in our times and leading to the gradual ascendancy of justice and wisdom over injustice and ignorance. This conscious transformation is further explored and studied in my forthcoming book, *Human-Transcendence: Of Love and Wisdom*.

With the publication of these two related books, I will have completed my major contribution to this conscious transformation. What more is needed is to transfer words into action – into a movement, or more to the point: a *quest*, against injustice and ignorance.

Of Pathics and Evil is the book that heralds this movement, this quest, by giving life to the voices of those who have suffered under the pathic spell.

This movement, this quest, this dawning, is now. Research it; it is all about us. Reflect upon it; it is within us. Let it happen; live your share of the good.

www.ingramcontent.com/pod-product-compliance
Lightning Source LLC
Chambersburg PA
CDHW060447030426
42337CB00015B/1517